Formal Methods Applied to Complex Systems

Series Editor
Jean-Charles Pomerol

Formal Methods Applied to Complex Systems

Implementation of the B Method

Edited by

Jean-Louis Boulanger

iSTE

WILEY

First published 2014 in Great Britain and the United States by ISTE Ltd and John Wiley & Sons, Inc.

ISTE Ltd
27-37 St George's Road
London SW19 4EU
UK

www.iste.co.uk

John Wiley & Sons, Inc.
111 River Street
Hoboken, NJ 07030
USA

www.wiley.com

Library of Congress Control Number: 2014939764

British Library Cataloguing-in-Publication Data
A CIP record for this book is available from the British Library
ISBN 978-1-84821-709-6

MIX
Paper from responsible sources
FSC® C013604

Printed and bound in Great Britain by CPI Group (UK) Ltd., Croydon, Surrey CR0 4YY

Contents

Introduction

I.1. Context

Although formal program analysis techniques have a long history (including the work by Hoare [HOA 69] and Dijkstra [DIJ 75]), formal methods were only established in the 1980s. These techniques are used to analyze the behavior of software applications written using a programming language. The correctness of a program (correct behavior, program completion, etc.) is then demonstrated using a program proof based on the calculation of the weakest precondition [DIJ 76].

The application of formal methods (Z [SPI 89], VDM [JON 90] and the B method [ABR 96, ARA 97]) for industrial applications and their suitability for use in industrial contexts dates back to the late 1990s. Formal specifications use mathematical notations to give a precise description of system requirements.

NOTE 1.– Z – A Z specification is made up of schematic diagrams and sets used to specify a computer system. A specification is a set of schematic diagrams.

NOTE 2.– The Vienna Development Method (VDM) – this is a formal method based on a denotational and operational vision (programs are seen as mathematical functions), unlike Z or the B method which are based on axiomatic set theory.

Introduction written by Jean-Louis BOULANGER.

One stumbling block is the possibility of implementation within the context of industrial applications (on a large scale, with cost and time constraints, etc.); this implementation requires tools to have attained a sufficient level of maturity and performance.

Note that for critical applications, at least two formal methods make use of recognized and widely available design environments covering part of the code specification process while implementing one or more verification processes: the B method [ABR 96], the LUSTRE language [HAL 91, ARA 97] and its graphic version SCADE[1] [DOR 08]. The B method and the SCADE environment have been used successfully in industrial tools.

To give an example, Atelier B, marketed and sold by CLEARSY[2], is a tool which covers the whole development cycle involved in the B method (specification, refining, code generation and proof). Note that Atelier B[3] can be freely downloaded since version 4.0.

Formal methods are based on a variety of formal verification techniques, such as proof, model checking [BAI 08] and/or simulation.

Although formal methods are now becoming increasingly widely used, they are still relatively marginal when viewed in terms of the number of lines of code involved. To date, far more lines of ADA [ANS 83], C [ISO 99] and C++ code have been produced manually than through the use of a formal process.

For this reason, other formal techniques have been implemented in order to verify the behavior of software applications written in languages such as C and ADA. The main technique, abstract program interpretation, is used to evaluate all the behaviors of a software application by static analysis. In

1 The SCADE development environment is marketed by ESTEREL-Technologies – see http://www.esterel-technologies.com/.

2 For more information on CLEARSY and Atelier B, see http://www.clearsy.com/.

3 Atelier B and the associated information may be obtained at http://www.atelierb.eu/.

recent years, this type of technique has been applied to a number of tools, including POLYSPACE[4], Caveat[5], Absint[6], FramaC[7] and ASTREE[8].

The effectiveness of these static program analysis techniques has greatly improved with increases in the processing power of personal computers. Note that these techniques generally require the insertion of additional information, such as preconditions, invariants and/or postconditions, into the manual code.

SPARK Ada[9] is an approach in which the ADA language [ANS 83] has been extended [BAR 03] to include these additional tools and a suite of tailored tools has been created.

I.2. Aims of this book

[BOW 95] and [ARA 97] provided the first feedback from industrial actors concerning the use of formal techniques, notably the B method [ABR 96], the LUSTRE language [HAL 91, ARA 97] and SAO+, the precursor of SCADE[10] [DOR 08]. Other works, including [MON 00, MON 02 and HAD 06], give an overview of formal methods from a more academic perspective.

Our aim in this book is to present real-world examples of the use of formal techniques.

For our purposes, the term "formal techniques" is taken to mean the different mathematically based approaches used to demonstrate that a software application respects a certain number of properties.

---

4 See http://www.mathworks.com/products/polyspace/ for further information concerning Polyspace.

5 See http://www-list.cea.fr/labos/fr/LSL/caveat/index.html for further information concerning Caveat.

6 See http://www.absint.com/ for further information concerning Absint.

7 Further details may be found at http://frama-c.com/.

8 See http://www.astree.ens.fr/ for further information concerning ASTREE.

9 The Website http://www.altran-praxis.com/spark.aspx offers additional information concerning SPARK Ada technology.

10 Note that SCADE started out as a development environment using the LUSTRE language before becoming a language in its own right from version 6 onward (the code generator for version 6 uses a SCADE model instead of a LUSTRE code as input).

Note that the standard use of formal techniques consists of producing specification and/or design models, but that formal techniques are increasingly seen as tools for verification (static code analysis, to demonstrate that properties are respected, to demonstrate good management of floating points, etc.).

This book is the fifth and final volume in a series covering different aspects:

– Volume 1 [BOU 11] concerns examples of industrial implementation of formal techniques based on static analysis, such as abstract interpretation, and includes examples of the use of ASTREE, CAVEAT, CODEPEER, FramaC and POLSYPACE.

– Volume 2 [BOU 12b] presents different formal modeling techniques used in the field of rail transport, such as the B method, SCADE, Simulink DV, GaTel and Control Build and other techniques.

– Volume 3 [BOU 12a] presents different tools used in formal verification: SPARK ADA, MaTeLo, AltaRica, Polyspace, Escher and B-event.

– Volume 4 [BOU 14] gives examples of the industrial implementation of the B method [ABR 96], SCADE, and verification using Prover Verifier. Note that this volume (which presents examples of application using the B method) constitutes a useful addition to university textbooks such as [LAN 96], [WOR 96] and [SCH 01].

I wish to thank all the industrial actors who have freely given of their time to contribute such interesting and informative chapters to this book.

I.3. Bibliography

[ABR 96] ABRIAL J.R., *The B Book: Assigning Programs to Meanings*, Cambridge University Press, Cambridge, August 1996.

[ANS 83] ANSI, Norme ANSI/MIL-STD-1815A-1983, Langage de programmation Ada, 1983.

[ARA 97] ARAGO, "Applications des Méthodes Formelles au Logiciel", Observatoire Français des Techniques Avancées (OFTA), Masson, vol. 20, June 1997.

[BAI 08] BAIER C., KATOEN J.-P., *Principles of Model Checking*, MIT Press, 2008.

[BAR 03] BARNES J., *High Integrity Software: The SPARK Approach to Safety and Security*, Addison-Wesley, 2003.

[BOU 11] BOULANGER J.-L. (ed.), *Static Analysis of Software*, ISTE, London, and John Wiley & Sons, New York, 2011.

[BOU 12a] BOULANGER J.-L. (ed.), *Industrial Use of Formal Method: Formal Verification*, ISTE, London, and John Wiley & Sons, New York, 2012.

[BOU 12b] BOULANGER J.-L. (ed.), *Formal Methods: Industrial Use from Model to the Code*, ISTE, London, and John Wiley & Sons, New York, 2012.

[BOU 14] BOULANGER J.-L. (ed.), *Formal Method, Applied to Industrial Complex Systems,* ISTE, London, and John Wiley & Sons, New York, 2014.

[BOW 95] BOWEN J.P., HINCHEY M.G., *Applications of Formal Methods*, Prentice Hall, 1995.

[COU 00] COUSOT P., "Interprétation abstraite", *Technique et Science Informatique*, vol. 19, no. 1–3, pp. 155–164, January 2000.

[DIJ 75] DIJKSTRA E.W., "Guarded commands, nondeterminacy and formal derivation of programs", *Communications of the ACM*, vol. 18, no. 8, pp. 453–457, August 1975.

[DIJ 76] DIJKSTRA E.W., *A Discipline of Programming*, Prentice Hall, 1976.

[DOR 08] DORMOY F.-X., "Scade 6 a model based solution for safety critical software development", *Embedded Real-Time Systems Conference*, 2008.

[HAD 06] HADDAD S., KORDON F., PETRUCCI L. (ed.), *Méthodes formelles pour les systèmes répartis et coopératifs*, Collection IC2, Hermes, 2006.

[HAL 91] HALBWACHS N., PAUL C., PASCAL R., *et al.*, "The synchronous dataflow programming language Lustre", *Proceedings of the IEEE*, vol. 79, no. 9, pp. 1305–1320, September 1991.

[HOA 69] HOARE C.A.R., "An axiomatic basis for computer programming", *Communications of the ACM*, vol. 12, no. 10, pp. 576–580, 583, 1969.

[JON 90] JONES C.B., *Systematic Software Development Using VDM*, 2nd ed., Prentice Hall International, 1990.

[LAN 96] LANO K., *The B Language and Method: A Guide to Practical Formal Development*, Springer Verlag London Ltd., 1996.

[MON 00] MONIN J.-F., *Introduction aux Méthodes Formelles*, Hermès, 2000. [Foreword by G. Huet]

[MON 02] MONIN J.-F., *Understanding Formal Methods*, Springer Verlag, 2002. [Foreword by G. Huet, Translation edited by M. Hinchey]

[SCH 01] SCHNEIDER S., *The B-Method: An Introduction*, Palgrave, 2001.

[SPI 89] SPIVEY J.M., *The Z Notation: A Reference Manual*, Prentice Hall International, 1989.

[WOR 96] WORDSWORTH J., *Software Engineering with B*, Addison-Wesley, 1996.

1

Presentation of the B Method

1.1. Introduction

The use of formal methods [BEH 93, ARA 97, HIN 95, MON 00, BOU 11, BOU 12a, BOU 12b] is increasing, especially in critical applications such as nuclear power plants, avionics and rail transport. Ensuring maximum safety while operating an application is a significant challenge.

The contribution of formal methods is that they present a mathematical framework for the development process, which provides a method for producing software that is correct by construction. This is because the development process can be verified by validation techniques such as proof or exploration of the model.

Figure 1.1. *Example of a Z diagram*[1]

Chapter written by Jean-Louis BOULANGER.

1 This Z diagram shows a file management system where the state is represented by a mapping function between the file names and their contents, and a set of files open in reading mode.

Of course, to achieve this we need a precise description of the properties that the computerized system must possess. There are different classes of formal methods: algebraic specifications (PLUSS or PVS), equational specifications (LUSTRE [HAL 91, ARA 97]) and model-oriented specifications (B [ABR 96], the Vienna Development Method (VDM) [JON 90] or Z [SPI 89]).

In contrast to model exploration-oriented validation (model-checking [BAI 08]) such as LUSTRE, the B method [ABR 96] is based on the proof of a proof obligation (or PO in the following) which guarantees the feasibility and the coherence of the model (validity of the refinement).

In the French railway industry, the use of formal methods [BEH 93, ARA 97, DEB 94, BOU 11, BOU 12a, BOU 12b], and in particular the B method, is increasingly common within the development of critical systems.

The software for these safety systems (rail signaling, automatic driving, etc.) must meet very strict quality, reliability, safety and robustness criteria.

One of the first applications of formal methods was made *a posteriori* on the SACEM[2] [GUI 90]. During the installation of the SACEM [GEO 90], the RATP[3] had carried out a Hoare proof [HOA 69] to demonstrate that the requirements had been taken into account; for more information, see [GUI 90]. The Hoare proof makes it possible to clearly show all of the postconditions, using a program P and a set of preconditions C.

The Hoare proof, which was carried out within the SACEM, showed a certain number of code properties, but it was not possible to link these with requirements related to safety (e.g. requirement for non-collision).

As a result, the decision was made to create a formal model in Z [SPI 89, DIL 95]. This formal model made it possible to break the properties down and to link the requirements with the code. Around 20 significant anomalies were discovered in this way by the team of experts responsible for the respecification in Z.

---

2 The SACEM (*Système d'Aide à la Conduite, à l'Exploitation et à la Maintenance* – Assisted Driving, Control and Maintenance System), which was installed in 1988, makes it possible to tell drivers the speed at which the train should be travelling (report of the lateral signalling in the cabin) via a screen installed on board, in order to aid driving.

3 See www.ratp.fr.

Projects such as the CTDC, KVS or the SAET-METEOR[4] [BEH 93, BEH 96, BEH 97, BOU 06], LST [DEH 94], CdG VAL (VAL for Véhicule Automatique Léger – Light Automatic Vehicle)[5] and the automation of Line 1 of the Parisian metro use the B method throughout the development process (from the specifications to the code).

1.2. The B method

1.2.1. *Presentation*

The B method was developed by Jean-Raymond Abrial[6] [ABR 96], and is a formal, model-oriented method like Z [SPI 89] and VDM [JON 90]. However, unlike these methods, it also allows incremental development of the specification up to the code through the concept of refinement [MOR 90], and this is through a unique formalism: the language of abstract machines.

```
MACHINE                         IMPLEMENTATION
          HelloWorld                      HelloWorld_n
OPERATIONS                      REFINES
Hello =                                   HelloWorld
          skip                  IMPORTS
END                                       BASIC_IO
                                OPERATIONS
                                          Hello =
                                          STRING_WRITE("Hello World")
                                END
```

Figure 1.2. *The "Hello" program in B*

At each stage of B development, proof obligations (POs) are generated in order to guarantee the validity of the refinement and the consistency of the

4 SAET-METEOR [MAT 98] has been in use since October 1998 on Line 14 of the Parisian Metro. The computer architecture of SAET-METEOR (*Système d'Automatisation de l'Exploitation des Trains* – Train Automation and Operation System – *Métro Est Ouest Rapide*) is presented in Chapter 2 of [BOU 09] and the development, V&V and safety demonstration process of the software are presented in Chapter 2 of [BOU 11c].

5 The first VAL was opened in Lille, France, in 1983. There are now also VALs in operation in Taipei, Toulouse, Rennes and Turin (since January 2006). There are over 119 km of lines and over 830 trains in use or in construction for VAL systems worldwide. VAL CdG combines VAL technology with complementary digital equipment based on the B method.

6 It should be noted that Jean-Raymond Abrial had participated in the development of both the Z and the B methods.

abstract machine. In this way, the B method makes it possible to develop safe software.

Like Z, the B method is based on set theory and first-order predicate logic. However, unlike Z, the B method has a *development* flavor in its way of specifying operations. In fact, operations are not specified in terms of pre- and postconditions, but by means of *generalized substitutions*.

In Figure 1.2, we introduce the specification of the *HelloWorld* program and its implementation *HelloWorld_n*.

1.2.2. *The concept of an abstract machine*

1.2.2.1. *Abstract machine*

A B-model is designed through composition, decomposition and refinement of abstract machines. The basic component of the B method is the abstract machine, which can be a high-level machine or a refinement of another machine. The final refinement may also be called the implementation.

The concept of an abstract machine is similar to the concept of a module and/or object, which is found in more traditional programming languages. The keyword here is “encapsulation”: the state evolution of an abstract machine should only take place through the behavior of the encapsulation.

Abstract machines are divided into three levels: the MACHINEs, which describe the highest level of specification; the REFINEMENTs, which include all the intermediary steps between the specification and the code; and the IMPLEMENTATIONs, which define the coding.

Figure 1.3 shows the structure of a MACHINE. The refinements and implementations follow the same model.

The B method defines a unique notation, known as abstract machine notation (AMN) (see [ABR 92]), which allows us to describe the above-mentioned three levels of abstraction. It should be noted that in order to transition from a high-level machine to implementation, we can go through one or several refinements. In this case, we talk about a development chain for the machine concerned.

```
MACHINE
        M (param)
CONSTRAINTS
        C
SEES
        N
SETS
        S;
        T={a,b}
CONSTANTS
        lc
PROPERTIES
        P
VARIABLES
        lv
INVARIANT
        I
ASSERTIONS
        J1; ...; Jn
INITIALISATION
        Init
OPERATIONS
        U <-- Op (p):=PRE Q THEN V END;
...
END
```

Figure 1.3. *Example of an abstract machine*

From the final refinement (implementation) onward, we have obtained a level of detail which is sufficient for us to use an automatic code generator (C [ISO 99], ADA [ANS 83], etc.) to obtain an executable code. The restrictions on the AMN at the implementation level make it possible to build a translator.

Abstract machines are made up of three parts: declarative, composition and executive. In Figure 1.4, the declarative part is shown in *italics*, the executive part is shown in **bold** and the composition part is shown in normal typeface.

1.2.2.2. *Declarative part*

The declarative part makes it possible to describe the state of the abstract machine through variables, constants, sets and, above all, through properties, which should always be verified by the state of the machine. This part is based on set theory and first-order predicates. We can call this a state model.

```
MACHINE
   STACK ( max_object )

SEES
   OBJECT

CONSTRAINTS
   max_object ∈ NAT1
VARIABLES
   stack
INVARIANT
   stack ∈ seq(Object) ∧
   size(stack) <= max_object

INITIALISATION
   stack := <>
OPERATIONS
   PUSH (XX) =
      PRE XX ∈ Object ∧ size(stack) < max_object
      THEN stack := stack ← XX END;

   XX ← POP = PRE size(stack) > 0
      THEN XX,stack := last(stack),front(stack) END
END
```

Figure 1.4. *Example of an abstract machine*

For the STACK machine in Figure 1.4, the state is made up of a sequence-type *stack* variable, with *Object*-type elements and a *max_object* constant, introduced by configuration, which makes it possible to configure the maximum number of elements from this stack. The sequence is the second type of basis after sets.

Expression	Name	Written	Meaning
B	Boolean	Boolean	Set of two values {true,false}
N	Natural number	NATURAL	{0.1,....}
NAT	Finite set of natural numbers	NAT	{0,1,...MAXINT}
Z	Integer	INTEGER	{..,-2,-1,0,1,2,...}
INT	Finite set of integers	INT	{-MAXIN, ..,-2,-1,0,1,2,...+MAXINT}

Table 1.1. *The basic sets*

The B language is not built on the manipulation of types, but rather on the manipulation of sets. For each variable, we calculate all the associated values. Table 1.1 introduces the basic sets.

The basic sets are associated with an operator set which makes it possible to construct more complex sets. Table 1.2 introduces a subset of set operators available for the creation of B models.

Expression	Name	Written	Means
$\varnothing$	The empty set	{}	The empty set
$\{e_1, e_2, e_3\}$	A list	$\{e_1, e_2, e_3\}$	A set which contains only the elements e_1, e_2 and e_3
P(A)	Set of the parts of A	Pow(A)	A set which contains all the parts of A
P * Q	Cartesian product	P * Q	The Cartesian product of P by Q.
$S \leftrightarrow T$	Set of all the relationships of S*T	S <-> T	Set of all the relationships from S to T, equal to P(S*T)
Id(S)	Identity of S	Id(S)	Set of the pairs $E \mapsto E$ or $E \in S$
	....		

Table 1.2. *The basic sets*

As we can see in Figure 1.4, the B language has a mathematical notation ($\in$, $\wedge$, ετχ). However, it also needs to have a computer notation (:, & , etc.), which makes it possible to enter elements using a normal keyboard. Table 1.3 shows an extract of the correspondence between B American Standard Code for Information Interchange (ASCII) notation and mathematical notation.

B ASCII notation	Mathematical notation	Meaning
<:	$\subseteq$	Included or equal
\/	$\cup$	Union
/\	$\cap$	Intersection
:	$\in$	Belongs to
::	$:\in$	Becomes an element of
f~	f^{-1}	Function or reciprocal relationship
f[E]	f(E)	Image of the set E by f
A<| f	$f_{\mid A}$	Restriction on the domain
!x.(.....)	$\forall x \ldots$	Universal quantifier
#x.(....)	$\exists x \ldots$	Existential quantifier
&	$\wedge$	logical "AND"
or	$\vee$	logical "OR"
not	$\neg$	logical "NOT"
{}	$\varnothing$	Empty set
%x.(...)	$\lambda x \ldots$	Lambda function
	....	

Table 1.3. *Correspondence between ASCII and mathematical notation*

Figure 1.5 shows an example of a specification which uses sets. There is a global set PEOPLE (PERSONNES) which characterizes all the people which can exist in the specification. This set must be finite, and this is why there is a constraint on the cardinal. The set "people" characterizes people who exist and the set "men" characterizes a specific subset of "people".

```
MACHINE
        EXAMPLE
SETS
        PEOPLE (nb_people)
CONSTANTS
        max_personne
PROPERTIES
        max_personne : NAT
&       card(nb_people) = max_personne
VARIABLES
        people, men
DEFINITIONS
        WOMEN == people - men
INVARIANT
        people <: PEOPLE
&       men <: people
...
INITIALISATION
        people, men = {}, {}
Required parameters are missing or incorrect.
...
END
```

Figure 1.5. *Example of set usage*

The clause DEFINITIONS introduces the set WOMEN which is the complement of the set *men*. This clause makes it possible to have "inline" definitions of programming languages (an "inline" code is expanded at compilation).

1.2.2.3. *Composition part*

The composition clauses (SEES, INCLUDES, IMPORTS and EXTENDS) make it possible to describe the various links between abstract machines. Each clause introduces visibility rules on the state and the operations of the abstract machine in question.

In our example in Figure 1.3, we introduce the visibility link (SEES) on the machine *OBJECT* in order to have access to the set *Object*.

1.2.2.4. *Executive part*

The executive part contains the initialization and the operations of the abstract machine. It is based on the generalized substitution language (GSL). This execution mechanism may be interpreted as an extension of the assignment as it exists in imperative languages (of the type ADA, PASCAL, C, etc.).

Table 1.4 shows a subset of the GSL [ABR 91]. Generalized substitutions are an extension of the work of Dijkstra [DIJ 76] on substitutions.

Simple substitution	x := E	[x:=E] R <=> substitution of all the free occurrences of x in R by E
Empty substitution	skip	[skip] R <=> R
Simultaneous substitution	S || T	[S || T] R <=> [S] R_S ∧ [T] R_t where R=R_S . R_t; T and S modify the distinct variable sets V_S and V_t; Vs (resp. V_t) is not free in R_t (resp. R_S)
Preconditioning	P | S	[P | S] R <=> P ∧ [S] R
Limited choice	S [] T	[S [] T] R <=> [S] R ∧ [T] R
Kept choice	P => S	[P => S] R <=> P =>[S] R
Choice not limited	@ x . S	[@ x.S] R <=> x.[S] R or x is not free in R

NOTE.– x describes a variable, E is an expression of set theory, P and R are predicates, and S and T are generalized substitutions.

Table 1.4. *A subset of generalized substitutions*

Generalized substitutions are predicate transformers. The predicate obtained by applying the substitution S on the predicate P is written as [S] P. In fact, as shown in Table 1.5, we define substitutions by their effect on a predicate, and this is known as weakest precondition (wp).

The substitution P is associated with the wp [P]R for all of R,
which is [P]R {P} R
following Hoare logic.
For example: let P and R be defined, respectively, by x:=x+1 and x:NATURAL
we obtain x+1: NATURAL {x:=x+1} x: NATURAL

Table 1.5. *Use of predicate transformation*

There are complementary calculation rules available for manipulating generalized substitutions, such as distributivity [S] (p &q) = [S]p & [S]q or [S](¬p) = ¬([S] p).

The behavior of our example (see Figure 1.4) basically consists of two operations (push and pop) that are constructed around the behavior of the sequences. The operations last, front and ← represent, respectively, access to the final element, the sequence without the final element and the concatenation to the right.

In order to find out whether the substitution of the body of the push operation can verify the invariant of the STACK machine, we can simply calculate the initial precondition so that the substitution stack := stack ← XX satisfies the invariant of the abstract machine. (see Figure 1.6)

On doit calculer [stack := stack ← XX] (stack ∈ seq(Object) ∧size(stack) <= max_object)
qui donne [stack := stack ← XX] (stack ∈ seq(Object)) ∧ [stack := stack ← XX] (size(stack) <= max_object)
et se réduit à (stack ← XX ∈ seq(Object)) ∧ (size(stack ← XX) <= max_object)

Figure 1.6. *Application of the push operation on the invariant*

In order to minimize the burden of the construction of abstract machines, some sugared constructions have been introduced at the AMN level. The basic substitutions (see Table 1.4) have a textual form available to them; for example, the preconditioning P | S is written as PRE P THEN S END.

Some more evolved structures, which are found in the so-called evolved languages, have been introduced, but they may be rewritten by combining the basic substitutions. The multiple substitution x,y := E,F and the classical conditional structure IF P THEN S ELSE T END are both examples of actions that can be found in the body of operations. They may be rewritten, respectively, with the simultaneous substitution x:=E || y:=F and the limited substitution P=>S [] not(P)=>T.

As previously stated, the AMN defines a single notation based on GSL, set theory and first-order logic. However, the set of substitutions cannot be used on all levels. For example, the substitution ANY xx WHERE P(xx) THEN S END (which means that ∀ xx.P(xx) => [S]) can be used at the abstract levels (machine and refinement), whereas the substitution WHILE B DO S END cannot be accepted at the most abstract level.

The B method is based on encapsulation. Therefore, the operations should provide the set of behaviors enabling the state of the machine to evolve. However, this is not always possible, as we will see in in the following.

1.2.3. *From machines to implementations*

1.2.3.1. *Principle*

Abstract machines that are used to describe the specification use non-deterministic constructs and all the power of set language and first-order logic. In this context, algorithmic constructions (sequence and loops) are forbidden for abstract machines.

In order to proceed toward an executable application, the process known as *refinement* needs to be introduced. This allows us to progressively replace the set data structures with structures close to those of programming languages. In this way, the non-determinism is removed and generalized substitutions analogous to sequence and loops (WHILE) are introduced.

All of these *refinement* stages are subjected to proofs of maintenance of the invariants and the conformity of the refined machines in relation to the more abstract machines.

1.2.3.2. *Refinement*

As can be seen in Figure 1.7, the refinement process (see [MOR 90]) has usually been represented as a sequence of independent steps, with which verifications are associated. A component i+1 (refinement or implementation) refines a component i (machine or refinement).

The refinement process begins with the definition of a machine that contains the abstract description of the need. The refinements allow us to make the need concrete and show the non-deterministic and non-sequential elements. The implementation is a B component that uses a subset of the B language named B0.

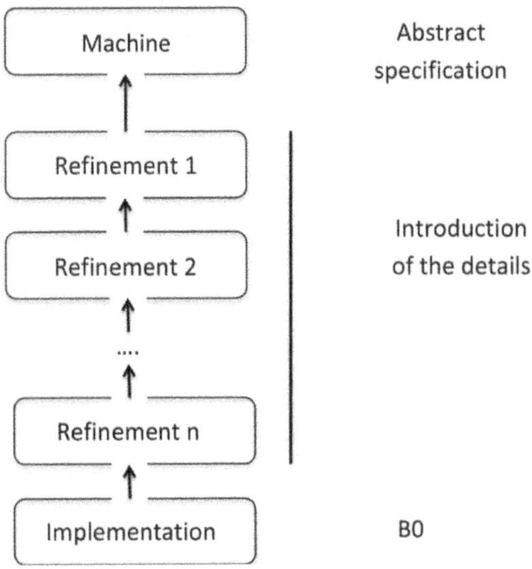

Figure 1.7. *From the description of the need to the implementation*

The sublanguage B0 is a language that is close to more traditional languages (C, ADA, etc.). B0 is thus easy to translate into programming languages.

Figure 1.8 shows an example of refinement (for more information about the process of refinement, see [MOR 90]). The specification indicates that the need is to find two numbers q and r such that a= q*b+r and r<b. It can be seen that the mathematical specification of the Euclidean division can be replaced (in the sense of refinement) by an algorithm that carries out the calculation through successive subtractions.

The suggested algorithm uses an instruction WHILE … DO END. The B language is here the B instruction, integrating the concept INVARIANT and the concept VARIANT. The VARIANT allows us to show the end of the loop and the INVARIANT allows us to verify the correct behavior of the loop.

1.2.3.3. *Process*

Figure 1.9 introduces the generally used process, which is focused on searching for a fault in the software application. The search for a fault is based on the concept of program execution. This approach seeks to show that the software is correct.

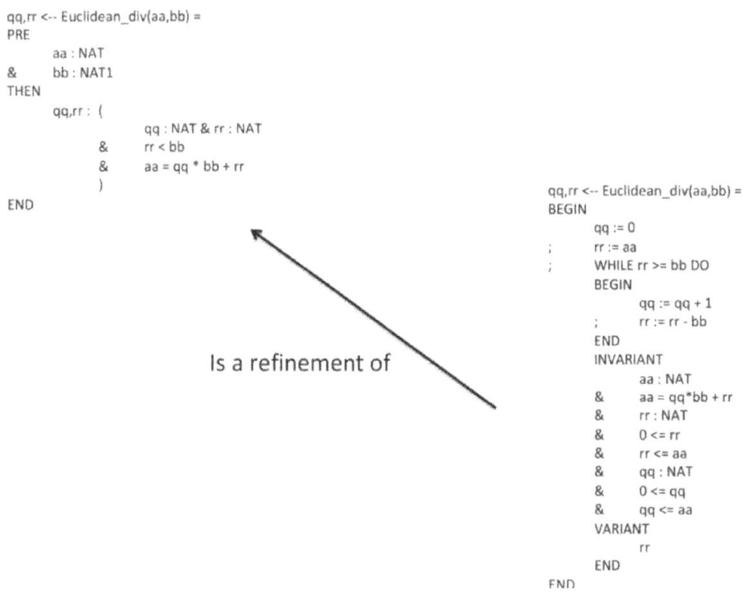

Figure 1.8. *Example of a refinement*

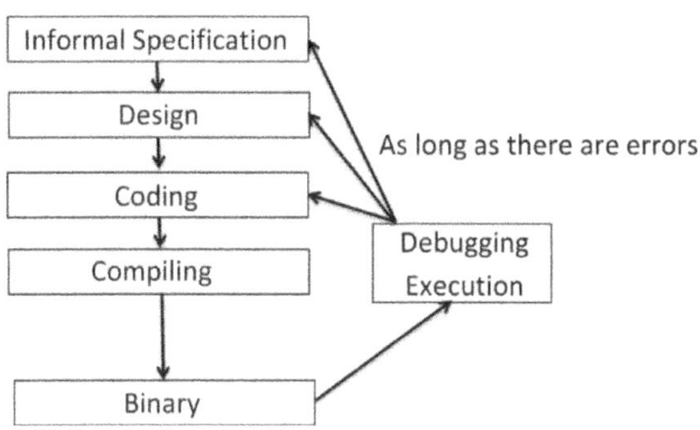

Figure 1.9. *Development cycle with the B method*

Using formal methods, the process is based on a different observation: "the software is correct by construction". As a result, the process is different because it is focused on analyzing the need and demonstrating that some properties are true during all executions (see Figure 1.10).

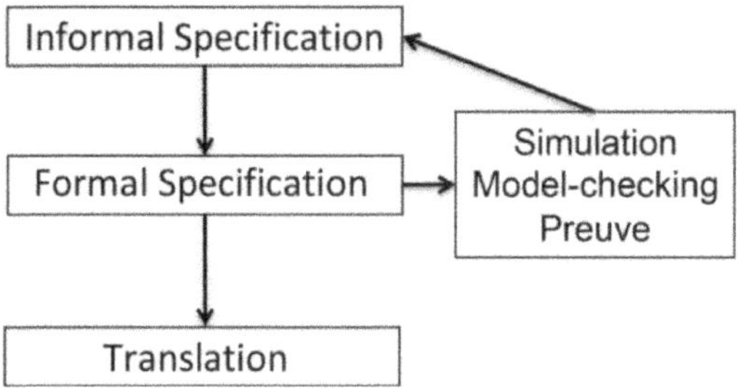

Figure 1.10. *Formal process*

As can be seen in Figure 1.11, the process consists of writing a modeling of the problem, simple and abstract. Then, to this modeling, as the stages known as refinement progress [MOR 90], we add more concrete and more complex elements, all the while proving the coherence of the new models created.

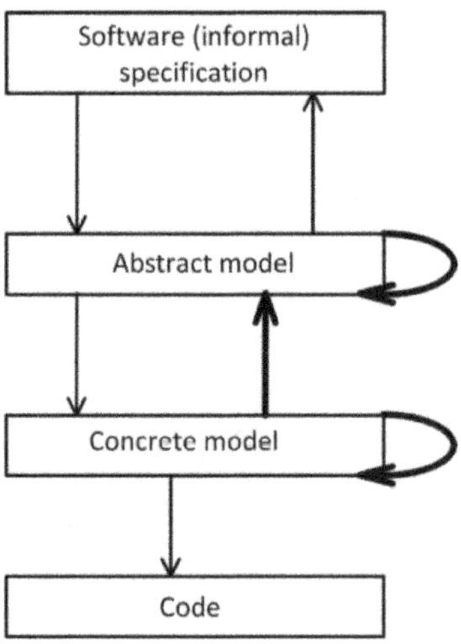

Figure 1.11. *Development cycle with the B method*

Implementation, the final stage, is free from abstract types of original data, which have become programmable structures such as tables and files. The following have been eliminated: the preconditions of subprograms, and the simultaneity and the non-determinism that were present in the abstract model. Structures for checking programming such as sequencing and loop have been introduced.

At this stage, automatic transformation into code may take place. This could be into ADA or C, or even into Assembleur code for certain tools: trying to match a formal specification directly with a traditional programming language is impossible because they have different thought patterns.

The concept of proof (in Figure 1.11, the thin arrows) is strongly linked to the B development and the specification is written as a function of these future obligations. The proof is involved at all levels of abstraction. After a machine is written, the proof of its internal coherence is carried out. If the result of this is positive, then the development may continue.

The proof is carried out in this way after each level of abstraction, verifying internal coherence and conformity with the level of abstraction above.

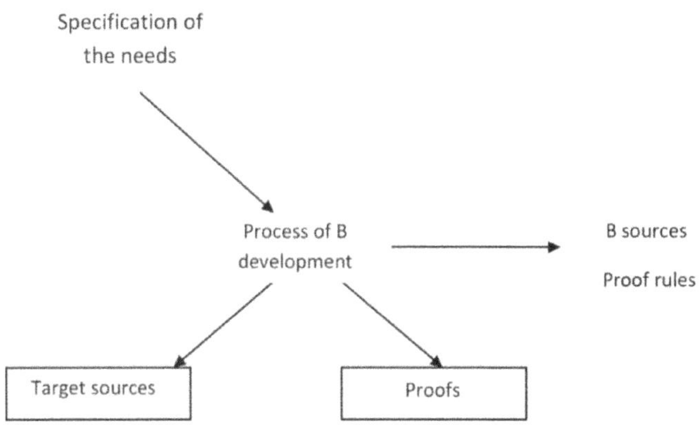

Figure 1.12. *B Process*

Figure 1.12 summarizes the creation process for a B model. In input are the specifications of the needs, and in output are the sources of the B model, the added rules, the POs, the proofs and the source codes.

1.3. Verification and validation (V&V)

1.3.1. *Internal verification*

1.3.1.1. *Principles*

As shown in Figure 1.13, external verification (consistency of the specification) and internal verification (validity of the refinements) are carried out through proof of the POs. POs are an essential part of the B method.

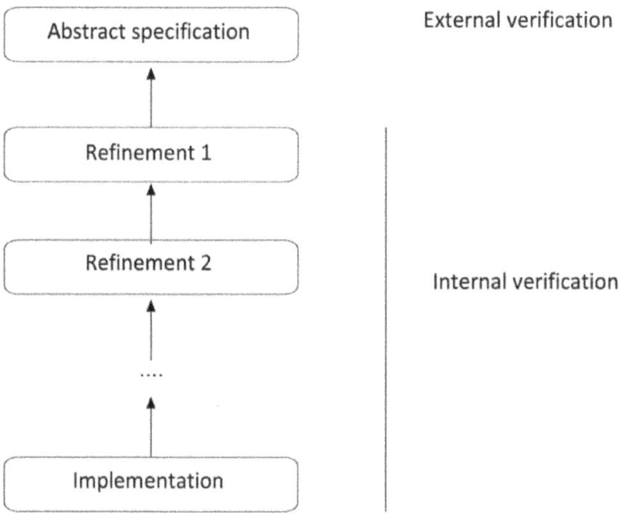

Figure 1.13. *Internal verification and external verification*

The B method introduces three verification phases for all abstract machines: syntactic analysis, verification of type and generation of POs. For implementations, there is an additional verification linked to the fact that the B component must comply with the B0 language in order to guarantee the translation into the target language.

1.3.1.2. *Syntactic and semantic analysis*

Syntactic analysis allows us to verify that the abstract machine has been correctly built, through ensuring that it complies with the syntactic rules of AMN. One of the syntactic rules verified in this way is linked to the restriction on the use of certain substitutions. For example, simultaneous substitution, denotated S || P, may not be used in an implementation.

Verification of type makes it possible to detect faults linked to undeclared or poorly declared objects, expressions that cannot be typed, incoherencies between various definitions of the same operation, or to violations of visibility rules introduced by the composition clauses. All expressions can be typed, since the set theory used in AMN is a simplification of classical set theory.

1.3.1.3. *Generation of proof obligations*

As we have already shown, at each development stage there is a stage of PO generation. POs are automatically generated by the tool.

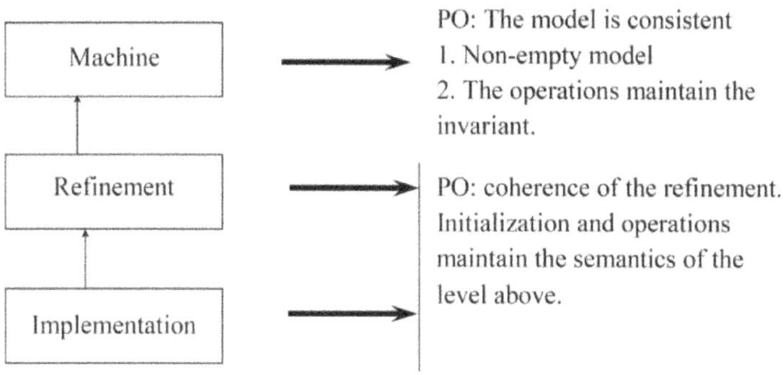

Figure 1.14. *Aims of proof obligations*

For a high-level abstract machine, the POs generated guarantee mathematical consistency. For refinements and implementations, the POs guarantee the validity of the refinement in relation to the machine at the next level in the development chain. In general, the complexity of the POs depends on the level of abstraction used (the more concrete, the more complex) and the structure of the application in terms of links between machines.

All the POs contain information that describes the context of the machine in their hypotheses. The context contains a set of constraints that define the formal parameters, and the properties concerning the sets and the constants of the abstract machine. It also takes into account that all the sets used are finite, not empty, and that all of their elements are distinct.

The context of an abstract machine is denotated by <Context>. The composition clauses may add information to the context, to the invariant and to the initialization which is in agreement with the visibility rules.

The verification of mathematical consistency introduces two types of POs. First, we need to show that the model is not empty. This is done by showing that the initialization creates the invariant.

<Context> ⇒ [Initialization] Invariant [1.1]

Second, we need to prove that each operation of the abstract machine maintains the invariant. In the case of an OPE operation defined by a substitution S under the precondition that if Q is OPE = PRE Q then S END, we obtain a PO of the following form:

$$\langle Context \rangle \wedge \text{Invariant} \wedge Q \Rightarrow [\,S]\ \text{Invariant}. \quad [1.2]$$

We may take the result of Figure 1.5 to be an example of this. It thus remains to be shown that:

(stack ∈ seq(Object) ∧size(stack) <= max_object) ∧

(XX ∈ Object and size(stack) < max_object)

⇒ stack<-XX ∈ seq(Object) ∧ XX ∈ Object ∧ size(stack<-XX) <= max_object

To show that an abstract machine is actually a refinement of a highest level machine in relation to a development chain, we need to show that its initialization and its operations maintain the semantics of their most abstract versions. The POs generated for the *n*th refinement are described by equation [1.3] for the initialization and by equation [1.4] for each operation.

$$\langle Context \rangle \Rightarrow [Init_n] \neg [Init_{n-1}] \neg I_n \quad [1.3]$$

$$\langle Context \rangle \wedge I_1 \wedge I_2 \wedge \ldots \wedge I_n \wedge Q_1 \Rightarrow Q_n \wedge [[u_n{:=}u_{n-1}]S_n] \neg [S_{n-1}] \neg (I_n \wedge u_n = u_{n-1}) \quad [1.4]$$

where $Init_i$, I_i, Q_i, S_i and u_i are, respectively, the initialization, the invariant, the precondition of the operation, the action of the operation and the formal parameter of the operation of the *i*th refinement.

We notice that there is no PO regarding the feasibility of the predicates introduced in the invariant, the preconditions of the operations, the constraints relative to the formal parameters, and the properties of the sets and the constants. In fact, feasibility is introduced by the construction of the other proofs or by the introduction of a specific PO in the case of need.

The verification of the existence of a variable that satisfies the invariant is indirectly introduced by the POs [1.1] and [1.3].

The existence of formal parameters that validate the precondition of an operation is carried out by the POs [1.2] and [1.4]. The existence of formal parameters that validate the constraints of the target machine is required when a machine uses the inclusion or importation of another machine.

All machines that include or import a configured machine must instantiate the formal parameters, and the PO [1.5] is generated in order to guarantee that the effective parameters validate the constraints.

<Context> ⇒ [Formal_parameter-:= Actual_parameter] (A∧Constraints) [1.5]

where A is a predicate indicating that the sets that have become parameters are finite and not empty, and where the predicate *Constraints* is associated with the clause of the same name.

The valuation of the sets and constants may be carried out at the highest level or at implementation (sets and constants submitted). The PO [1.6] guarantees that, at the implementation level, the properties are true for the values given to these objects:

<Subset_of_Context> ⇒[Deferred SET, Deferred VAR:= Values] Properties [1.6]

where *Properties* is the predicate associated with the clause PROPERTIES. <Subset_of_Context> relates to the part of the context used to create the Values.

Using constructive proof implies that certain verifications are carried out at the implementation level. In the case of parameterized machines, these verifications are reported until inclusion (machine or refinement) or importation (implementation) in a machine which is part of another development chain.

In the above, we have seen that we can use the structure WHILE at the final realizations level. As we are in a proof environment, a certain number of complementary POs are generated to guarantee that WHILE (see Figure 1.8) and its termination are executed correctly.

Finally, the following should be noted: while we are analyzing the POs, the number of predicates from the analysis grows when the number of the levels of refinement and the number of links introduced by the composition clauses increase.

The POs are represented by a goal to be achieve under the condition of the presence of assumptions. These are established starting from the preconditions and the definitions contained in the refined component, but also using the information read in the viewed or imported machines.

1.3.2. *Validation or external verification*

When the B-model is written and proved, we may believe that it is correct, but in fact it is not so simple. The proof guarantees that the B-model is coherent and respects the properties introduced in precondition, invariant and postcondition. However, the validation deals with the correctness with regard to the need.

The B method does not cover the validation; we need to introduce some specific activities:

– to review the B-model to verify that the textual specification is assumed by the model;

– to demonstrate that the properties (contained in the model) cover all parts of the model. It is possible to introduce some obvious properties or partial properties (which cover just a part of the model);

– to test (overall software tests) the complete software (generated automatically) to demonstrate that the complete application fulfills the requirements of the textual specification.

1.4. Methodology

The development of an application in B is not code-oriented, but rather it is proof-oriented. This is why all application development methodology in B must be proof-oriented. Indeed the POs generated should be as small as possible and their numbers whether large or small should be provable.

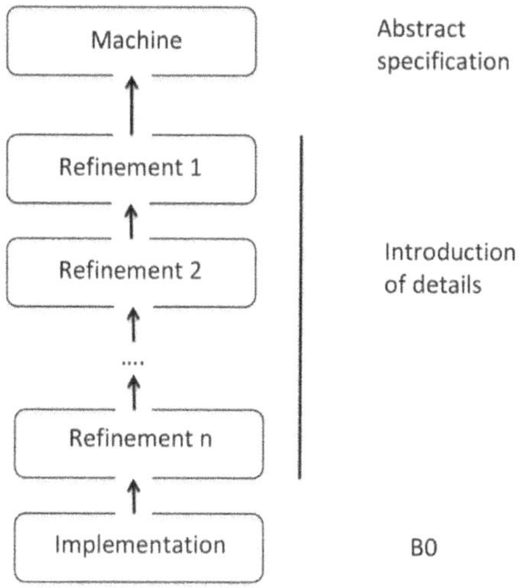

Figure 1.15. *Refinement chain*

1.4.1. *Development by layer*

Figure 1.15 shows the classical process for development using a formal method. We begin by writing the specification of the system to be created, and then we carry out successive refinements until the code is obtained.

In order to validate the specification, there is a unique external verification at the level of the specification and there are internal verifications at each refinement. Putting a process such as this in place for development in B introduces a significant network of links (SEES, INCLUDES, PROMOTES and EXTEND) between the machines (composition part of the machines) at the highest level of abstraction.

In addition, such a process rapidly reveals variables and invariants which characterize the composition part in high-level machines. This weighs down the predicates brought into play in the POs and thus makes the POs more complicated.

The B development must start from the highest possible level of abstraction and progressively introduce the details of implementation in the form of operation and data refinements. In this way, a layered development is obtained (see Figure 1.16).

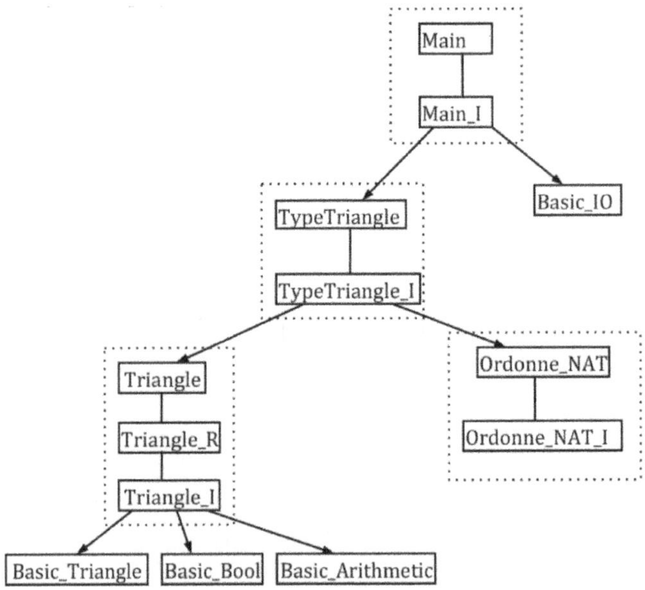

Figure 1.16. *Layered development*

In fact, in layered development [WAE 95], we progress from an abstract stage to a concrete stage that leads to the appearance of new abstract stages. This is the way in which the concept of a development chain and a breakdown based on services appears.

A development chain brings together all the stages, from specification to implementation, for a given module (shown by the dotted rectangle in Figure 1.16). The structuring of the layered model is performed through SEES and IMPORTS links. The SEES link (shown by a line) allows MACHINE and REFINEMENT to access the data structures. The IMPORTS link (shown by the arrow) makes it possible to access the operations during the final realization.

The sheets of the graph obtained in this way are basic machines that are already proved and that have been created in different target languages.

This type of development offers a model rather than a specification of the problem. As an immediate consequence, we have an external validation, which will need to be fragmented on the set of high-level abstract machines.

The three advantages of the layer development are:

– The first is linked to the fact that the availability of high-level abstract machines that are used in the composition clause is enough to prove a development chain. This is close to the concept of a module or package which is found in languages such as ADA.

– The number of links between abstract machines is limited, which decreases the complexity of the POs. We focus solely on the SEES and IMPORTS links.

– The graph obtained is a non-transitive acyclic graph. This limits the impact of a modification of a high-level abstract machine. The modification of a refinement or an implementation does not have an impact outside its development chain.

1.4.2. *Role of the breakdown in the makeup of the POs*

In section 1.3.1.3, we presented the POs generated by the B method, and we observed that the number of links between machines introduced a complexity in terms of the predicate brought into play in the PO. In fact, the composition links are of two categories: the links at the abstract level (machine and refinement) and the links at the concrete level (implementation).

Another aspect of the role of the breakdown is the algorithmic refinement. If we begin with a specification that is insufficiently abstract, the complexity of the POs very quickly increases. As F. Meija (DEH 94, DEH 94a) pointed out in his articles, the choice of an operation's refinement structures is important. In the case of a conditional structure (IF THEN ELSE END or CASE OF END), we should not attempt to make a situation disappear.

1.4.3. *Development cycle of a B project*

Introducing a PO with the development provides an important alternative to the program test usually carried out during the development.

Figure 1.17 shows the development cycle of an application in B. We can see that there is no compilation, and therefore no execution, before the final phase. In fact, as we do not have an effective animator which could evaluate the behavior of the B-model during the development, we cannot carry out external verification of the model.

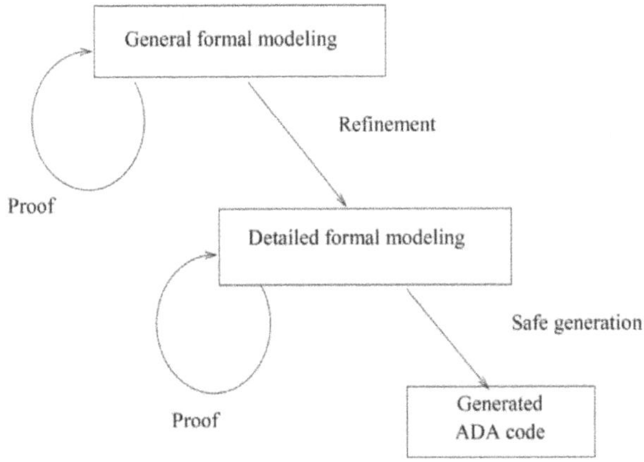

Figure 1.17. *B Development cycle*

The presence of the formal proof of conformity of the developed code with the specifications has allowed us to significantly reduce the test phases of the V cycle. This is shown in Figure 1.17.

The use of the B method for SAET-METEOR (see [BOU 06, Chapter 3]) showed that it is possible to replace test activities (unit test (UT) and integration test (IT)) by proof activities.

NOTE.– if it is required to create a manual code (low-level function, link with components developed outside of B, etc.), it will be necessary to model these elements within B and to show that the component developed manually (or re-used) respects this specification. This verification is modeled by the dotted arrow (see Figure 1.18) that leads the manual code toward higher levels and by the need to conduct at least unitary tests on these portions of the code. It will then be necessary to carry out a phase of integration tests to show that the manual code and the generated code interact correctly.

Figure 1.18 shows an informal specification. This specification will be partially taken into account by the B-model and will be the input for the creation of functional tests showing that the correct software has been created. The traceability phases are identified by the dotted arrows. We must show that we have correctly taken all the needs into account at each stage.

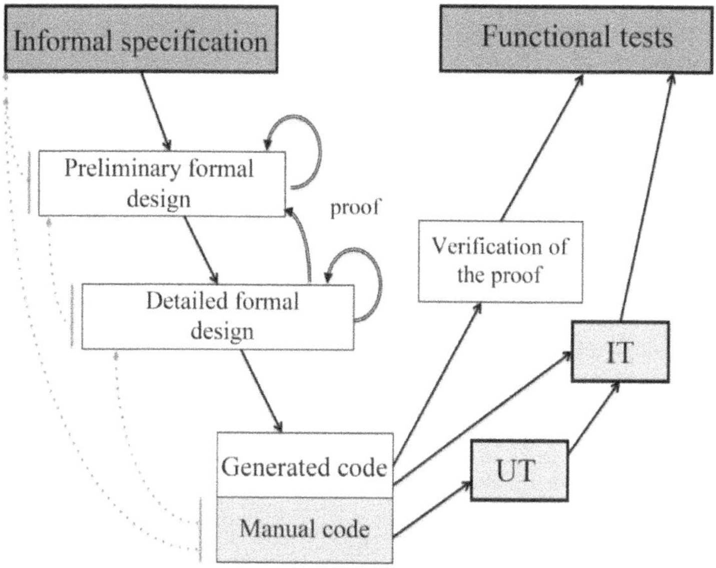

Figure 1.18. *B Development cycle*

The proof activities are shown by the double arrows in the figure. They may require the addition of lemmas during the interactive proofs. This is why it has been necessary to add a verification phase for the proof activity and for the lemmas.

However, without restarting the debate about the use of formal methods in safety software applications, in [BEH 96] it is stated that the unit and integration tests are redundant with the complete proof and safe code generation. Waeselynck [WAE 95] recommends preserving all the test phases in the expectation of returning to the methodology and the validation of B tools. This discussion is always valid if the development is carried out in a context outside a processor based on safe code (for PSC architecture, see Chapter 2 of [BOU 09] and Chapter 1 of [BOU 11a]).

It should be noted that creating and validating a B-model does not guarantee that the code generator, the production tools of executable programs (compiler, linker, etc.), the installation tools, the management tools for configuration, the target material architecture, etc., do not transform the execution and therefore nullify the proofs that have been carried out.

This point is mentioned in several chapters of this book. A qualification report for the tools used needs to be produced. However, the production of a qualification report for a code generator and/or a proof tool is not an easy task.

1.5. Feedback based on experience

1.5.1. *A few figures*

Table 1.6 provides information on the complexity of the B developments carried out in the railway sector. The table does not describe all of the railway applications that have been created using the B method, but it allows us to take stock of the complexity of the developments created with the B method.

System name	Lines of code B	Lines of generated code	Language	Number of proof obligations
CDTC	5,000	3,000	ADA	700
KVB	60,000	22,000	ADA	10,000
KVB-SN	9,000	6,000	ADA	2,750
KVS	22,000	16,000	ADA	6,000
SACEM-simplified	3,500	2,500	Module 2	550
SAET-METEOR	115,000	90,000	ADA	27,800
Eurocoder	10,000	4,500	ADA	4,200
CdG-VAL	PADS: 186,440	30,632	ADA	62,056
	UCA: 50,085	11,662	ADA	12,811

Table 1.6. *Example of complexity of a B-model [BOU 06]*

1.5.2. *Some uses*

1.5.2.1. *The current situation*

The B method was initially used for railways. As opposed to Safety-Critical Application Development Environment (SCADE) (see [BOU 12b, Chapter 2]), which is based on an equational language, the B method was defined for the description of sequential, non-interruptible programs. Its ability to describe complex algorithms is one of its key strengths; another strength of the B method is that it delivers one single notation that goes from specification to implementation.

The railway equipment which manages line occupation (called ground equipment) is difficult to model with equations. Therefore, we need to describe algorithms which will manipulate complex structures describing line topology (see [BOU 12a, Appendix 2.7]) and the characteristics of trains and equipment.

The main users of the B method are ALSTOM and SIEMENS; however, AREVA, in the Communication-Based Train Control (CBTC) project[7], is in the process of using the B method.

There have been several attempts to apply the B method in the automobile and space industries.

1.5.2.2. *SAET-METEOR*

Line 14 of the Paris Metro is managed by SAET-METEOR, and more particularly by the automatic train protection sub-system (see Figure 1.19) which is distributed along the line and within the equipped trains.

The control system has complete control over the automatic operation trains (acceleration, emergency stop, etc.). However, the manual operation trains are autonomous and can override a stop order transmitted by signaling. The line is managed by an automatic line pilot (PA-Ligne) and is divided into automation sections [LEC 96].

The control system is thus made up of three software applications developed with the B method and with a safety level of SSIL3-SSIL4 as specified by the standard CENELEC EN 50128 [CEN 01, CEN 11][8]

It is noteworthy that since SAET-METEOR began operation in 1998, the safety software has had no problems, so that no change to the safety software has been necessary.

---

7 "Communication Based Train Control": an operation, driving and safety system for trains and metros. CBTC is a system made up of embedded equipment onboard trains and fixed equipment communicating between them (usually by radio). CBTC is subject to a standard [IEE 04].

8 For more information, see http://www.cenelec.eu/.

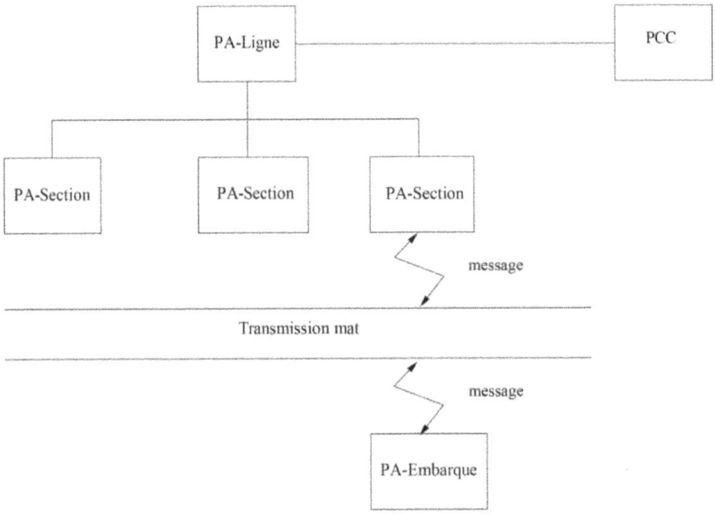

Figure 1.19. *Breakdown of the SAET-METEOR Automatic Pilot*

The robustness of the process implemented for the SAET-METEOR project made it possible to reproduce all of the work for the extension of the line from Madeleine to Saint-Lazare. This extension has been open to the public since 16 December 2003. On 26 June 2007, RATP opened an extension to Olympiades (13th *arrondissement*, Paris).

1.5.2.3. *VAL CdG*

The VAL CdG (Figure 1.20) is based on Siemens[9] VAL technology[10] and it combines the classical VAL (purely electronic) with a VAL controlled by a two-direction automatic pilot (PADS) and an alarm control unit (UCA).

CdG VAL comprises two lines (Line 1 and LISA), which have been in operation since April 2007. The line is open 24 hours a day.

The PADS and UCA were developed with the B method and with a safety level of SSIL3-SSIL4 as described in the standard CENELEC EN 50128 [CEN 01, CEN 11].

9 For more information, see www.siemens.com.

10 The VAL, the first fully automatic driverless metro in the world, was opened in Lille, France, in 1983, and now also operates in Taïpei, Toulouse (Line 1) Rennes, Toulouse (Line 2) and Turin, Italy. There is also a VAL at the airports Chicago O'Hare and Paris-Orly.

Figure 1.20. *The CdG VAL at the platform*

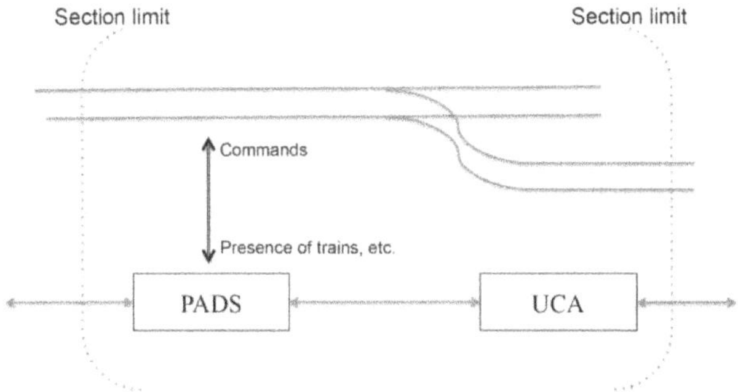

Figure 1.21. *Architecture of the VAL CdG*

1.5.2.4. *Eurobalise coder*

For our third example, we will take some field equipment that links a central station and the balises (a balise is an electronic beacon or transponder, placed between the rails, that gives orders to the trains).

For this application, there is only one formally developed software application, which was developed with the B method [ABR 96] and one treatment unit. The software application has been created with a safety level of SSIL3-SSIL4 as described in the standard CENELEC EN 50128 [CEN 01, CEN 11].

The B method is a formal method which guarantees (through mathematical proofs) that the software is correct with respect to a property.

This guarantee is very useful, but it does not cover the code generator, the generation chain for the executable program (compiler, linker, etc.) and the means of loading.

As shown in Figure 1.22, with this application, there are two code generators and two code generation chains for executable programs (two compilers). This makes it possible to have two different versions of the executable program. It is thus possible to show that the address tables (variables, constants, functions, parameters, etc.) of the two executable programs are indeed different. Each version of the application is loaded in different memory spaces.

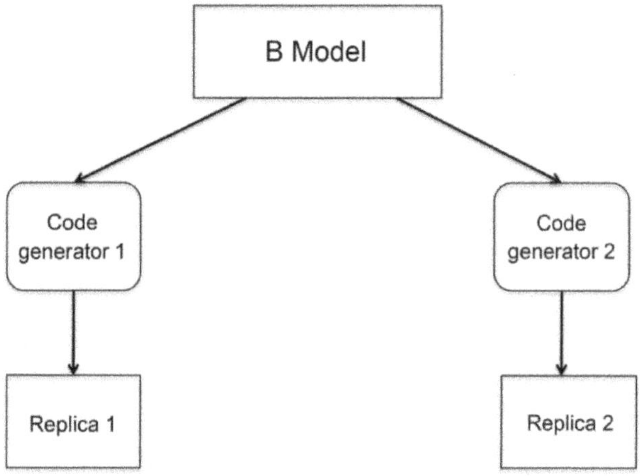

Figure 1.22. *Diversification*

1.6. Conclusion

A complete course on the B method is beyond the scope of the current chapter; however, we have been able to present the basic principles of this formal method. A formal method is based on a syntax, a semantics and a verification method.

The B method is a formal programming method that aims to specify and produce software safely.

One of the significances of the B method is that it offers a homogeneous notation for the specification and the design of a software application.

For the B method, the verification principle is the proof. The specifications obtained in this way are free of the most usual bugs and, through the principle of refinement of the specifications, it is possible to construct algorithms and show that these algorithms verify the specification. The crucial difference between the B method and the classical development lies in the fact that with formal methods the program is correct by construction.

The test thus becomes an "obsolete" activity, which is a good news given the cost of testing. However, this is only true if a certain number of assumptions are verified, such as the demonstration that the generation chain for the executable program (code generator, compiler, etc.) does not introduce any fault, and that it is possible to trust the verification tools (proof obligation generator, prover, etc.).

1.7. Glossary

AMN abstract machine notation

CENELEC *Comité Européen de Normalisation ELECtrotechnique* (European Committee for Electrotechnical Standardization)

GSL generalized substitution language

IT integration tests

METEOR *Metro Est Ouest Rapide* (High-speed East-West metro)

PA *Pilote Automatique* (autopilot)

PO proof obligation

PADS *Pilote Automatique Double Sens* (two-way autopilot)

SACEM *Système d'Aide à la Conduite, à l'Exploitation et à la Maintenance* (Assisted Driving, Operation and Maintenance System)

SAET *Système d'Automatisation de l'Exploitation des Trains* (Train Automation and Operation System)

SCADE Safety-Critical Application Development Environment

SIL safety integrity level

SSIL software SIL

UCA	*Unité de Contrôle des Alarmes* (alarm checking unit)
UT	unit test
V&V	verification and validation.
VAL	*Véhicule Automatique Léger* (light automatic vehicle)
VDM	Vienna Development Method
WP	weakest precondition

1.8. Bibliography

[ABR 91] ABRIAL J.R., LEE M.K.O., NEILSON D.S., *et al.*, "The B-Method", *The proceeding is VDM'91*, vol. 2, pp. 398–405, 1991.

[ABR 92] ABRIAL J.R., "On constructing large software systems", *IFIP 12th World Computer Congress*, vol. A-12, pp. 103–112, September 1992.

[ABR 96] ABRIAL J.R., *The B-Book*, Cambridge University Press, 1996.

[ANS 83] ANSI, Standard ANSI/MIL-STD-1815A-1983, Ada programming language Ada, 1983.

[ARA 97] ARAGO, "Applications des méthodes formelles au logiciel", *Observatoire Français des Techniques Avancées (OFTA), ARAGO 20*, Masson, June 1997.

[BAI 08] BAIER C., KATOEN J.-P., *Principles of Model Checking*, MIT Press, 2008.

[BEH 93] BEHM P., "Application d'une méthode formelle aux logiciels sécuritaires ferroviaires", *Atelier Logiciel Temps Réel, 6ème Journées Internationales du Génie Logiciel*, 1993.

[BEH 96] BEHM P., "Développement formel des logiciels sécuritaires de METEOR", in HABRIAS H. (ed.), *Proceedings of the 1st Conference on the B Method, Putting into Practice Methods and Tools for Information System Design*, Nantes Computer Science Research Institute (IRIN), pp. 3–10, November 1996.

[BEH 97] BEHM P., DESFORGES P., MEIJA F., "Application de la méthode B dans l'industrie ferroviaire", *ARAGO 20*, pp. 59–88, 1997.

[BOU 06] BOULANGER J.-L., Expression et validation des propriétés de sécurité logique et physique pour les systèmes informatiques critiques, PhD Thesis, University of Technology of Compiègne, 2006.

[BOU 09] BOULANGER J.-L. (ed.), *Sécurisation des architectures informatiques – exemples concrets*, Hermes-Lavoisier, 2009.

[BOU 11a] BOULANGER J.-L. (ed.), *Sécurisation des architectures informatiques industrielles*, Hermes-Lavoisier, 2011.

[BOU 11b] BOULANGER J.-L. (ed.), *Static analysis of software*, ISTE, London, John Wiley & Sons, New York, 2011.

[BOU 12a] BOULANGER J.-L. (ed.), *Industrial use of formal method: formal verification*, ISTE, London, and John Wiley & Sons, New York, 2012.

[BOU 12b] BOULANGER J.-L. (ed.), *Formal methods: Industrial use from model to the code*, ISTE, London, John Wiley & Sons, New York, 2012.

[CEN 01] CENELEC EN 50128, "Railway applications – communications, signalling and processing systems – software for railway control and protection systems", CENELEC, May 2001.

[CEN 11] CENELEC EN 50128, "Railway applications – communications, signalling and processing systems – software for railway control and protection systems", CENELEC, May 2011.

[DEH 94] DEHBONEI B., MEJIA F., "Formal development of software in railways safety critical systems", in MURTHY T.K.S., MELLITT B., BREBBIA C.A., *et al.* (eds.), *Railway Operations*, Computational Mechanics Publications, vol. 2, pp. 213–220, 1994.

[DEH 94] DEHBONEI B., MEJIA F., "Formal methods in the railways signalling industry", In Springer-Verlag, (ed.), FME'94, *Industrial Benefits of Formal Methods of Lecture Notes in Computer Science*, Springer, Verlag), vol. 873, pp. 26–34, 1994

[DIL 95] DILLER A., *Z: An Introduction to Formal Methods*, John Wiley & Sons, March 1995.

[DIJ 76] DIJKSTRA E.W., *A Discipline of Programming*, Prentice Hall, 1976.

[GEO 90] GEORGES J.-P., "Principes et fonctionnement du Système d'Aide à la Conduite, à l'Exploitation et à la Maintenance (SACEM). Application à la ligne A du RER", *Revue Générale des Chemins de fer*, vol. 6, June 1990.

[GUI 90] GUIHOT G., HENNEBERT C., "SACEM software validation", i*Proceedings of 12th IEEE-ACM International Conference on Software Engineering*, March 1990.

[HAL 91] HALBWACHS N., CASPI P., RAYMOND P., *et al.*, "The synchronous dataflow programming language Lustre", *Proceedings of the IEEE*, vol. 79, no. 9, pp. 1305–1320, September 1991.

[HIN 95] HINCHEY M.G., BOWEN J.P. (eds.), *Applications of Formal Methods*, International Series in Computer Science, Prentice Hall, 1995.

[HOA 69] HOARE C.A.R., "An axiomatic basis for computer programming", *Communications of the ACM*, vol. 12, pp. 576–583, October 1969.

[IEE 04] IEEE, 1474.1, IEEE Standard for Communications-Based Train Control (CBTC) Performance and Functional Requirements, 2004.

[ISO 99] ISO, ISO/IEC 9899:1999, Programming languages – C, 1999.

[JON 90] JONES C.B., *Systematic Software Development Using VDM*, 2nd ed., Prentice Hall International, 1990.

[LAN 96] LANO K., *The B Language and Method: A Guide to Practical Formal Development*, Springer Verlag London Ltd., 1996.

[LEC 96] LECOMPTE P., BEAURENT P.-J., "Le système d'automatisation de l'exploitation des trains (SAET) de METEOR", *Revue Générale des Chemins de fer*, vol. 6, pp. 31–34, June 1996.

[MAT 98] MATRA and RATP, "Naissance d'un Métro. Sur la nouvelle ligne 14, les rames METEOR entrent en scène. PARIS découvre son premier métro automatique", *La vie du Rail & des Transports*, Hors-Série no. 1076, October 1998.

[MON 00] MONIN J.-F., *Introduction aux méthodes formelles*, Hermès, 2000.

[MOR 90] MORGAN C., *Deriving Programs from Specifications*, Prentice Hall International, 1990.

[SCH 01] SCHNEIDER S., *The B-Method: An Introducton*, Palgrave, 2001.

[SPI 89] SPIVEY J.M., *The Z Notation: A Reference Manual*, Prentice Hall International, 1989.

[WAE 95] WAESELYNCK H., BOULANGER J.-L., "The role of testing in the b formal development process", *The proceeding is VDM'91, ISSRE'95*, Toulouse, 25–27 October 1995.

[WOR 96] WORDSWORTH J., *Software Engineering with B*, Addison-Wesley, 1996.

2

Atelier B

2.1. Introduction

Atelier B has been used on many occasions in developing safety programs that are used for functions at the SSIL3 and SSIL4 levels[1]. The autopilot (known as SAET-METEOR, see [BOU 11a], Chapter 3) of Line 14 of Paris's Metro was the first high-visibility project to use Atelier B, and this project was instrumental in the qualification of the tool by the AQL[2] department of the RATP[3]. This qualification process involved extensive testing, reviews of the development documentation and close examination of the source code.

For certain sensitive tools, such as mathematical proof tools, specific measures had to be taken, as mathematical proof replaces a large number of unit and integration tests. For example, a new theorem prover, based on different solution principles and including its own validation process, was needed to validate the mathematical rules; a group of experts was also established for manual validation of those rules that could not be validated automatically.

This version of the Atelier, version 3.6.4, has since been used for other automatic metro systems, both in France and abroad. Development of Atelier B has continued in parallel to make use of new techniques. Version 4.0

Chapter written by Thierry LECOMTE.

1 There are five SSILs (software safety integrity levels), from 0 to 4: see standard CENELEC EN 50128 [CEN 11].

2 *Atelier de qualification logiciel*, program qualification tool.

3 See http://www.ratf.fr.

constituted a technological departure from earlier versions in using the Qt environment, enabling distribution of the application using the Windows, Linux, Solaris and MacOS operating systems. Two versions of Atelier B are currently available: a free community version, which is partly open-source, and a commercial version, which includes extensive technical support.

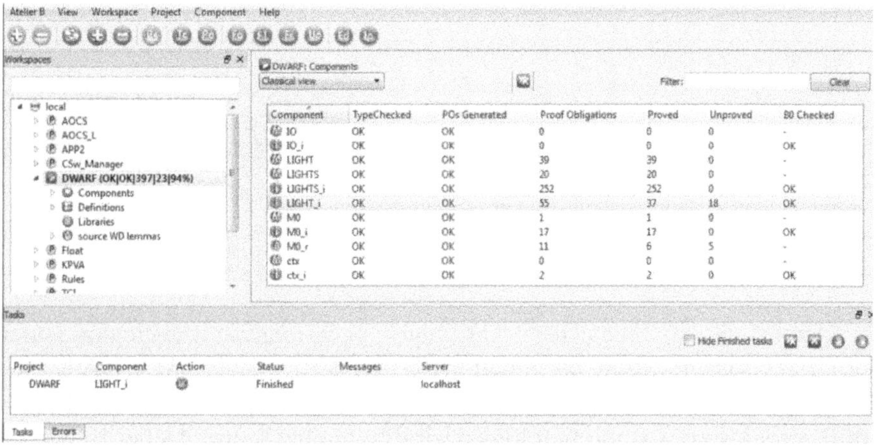

Figure 2.1. *Central interface of Atelier B*

This environment may be used to manage B projects for the development of sequential projects and for B-event projects for modeling non-sequential systems and software[4]. In addition to the functions expected of a software engineering suite, Atelier B allows us to verify the conformity of implementable models in relation to their specifications using mathematical proof. The mathematical predicates (or proof obligations) which must be demonstrated in order to guarantee this conformity are generated automatically.

These proof obligations are then processed by an automatic theorem demonstrator. The validity of a B project is dependent on the demonstration of all of the proof obligations. The obligations, which are not demonstrated automatically, must be inspected to determine if the model is at fault (errors in the specification and/or implementation), or if the theorem demonstrator lacks the heuristics needed for automatic demonstration of the proof obligation.

4 Managed via interruptions, parallel and distributed aspects.

In these cases, the human operator must assist the tool by providing commands, within the context of an interactive demonstration, for correct orientation of the mathematical demonstration. The user also has the option to define generic mathematical rules, which are then used in the construction and reuse of demonstration schemas.

This demonstration activity is carried out throughout the development process, enabling early detection of errors or incoherencies in the specification or implementation without needing to wait for the final code to be available.

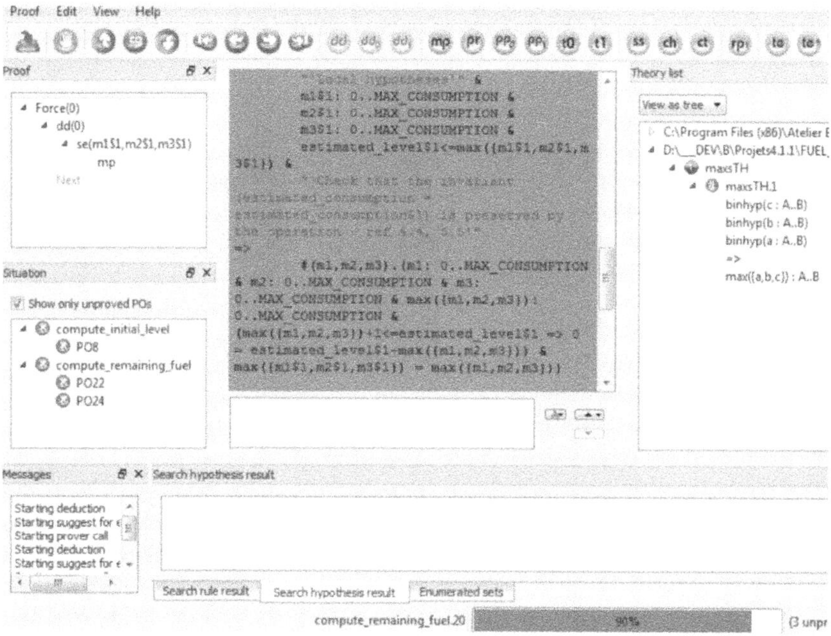

Figure 2.2. *Interactive prover in Atelier B*

2.2. Automatic refinement

In the 1990s, Matra Transport International[5] studied the possibility of producing an implementation of a B model[6] as automatically as possible

5 Now part of Siemens Transportation Systems.

6 The portion of the model suitable for direct translation into a code language such as Ada and C.

[BUR 99]. This technique, known as automatic refinement, has been used on a number of occasions, notably for the New York metro (Carnarsie Line) and the automatic shuttle at Paris Charles de Gaulle airport (the VAL-CDG, which was brought into service in April 2007).

The RIMEL project[7] involved the development of an automatic refinement tool known as B automatic refinement tool (BART), specifically designed for integration into Atelier B. This refinement tool reused principles from the tool developed by Matra Transport International, using iterative application of model transformation rules to replace set, relationship and partial function-type data with other data based on scalars, tables and tables of tables, modifying the associated algorithms as needed.

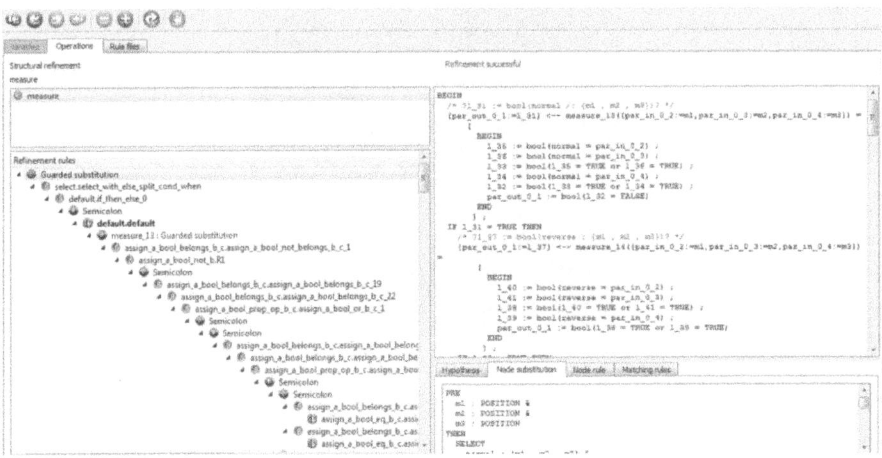

Figure 2.3. *Implementation of BART*

These transformations are carried out gradually, generally by introducing more intermediate steps than a human programmer would use; this leads to the production of simpler, but more numerous, mathematical proof obligations.

BART operates using pattern matching principle. Thus, the rules describe certain motifs that should be found in the input file, and the way in which these motifs should be replaced as part of the refinement process.

7 ANR-SETIN project (http://rimel.loria.fr).

Refinement rules are applied repeatedly, and may generate new machines or implementations. This continues until one of the two following conditions is verified:

– The generated components correspond to a translatable B0 implementation. This constitutes a successful automatic refinement.

– No further rules can be applied. Human intervention is then needed to add new refinement rules and/or modify the existing rules. This interactive refinement phase uses a specific interface, displaying the part of the B model which is being transformed, the information in the B model available for use by the rules, potentially applicable refinement rules and the transformed model at the current point of execution.

The whole generation process may be reiterated for certification purposes to show that the B models used for code generation were effectively produced by automatic refinement. The refinement engine and refinement rules do not require intensive validation as the validity of the generated models is guaranteed by mathematical proof.

```
RULE scalar_ini0
REFINES
    @a :: @b
WHEN
    ENUM(@b) &
    @c : @b
IMPLEMENTATION
    @a := @c
END;
```

```
RULE assign_a_b_6
REFINES
    @a := @b
WHEN
    B0(@a) &
    DECL_OPERATION(@c <-- @d | BEGIN @c := @b END)
IMPLEMENTATION
    @a <-- @d
IMPLEMENT
     @a
END;
```

Figure 2.4. *Example of rules used in BART*

258 refinement rules are supplied with BART (an example is given in Figure 2.3). These constitute a reference database, which is then extended on the basis of user requirements.

2.3. Code generation

Code production tools are an important aspect of the B method, as they are used to generate programs corresponding to the specification expressed in the form of a B model [ABR 96].

The code generation phase is critical, as a faulty code generator will produce a non-compliant program and thus destroy the formal development cycle. For this reason, code generators are never used alone, and additional measures are taken to avoid anomalies of this kind.

For example, duplicate generators (see Figure 2.4) may be used to construct a double chain, producing two separate source codes from the same B model. For doubling purposes, we may use libraries (pathways, compilations) based on different techniques/approaches, and produce visibly different codes (instructions for independent transformations may be swapped, additional instructions with no functional impact on the results may be added, etc.). These techniques also allow us to deal, in part, with production errors in the final binary code during the compilation stage.

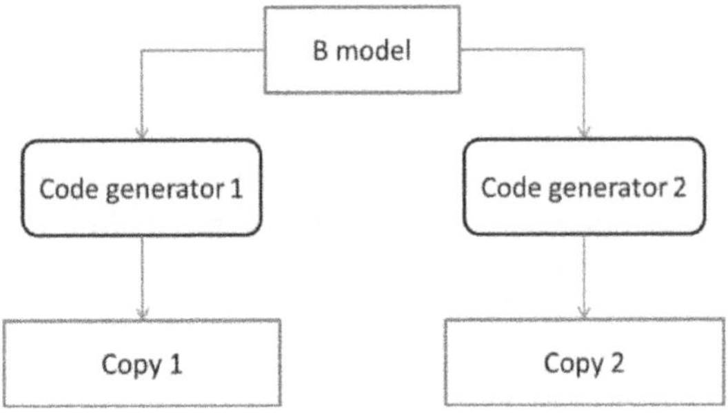

Figure 2.5. *An example of double generation*

These programs are executed using a wide variety of platforms, and a wide variety of different code generators are also available. Each execution platform generally corresponds to a specific code generator. The BOM project[8], for instance, studied the generation of C code and Java bytecode for chip card type applications, where memory usage must be kept to a minimum. The results of this project were partly reused in developing a new, public C code generator, intended for release with version 4.0 of Atelier B.

This generator, ComenC, was based on a limited definition[9] of the implementable B language (B0) and the Cocktail tool suite[10], aiming to produce readable C source code with limited use of pointers, for use in the development of safety applications respecting the CENELEC EN 50128

8 See http://lifc.univ-fcomte.fr/~tatibouet/PERSO/WEBBOM/RESSOURCES/index.html.

9 This definition notably disallowed multiple uses of the same abstract B machine within a single development project.

10 See http://www.cocolab.de/en/cocktail.html.

[CEN 11] and CEI/IEC 61508 standards[11,12]. A new code generator, C_4B, based on Coco/R[13] framework has been set up and integrated into Atelier B 4.1, as a replacement for ComenC. C_4B offers more flexible code generation (basic data types implementation) and imposes less B0 constraints. Moreover, C_4B is fully developed in C++ and as such it is more easily maintainable.

A policy of widespread distribution was established, with presentations and courses given in a number of French universities and engineering schools, with the aim of improving the accessibility of safety application development using formal B models. Eventually, the restrictions applied to the B0 language were found to be too restrictive, posing considerable problems for program developers.

Work then began on a new code generator, $ComenC_2$. Based on the B Compiler, this generator offered support for multi-instance machines, and allowed users to parameter certain translation choices through the use of translation profiles.

```
EVENTS

  RTC_swap
    ref Swap
=
  ANY
    time
  , morrow
  , victor
  , leftspan
  WHERE
    time     : INTEGER
  & morrow   : INTEGER
  & victor   : PROCESSES
  & leftspan     : INTEGER
  & clock0 < time
  & time < morrow
  & clock0..morrow /\ dom(Schedule) = {time}
  & (elected0 : Tasks  => time <= clock0+term0(elected0))
  & (elected0 : Tasks  => leftspan = term0(elected0)-(time-clock0))
  & term0[Schedule[{time}]] = {0}
  & victor : Schedule[{time}] \/ term0~[NATURAL1]
  & (victor = elected0  =>  0 < leftspan)
  THEN
    clock0 := morrow
  || elected0 := victor
  || term0 := term0 <+ ({Phantom}<<|{elected0 |-> leftspan} \/ (Schedule[{time}]<|Deadline))
  END
```

Figure 2.6. *Example of an event-B model*

11 See http://www.cenelec.eu/Cenelec/Homepage.htm.

12 See http://www.iec.ch/.

13 http://www.ssw.uni-linz.ac.at/Coco/.

Support for the event-B language was introduced with Atelier B 4.0, and it is now possible to model systems (in the broad sense of the term) using representations based on events and the expression of permanent or transitory properties through mathematical predicates. This approach has been applied to a range of domains and technical objects, essentially for analytical purposes and not for code purposes, as in the case of the B "for software" language.

Nevertheless, a number of code-oriented applications have been developed recently. Notable examples include code production for:

– Programmable automata: for triggering the platform doors for line 13 of the Paris metro [SAB 08]. A system model was used to identify a safe algorithm for controlling the opening mechanisms of the platform doors with a chosen set of disturbances. The corresponding code for the automaton was then produced using a Ladder[14] code generator, developed for the project. To do this, a subset of the Event-B language was defined, alongside translation plans using analysis of data flows. These plans were programmed using the B Compiler. The code generator was not qualified or certified: the generated Ladder code was manually re-read and compared to the specification documentation.

– *Microelectronics systems:* in the course of the Forcoment project[15] [BEN 09a, BEN 09b], it was seen that an event-based model of a function may be transformed into a hardware description. The code generator developed as part of this project produces a synthesizable VHDL model (corresponding to a subset of the VHDL language, with clear semantics) based on an event-B model and the parameterization of the translation process, used, for example, to identify input, output, clocks, registers, etc., and to orient the translation of integer-type data (which may also be handled using bit-to-bit operations and which need to be represented in the form of bit vectors). Unlike C and Ada code generators (which use the "one for one" translation principle), there is a certain semantic distance between the event-B model and the generated VHDL model. Further work is needed to validate this approach, in addition to the two cases in which it has been applied, for which the generated VHDL has been shown to satisfy functional validation tests.

14 One of the five programming languages for programmable automata according to the IEC61131-3 standard.

15 See http://www.methode-b.com/php/projet-forcoment-fr.php.

2.4. Proof and model animation

Proof tools are crucial, as they guarantee the validity of an implementation in relation to its specification, thus replacing most of the testing phase for the obtained software. Paradoxically, these tools undergo minimal evolution in order to guarantee "proof replay" when later versions of Atelier B are used for evolutions of a proved pre-existing model.

In the case of system modeling, where code production is not the main objective, it is difficult to verify whether or not the developed model is correct (i.e. no important properties have been forgotten) and whether or not it corresponds to the real system (i.e. whether it behaves in the same way as the real system). It is therefore possible to prove an incorrect model if no references are available for validation.

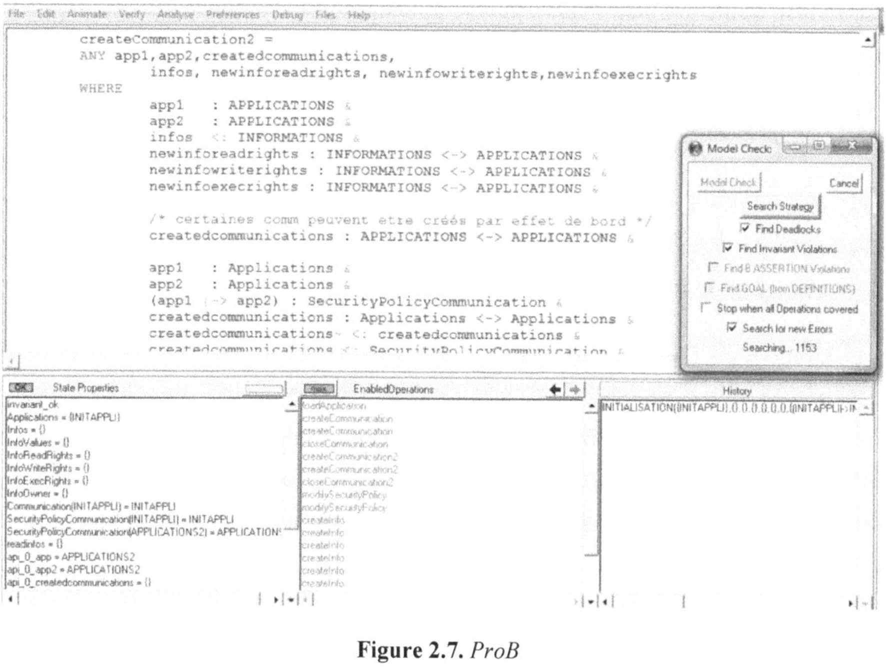

Figure 2.7. *ProB*

This is the reason for the recent development of model animation techniques, used to validate models of this type (which can contain hundreds of events). ProB[16] is a notable example, which acts both as a model-checker and a model animation tool. ProB goes through the state space of model variables to check that all possible value combinations verify the properties of the model.

Heuristics and optimization techniques may be used to limit the number of evaluated states, enabling the use of this tool for large-scale models, for example in the validation of topological data for the description of metro lines [LEU 10].

2.5. The move toward open source

In the early 2009, the decision was made to make the most recent Atelier B tools open source in order to promote the spread of B and its use by third parties in both academic and industrial contexts. At that time, only the B predicate animation kernel[17] was available under the GPLv3 license. The following elements were then made accessible:

– the B compiler;

– the BART automatic refinement tool;

– the C_4B C code generator;

– the graphical interface of Atelier B.

Along with these license changes, the distribution method for Atelier B was changed to a Qt-style dual usage license, offering:

– a free community version, without support, updated approximately once every two years;

– a professional version, including support services and regular updates.

These measures promoted the evaluation of the B method, with 18,000 recorded downloads from the first version of Atelier B 4.0 onward. Moreover, a large number of contributions to these tools and the associated

16 See http://www.stups.uni-duesseldorf.de/ProB/index.php5/The_ProB_Animator_and_Model_Checker.

17 PredicateB: library used for the evaluation of predicates and expressions and for executing substitutions in the B language. This library is both used by the RATP Ovado and ClearSy SDV tools, in addition to the ProB model checker, for validating constants representing the track topology of a metro line.

documentation have been made available under the "creative commons – paternity" license.

Notable examples include a localized Japanese version of Atelier B, developed by Sapporo University, and a Brazilian (Portuguese) version produced by AeS, a small company in Sao Paulo. Atelier B is available for free download at http://www.atelierb.eu.

2.6. Glossary

AQL *atelier de qualification logiciel* (software qualification workshop)

BART B automatic refinement tool

CENELEC *Comité Européen de Normalisation Electrotechnique* (European Committee for Electrotechnical Standardization)

IEC International Electrotechnical Commission

RATP *régie autonome des transports parisiens* (autonomous operator of parisian transports)

SSIL software safety integrity level

2.7. Bibliography

[ABR 96] ABRIAL J.R., *The B-Book*, Cambridge University Press, 1996.

[BEN 09a] BENVENISTE M., "A proved 'correct by construction' realistic digital circuit", *Recent Innovation and Applications in B, FM Week*, Eindhoven, 3 November 2009.

[BEN 09b] BENVENISTE M., "A proved 'correct by construction' memory protection unit", *SmartEvent 2009*, Sophia Antipolis, 22–25 September 2009.

[BOU 11] BOULANGER J.-L. (ed.), *Techniques industrielles de modélisation formelle pour le transport*, Collection IC2, Hermes-Lavoisier, 2011.

[BUR 99] BURDY L., MEYNADIER J.-M., "Automatic refinement", *FM'99 – B Users Group Meeting – Applying B in an Iindustrial Context: Tools, Lessons and Techniques*, pp. 3–15, 1999.

[CEN 11] CENELEC EN 50128, Railway applications – Communication, signalling and processing systems – Software for railway control and protection systems, July 2011.

[IEC 98] IEC, "IEC 61508: Sécurité fonctionnelle des systèmes électriques électroniques programmables relatifs à la sécurité", *Norme internationale*, 1998.

[LEU 10] LEUSCHEL M., "Validation of railway properties with ProB", *Workshop on B Dissemination*, Natal, Brazil, 8 November 2010.

[SAB 08] SABATIER D., PATIN F., POUZANCRE G., *et al.*, "Utilisation de la méthode formelle B pour un système SIL3: la commande des portes palières sur la ligne 13 du métro parisien", *LambdaMu'15*, 28 November 2008.

3

B Tools

3.1. Introduction

In this chapter, we will give a brief overview of the operations of a B environment, specifically Atelier B, supplied by CLEARSY[1].

Unlike other formal methods, the B development cycle is fully covered by two commercial tools (covering specification, refinement, code generation, generation of proof obligations (POs) and proof assistants).

The first of these tools is Atelier B, sold and marketed by CLEARSY, and B-Toolkit, sold and marketed by B-Core (UK) Ltd. Note that the B-Toolkit is no longer commercially available.

This chapter will be broken down into three sections:

– general principles;

– presentation of Atelier B;

– presentation of open source tools.

3.2. General principles

All formal methods must be based on precise syntax and semantics, and the B method is no exception [ABR 96b]. The method includes a full

---

Chapter written by Jean-Louis BOULANGER.

1 For more information on CLEARSY and Atelier B, see http://www.clearsy.com/.

description of the different internal validation phases for abstract machines (syntax analysis, typing and PO generation). This gives us a precise idea of what should be included in a development suite. Figure 3.1 shows an outline of a development suite for the B method.

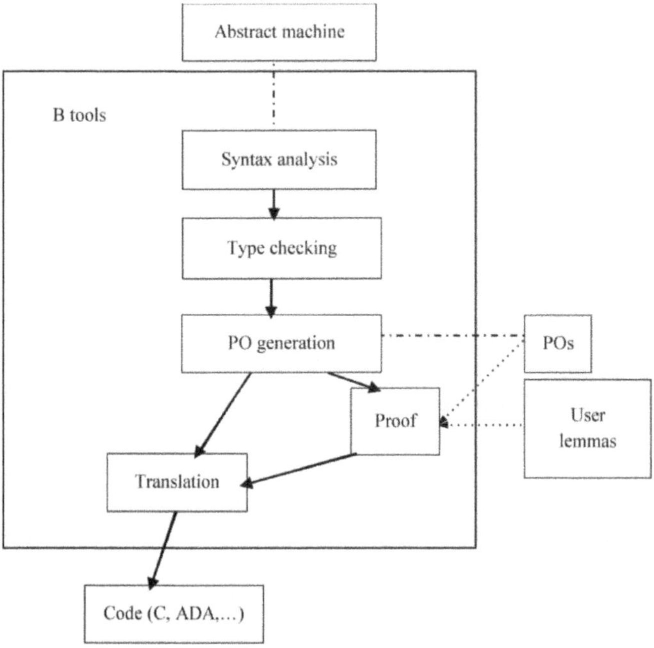

Figure 3.1. *Outline of a tool for use with the B method*

The arrows show the order of activation of different phases, while the dotted lines represent access to input files: an abstract machine, POs or user lemmas, or output files: generated code or POs. The tool must take account of dependencies introduced by composition clauses (sees, includes, etc.).

3.3. Atelier B

3.3.1. *Project management*

Note that Atelier B[2] is available free of charge from version 4.0 onward. It includes an integrated development environment (IDE), as shown in

2 Atelier B and the associated information may be downloaded from http://www.atelierb.eu/.

Figure 3.2. This IDE allows us to create B projects and components (machines, refinements and implementations) via the + and – buttons (see Figure 3.2).

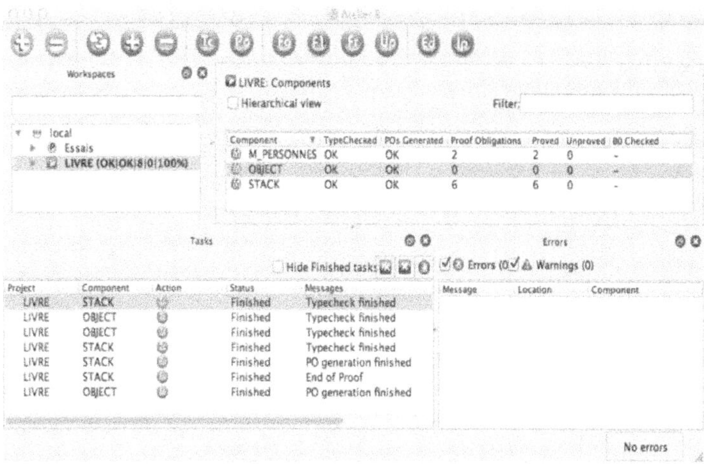

Figure 3.2. *Atelier B*

The "workspace" section shows the list of current projects. For a selected project (e.g. LIVRE), we see the list of components and the verification summary:

– type verification;

– generation of POs;

– number of POs to prove;

– number of unproved POs;

– number of proved POs;

– compatibility verification for B0[3].

Atelier B also includes a component editor, shown in Figure 3.3. This editor offers assistance in creating B models, showing the connections between mathematical and textual symbols on the right-hand panel (B symbols).

3 B0 is a subset of the B language used for direct translation into classic programming languages.

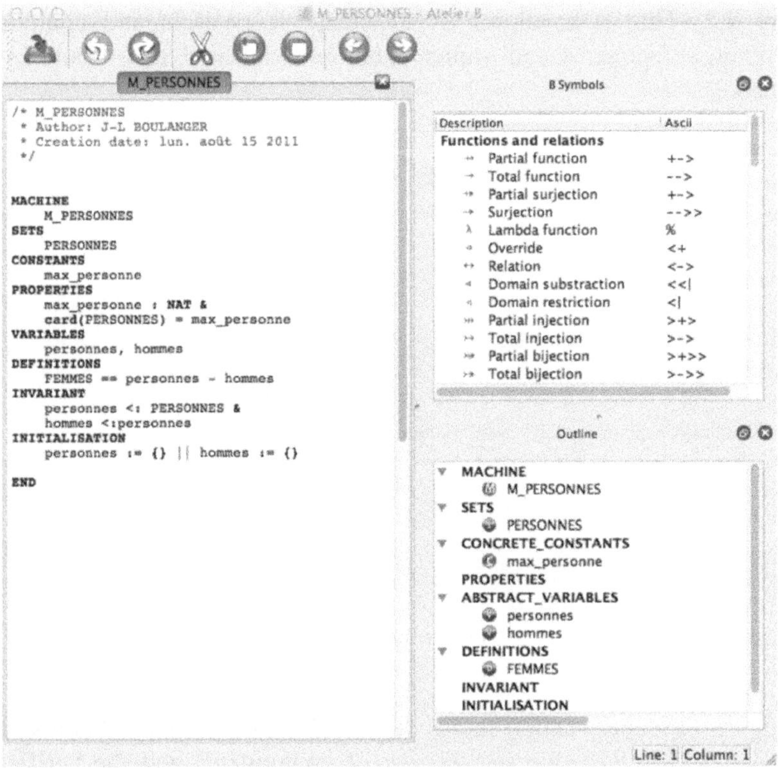

Figure 3.3. *The component editor*

This editor carries out verifications (syntax, typechecking, etc.) on components during the input process. The results are shown in the "Outline" panel.

Atelier B carries out verification and highlights anomalies each time a component is saved.

3.3.2. *Typechecking and PO generation*

3.3.2.1. *Typechecking*

Atelier B carries out verification either when a B component is saved or in response to a user request using the type check (TC) button (see Figure 3.2).

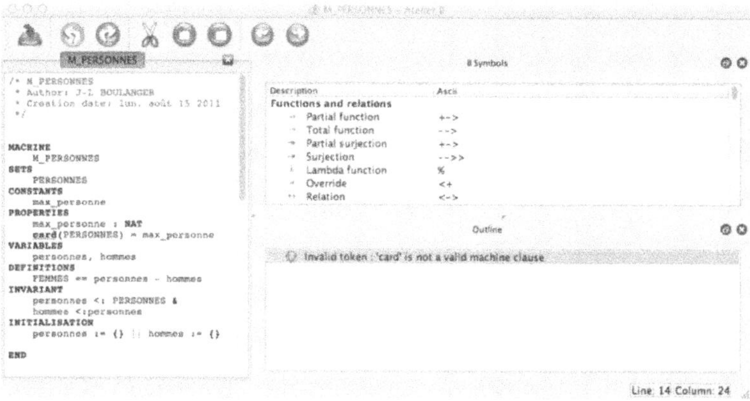

Figure 3.4. *Example of a syntax error*

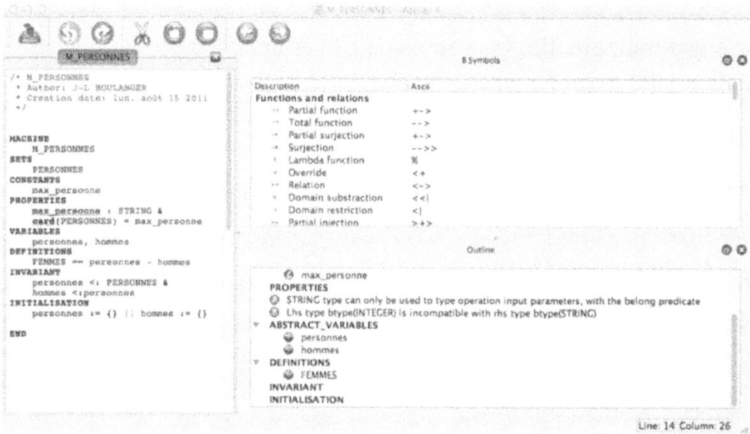

Figure 3.5. *Example of a typing error*

In the case shown in Figure 3.5, an error has been introduced by indicating that the constant max_personne is a string. This is incompatible with the use of the constant.

3.3.2.2. *PO generation*

Each B component (machine, refinement or implementation) is subject to a proof obligation generation phase (see Figure 3.6). The POs are automatically generated by the tool using the PO button (see Figure 3.2).

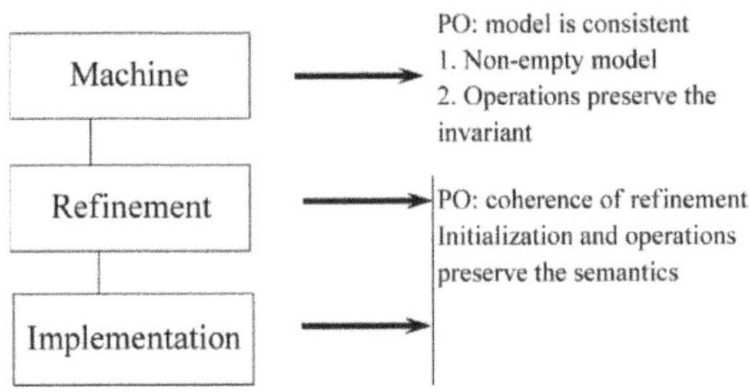

Figure 3.6. *Objectives of proof obligations*

For a high-level abstract machine, the generated POs guarantee mathematical consistency. For refinements and implementations, the POs guarantee the validity of the refinement in relation to the machine situated on the next level up in the development chain.

As a general rule, the complexity of POs depends on the chosen level of abstraction (the more concrete the case, the higher the complexity level) and the structure of the application in terms of connections between machines.

3.3.3. *Code generation*

3.3.3.1. *Verification of B0*

Code can only be generated for implementations. These implementations use a sub-set of the B language, noted B0. This subset of B is similar to imperative programming languages (ADA, C, Java, etc.).

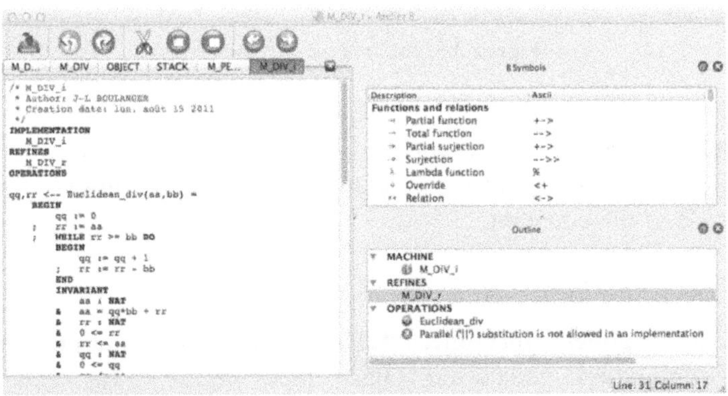

Figure 3.7. *Example of an implementation error*

When an implementation is saved or added to a project, the tool verifies that only B0 has been used.

3.3.3.2. *Code generation*

The commercial version of Atelier B comes with ADA and C code generators, which have been used for projects with high safety levels (SSIL3-SSIL4[4] in the CENELEC EN 50128 standards[5] [EN 01, EN 11]).

In the case of SAET-METEOR (see [BOU 12], Chapter 2), the B model [ABR 96] was translated into a safe ADA version [ANS 83] automatically by the tool.

The safety aspect is obtained through the use of a subset of ADA and a coded safety processor (named PSC, see [BOU 10] Chapters 3 and 11) guaranteeing the safety of the execution.

Formal methods present a number of advantages in terms of code generation:

– The conformity of the produced code to formal specifications has been proved. Therefore, it is possible to eliminate unit tests and integration tests.

– The obtained code is coherent (no useless variables, no typing problems, no dead code, no unvisited tests, no infinite loops, no side-effects, etc.). This allows early detection of a large number of classic faults.

– Formal methods offer a rigorous, high-quality approach.

3.3.4. *Prover*

Atelier B offers an automatic prover and an interactive assistant for manual proof.

3.3.4.1. *Automatic prover*

The automatic prover applies rule databases to each obligation, rewriting the goal and hypotheses until they coincide. The major drawback of these

4 SSIL: Software Safety Integrity Level. Standard [EN 01, EN 11] identifies five safety levels, from 0 (the lowest) to 4 (the highest).

5 The 2001 version of standard EN 50128 ([EN 01]) was updated in 2011 ([EN 11]), but both versions remained applicable until 2014 (this deadline has since been extended until 2017).

rewritings is that the suite does not retain the trace of the original goal, which sometimes leads to unwarranted failures.

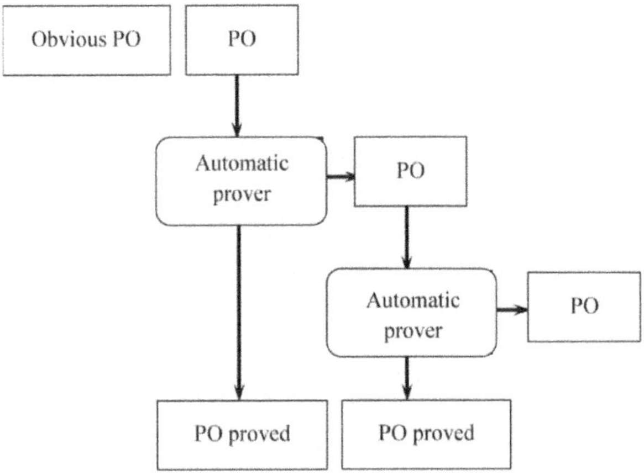

Figure 3.8. *Application of the proof process*

As we see from Figure 3.8, obvious POs are detected by the tool and considered proved. The figure also demonstrates the use of the prover in automatic mode for POs. At the end of this phase, a subset of POs may remain unproved (often around 20% for a well-founded project). The interactive proof assistant may be used to treat these cases. The first phase consists of using existing lemmas and tactics; in the second phase, we may need to introduce new lemmas, in the form of hypotheses or new proof tactics.

The prover may fail to demonstrate POs for one of two reasons:

– the proof obligation is false (e.g. if attempting to prove a goal of $100 < 50$), indicating a design error;

– the obligation is correct, but the rule basis is insufficient to establish the fact.

The tactics used by the automatic prover generally become more costly in terms of calculation time as the required demonstrations increase in complexity. The most exhaustive tactics can generate infinite loops in demonstrations.

Therefore, we need to manage the implemented tactics, and the tactics used by the prover have been grouped into "strength" categories for this reason: rapid, 0, 1, 2 and 3.

In most cases, the addition of tactics defined in the tool is sufficient to prove the majority of obligations generally from 80% to 100% for automatic proof.

3.3.4.2. *Principles of proof in interactive mode*

A certain number of additional rules are available, but will only be applied in response to a user request using the interactive proof option.

As the rule database of the automatic prover does not allow us to solve all possible cases; it is sometimes necessary to add rules using the interactive prover. A number of possibilities are then available to the user.

First, the user may apply rules defined in the Atelier, which are not applied systematically as they lead to considerable increases in solution time. If these added rules are not sufficient, the user may create new rules. Care is required when producing these rules, as they cannot be validated in full and it is possible to write rules allowing the solution of false obligations.

Added rules are subject to a specific verification process in order to demonstrate their correctness.

Note that interactive mode also allows the implementation of a specialist predicate prover (PP).

3.3.4.3. *Implementation of proof in interactive mode*

The interactive prover interface is shown in Figure 3.9. This interface may be used to handle POs for a given component. In the lower section of the interface, we see that the verification of the component M_PERSONNES involves proving two POs linked to the initialization.

In this example, we see that PO1 has been proved: this obligation consisted of demonstrating that the empty set is included in the Personnes set, which constitutes an obvious proof.

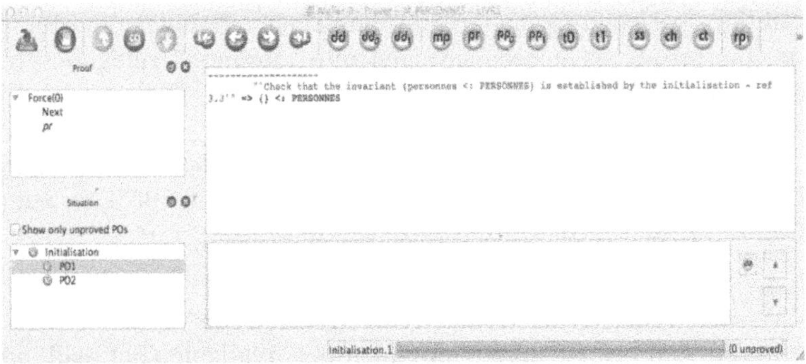

Figure 3.9. *Interactive prover*

3.3.5. *Tool qualification*

A qualification procedure for Atelier B was implemented in the context of the CASCADE European research project [MAR 95] and the industrial SAET-METEOR[6] (*Système d'Automatisation de l'Exploitation des Trains – METro Est Ouest Rapide*, for further details see [MAT 98, LEC 96]) project.

This procedure involved a number of industrial actors (Alstom, Siemens[7] Transportation Systems (then trading as Matra Transport International), the RATP and the SNCF) and the Inrets.

In addition to verification and validation work (validation of acquisition phases, validation of the rule base used by the provers, validation of the ADA code generator, etc.), a number of more specific activities were carried out, including expert rule reviews, implementation in a variety of industrial projects, and specific analytical activities.

This work showed that Atelier B was qualified for SSIL3-4 safety levels in the context of the SAET-METEOR project, using version 3.x.

Several versions of Atelier B have been produced since 1998, some of which have been qualified. The new qualifications are based on the existence of reference projects (such as SAET-METEOR), and all activities can be

6 For more information on the use of formal methods in the SAET-METEOR project, see [BOU 12] Chapter 2.

7 See http://www.siemens.com for more information.

replayed for these projects to verify that the same results are obtained. This qualification approach combines the use of feedback with qualification testing, based on replays of projects already in use in a commercial context.

Several changes have been made to Atelier B from version 4.0 onward (introduction of automatic refinement, changes to the interface, availability for different operating systems, etc.). Some of these changes have made it harder to carry out replay-based qualification, and more substantial qualification efforts are required. This is the reason behind the use of a double code generation chain for certain projects (lowering the safety levels required from each code generator).

3.4. Open source tools

3.4.1. *Presentation*

Researchers create tools in order to test possibilities and mix different methods and practices. In the case of B, The B-Book [ABR 96] was published during the final stages of the first major project to use the language in an industrial context (SAET-METEOR was brought into service in 1998).

A description of the B language therefore became available to academics at the same time as Atelier B. Atelier B is based on the B kernel, a language execution mechanism based on pattern-matching. The subjacent language is based on the theory and rules of pattern-matching. Atelier B produces files in a format associated with this context, making them difficult to interpret (the format is not given in the tool documentation) and creating interfacing issues when attempting to use Atelier B with other tools.

Faced with this problem, researchers began working on tools designed to manage the B language and facilitate interfacing, such as the ABTOOLS, BRILLANT[8] [COL 10], JBTools, BOB, MATISSE and RODIN projects.

The BRILLANT [MAR 03] project, based on the use of OCaml and Extensible Markup Language (XML), will be presented in Chapter 8 of this book. The RODIN project will be the subject of further discussion in Chapter 9.

---

8 For more information on the BRILLANT project, see http://gna.org/projects/brillant.

Other projects, such as BCARE (see [BOU 14], Chapter 7) aim to offer the means of validating proof activities. An interface between Atelier B and proof tools has been developed very recently, see [MEN 12].

Space and time considerations mean that we will not be able to present the full range of available open source tools in this chapter. For this reason, the BRILLANT project will be discussed separately, and we will focus our attention here on the ABTools environment. Other projects and initiatives are cited throughout the book.

3.4.2. *ABTools*

3.4.2.1. *Presentation*

In this section, we will show how the ABTools environment [BOU 01], a tool suite for the B method [ABR 96], may be used for rapid creation of a prototype associated with an extension of the B language. This environment was developed using the ANother Tool for Language Recognition (ANTLR) compiler generator [PAR 93].

Research work on the B language has tended to focus on the creation and implementation of extensions. These extensions aim to extend use of the B method [ABR 96] to other domains (mathematical aspects [ABR 02], system aspects, real time, etc.).

Note that two commercial tools were developed, CLEARSY's Atelier B and BCORE's BToolkit[9]. These commercial tools were not open and did not allow users to test extensions to the B language. Our tool does not aim to compete with the commercial suites, but to provide the open source tools for the study and development of extensions to B.

Our work focuses on the creation of a full environment taking account of the whole of the B language and the associated restrictions, designed to enable the rapid and easy implementation of extensions. The ABTools environment was generated using ANTLR, a compiler generation environment.

9 The BCORE tool is no longer available.

The verification process associated with the B method consists of using proof to demonstrate the coherence of the proposed model. The coherence of a B model is defined via the generation of mathematical lemmas known as POsPO. The PO generation process is based on the semantic definition of the B language (generalized substitution).

This section will be broken down into three parts, beginning with a presentation of ANTLR. In the second part, we will provide a description of the ABTools environment. The final part concerns the PO generation process and its implementation in the context of our environment.

3.4.2.2. *The ANTLR compiler generator*

ANTLR[10] is distributed by Terence Parr [PAR 93] under an open source license. ANTLR is not simply a compiler generator, but a full compiler development environment.

To date, the ANTLR environment has been used for the implementation of various languages including C, Java, Verilog and SDL-2000 [SCH 98]; most of the associated grammar is available on the official website. The environment is even suitable for direct integration into commercial tools.

ANTLR offers coverage of all phases of the compilation process: lexing, parsing, typing and code generation (Java, C, etc.), along with documentation generation (using TEX, HyperText Markup Language (HTML), XML, etc.).

The object character of the ANTLR environment permits high levels of flexibility, and any new grammar may be considered as an extension (through inheritance and/or overloading) of a grammar which has already been validated.

	Input stream	Output stream
Lexer	Character	Token
TokenStreamFilter	Token	Token
Parser	Token	Abstract syntax tree
TreeParser	Abstract Syntax Tree	Abstract syntax tree

Table 3.1. *Basic set*

10 More information on ANTLR is available at http://www.antlr.org/, including articles, grammars, database tools and full environment, ANTLRWorks.

Table 3.1 shows the four stages of language recognition using ANTLR. During the first stage, the Lexer analyzes the input character flow, and produces output in the form of tokens, each with a type and a value. This token flow is generally used directly as input by the parser, which constructs the abstract syntax tree (AST).

It is also possible to manipulate the token flow in order to add, remove or modify tokens using a filter (the TokenStreamFilter). The TreeWalker may also be used to evaluate the AST; this evaluation can lead to the creation of a new AST.

ANTLR provides a single language to describe each stage in the recognition process, based on the notion of objects. Therefore, it is possible to create new grammars by inheritance and overloading of existing grammars.

Using the textual description of the analyzers (lexical, syntax or treewalker), the ANTLR environment can then generate the target code of a tool implementing the analyzer. Till date, it is able to generate source code for any two languages from Java, C++ and C#. This choice has a direct influence on the grammar, as the action language, used in the rule base, is also the target language.

ANTLR offers documentation functions, which are compatible with javadoc, and allows generation of an html version of the analyzer. XML files can also be generated using object serialization functions.

Re-entry is a key characteristic of ANTLR-generated parsers. The term implies that in an analytical context, any rule from a tool (lexer, parser or treeParser) can be recalled in an action block. This is possible because each rule from the grammar is associated with a method.

3.4.2.3. *The ABTools environment*

3.4.2.3.1. Presentation

Figure 3.10 shows a development environment for the B language. The treatment of B is characterized by the following phases:

– lexical and syntactic analysis;

– semantic analysis (typechecking, respect of B0 constraints, etc.);

– PO generation;

– proof of POs;

– code generation;

– generation of project documentation.

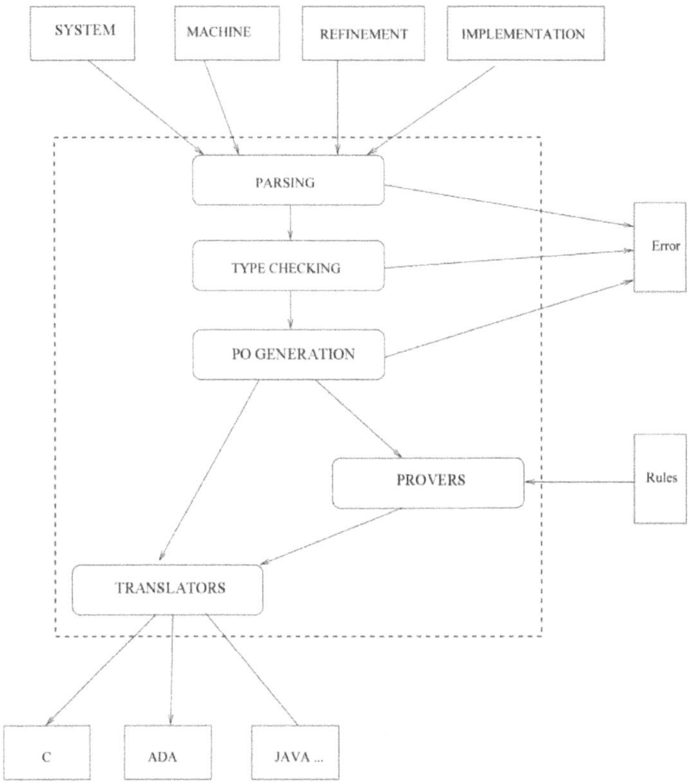

Figure 3.10. *A B environment*

The ABTools environment, as shown in Figure 3.11, is currently made up of five elements: a lexical analyzer, a syntax analyzer, a decompiler (American Standard Code for Information Interchange (ASCII), LaTeX, XML), a typechecker (which verifies types and generates a symbol table) and the PO generator.

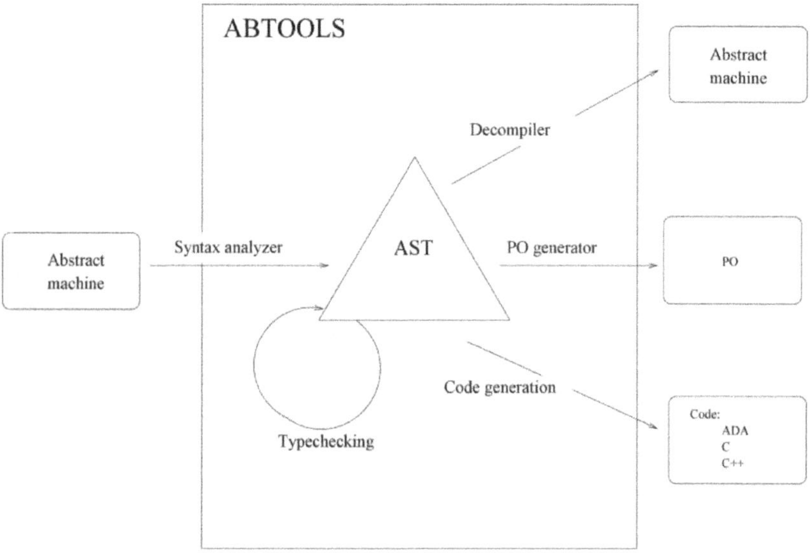

Figure 3.11. *The ABTools environment*

A more detailed presentation of the ABTools environment is given in [BOU 01]. Note that the proof aspect is not covered by our environment, which is designed for use in generating POs in different formats (ASCII, XML, etc.). Proof is covered by specific tools such as Isabelle/Hol, Phox, etc.

We chose to develop a Java application to ensure the portability of our environment, allowing the creation of a graphical interface and a web application via the creation of an applet. If efficiency problems arise, our application may also be compiled using gcj[11].

3.4.2.3.2. Lexical and syntactic analysis

Presentation

The lexical and syntactic analyzers were defined using an LALR(k) grammar, and the B-language grammars we implemented were of the

11 gcj (http://gcc.gnu.org/java/) is an application for Java to C code conversion, included in GCC.

LALR(k) type. For the first grammars, we obtained a value of k = 10 due to a large number of syntax conflicts. We are now down to k = 2.

As we demonstrated in [BOU 99], certain syntax issues need to be resolved when creating a grammar for the B method. To carry out syntactic analysis of a complex B component, for example, we considered that the definitions were syntax objects in their own right, imposing limits on what may be written in a definition. More generally, this work required us to formalize certain imprecise aspects of the B language.

Characteristics of our grammar

Our grammar defines a parser, which is an extension of the basic parser in ANTLR, as we see from the following code extract.

```
class BParser extends Parser;
options {
 exportVocab    = B;    // Call its vocabulary "B"
 k              = 2;    // k tokens lookahead
 buildAST       = true;
 ASTLabelType   = "MyNode";
}
```

The constructed parser exports a vocabulary known as B and produces a syntax tree where each node is an object in the MyNode class. The MyNode class enables us to manage more complex data structures and provides associated services.

As the following code extract shows, our grammar is able to take account of the three types of abstract machines and process empty files. Empty files generate a syntax error message. A specific module developed in Java is used to generate errors discovered during different stages of the analysis of a B component and produce reports.

```
component:
                  machine
          | refinement
          | implementation

          |   /* Empty source files are *not* allowed.  */
              { errors.WSyntaxic   ( "B.g", "The file is empty" ); };
```

All of the possibilities offered by ANTLR were put to use in order to obtain an LALR(2) grammar. The best means of solving syntax problems consists of conditioning problematic rules.

In terms of the visibility clauses between abstract machines, machines may or may not be renamed; the rule shown above accepts both situations. Note that management of the abstract machine table is included in the action part of the conditional.

```
nameRenamedWithSave[String type]        :
 (B_IDENTIFIER B_POINT) => B_IDENTIFIER (B_POINT^
nameRenamedWithSave[type] )
| t1:B_IDENTIFIER { add_AM((MyNode)#t1,type); };
```

The lexer is defined as an extension of the basic lexer. In accordance with the B language, the description of the lexer mentions the fact that the identifiers are case sensitive. The k characteristic has a value of 5, which is directly linked to the longest subchain shared by keywords in B.

```
class BLexer extends Lexer;
options {
exportVocab          = B   ;                        // Call its vocabulary "B"
caseSensitive        = true ;              // In B, the case is significant
caseSensitiveLiterals = true ;             // In B, the case is significant
testLiterals           = true ;            // automatically test for literals
k = 5   ;                     // k characters of lookahead
}
```

Each keyword in B may be entered explicitly in the lexer description, as shown by the extract below, or implicitly in the parser.

```
B_PARTIAL              : "+->" ;
B_RELATION             : "<->" ;
B_TOTAL                        : "-->" ;
B_PARTIAL_INJECT               : ">+>" ;
B_TOTAL_INJECT                 : ">->" ;
B_PARTIAL_SURJECT  : "+->>";
B_TOTAL_SURJECT    : "-->>";
B_BIJECTION        : ">->>";
```

Non-determinism

As we indicated in [BOU 99], several tokens are used in different contexts (see Table 3.2).

Symbol	Different uses	Language
";"	Substitution sequencing Relationship composition Separation in set or definition lists	Substitution Expression Clause etc.
"="	Equality test in a condition Set definition Evaluation Start of the body of an operation	Predicate Expression Clause
":"	Membership Becomes such that Evaluation of a record field	Predicate Substitution Expression
"||"	Parallel substitution composition Parallel relationship composition	Substitution Expression
"-"	The difference between two arithmetic expressions Unary negative operator The difference between two set expressions	Expression Expression Expression

Table 3.2. *Basic set*

The decision rules allow us to return to a situation where we have full understanding, but the syntax tree will always contain these ambiguities. ANTLR allows us to rename tokens when constructing a tree; for example, the following rule recognizes a B operation and renames the token = (B_EQUAL).

```
operation_Mch  :
  operationHeader  c:B_EQUAL^ {#c.setType(OP_DEF);}
substitution_Mch;
```

As we have seen, a restriction has been applied to the notion of definitions in order for the syntactic analysis (parsing) phase to be determinist.

```
formalText_Mch  :
        expression  |
        substitution_Mch  |
        operation_Mch
```

This definition introduces the notion of levels; the language used in a machine is not the same as that used for refinement or implementation.

Semantic checks by the parser

The parser is able to carry out certain semantic checks, ensuring that the correctly-parsed component verifies certain "good" properties.

The B language makes extensive use of identifier lists, enabling reasonably succinct writing of abstract machines.

```
VARIABLES
    AA, BB, CC
INVARIANT
    AA, BB, CC : INT*INT*INT
```

RU1: Uniqueness rule. Take the list of variables LV. The variables must be distinct from one another.

Clause name	ABTOOLS rule name	MR reference[12]
Substitution becomes equal	simple_affect simple_affect_ref	Section 6.3 Restrictions
Non-bounded choice	See Rq1	Section 6.10 Restrictions
Local definition	See Rq1	Section 6.11 Restrictions
Becomes element of	simple_affect_ref	Section 6.12 Restrictions
Becomes element such that	See Rq1	Section 6.13 Restrictions
Local variable	See Rq1	Section 6.14 Restrictions

Table 3.3. *Application of rule RU1*

Rq1: The variable list acts in a zone (clause, substitution, see Table 3.3) known as the zone of declaration. Each variable is added after existence checks using the symbol table. No further checks are required and, therefore, RU1 is verified by default.

Checks for rule RU1 are included in the typechecker (file Typing.g).

12 The MR is the reference manual supplied with Atelier B.

To take another example, let us consider rule RA1, which concerns variables subject to affectation. Table 3.4 shows the limits of application of this rule.

RA1: Accessibility rule. Taking the variable list LV, each variable of LV must be accessible in write mode.

Clause name	ABTOOLS rule name	MR reference
Substitution becomes equal	simple_affect	§6.3 Restrictions
Becomes element of	simple_affect	§6.12 Restrictions
Becomes element such that	simple_affect	§6.13 Restrictions

Table 3.4. *Application of rule RA1*

Other rules are also implemented within the ABTools environment.

Treatment of additional files

The B language allows information to be encapsulated and shared using access clauses. These access clauses show the behavior and environment of other abstract machines.

DEFINITION.– *All abstract machines cited in an access clause will be labeled as "in use".*

In a parsing context, we can check the syntactic and semantic correctness of the "in use" abstract machines. To do this, we simply need to memorize the list of "in use" machines.

In order to treat visibility connections, we have introduced a table that used to manage the abstract machines visible to a given machine or defined in the context of a project. This table is created and dependences are read as and when requested by the user (switch -loadLinked).

key MAIN_0.mch Element AM Name : MAIN_0.mch | AM File : ../
STD_LOGIC_1164/|
key ENTRIE_0.mch Element AM Name : ENTRIE_0.mch| AM File : ../
STD_LOGIC_1164/|

A B component may use a definition file in addition to the in-use machines. A certain number of definitions can be placed into a file to enable their reuse.

This file is an ASCII file with no particular structure, containing a definition clause. If the file is accessed, the parser will add the set of definitions to the definition clause.

3.4.2.3.3. Tree manipulation

In ANTLR, syntax trees are examined and managed via grammars known as TreeWalkers. The examination of the tree is carried out as part of the second phase, so we no longer need to check the conformity of the input AST; for this reason, our grammar only concerns the treewalking aspect.

Decompilation of the syntax tree

Decompilation is carried out using a treewalker. We have used object technology to produce a single TreeWalker, which currently allows us to generate ASCII, TeX and XML versions of the AST.

```
class TreeWalker extends TreeParser;
 options {
        importVocab     = B;
        buildAST                = false;
        ASTLabelType    = "MyNode";
        k               = 1;
}
```

The following rules show that the TreeWalker is, first and foremost, a set of rules which allow us to “walk through” the AST. Sections of code may be associated with these rules through the use of action blocks.

```
machine :
#(     "MACHINE"
                { index.Add();
        printToStringln(out.Clause("MACHINE"));}
       paramName
       clauses
                { printToString(out.Clause("END"));}
);
```

Our decompilation TreeWalker is contained in the file Treewalker.g.

Typechecking

The typechecking phase is applied to an AST, and allows us to check that types have been used correctly. This phase allows us to add type information to the AST.

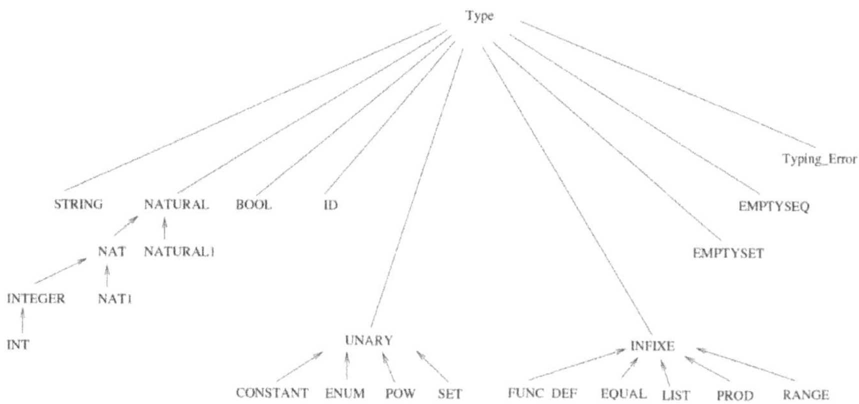

Figure 3.12. *Type tree*

Figure 3.12 shows a tree diagram of the B types used. Each B type constructor is associated with a Java class. The diagram takes the form of an inheritance graph.

The typechecker is coded using a treewalker, named Typing.g, as we see from the following extract:

```
class Typing extends TreeParser;
options {
        importVocab     = B;
        buildAST                = false;
        ASTLabelType    = "MyNode";
        k               = 1;
}
```

The typechecker carries out a number of actions within the AST:

– declaration of encountered objects (variables, sets, constants and operations), along with verification of the uniqueness of each identifier;

– typechecking;

– type inference in certain, highly specific cases (VAR ii IN ss END clause);

– typechecking of all declared elements.

All of these actions are implemented by the action part of the rules.

```
set_interval_value:
#(tt:B_EQUAL   a:B_IDENTIFIER
{
  Type newType = new Type();
  pushScope(#a.getText());
}
  newType =interval_declaration
{
  newtype.setLineNumber(#tt.getLineNum());
  #tt.setBType(newtype);
  addId(a,newType);
  popScope();
} );
```

The type may either be calculated locally or be the subject of calculations in another rule; we use rules with parameter return in order to transfer types. If anomalies occur, the number of the affected lines is propagated to the type token itself to facilitate tracking.

New identifiers are taken into account using the definition context, managed as a pile: see operators pushScope(id) and popScope(). The associated symbol table is updated throughout the typechecking process, using the instruction addId(id,type).

```
 MACHINE         ANY
 CONSTANTS       xx
 PROPERTIES      xx : INT
 INITIALISATION            ANY xx WHERE xx : INT & xx = 0 THEN skip
END
 END
```

For illustrative purposes, the passage from the abstract machine shown above[13] in the context of our environment (ABTOOLS -symbolTable any.mch command) produces the following symbol table:

13 We will not go into detail concerning the relative merits of this abstract machine here.

```
list of variables:
key  any::ANY::xx Element xx(INT)
key  any Element any(FUNC_DEF(CONSTANT(Not Defined),Not
Defined))
key  any::xx Element xx(INT)
```

The name of the machine itself forms part of the symbol table. The type FUNC_DEF(CONSTANT(Not Defined),Not Defined) signifies that it is a parameter-free function. Similarly, the xx identifier is defined in two distinct contexts.

ANTLR allows the use of re-entry grammars, enabling us to verify that all declared objects are typed. This process involves two phases: first, object declaration (constants and variables) and, second, the retrieval of type information and the detection of non-typed and/or unused objects (constants and variables).

An extract from the *Properties* rule is given below. The action section checks the typing of each constant (abstract or concrete).

```
properties     :
#("PROPERTIES"
{
        Type type = new Type();
}
type = tt:predicate
{
        typeControleTreatement (tt, type);
        if (constant != null)          list_var_bis(constant);
        if (abstract_constant != null)  list_var_bis(abstract_constant);
        if (visible_constant != null)   list_var_bis(visible_constant);
        if (hidden_constant != null)    list_var_bis(hidden_constant);
        if (concrete_constant != null)  list_var_bis(concrete_constant);
} );
```

This syntax rule allows semantic checking (described in the reference manual), which indicates that the introduction of a constant should be followed by the Properties clause.

3.4.2.3.4. Generation of POs

As we see from Figure 3.13, the generation of POs is a three-stage process. Each step is associated with a treewalker, each of which introduces its own vocabulary. The three phases are as follows:

– construction of a new tree representing the theoretical proof obligation;

– replacement of syntactic sugar by base substitutions;

– tree reduction by applying substitutions.

The second phase involves removing the syntactic sugar introduced by J.R. Abrial to define the B language in order to revert to the generalized substitution language. The Goal rule shown below shows the passage from [INSTRUCTION]P to [GSL]P.

```
goal! : #(SUBST_TO      ii:instruction      pp:predicate
          { #goal = #(SUBST_TO, #pp,  #ii); }
);
```

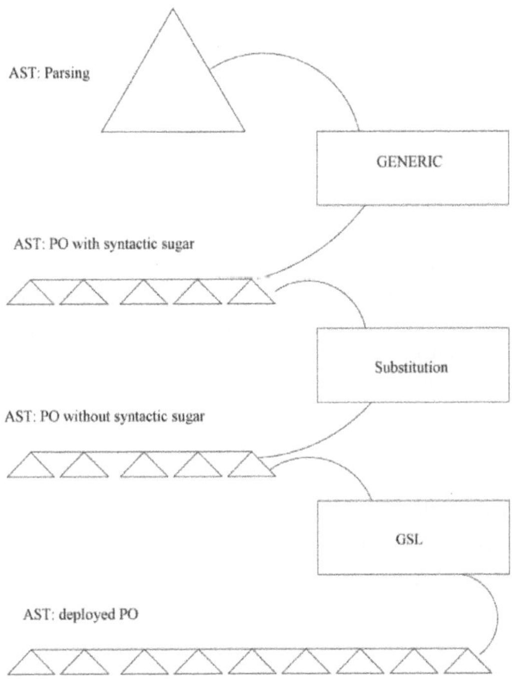

Figure 3.13. *The three stages of PO generation*

The equivalence between a subset of substitutions used in B and generalized substitutions is shown in Table 3.5.

BEGIN S END	S
PRE Q THEN S END	P|S
ANY z WHERE P THEN S END	@ z.(P=>S)
VAR x IN S END	@ x.S

Table 3.5. *Syntactic sugar*

The coding of this equivalence is shown below in an extract from the grammar substitution.g.

```
instruction   :
   #("skip")
 | ! #("BEGIN" i4:instruction
      { #instruction = #i4;}
    )
 | ! #("PRE" p5:predicate i5:instruction
      { #instruction = #(GSL_SUCH, p5, i5); }
    )
 | ! #("ANY" l10:listTypedIdentifier p10:predicate i10:instruction
      { #instruction = #(GSL_FOR_SUCH,l10, #(GSL_GUARD, p10,i10));}
    )
 | ! #("VAR" l14:listTypedIdentifier i14:instruction
      { #instruction = #(GSL_FOR_SUCH,l14,i14); }
    )
```

Once the POs have been normalized, they can then be deployed. This stage is based on the semantics of generalized substitutions. Table 3.6 shows the main substitutions and the associated semantics.

Substitution	Result
[skip]R	R
[S||T](P ∧ Q)	[S]P ∧ [T]Q
[P | S]R	P ∧ [S]R
[S[ ]T]R	[S]R ∧ [T]R
P ==> S]R	(P ==> [S]R)
[@x.S]R	∀z.[S]R
[x,y := E,F]R	[x := E||y := F]R

Table 3.6. *Semantics of generalized substitutions*

The code extract shown below highlights the equivalence between formal rules and the translation into grammar form.

```
gsl [MyNode pr]  returns [MyNode result]
{
MyNode res;
result = new MyNode(); }:
 !#(GSL_SUCH     p1:predicate         res=gsl[pr]
    {result= #(B_AND,    #p1, #res);})
| !#(GSL_FOR_SUCH  ll:listTypedIdentifier res=gsl[pr]
    {result= #(B_FORALL, #ll, #res);})
| !#(GSL_GUARD    p2:predicate         res=gsl[pr]
    { result  = #(B_IMPLIES, #p2, #res);})
| !#("skip"
    { result  = pr;})
```

The set of substitutions is modeled in the form of a single rule, entitled gsl, made up of several alternatives.

3.4.2.4. *Scalability*

A number of interesting extensions to the B method have been developed. It is important to be able to implement these extensions quickly and easily for validation purposes.

ANTLR allows us to achieve this goal as the grammars used may be extended by inheritance. New grammars are constructed by overloading certain rules and by adding supplementary rules.

3.4.2.4.1. Classic B

“Classic” B is described in The B-Book [ABR 96]. This is the first of the B languages implanted in our project, respecting [STE 98].

To give a first example of scalability, we implanted certain extensions proposed in [BOU 99]. In this chapter, we will describe an improved version of B known as BPrime.

3.4.2.4.2. B Prime

This version of the B language allows us to type variables at the moment of declaration. Figure 3.14 shows an example where the typing information invariant has been removed, allowing the INVARIANT clause to be reserved for more important or more critical properties.

```
VARIABLES
    N1, N2, N3

INVARIANT
   N1 ∈ NAT ∧
   N2 ∈ NAT ∧
   N1 > N2 ∧
   N3 ∈ NAT ∧
   (N1 + N2) > N3
```

```
VARIABLES
   N1 ∈ NAT ∧
   N2 ∈ NAT ∧
   N3 ∈ NAT

INVARIANT
  N1 > N2∧
  (N1 + N2) > N3
```

Figure 3.14. *Explicit typing*

The implementation of this extension in our environment consisted of creating a new grammar, BPrime.g. This grammar inherits the grammar described above, with overloading of certain rules.

It takes the following form:

```
 class BPrimeParser extends BParser;
 options {
exportVocab = BPrime;
k =2;
buildAST = true;
ASTLabelType = "MyNode";
}

 variables : (        "VARIABLES"^ |
                      "ABSTRACT_VARIABLES"^ |
                      "VISIBLE_VARIABLES"^
               )       listTypedIdentifier ;

 listTypedIdentifier : typedIdentifier (B_COMMA^ typedIdentifier)* ;

 typedIdentifier    : nameRenamed (B_INSET^ cbases)? ;
```

This new grammar inherits all of the rules associated with the BParser. It overloads the variables rule and introduces two new rules, listTypedIdentifier and typedIdentifier. This development also needs to be applied to the other tools (the decompiler and the typechecker).

Systematic separation of grammars is not useful in treewalkers, as these tools presume that the abstract trees are correct. The BPrime language extends this notion of implicit typing to the CONSTANT clauses (abstract or otherwise), to operation profiles and to the ANY, VAR and WHILE substitutions, as seen in Figure 3.15.

```
// AUTHOR : Boulanger Jean-Louis
/* Example of a machine described using BPRIME */
MACHINE    Exemple_BPrime
VARIABLES  aa : NAT , bb : NAT  // Explicit typing of variables
INVARIANT  aa < bb  // Invariant only contains properties
OPERATIONS
        r1 : NAT, r2 : NAT <-- EX ( p1 : NAT, p2 : NAT) =
        PRE p1 < p2 THEN
            ANY     a1 : NAT, a2 : NAT
             WHERE  (a1 < a2) &  (a1 < p1) &  (a2 < p2)
             THEN   r1, r2 := a1, a2
             END
        END
END
```

Figure 3.15. *Example of a B component with explicit typing*

The BPrime language introduces two further developments:

– use of comments, as in C++ (see Figure 3.16);

– use of the character "," as a set separator in the SETS clause.

```
CPPComment
  options { paraphrase = "a C++ comment"; }:
          "//"
          ( ~('\n') )*
          {_ttype = Token.SKIP;}
;
```

As we see from the code extract shown above, the first modification affects the lexer via the CPPComment rule. This rule indicates that any character between the // token and the end line character will be ignored.

Figure 3.16 shows an example of an abstract machine described using BPrime.

3.4.2.4.3. System B

In [ABR 96b], J.-R. Abrial demonstrated the possibility of using the B method for distributed systems. In [ABR 98], Abrial offers a full, true extension of the B method to the notion of events and dynamic constraints.

```
SYSTEM          toy_with_scheduler_dynamics_and_modality
VARIABLES         xx, yy, cc, dd
INVARIANT         xx, yy, cc, dd : NA*NAT*NAT*NAT
               &  (cc >0 or dd>0)
DYNAMICS          xx <= xx' & yy <= yy'
INITIALISATION  xx,yy := 0,0 || cc,dd :: NAT1*NAT1
EVENTS
evt_xx = SELECT  cc>0 THEN xx,cc:=xx+1,cc-1 || dd::NAT1 END;
evt_yy = SELECT  dd>0 THEN yy,dd:=yy+1,dd-1 || cc::NAT1 END
MODALITIES
SELECT  cc > 0 LEADSTO cc = 0 WHILE evt_xx VARIANT cc END;
SELECT  dd > 0 LEADSTO dd = 0 WHILE evt_yy VARIANT dd END
END
```

Figure 3.16. *A system*

This extension introduces new clauses (SYSTEM, EVENTS, DYNAMICS, VARIANT and MODALITIES), new substitutions and a new type of predicate. Figure 3.17 shows an example taken from [ABR 00].

3.4.2.4.4. Event B

A new definition of a form of B using the notion of events was introduced as part of the MATISSE project ([MAT 01a] and [MAT 01b]). This language, known as Event B, builds on the basis established in System B, while developing the MODALITIES clause and the notion of events (refinement, decomposition and regrouping).

The establishment of this extension within the ABTools environment was presented in the course of the *Journées B* meeting organized by the GDR-ALP group on June 13–14 2002.

The ABTools environment does not currently support the B EVENT language as defined in the context of the RODIN project.

3.4.2.5. *Results*

This presentation of the ABTools environment has demonstrated the capacities of the ANTLR compiler generation environment, which allowed us to create a first version of our B environment and test certain extensions.

The parsers included in the ABTools environment (B, BPRIME, System B and Event B) are described by an LALR(2) grammar. The other tools are described by an LALR(1) grammar.

The typechecker finalization phase has been completed and work has begun on the generation of POs.

Work is also underway concerning code generation. After formalization of the passage from B0 to the target language(s), code is generated by adapting the decompiler. Note that a translator has been created for the passage from B to JML; this translator is now operational and is included in the ABTools environment.

No major difficulties have been encountered, and the use of ANTLR in constructing our B environment may be considered successful.

All of the developments described in this chapter are available at http://sourceforge.net/projects/abtools/. The significance of these results is increased by the ease of implementing extensions.

The current version of the ABTools environment was developed with ANTLR version 2.7. Work is currently in progress on a move to ANTLR version 3.0 [PAR 08].

3.5. Conclusion

In this chapter, we have presented different types of tools used for the implementation of the B language.

Both the commercial and freely-distributed versions of Atelier B constitute high performance tools for learning the B language and for complex developments, but interfacing with other tools is difficult, although it is possible to use open source tools to prove POs generated using Atelier B (see [MEN 12]).

We have also presented the ABTools environment, used to test extensions to the B language by generalizing existing grammars. The BRILLANT project (Chapter 12) is also significant, as it allows tool interfacing via XML exchange files.

3.6. Glossary

ABTOOLS Another's B Tools

AMN Abstract Machine Notation

ANTLR ANother Tool for Language Recognition

AST Abstract Syntactic Tree

CENELEC[14] *Comité Européen de Normalisation ÉLECtrotechnique*, European Committee for Electrotechnical Standardization

GSL Generalized Substitution Language

IDE Integrated development Environment

METEOR *METro Est Ouest Rapide*, train operation system used by the Paris metro

PO Proof Obligation

SAET *Système d'Automatisation de l'Exploitation des Trains*, Automation system for train operations

SSIL Software SIL

V&V Verification and Validation

WP Weakest Precondition

3.7. Bibliography

[ABR 96a] ABRIAL J.-R., "Extending B without changing it (for developing distributed systems)", in HABRIAS H. (ed.), *Proceedings of 1st Conference on the B Method, Putting into Practice Methods and Tools for Information System Design*, IRIN Institute for Research in Computers, Nantes, pp. 169–191, November 1996.

14 See http://www.cenelec.eu/.

[ABR 96b] ABRIAL J.R., *The B-Book*, Cambridge University Press, 1996.

[ABR 98] ABRIAL J.-R., MUSSAT L., "Introducing dynamic constraints in B'98", *Recent Advances in the Development and Use of the B Method Lecture Notes in Computer Science,* vol. 1393, pp. 83–128, 1998.

[ABR 00] ABRIAL J.-R., Event driven sequential program construction, School Scholars programming, March 2000.

[ABR 02] ABRIAL J.-R., CANSELL D., LAFITTE G., "'Higher- order' mathematics in B", *ZB 2002 – Formal Specification and Development in Z and B*, pp. 370–393, 2002.

[ANS 83] ANSI, Standard ANSI/MIL-STD-1815A-1983, Ada programming Langage, 1983.

[BOU 99] BOULANGER J.L., GEORGE M., BRUNO T., Revisiting B language syntax, Technical Report 99-07, CNAM Laboratory CEDRIC, 1999.

[BOU 01] BOULANGER J.L., "ABtools, une suite d'outils pour la méthode B développé avec ANTLR", *Journées "Outils pour et autour de la méthode B*", 15–16 October 2001.

[BOU 10] BOULANGER J.L. (ed.), *Safety of Computer Architectures*, ISTE, London, and John Wiley & Sons, New York, 2010.

[BOU 12] BOULANGER J.L. (ed.), *Formal Methods Industrial Use from Model to the Code*, ISTE, London, and John Wiley & Sons, New York, 2012.

[BOU 14] BOULANGER J.L. (ed.), *Formal Methods Applied to Industrial Complex Systems*, ISTE, London, and John Wiley & Sons, New York, 2014.

[COL 10] COLIN S., PETIT D., MARIANO G., *et al.*, "BRILLANT: an open source platform for B", *Workshop on Tool Building in Formal Methods (held in conjunction with ABZ 2010)*, February 2010.

[EN 01] EN 50128, Railway applications – communications, signalling and processing systems – software for railway control and protection systems, CENELEC, May 2001.

[EN 11] EN 50128, Railway applications – communications, signalling and processing systems – software for railway control and protection systems, CENELEC, July 2011.

[LEC 96] LECOMPTE P., BEAURENT P.-J., "Le système d'automatisation de l'exploitation des trains (SAET) de METEOR", *Revue Générale des Chemins de fer*, vol. 6, pp. 31–34, June 1996.

[MAR 95] MARIANO G., BOULANGER J.-L., KOURSI M.E.L., Recueil des rapports d'anomalies sur le développement de l'AtelierB, Report prepared under the project ASCOT N2 INRETS-ESTAS No. 95–48, 1995.

[MAR 03] MARIANO G., BOULANGER J.-L., "BRILLANT: modèle de développement libre et recherche scientifique: une dynamique autour de B?", *Club SEE "Systèmes Informatiques de Confiance"*, Réunion à l'ENST (Paris), Thème: "Méthodes formelles", 19 June 2003.

[MAT 98] MATRA, RATP, "Naissance d'un Métro, Sur la nouvelle ligne 14, les rames METEOR entrent en scène. PARIS découvre son premier métro automatique", *La vie du Rail & des transports*, Numéro 1076 -Hors-Série, October 1998.

[MAT 01a] MATISSE, Event B reference manual, Technical report, Methodologies and Technologies for Industrial Strength Systems Engineering, 2001.

[MAT 01b] MATISSE, Event B to B translator user manual, Technical report, Methodologies and Technologies for Industrial Strength Systems Engineering, 2001.

[MEN 12] MENTRÉ D., MARCHÉ C., FILLIÂTRE J.-C., *et al.*, "Discharging proof obligations from Atelier B using multiple automated provers", *ABZ Conference*, Pisa, Italy, June 2012.

[PAR 93] PARR T.J., Obtaining practical variants of LL(K) for K>1 by splitting the atomic K-Tuple, PhD Thesis, Purdue University, 1993.

[PAR 08] PARR T.J., *The definitive ANTLR reference – building domain specific languages*, The Pragmatic Programmers, 2008.

[SCH 98] SCHMITT M., The development of a parser for SDL-2000, Technical report, Institute for Telematics, Medical University of Lubeck, Ratzeburger Allee 160 23538, Lubeck Germany, 1998.

[STE 98] STÉRIA, Le langage B: manuel de référence, Technical Report V 1.8, RATP SNCF INRETS, June 1998.

4

The B Method at Siemens

4.1. Introduction

4.1.1. *Siemens Industry Mobility*

Siemens SAS Industry Mobility is an international center of excellence for the creation of fully automatic subway systems and is a world leader in automated urban transport systems. The company is the result of Siemens' takeover of the transport branch of the Matra group between 1995 and 2001. The Société Générale de Mécanique-Avion-Traction, founded in 1937 (the name was contracted to Matra in 1941), initially specialized in the military sector before rapidly acquiring significant capacities in space-related activities.

The guidance and remote control systems developed in the context of space and military projects were then applied to other domains, notably in the field of urban transportation. Matra anticipated urban transformation and was ideally placed to participate in land-use planning activities. In the mid-1970s, this strategy led to the creation of two large-scale projects: Aramis and VAL.

The first of these projects was a Personal Rapid Transit (PRT) project using small vehicles (10 seats), circulating in sets. It was never implemented on a commercial scale, but certain ideas were adopted for future systems. The VAL (*Véhicule Automatique Léger*, Light Automatic Vehicle) – the world's first fully automatic subway system – was a great commercial

---

Chapter written by Daniel DOLLE.

success. The VAL was a small-scale, driverless subway vehicle, completely safe, highly reliable and economically profitable. The first line was inaugurated in 1983, and linked Villeneuve d'Ascq (France) to the center of Lille. Other towns and cities were quick to adopt the VAL, including Toulouse, Rennes, Orly Airport and Turin, in Europe, and cities as diverse as Taipei, Uijeongbu in Korea and Chicago O'Hare airport elsewhere in the world. In the initial design, the safety functions of the VAL were not covered by software, but by electronic components with intrinsic safety: any and all faults left the system in a safe state.

Software-based safety functions were used for the first time in 1989 for SACEM (*Système d'Aide à la Conduite, à l'Exploitation et à la Maintenance* – an assisted driving, control, and maintenance system), developed in association with GEC-Alsthom and CSEE. The SACEM system [GEO 90] was designed to reduce the interval between trains in the central section of the *Réseau Express Régional* – regional express network (RER) in and around Paris from 2 min 30 s to 2 min.

The arithmetic coding technique[1] used to guarantee the safety of system software at the time has proved to be particularly durable, and the same principles are still used in Siemens systems today. Line D of the Lyon subway system, brought into service in 1992, marked a turning point as the first fully automatic wide gauge metro.

The SACEM safety software [GUI 90] was developed using traditional methods, but the RATP required particularly rigorous validation: program proof (as used by Hoare [HOA 89]) as a first stage, followed by a formal respecification. This work was extremely costly, but was successful in detecting errors; the experience convinced the RATP[2] of the need to apply formal methods from the software specification phase onward. This requirement was present in the specification for the SAET-METEOR system ordered by the RATP for Line 14 of the Paris metro [MAT 98].

The SAET-METEOR, brought into service in 1998, is a fully automatic, driverless line. Its major distinguishing factor is the fact that fully automatic and manually driven trains are permitted to run on the same line, making the

1 For more information on the *Processeur Sécuritaire Codé* (PSC)-coded safety processor, see [BOU 09, Chapter 2], [BAR 08] and [BOU 11, Chapter 1].

2 For more details, see www.ratp.fr/.

system extremely complex. The system (station stops, braking, train spacing, door opening, point commands, etc.) is managed by safety software, developed using a formal approach centered on the B method [ABR 96] The development process used for these programs, based on proof, allowed the removal of unit tests and produced remarkable results: all errors were found before validation tests took place.

Note that in the context of its first use, the B method was applied on an "industrial" scale: 115,000 lines of B, divided into 1,150 components, 27,800 proof obligations (POs) and 1,400 proof rules. This application was preceded by in-depth work on methodological definition, leading to the production of almost 300 pages of best practice guidelines for use by developers and the operational safety team.

4.1.2. *The CBTC system*[3]

Urban transport systems are made up of elements in which software may play a variety of roles. Examples include the computer commanding the slip control/protection system for rolling stock, passenger information systems, the central odometer system used in localizing trains, the ticket distribution system, the timetable calculator, etc. These elements are not all subject to the same criticality levels in relation to correct system operations and to safety, and the part played by Siemens in their creation varies.

The IEEE 1474.1 standard [IEE 04] provides a framework for the presentation of applications developed by Siemens using formal methods. The standard concerns the latest generation of automatic urban transport systems, i.e. communication-based train control (CBTC).

These systems are based on three principles:

– trains are localized precisely, independently of track circuits;

– the automatic systems on board trains and on the wayside exchange information continuously via a high capacity communications system;

3 Communication-based train control: a system applied to train use, piloting and safety. The CBTC system is made up of on-board equipment and wayside equipment in constant communication (generally over a radio link). CBTC has been subject to standardization [IEE 04].

– vital functions are implemented by on-board and wayside computers.

This standardized definition is used in the Siemens Trainguard MT CBTC. The product has been designed for use in both the creation of new automatic lines and the renovation of existing lines.

The architecture of CBTC systems is based on a kernel including the following equipment:

– on-board autopilots (APs);

– wayside APs, each controlling a section of the line;

– IOM: input/output modules which manage the acquisition or command of binary electrical signals on the wayside;

– line APs, which ensure the safety of whole lines in the cases of full automation;

– a wayside/train communications network which uses a free propagation radio system, based on spread spectrum modulation.

Depending on whether the project concerns a renovation, an extension or the creation of a new line, this kernel interacts with products, either preexisting elements or elements created by Siemens, which carry out the following functions: signaling, command post-supervision, platform door control, safe distribution of traction current and audio-visual system functions.

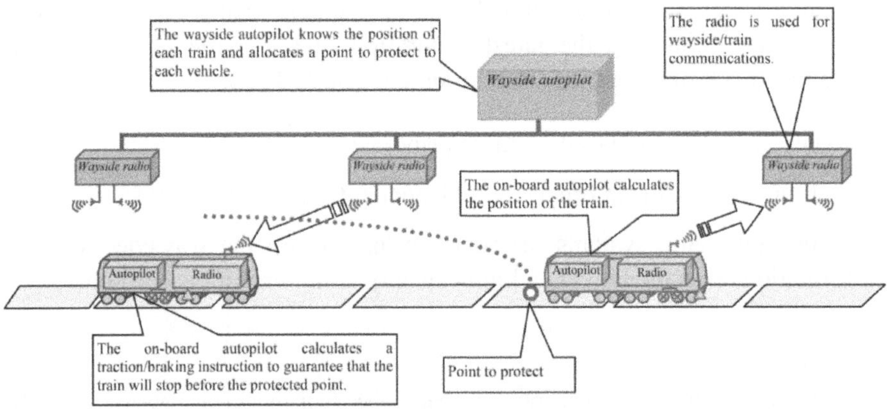

Figure 4.1. *Example of CBTC*

In the Siemens CBTC system, the on-board AP in each train calculates its own position on the line and transmits the information to the relevant wayside APs. These units establish a constantly updated cartography of the relevant portion of track, and assign a movement authority limit to each train. This point corresponds to the rear of the previous train. The on-board AP then establishes an optimum speed profile, ensuring that the train will stop safely before the protected point. The minimum space between trains therefore corresponds to the braking distance plus a safety margin. This distance may be considered as a safety zone which moves with the train, and is known as a "moving block".

The role of the line AP is to manage situations affecting the safety of the whole line or the whole fleet. It ensures the safety of controls transmitted by central command system operators to the on-board APs. It also participates in restoring traction power following faults in wayside APs, identifying all of the trains on the line.

4.1.3. *Characteristics of B programs*

The software architecture of a wayside or on-board AP includes the following elements:

– A set of components known as the "base computer" provides safe treatment services and low-level drivers using an ordinary real-time operating system (OS). This base computer is shared by all equipment.

– A specific communications layer for each piece of equipment, containing the protocols used for non-safety-related transmissions.

– A functional application program, which only carries out processes with no safety constraints. This includes the maintenance, diagnosis and support functions included in each device. In the case of on-board APs, this also includes functions such as train piloting and motor commands.

– A safety application program, responsible for all processes involving the safety of persons and goods. This is the only program to be specified in B, based on a very simple design: a single task is carried out cyclically, with the acquisition and treatment of input followed by the creation of output. The low reactivity dynamics of rail systems allows us to use cycle times which are relatively long for real-time applications, from 100 to 400 ms.

These architectural elements are further divided into core product or project-specific software. Our systems respond to a wide variety of usage requirements, and our programs are therefore designed as platforms suitable for reuse with specific elements created to fulfill the needs of different clients.

4.1.4. *The target calculator*

The B method, as used by Siemens, allows us to produce a code which fulfills the relevant functional requirements. We also need to guarantee the safe execution of this code. Our calculation platform is unable to prevent errors during execution or compilation, but it is almost always able to detect them. When this happens, the energy supply to the output is cut off. This situation has knock-on intrinsic safety effects on the equipment carrying the device, which is put into a safe state: for wayside equipment, the power supply is cut off, and for on-board equipment the train is forced to stop. This technology guarantees that if the system ceases to operate correctly, it will be placed in a safe state.

Our calculation platform – the coded safety processor (CSP)[4] – uses a probabilistic approach to detect discrepancies between software source code and its execution. Each item of software data is made up of two parts: 32 bits of information and N redundant bits. The overall safety level depends on N and not on the technology used for the calculation. This value is independent of the reliability of the material and does not require any particular compiler validation activity.

The redundant part of a piece of data is the sum of three terms:

– an arithmetic coding of the 32 bits of information, which allows us to detect alterations in memory or when copying data;

– a signature, which detects errors in the order of instructions. This signature is static and independent of the 32 bits of information; it is calculated offline;

– a characteristic date for each calculation cycle, ensuring that only the latest data values will be used.

---

4 For more information on the CSP, see [BOU 09, Chapter 2], [BAR 08] and [BOU 11a, Chapter 1].

The source code is subject to static analysis by a signature predetermination tool (SPT), which assigns a signature to each input data value and calculates the expected signatures for each output data value. These precalculated signatures are then included in the executable. The safety of the coded processor depends on the independence of the source code analyses carried out by the compiler and the SPT. We presume that no shared common error modes exist, as the two tools were developed independently.

During the execution, all calculations are carried out by calls to an elementary function library (arithmetic, connection condition calculations, loops, etc.) which updates both the 32 bits of useful information and the N redundant bits. At the end of each calculation cycle, a failsafe hardware component – the dynamic controller – compares the obtained signatures with the expected values.

If a contradiction is detected, the dynamic controller forces the equipment into safe mode. For reasons of efficiency, variables are not verified independently, but are used in the creation of a synthetic variable which assembles any errors. As long as the calculation cycle remains below 2^{-N}, the probability of an error being detected is $1 - 2^{-N}$. In our implementation, 2^{-N} is close to 10^{-14}; therefore, errors are almost certain to be detected.

The dynamic controller also allows us to check the execution time for a calculation cycle. Input data must be received exactly once in a time period fixed by an intrinsically safe clock in order for the dynamic controller to remain in a permissive state.

4.2. The development process using B

4.2.1. *Development*

The classic software development cycle involves specification, design, coding, testing and maintenance phases. The formal development cycle involves a slightly different set of phases: specification, formalization, coding, proof, validation and maintenance.

– The starting point for a development is a set of informal or semi-formal documents, specifying the requirements for a program.

– These documents are translated into a formal model using B [ABR 96], known as the abstract model.

– The abstract model is completed by refining all machines to the point of implementation, with the addition of abstract data reading services to existing machines. This results in the production of a concrete model, which is then translated into a compilable language.

– Proof is then used to guarantee that the concrete model conforms to the abstract model, and that the two are coherent.

– The conformity and completeness of the formal specification in relation to the informal documents are then verified by re-reading and testing.

These activities will be discussed in more detail in the following sections.

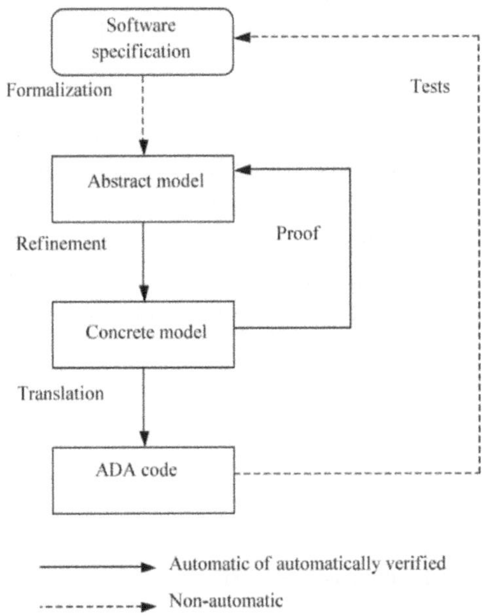

Figure 4.2. *Process*

4.2.2. *Informal specification*

The program is specified in a text document organized according to the principles of functional analysis (structured analysis and design technique (SADT) – [LIS 90]). The aim of this document is to provide a clear and thorough description of what is expected of the program, expressed using natural language, state automata or B formulas, depending on the case.

In our experience, a functional specification can be transformed quite directly into a B model:

– each function is translated into a B machine;

– this machine contains a single writing operation, which calculates output as a function of input for each cycle;

– a function, divided into subfunctions, is translated as an implementation which imports the machines translating each subfunction;

– the output flows of a function become the variables of the associated machine;

– the input functions are transformed into direct accesses to the corresponding output flows, with a SEES clause.

The data dictionary, which provides a precise definition of each piece of data and indicates its B type, is a particularly critical element of the informal specification. Data are generally found in the abstract model, and the definitions contained in the dictionary are essential in ensuring model readability.

The program specification is a pragmatic combination of textual, semi-formal and formal elements, and is generally created by experienced engineers. Specialists with extensive knowledge of B will naturally be tempted to use B notations for reasons of precision and succinctness. However, it is important to find a compromise which will be acceptable to all readers of the document:

– the system team, responsible for verifying the conformity of the program specification to preexisting documents (system or equipment specifications);

– the development team, responsible for formalizing the specification;

– the team responsible for specifying program test scenarios;

– the functional safety team, responsible for verifying the program specification in relation to existing documents and for verifying the abstract model in relation to the specification.

The system and test teams are likely to have limited knowledge of B, so it is better to express requirements using natural language. Pseudo-code should ideally be used in relation to input/output flows.

4.2.3. *Formalization of the specification*

4.2.3.1. *General principles*

The aim of formalization is to express the contents of the requirement specification for a program using B. This process is based on the following guiding principles:

– describe the requirement as completely as possible;

– describe the requirement as clearly as possible;

– leave developers as much freedom as possible;

– facilitate proof activities.

The specification model is considered to be complete when all of the requirements have been transferred to the abstract model, which can then be refined without access to the specification documents. To achieve this, we aim to identify the information below in the specification document and transfer it to the formal model:

– data representing program states, the inputs/outputs of functions or its configuration;

– treatments specifying the calculation of function output from input and modifications to the state variables, used in the B substitutions;

– properties are assertions which are redundant with the treatments. They are formalized in the invariants, properties and postconditions of the B model. Ideally, these properties should express the fundamental aspects of the program under development;

– hypotheses are assumptions concerning the outside environment of the program. They may be used in modeling choices or may appear as postconditions for basic machines;

– limitations specify the validation conditions of data, and must be used in the preconditions for data reading operations.

4.2.3.2. *Cutting machines*

The model architecture is constructed in a way so as to enable gradual division of the complexity of a specification. Cutting machines are an essential element in this process, and will be presented in the following paragraphs before we consider the decomposition process.

A cutting machine is a machine that contains the minimum information required to prove machines which import or see it. A machine of this type does not constitute a complete specification, and is associated with a refinement, specifying the information which is needed to implement the machine.

Cutting machines simplify the proof of implementations which import them; for example, it is often possible to "hide" control structures in a refinement, reducing the number of lemmas in the importing implementation.

```
MACHINE
   example_1
ABSTRACT_VARIABLES
   xx
OPERATIONS
   oper =
      SELECT C1 THEN
         xx := E1
         ...
      WHEN Cn THEN
         xx := En
      END
END
```

```
MACHINE
   example_2
ABSTRACT_VARIABLES
   xx
OPERATIONS
   oper =
      BEGIN
         xx : (simple)
      END
END
```

```
REFINEMENT
   example_2_r
REFINES
   example_2
ABSTRACT_VARIABLES
   xx
OPERATIONS
   oper =
      SELECT C1 THEN
         xx := E1
         ...
      WHEN Cn THEN
         xx := En
      END
END
```

Figure 4.3. *Example of a cutting machine*

Figure 4.3 shows the replacement of a machine example_1 by a cutting machine example_2 and its refinement example_2_r:

If the postcondition *xx: (simple)* is sufficient to prove the implementation which calls up *oper*, we can replace *example_1* with *example_2*. However, the SELECT instruction must be retained, as it ensures the completeness of the specification: this instruction is placed in a refinement of example_2. The global proof is simplified as the different conditions of the SELECT instruction are hidden from the implementation using *oper*.

4.2.3.3. *Architecture of the abstract model and the decomposition approach*

The division of the B model should be carefully considered in architectural terms from the top down in order to facilitate traceability in relation to the informal specification.

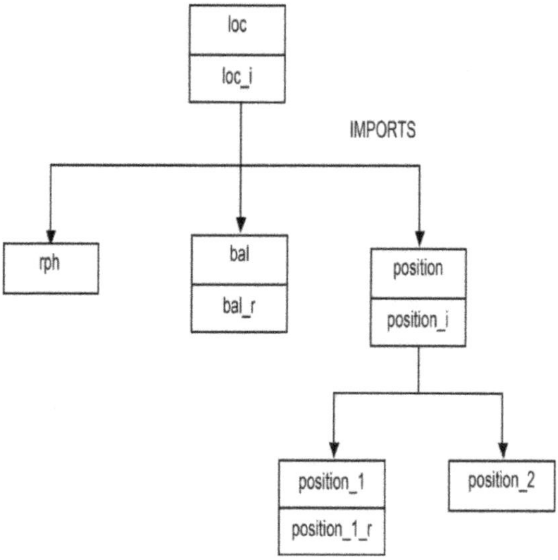

Figure 4.4. *Decomposition*

The formalization approach operates from the top down:

– If the requirement to specify is simple, it is described completely in a single machine, and the decomposition process is complete.

– If the requirement is too complex to specify in a single machine, it needs to be divided into two parts: one which is needed to prove the components using the machine (exterior view) and the information needed to fully capture the requirement (interior view).

The exterior view is placed into a cutting machine. At this point, two different situations are possible. If the interior view can be inserted into a refinement, the decomposition process is complete. Otherwise, the requirement must be divided into simpler requirements, each of which must be specified in a new machine. The cutting machine is refined by an implementation which calls the operations of the new machines, generally in sequence. The decomposition process is repeated for the new machines.

This approach is illustrated in Figure 4.4:

– The cutting machine loc is refined by the implementation loc_i which imports the rph, bal and position machines.

– The rph machine constitutes a full specification, as it is very simple.

– The bal machine is a cutting machine with the addition of a refinement, bal_r.

– The position machine is a cutting machine, as the problem is sufficiently complex to require further decomposition.

The completion criterion for decomposition was initially based, essentially, on size: an operation of more than 100 lines was generally considered to be a suitable candidate for decomposition. Developers currently enjoy considerable freedom in this respect.

Elements of an abstract model may be produced in two stages. In these cases, the first stage consists of creating an abstract and compact formalization to ensure correct understanding of the problem. The developer may then reduce the level of abstraction of "difficult" components as and when required if the refinement of this formalization is too difficult to prove.

4.2.4. *Refinement and coding*

4.2.4.1. *General principles*

The aim of this activity is to produce B implementations to refine the abstract model. This task is carried out using the following principles:

– As many components as possible should be refined and implemented in B.

– The obtained code should be efficient in terms of execution time and memory use.

– The difficulty of proof should be kept under control, while avoiding an excessive increase in the number of components.

Refinement consists of adding to the abstract model in order to transform data and control structures into transcodable data and instructions. This may lead to minor modifications of the specification model.

The refinement process is complete when all possible components have been implemented and the completed model has been proved and transcoded.

4.2.4.2. *Stages in the refinement process*

The refinement process should produce implementable data and control structures: sets and relationships in the specification model should be transformed into arrays, and the ANY, CHOICE and SELECT structures need to be reduced to IF or CASE instructions.

It is theoretically possible to create a correct B model in which these two refinements are carried out simultaneously in a single step: each leaf in the importation tree (machine or refinement) would be refined by a single implementation.

In practice, this approach requires us to carry out proofs with an excessive level of complexity; we generally proceed by stages, separating data refinement from structure refinement.

The starting point for a refinement step is a B component (machine or refinement) which fully expresses a requirement using operations acting on abstract variables. Each step consists of implementing certain operations and variables of the starting component (mach_1) and moving the others to an imported component (mch_2). The non-implemented operations are promoted to implementation (mch_1_i) and their specification is copied from mch_1 to mch_2.

The size of each step must be carefully assessed:

– if too much is carried out in a single step, implementation will be difficult;

– if too little is carried out in each step, a considerable number of duplications will occur and consistency will be difficult to manage.

In practice, the following principles are applied:

– Proof is generally simpler when using abstract data structures rather than concrete data structures. For this reason, when an operation contains a control structure (SELECT, CHOICE, ANY, etc.), it is generally better to implement the operation and to move the variables to the imported machine.

– Operations without a control structure but which contain complex expressions (set unions or relationship images, for example) are implemented by an abstract iteration.

– Implementable variables and operations should be implemented early on in order to avoid duplications in the model.

– It is generally advisable to implement reading operations at the end of the process.

The general approach takes the following form:

– choose the most complex of the remaining operations and implement it;

– if certain variables have had to remain abstract for this implementation, move these variables to an imported machine;

– move those operations which need to be moved (reading operations for displaced variables, for example);

– start the process again for as long as there are operations to implement.

Note that:

– we pass directly from machines to implementations; the introduction of refinements during coding is not generally useful;

– the invariant of a variable moved into an imported machine may be reduced to its type. Properties concerning the requirement are covered by operations and may disappear completely. Purely software-related properties which may be necessary for proof can be transformed into preconditions for the operations which require them.

4.2.4.3. *Loops and abstract iteration*

In B, loops are only authorized in implementations, and as such they can only use concrete data and control structures. However, the ability to manipulate abstract data (functions, relationships, sets, etc.) is essential in the abstract model and highly desirable in the concrete model. At Siemens, the notion of abstract iteration is used as a response to this requirement.

An abstract iterator is a machine which allows us to "walk through" a data structure without showing the implementation. Iterators do not carry out any treatments other than data examination, and the same iterator can be used in loops carrying out completely different treatments. The architecture of this solution is shown in Figure 4.5.

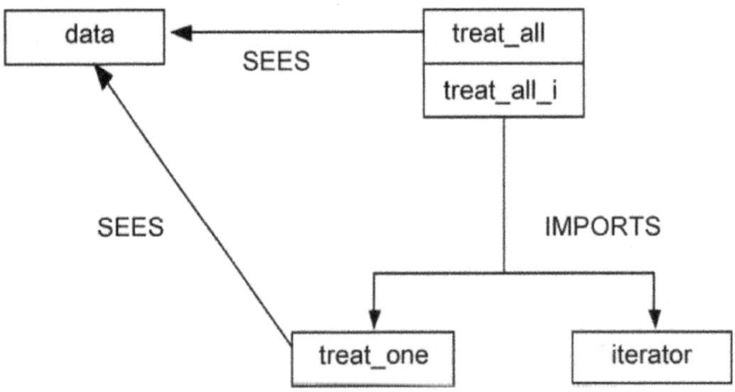

Figure 4.5. *Example of iterator use*

The treat_all machine contains an operation which requires examination of all the elements of a declared set in a given machine. This is carried out by using a loop of treat_all_i to call up the operation of treat_one for each element of the data. The iterator itself is presented below. It provides two variables, representing a partition of the set for examination (the subset that has already been examined and the subset that still requires examination) and two operations, used to initialize the examination and to select an element.

The use of abstract iterators tends to lead to simple proofs, as it distinguishes between:

– the examination refinement proof (in the implementation of the iterating;

– the proof of the treatment requiring the examination (in the implementation of treat_one);

– the proof of the refinement of the examined data (as treat_one only handles abstract data).

The writing of the invariant and the loop is also generally simplified, as the difficult aspect – the description of the progress of the calculation procedure – is carried out using abstract data.

```
MACHINE
   iterator
SEES
   types

ABSTRACT_VARIABLES
   data_to_process,
   processed_data

INVARIANT
   data_to_process <: t_data &
   processed_data <: t_data

INITIALISATION
   processed_data    :: POW(t_data) ||
   data_to_process :: POW(t_data)

OPERATIONS
   continue <-- initiate_iteration_t_data =
   BEGIN
      processed_data := {} ||
      data_to_process := t_data ||
      continue := bool(t_data /= {})
   END;

   continue, elt_data <-- continue_iteration_t_data =
   PRE
      data_to_process /= {}
   THEN
      ANY n_t_data WHERE
          n_t_data : data_to_process
            THEN
         processed_data:= processed_data \/ {n_t_data}    ||
         data_to_process := data_to_process - {n_t_data}||
         elt_data := n_t_data ||
         continue := bool(data_to_process /= {n_t_data})
      END
   END
END
```

Figure 4.6. *Example of an iterator using B*

4.2.4.4. *Data refinement*

The variables and constants in the abstract model are generally not transcodable. Their refinement consists of expressing abstract data through concrete data, suitable for use in implementations, and implementing the operations using this data.

	ABSTRACT	CONCRETE
Data	a <: t_x	a_r : t_x_i --> BOOL
Gluing	a = a_r~[{TRUE}]	
Operations	a := a ∨ {x}	a_r(x) := TRUE
	a := a – {x}	a_r(x) := FALSE
	res := bool (x : a)	res := a_r(x); assert (a_r(x) = TRUE => x : a)
	a := exp	cont <-- initiate_iteration_t_x; WHILE cont = TRUE DO cont, x<-- continue_iteration_t_x; a := (a – {x}) ∨ (exp ∧ {x}) INVARIANT cont = bool(x_to_process /= {}) & x : t_x & x_to_process ∨ x_processed = t_x & a ∧ x_processed = exp ∧ x_processed VARIANT card (x_to_process) END
	a := (a – {x}) ∨ (exp ∧ {x})	l := bool(x : exp); a_r(x) := l

	res := bool(a = {})	res := TRUE;
		cont <-- initiate_iteration_t_x;
		WHILE cont = TRUE DO
		cont, x<-- continue_iteration_t_x;
		l := bool(x : a);
		IF l = TRUE THEN
		res := FALSE;
		cont := FALSE
		END
		INVARIANT
		cont = bool(x_to_process /= {} &
		a ∧ x_processed = {}) &
		x : t_x &
		x_to_process ∨ x_processed = t_x &
		res = bool (a ∧ x_processed = {})
		VARIANT
		card (x_to_process)
		END

Initialization	a := {}	a_r := t_x_i * {FALSE}

Table 4.1. *Refinement processes*

The concrete data is limited by the target language of the transcoding process. In our case, we have:

– t_scalar:

The predefined integers (INTEGER, NATURAL, NAT, INT), Booleans, enumerated values and integer intervals.

– t_scalar --> t_scalar:

One-dimensional tables.

– t_scalar_1 * t_scalar_2 --> t_scalar_3 or

– t_scalar_1 --> t_scalar_2 --> t_scalar_3

Two-dimensional tables.

Around 10 refinement schemes are in widespread use. Table 4.1 shows the refinement of an abstract set from a Boolean table representing its characteristic function.

Note the use of abstract iterators, which allows us to separate data refinement from treatment refinement: the concrete variable a_r is not involved in any loops.

4.2.5. *Proof*

4.2.5.1. *General principles*

The aim of the proof process is to demonstrate the POs of the B model being developed and correct any false POs that come to light. Like testing, proof is a validation activity; at Siemens, the choice was made to leave this activity to the developers themselves rather than to an independent team. This generates considerable savings in terms of time, as parts of the proof process can be carried out in the course of model development.

Proof activities are first used in developing the model, not for exhaustive proof at this stage, but to eliminate as many errors as possible. Proof activities then continue into later stages for model validation.

4.2.5.2. *Proof in practice*

When proving a B model, we must:

– demonstrate all of the POs;

– record these demonstrations in order to show them to the validation team or any other group responsible for verifying the model consistency.

Atelier B produces POs automatically, and offers powerful automatic provers which are able to deal with around 85% of lemmas.

Each of the remaining lemmas, each containing hundreds of hypotheses and as many as 2,500 hypotheses for certain components, is then subject to an “interactive” proof approach in which the developer aims to rewrite the lemma in order to obtain a trivially correct lemma.

The rewriting stage may be carried out in three different ways:

– by applying predefined heuristics from Atelier B;

– by applying a rewriting rule chosen from a database of validated rules;

– by defining and applying a new rewriting rule.

The different stages in the interactive proof process are saved in a file which may be examined to ensure the exactitude of the demonstration. The introduction of new rewriting rules is a sensitive point in the process: these rules must be carefully and thoroughly verified in order to avoid proving a false lemma by a falsc rule. Two processes are used in parallel to verify added rules:

– peer review during development involves an initial verification stage and ensures that the added rules present complexity levels compatible with complete validation;

– during model validation, each new added rule is demonstrated by an independent team, and this demonstration is saved in a monitoring file.

The validation process stops at this point, as it is not necessary to verify the demonstration of rules to demonstrate the lemmas in a model.

4.2.5.3. *Ease of proof*

Several elements contribute to reducing the efforts involved in proof. By order of importance, they are:

– The architecture of the abstract model;

- Proof facilitation is taken into account when constructing the model, using cutting models wherever necessary. This allows us to avoid excessively complex B constructions, for example, which would generate difficult POs.

– A limited number of refinement processes;

- Around 10 data refinement processes are sufficient to produce our applications. Our methodological guidelines advise limiting the number of treatment refinements, and our automatic refinement tool is also parsimonious. This means that most POs can be grouped into a few, very similar families, which are easier to understand and prove. This tendency toward uniformity is highlighted further by the use of automatic refinement.

– Capitalization of proof;

- The costs associated with interactive proof are essentially due to writing and validating new rules. Our base of validated rules naturally encourages developers to reuse existing rules, rather than to create new rules requiring validation. At each stage of the interactive proof process, the developer may consult the rule base to see which rules may be applied and simulate the results of the application. If none of the existing rules respond to the requirements and a new rule is needed, the new rule will be added to the rule base after validation and may then be reused for future projects.

We currently have access to a base of 5,100 rules, around one-third of which is made up of predefined rules from Atelier B; the other two-thirds are the result of our work on a variety of projects over the last 18 years.

4.3. Monitoring

4.3.1. *Development review*

The purpose of reviews is to identify faults in B models and their documentation as early as possible. Reviews are carried out throughout the development process, with the aim of verifying whether or not input documents (B models or software specifications) are of sufficient quality to allow work to progress.

In more concrete terms, reviews help to ensure that:

– the software specification document is self-supporting, and can be used both for development and for safety validation;

– the abstract model formalizes all requirements expected of the program;

– the development follows the recommendations of our best practice guidelines, the B development guide;

– the model enables the operational safety team to carry out validation activities in the best possible conditions.

The review process aims to provide a level of coverage such that all formal developments will be seen by at least two people, the developer and a reviewer, before being passed to the operational safety team.

4.3.1.1. *Review objectives*

We can identify three main classes of model reviews based on their main objectives:

– abstract model reviews which aim to verify that all requirements have been formalized;

– concrete model reviews which aim to remove performance risks and verify that the model is easily provable;

– proof reviews which aim to verify that the proof rules are correct.

Document-based reviews form an integral part of the quality approach used by Siemens, but do not present any specific characteristics linked to the use of B.

4.3.1.2. *Initiation criteria*

The effort involved in the review process should be adapted on the basis of the expected gains. Review initiation is left to the discretion of those responsible for development, based on the use of a number of indicative criteria:

– priorities for model reviews include new specification modelings and functions which have been substantially modified;

– development packages received from external sources should be subject to systematic review;

– the abstract model should be reviewed before work begins on the concrete model;

– any developments carried out by inexperienced personnel should be reviewed;

– a proof review should be carried out before delivering a model to the operational safety team;

– excessively “large” components should be reviewed. The exact definition of “excessively large” is left to the development team, but a review should certainly be envisaged in the following cases:

- components producing more than 1,000 POs,

- components of more than 1,000 lines,

- components for which the proof time, on relaunching saved interactive proofs, is more than 30 min.

In our experience, the short-term quality/cost balance for model reviews is very good as it allows faults to be corrected at an early stage. The medium- and long-term benefits are also considerable, as inexperienced developers are able to benefit from the remarks of more experienced colleagues.

4.3.2. *Testing*

At Siemens, tests are currently carried out on code written in Ada [ANS 83]. Our process involves simulating the environment of safety applications and verifying that the applications behave in accordance with the program specification. This classic approach is applied to all of our developments. We use the same simulation techniques and the same test language for safety applications developed in B and for non-safety applications.

The major drawback of this approach is that testing takes place late in the process, and can only be implemented once the concrete model has reached a relatively advanced stage. Moreover, testing Ada code is the same as testing the concrete model: this is not cost effective, as the proof and safety actions carried out on the translation guarantee that the Ada code will conform to the abstract model. It would be interesting to explore the possibility of testing the abstract model, for example, by using the animation functions offered by Atelier B.

4.3.3. *Safety validation*

An operational safety team, independent of the development teams, carries out activities to verify that the systems delivered by Siemens respect the performance levels required by the client and by the applicable regulations in terms of reliability, availability, maintainability and safety. These activities cover the phases from creation to use; in this case, however, we are only interested in activities related to vital software.

Operational safety activities are structured around two key hypotheses:

– either the program is in a maximally safe state or its execution conforms to the source code;

– the source code conforms to the specification expressed in the abstract model.

The use of these hypotheses allows us to remove certain activities involved in the safety aspect of classic developments. These include failure mode and effects analysis (FMEA), unit tests and integration tests.

The use of coded processor technology guarantees the first hypothesis. The second hypothesis is covered by specific validation activities which will be discussed in the following sections.

4.3.3.1. *Specification analysis*

Software validation is only meaningful if the point of departure has itself been validated. Specification analysis consists of verifying the completeness of the document: it must contain all requirements included in earlier documentation (system or equipment specifications) and those resulting from safety analyses of these earlier documents. The document is also checked for internal consistency.

4.3.3.2. *Proof validation*

This purpose of this activity is to verify that the proof is complete and free of errors. The completeness aspect is covered by a simple check that the proof files supplied by the development team are sufficient to prove all of the lemmas in the application. The second aim is achieved by verifying proof rules added by the developers.

Each rule not contained in the prevalidated rule base will be the subject of a demonstration recorded in a validation file. In the best cases, this demonstration is obtained using an automatic prover; otherwise, the demonstration is produced by the person responsible for validation.

4.3.3.3. *Analysis of the abstract model*

The aim of abstract model analysis is to verify the completeness of this model in relation to its specification document. The analytical process involves crossed re-reading of the entire abstract model and the specification document, and results in the production of a set of traceability tables. Note that there is no need for the operational safety team to re-read the concrete model, as conformity to the abstract model is guaranteed by the proof process.

4.3.3.4. *Analysis of basic machines*

A basic machine is any component of a formal model which is not implemented in B. Basic machines form the "borders" of the formal model, and are used each time the model needs to access a non-formalized resource. This is the case when using services provided by the computer operating system, particularly when processing application input/output.

Two types of errors which can affect a basic machine cannot be detected by proof:

– the machine may stipulate contradictory properties, as the coherency of the INVARIANT clause of a machine is only proved by the implementation of its initialization, and this proof does not exist for basic machines;

– it may state properties which are not verified by the executable code which implements the machine.

Basic machines and the Ada code which directly implements them are reviewed by the operational safety team to detect situations of this type. To facilitate this validation, developers are given the following advice for basic machines:

– only declare concrete variables or constants;

– use substitutions which are as indeterminist as possible;

– reduce the contents of the PROPERTIES and INVARIANT clauses to the strict minimum.

4.3.3.5. *Production chain verification*

The objective of this activity is to guarantee that executable components installed *in situ* are constructed with all due care, based on B models with verified proof, and that the safety applications they contain have been tested in a satisfactory manner. Monitoring and analysis activities are also carried out with each evolution of Atelier B and the relevant transcoding tools.

4.3.3.6. *Operational tests*

The purpose of this activity is to define test cases which will reinforce convictions that a program conforms to the specification. These test cases need to cover all safety functions contained in the specification. They must also cover all conditions which place or maintain application variables in a restrictive state. Note that the aim of the activity is to test the software itself, not a particular configuration. The data used to configure the program for testing may therefore be different from the data used for the final on-site configuration.

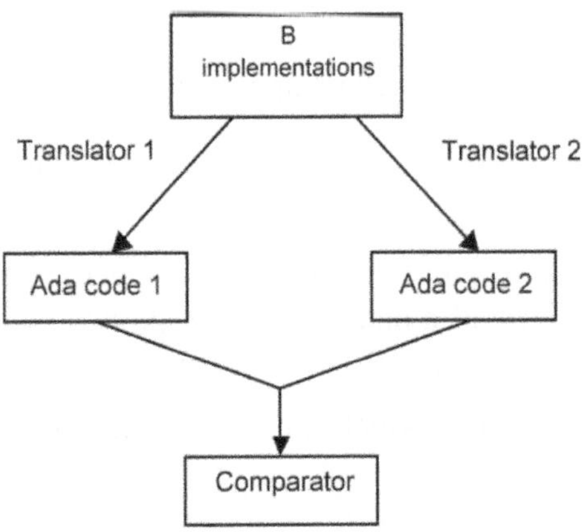

Figure 4.7. *Double generation chain*

4.4. Digging deeper

4.4.1. *Translation from B to Ada*

The coded processor ensures that the execution of the program conforms to the source code. The source code also needs to conform to the B implementation which it translates. For this reason, we compare the results of two functionally equivalent but independent translators.

The credibility of this approach is dependent on a number of points:

– the specification of the translators must be error-free;

– the two translators must not possess common error modes;

– the comparator must be safe;

– the produced code must not be modified after comparison.

The specification of the translators is particularly critical: an error in the translator specification document would lead to a shared translation error in both translators, which the comparator would be unable to detect. We therefore aimed to create a translation definition using simple syntactic transformations wherever possible. The resulting document is relatively succinct – 70 pages – and was subject to particularly rigorous verifications.

Two separate teams created and validated the transcoders in order to avoid common error modes resulting from human errors. This constraint was applied to both the initial development and the subsequent modifications to the transcoders.

Protection is also required against the possibility of shared modes in the tools used to create the translators; for this reason, different syntactic analyzers, programming languages and compilers were used in the two cases.

The two obtained pieces of Ada code [ANS 83] must then be compared to check that the two translators obtain the same result. The diagram below shows the use of the SPT to compare the Ada codes.

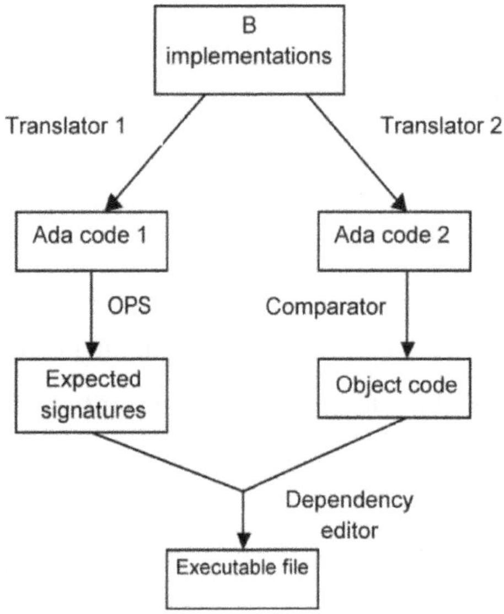

Figure 4.8. *Double generation chain for use of the CSP*[5]

One set of sources is compiled and the other set is analyzed by the SPT. Any errors (in translation, compilation or execution) will lead to a difference between the precalculated signatures and those obtained by the execution; the probability of detection is very high, and in these cases, all wired output are placed into a restrictive state by the dynamic controller.

The operational safety team verifies that the production chain clearly separates the two blocks of Ada code and that they have not been modified after their translation from B for all software deliveries.

4.4.2. *Abstract models and concrete models*

The notions of abstract and concrete models are helpful in presenting the B development cycle, but a more subtle interpretation is possible. The concrete model is produced from the abstract model using refinement activities, but these activities often entail modifications to the abstract model

5 The technology used in the coded safety processor is described in [BOU 09, Chapter 2]. This processor [FOR 89] was initially implemented in the context of the SACEM project in the 1980s [GEO 90, MAR 90, HEN 94].

itself. This occurs because creation of a program sheds new light on the specification and may reveal errors. More technical reasons may also lead to modifications in an abstract model: two examples are shown below.

It is difficult to produce the "right" variable reading operations early in the creation process. When working with B, variable reading operations are only used in implementations; although they form part of the abstract model, they are barely used at this stage, if at all. Potential shortcomings in these operations will, therefore, not be detected before the concrete model is produced. This is shown by the example given below in which we attempt to select a reading operation to associate with the partial function x: t_index +-> t_content.

It is not difficult to imagine a large number of other possibilities, and selection only becomes possible during the implementation of treatments using x. Machines declaring x will also be completed at this point.

<table>
<tr>
<td>res <-- read_1(i) =
PRE
    i : dom(x)
THEN
    res := x(i)
END</td>
<td>res, ok <-- read_2(i) =
PRE
    i : t_index
THEN
  IF i : dom (x)
  THEN
    ok := TRUE ||
    res := x(i)
  ELSE
    ok := FALSE ||
    res :: t_content
  END
END</td>
<td>res <-- read_3(c) =
PRE
  c : t_content
THEN
  res :(res : t_index
&
      (c : ran(x) =>
       res |-> c : x))
END</td>
</tr>
</table>

Table 4.2. *Example of a reading operation*

Optimization of the concrete model may also lead to modifications to the abstract model. Certain production choices may be guided by the developer's knowledge of the software environment.

Rather than coding a very general but inefficient solution, developers use hypotheses to obtain higher levels of performance from their code. These hypotheses are generally not present in the first version of the abstract model; we must therefore add them at the correct position. This position is often in the input variables of the application. The hypotheses may then be discussed with systems and operational safety engineers to check that they are both relevant and harmless.

4.4.3. *Functional calculation with safety monitoring*

The safety calculator used by Siemens is costly in terms of execution time, and it is sometimes necessary to maintain identical safety levels without using this calculator. One technique consists of replacing a vital calculation with an equivalent, but less costly, classic calculation.

In order to maintain safety levels, we need to verify the validity of the calculation, forcing the program into a restrictive state in case of failure. The payoff for these performance gains is a risk of reduced availability due to the replacement of a proved, safe and available treatment by a treatment for which verification may fail on execution.

Three variations of this technique are presented below. Note that the cases using partial proof and proof by model polarization do not formalize software availability.

4.4.3.1. *Total proof*

Let F be a complex function, but with a predicate P which is easy to calculate, such that P (x, y) <=> y = F(x) is true. The calculation operation = y:= F(x) may be refined.

We start by writing a basic machine containing the functional operation:

```
p_y_f <-- compute_f (x) =
  PRE
    x : t_x
  THEN
    p_y_f :: INTEGER
  END
```

This operation is specified in indeterminist form, as the calculation is not carried out in B and its result thus presents no safety guarantees.

The safety operation is then implemented by a call to the functional calculation, followed by verification of the predicate:

```
calcul =
  BEGIN
    y <-- compute_f(x;
    IF not (P) THEN
      failure
    END
  END
```

4.4.3.2. *Partial proof*

The previous technique is said to be "total" as the safety controls guarantee that we will find a value of y where y = F(x).

In most cases, F includes calculations associated with system availability and performance:

y = F(x) <=> P(x, y) where

P(x,y) is defined by Safety (x,y)& Availability(x,y) & Performance(x,y)

If we decide to only formalize the safety aspect, the specification model can include:

```
compute = y: (Safety(x, y))
```

Refined by:

```
compute =
  BEGIN
    y <-- compute_f(x);
    IF not Safety(x, y) THEN
      failure
    END
  END
```

4.4.3.3. *Proof by polarization*

A final variation of the technique may be applied when a full problem specification takes the following form:

```
IF condition THEN
  permissive_action
ELSE
  restrictive_action
END
```

and the following conditions are satisfied:

– the condition predicate is costly to evaluate;

– another predicate, condition', with a lower evaluation cost, is available, such that:

condition' => condition

– the execution of restrictive_action when condition is true does not create safety issues.

If we only formalize the safety aspect, the specification model can include:

```
SELECT condition THEN
  permissive_action
WHEN 0 = 0 THEN
  restrictive_action
END
```

Refined by:

```
compute =
  VAR l_y_f
  IN
    y <-- compute_f(x);
    IF condition' THEN
      permissive_action
    ELSE
      restrictive_action
    END
  END
```

This technique is most widely used in the cases where condition takes the form #z.P(z): it is generally quicker to verify that P is true for a given value of z than to verify that P is false for all values of z.

The refinement therefore becomes:

```
compute =
  BEGIN
    y <-- compute_f(x);
    IF P(y) THEN
      permissive_action
    ELSE
      restrictive_action
    END
  END
```

We have shown that P(y) => #z.P(z).

4.4.4. *Configuration*

The automatic pilots produced by Siemens may be configured using properties which describe the properties of different system objects.

This covers information such as:

– track topology;

– the position of objects along the track;

– slopes and curves for each point on the track;

– the speed profile authorized by civil engineering constraints;

– the nature of each piece of information in messages with generic formats;

– characteristics of rolling stock (mass, length, guaranteed braking capacity, etc.).

This configuration data can be specified in B, but the resulting programs lack flexibility: any modification of the data (following track maintenance or line extension, for example) would require the program to be (at least partially) reproved and retranscoded. Furthermore, this would have no effect on the main difficulty with configuration data: ensuring that it is an accurate image of the situation in the field. For these reasons, the strategy chosen by Siemens involves modeling only those properties that are needed for the proof. This data is then modeled:

– either as constants in the basic machines: this is the case for fixed equipment which is initialized by reading configuration files;

– or as variables in the basic machines which manage the input data flow: this is the case for onboard equipment, which receives messages describing the current zone as it moves along the track.

Configuration validation, therefore, involves two relatively distinct aspects:

– data must conform to the reality in the field;

– data must conform to the relevant properties expressed by the formal model.

The first point is a surveying issue with no bearing on the use of formal methods. The second point is covered by the operational safety team, using tools to automatically verify the conformity of configuration data with the hypotheses used in the B model. These tools operate by describing the values of configuration data in B and adding hypotheses extracted from the main model. Specialized provers are used to demonstrate these hypotheses.

This approach is illustrated in the following example. The `data` constant is declared in a basic machine with a certain number of properties.

```
CONCRETE_CONSTANTS
  data
PROPERTIES
  data: t_zacq_fu_mr_i --> t_segment_i &
  !xx.(xx : t_zacq_fu_mr =>
      data(xx) : t_ segment_pas \/
               {c_segment_indet}) &
  t_zacq_fu_mr =
    dom(t_zacq_fu_mr <| data |> t_segment)
```

These properties are based on the following declarations:

```
SETS
  t_zacq_fu_mr_i , t_segment_i
CONCRETE_CONSTANTS
  . c_segment_indet
ABSTRACT_CONSTANTS
  t_zacq_fu_mr, t_ segment
PROPERTIES
```

```
c_ segment_indet : t_segment_i &
t_ segment <: t_segment _i &
c_t segment_indet /: t_segment &
t_zacq_fu_mr <: t_zacq_fu_mr_i
```

A certain number of these constrants are evaluated in B, while others are only evaluated in the basic machines. All of the evaluations are grouped together, transformed into B where necessary and added to the properties of the initial model. For example:

```
PROPERTIES
  c_segment_indet = 0 &
  t_segment_i = 0 .. 255 &
  t_zacq_fu_mr_i = 0 .. 50 &
  t_segment = 1 .. 45 &
  t_zacq_fu_mr = 1 .. 3 &
  data = (0 .. 255) * {0} <+
        {1 |-> 23, 2 |-> 45, 4 |-> 67}
```

We must then simply prove the obtained model to validate the data. In this case, proof allows us to see, for example, that the tuple 4 |-> 67 is not suitable.

4.4.5. *Limitations*

4.4.5.1. *The main program*

The transcoding of the main machine into Ada/CSP does not produce an Ada compilation unit which can be directly used as a main program. The main machine is therefore written directly in Ada; this is a simple process and does not pose any significant validation issues.

4.4.5.2. *Time*

The purpose of the abstract model is to encapsulate all of the safety requirements applicable to the program. B does not include a construction which allows explicit expression of time constraints. However, these constraints may be modeled implicitly based on a hypothesis of the cyclical implementation of the program. In our case, the dynamic controller, i.e. a hardware component, guarantees periodic activation of the program.

4.4.5.3. *Real numbers*

The functions assigned to wayside computers can be modeled naturally using predicate logic and set theory, and B is almost ideal for this type of application. The numerical calculations required by onboard applications (odometers, energy calculations, etc.) are difficult to model as B is not able to handle real numbers, only integers.

Our modeling consists of representing real numbers by an integer mantissa associated with a scaling factor which remains implicit in the model. The real number x is therefore modeled as x_mantissa: INT and a scale factor F such that:

x_mantissa * F <= x < (x_mantissa + 1) * F

The modeling activity therefore consists of defining the "right" scale factors to use. These factors must allow us to represent the desired physical values (i.e. the calculation should not overflow) with the desired level of precision.

4.4.5.4. *Availability*

The formalization must cover safety requirements in detail, but will not necessarily cover all the availability requirements. It is not necessary to formalize availability requirements if they are clearly separated from safety requirements in the relevant informal documents. In other cases, unless significant technical difficulties are encountered, availability requirements should be modeled in the same way as the safety requirements.

4.4.5.5. *New properties*

The specification formalization process may highlight properties that are contained implicitly in earlier documents but that seem significant to the formalization engineers. In the cases where these properties concern variables and are expressed in the form of invariants, it is generally useful to add them to the model to assist understanding of its operation.

When these properties concern constants which are not evaluated in B, it is best to avoid expressing them in B as they will not be validated by proof: they will be used as hypotheses in the basic machines describing the configuration data.

4.5. Automatic refinement

4.5.1. *History*

The bulk of the formal development aspect of the SAET-METEOR project was completed in 1996. This was the first development by Siemens (then operating as Matra) to use formal methods, and the risks associated with the use of this new technology were significant.

In an attempt to limit these risks, methodological work was carried out in parallel to the development process to identify and spread principles for best practice. A guide was produced which provided relatively directive refinement schemes, both for data and treatments. Following these indications, formal developers used a number of intermediate steps in refining treatments, ending with data refinement. The architecture of this process is similar to that shown in Figure 4.9.

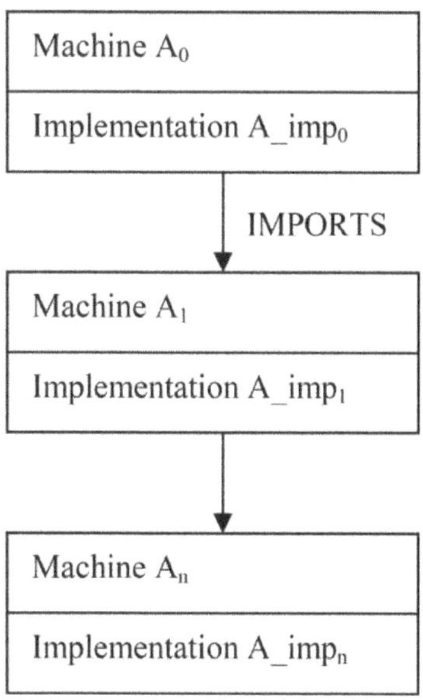

Figure 4.9. *Architecture example*

In this architecture, each operation Op of Ai is implemented in A_impi by calls to operations of Ai+1. : Op1; … ; Opn. As each of these new operations uses the same abstract variables as Op, the refinement is relatively easy to prove. This technique reduces the proof workload, but presents the major drawback of being highly repetitive: each new machine contains part of the contents of the previous machine. This means that the maintenance costs associated with the model are high.

The possibility of using tools to produce refinements was studied from an early date. A first attempt, entirely coded in C, was applied to the abstract model of the line AP for SAET-METEOR.

This first prototype showed that the general approach was valid, and that the reduction in performance generated by the passage from a concrete model coded "by hand" to an automatically refined model was acceptable. This experiment also showed the inadvisability of using fixed refinement rules in the tool, as any modifications to the refinement strategy would require modification of the tool itself.

The next stage was the replacement of the prototype by an interpreter, applying an external rule base. The use of this tool was rapidly extended to all of our projects and now it forms an essential part of our approach. The interpreter is a stable program which has changed very little since its creation in 1999. The rule base is used for all of our applications and is enriched in the course of each project. To date, it contains around 500 rules.

The expertise used in creating our projects is therefore reused, even in the cases where the code itself cannot be recycled.

4.5.2. *Operational principles*

The input into the refinement tool is a component of the abstract model (machine or refinement). The output generated by the tool is an implementation of the component. As the implementation can itself import a new machine, the process is repeated until a terminal implementation has been obtained.

Refinement stages follow the pattern below:

– The tool analyzes the variables of the starting component and determines their implementation. This is illustrated by the following simplified refinement rule:

```
RULE set_variable IS
  ABSTRACT_VARIABLE a
  TYPE integer_set(a,n)
  WHEN
    a ⊂ 1..n
  CONCRETE_VARIABLE
    a_r
  INVARIANT
    a_r ∈ 1..n → BOOLEAN &
    a = a_r⁻¹[{TRUE}]
END
```

The rule is applied to the refinement of a variable "a" with an invariant "a ⊂ 1..n" and implemented by a variable "a_r" using a gluing invariant. The construction "integer_set(a,n)" is treated as a predicate – the hypothesis – for substitution refinement: it records the applied data refinement.

One limitation of the tool is that variable refinement is chosen independently of the intended use. The selected refinement is always the most general in that the gluing invariant does not lose information. In our example, if the only uses of "a" were "max(a)", "a" could be implemented more efficiently with a_max: INT with the gluing a_max = max(a). This limitation remains theoretical and does not pose any problems in practice.

– The substitution refinement rules are applied in a context defined by refinements of variables and the hypotheses verified at the point of refinement. Suppose that we wish to refine the affectation contained in the IF below.

```
INVARIANT
  my_set ⊂ 1..99
OPERATIONS
 my_operations =
  IF 3 ∈ my_set THEN
    my_set := my_set ∪ {my_var}
  END
```

The context in which the substitution refinement rules will be applied contains "integer_set(my_set,99)" (the rule shown above has been applied) and 3 ∈ my_set. The following rule may therefore be applied:

```
RULE assign_set_variable IS
WHEN integer_set(a,n)
REFINE
  a := a ∪ {b}
INTO
  local_variable_1 := b;
  IMPLEMENTATION(
    a_r(local_variable_1) := TRUE)
END
```

This rule copies "b" into a local variable and updates the table which implements "a". The second instruction does not require further refinement, and is labeled as an implementation. The first instruction is not labeled and may be refined as needed, for example in the cases where b is a complex expression. In our example, this is not necessary, and the implementation would therefore contain the following substitutions:

```
l_1 := my_var;
my_set_r(l_1) := TRUE;
```

Note that the tool does not analyze the operations of the seen machines. When it implements access to a variable of a seen machine, it imposes its own reading operation, and the developer must ensure that this is present in the seen machine. Our rule base is based on a limited number of naming conventions to facilitate this task.

A possible extension would be to enable modification of seen machines to add or modify reading operations. This would allow the tool to modify the abstract model, but it would also require tool validation activities which are not currently necessary.

One notable property of the refinement tool is that it does not need to be monitored by the operational safety team: an error in the rules or in the interpreter itself will always be detected during proof of the concrete model.

4.5.3. *Interactive refinement*

The refinement tool can operate in interactive mode, and this approach is used in the following situations:

– when the tool is unable to find applicable rules;

– when the refinement does not converge;

– when the code produced cannot be proved or is not efficient.

In interactive mode, the developer can adjust the refinement by examining the context and the rules applied to each stage. The developer can also modify refinement tools and store them with the refined component, or, more rarely, add them to the rule basis if he or she considers them to be reuseable.

4.6. Conclusion

The first aim of subway operators and their clients is to provide access to safe transportation. Siemens has responded to this expectation using a rigorous development process (capability maturity model integration (CMMI) level 3) and by employing cutting-edge techniques. The B method, used by Siemens for over 18 years, is a key element in this approach.

From the moment it was first used in the SAET-METEOR project, the method and its tools presented a sufficient level of maturity to produce safe software with controlled development costs. Since then, the implementation of automatic refinement has allowed us to multiply the size and complexity of our applications by 4, while reducing the size of development teams and the time needed to create our systems.

The increasing complexity of our systems is the main concern in relation to the future of the B method. From a software perspective, the subject has been thoroughly tackled, and current working methods are sufficient to make the necessary improvements to our Trainguard MT CBTC platform [IEE 04].

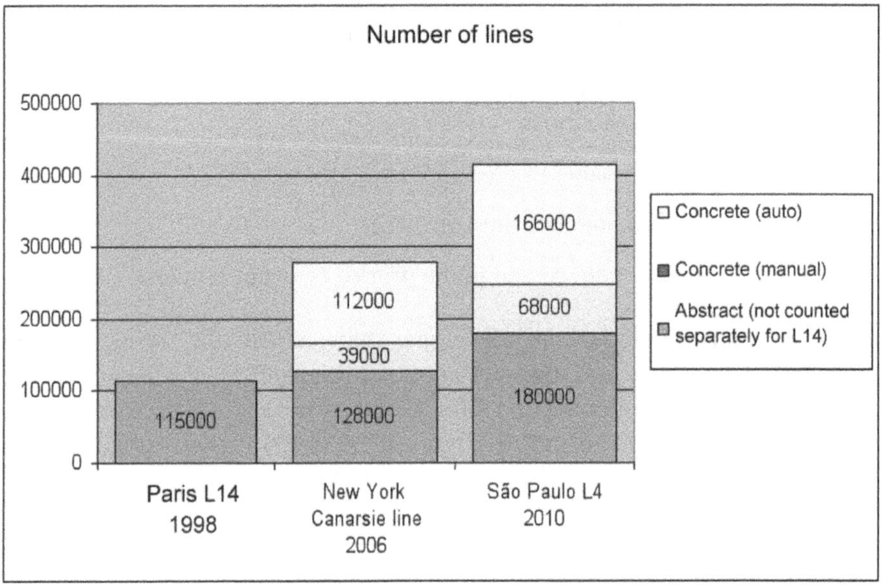

Figure 4.10. *Evolution in the size of B models*

Work on version 3 of the product is currently in its final stages. This new version will be used in our current projects, including renovation of the PATH network connecting Manhattan to New Jersey and the automatization of the Helsinki metro. Our systems are becoming increasingly modular, based on the reuse and association of components. These systems need to be subject to the same rigorous approach used in software development.

We are currently able to prove that our software is correct. In the future, it should be possible to use proof to guarantee the most important properties relating to the material objects of our systems. This represents a significant change of mentality for systems engineers (more so than for software engineers). Despite significant developments, Event B is still considered as a research project, rather than an industrial tool, at Siemens, based, for example, on its use in the European Deploy project[6].

6 For more details on the Deploy project, see http://www.deploy-project.eu/.

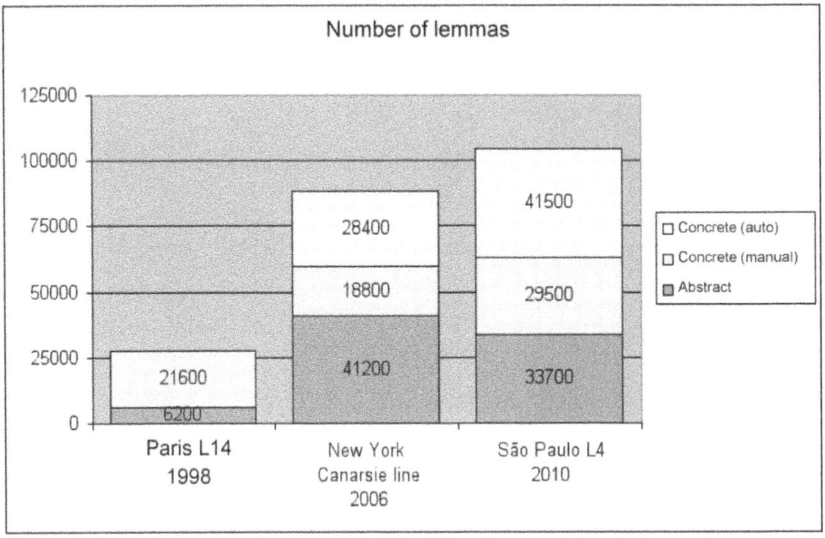

Figure 4.11. *Evolution of the number of POs in B models*

4.7. Glossary

CBTC	communication-based train control
CMMI	capability maturity model integration
IOM	input/output module
METEOR	*Metro Est Ouest Rapide* (High-speed East-West metro)
SPT	signature predetermination tool
OS	operating system
AP	autopilot
PAE	*Pilote Automatique Embarqué* (on-board autopilot)
PAS	*Pilote Automatique Secteur* (sector autopilot)
PO	proof obligation
PRT	personal rapid transit
RATP	*Régie Autonome des Transports Parisiens* (Autonomous Operator of Parisian Transports)
RER	*Réseau Express Régional* - regional express network

SACEM *Système d'Aide à la Conduite, à l'Exploitation et à la maintenance* (Assisted driving, control, and maintenance system)

SADT structured analysis and design technics

SAET *Système d'Automatisation de l'Exploitation des Trains* (Automation System for Train Operations)

VAL *Véhicule Automatique Léger* (Light Automatic Vehicle)

4.8. Bibliography

[ANS 83] ANSI, Standard ANSI/MIL-STD-1815A-1983, Ada programming language, 1983.

[BAR 08] BARO S., "A high availability vital computer for railway applications: architecture & safety principles", *Proceedings of Embedded Real-Time Software (ERTS '08)*, 2008.

[BOU 09] BOULANGER J.-L. (ed.), "Sécurisation des architectures informatiques – exemples concrets", Hermes-Lavoisier, 2009.

[BOU 11] BOULANGER J.-L. (ed.), "Sécurisation des architectures informatiques industrielles", Hermes-Lavoisier, 2011.

[CHA 96] CHAUMETTE A.-M., LE FEVRE L., "Système d'automatisation de l'exploitation des trains de la ligne METEOR", *REE*, 8 September 1996.

[FOR 89] FORIN P., "Vital coded microprocessor principles and application for various transit systems", *IFAC – Control, Computers, Communications in Transportation*, pp. 137–142, 1989.

[FOR 96] FORIN P., "Une nouvelle génération du processeur sécuritaire code", *Revue Générale des Chemins de fer*, vol. 6, pp. 38–41, June 1996.

[GEO 90] GEORGES J.-P., "Principes et fonctionnement du Système d'Aide à la Conduite, à l'Exploitation et à la Maintenance (SACEM). Application à la ligne A du RER", *Revue Générale des Chemins de fer*, vol. 6, June 1990.

[GUI 90] GUIHOT G., HENNEBERT C., "SACEM software validation", *Proceedings of the 12th IEEE-ACM International Conference on Software Engineering*, March 1990.

[HEN 94] HENNEBERT C., "Transports ferroviaires: Le SACEM et ses derives", *ARAGO 15, Informatique tolérante aux fautes*, Masson, Paris, pp. 141–149, 1994.

[HOA 69] HOARE C.A.R., "An axiomatic basis for computer programming", *Communications of the ACM*, vol. 12, pp. 576–583, October 1969.

[IEE 04] IEEE, 1474.1, IEEE Standard for Communications-Based Train Control (CBTC), Performance and Functional Requirements, 2004.

[LIS 90] LISSANDRE M., *Maîtriser SADT*, Armand Collin, 1990.

[MAR 90] MARTIN J., WARTSKI S., GALIVEL C., "Le processeur codé: un nouveau concept appliqué à la sécurité des systèmes de transports", *Revue Générale des Chemins de fer*, vol. 6, pp. 29–35, June 1990.

[MAT 98] MATRA and RATP, "Naissance d'un Métro. Sur la nouvelle ligne 14, les rames METEOR entrent en scène. PARIS découvre son premier métro automatique", *La vie du Rail & des transports*, no. 1076, October 1998.

5

Industrial Applications for Modeling with the B Method

5.1. Introduction

The B method [ABR 96] was introduced at the end of the 1980s to produce software that is correct by construction. At that time, it was promoted and supported by RATP[1], and the B method and the tool which implements it, Atelier B, were at first applied within the transport industry.

The method's first real success [BEH 93, BEH 96, BEH 99] was the development of the automatic control of the SAET-METEOR metro (see [BOU 12, Chapter 3]), installed on Line 14 of the Paris metro. Over 110,000 lines of B were written for this project, allowing the automatic generation of 86,000 lines of Ada code. This development was followed by many others such as the Beijing metro built for the Olympic Games, the Canarsie Line in New York or, nearer home, the automatic shuttle linking the terminals of Charles de Gaulle Airport (called CdG-VAL, see [BAD 05]).

During the CdG-VAL project, an innovative technique was used: automatic refinement (Figure 5.1). The definition of modeling guides with B on the one hand and of refinement patterns on the other hand were used to automate the transformation process of a B model into its implementation, through a sequence of small steps.

Chapter written by Thierry LECOMTE.

1 See http://www.ratf.fr.

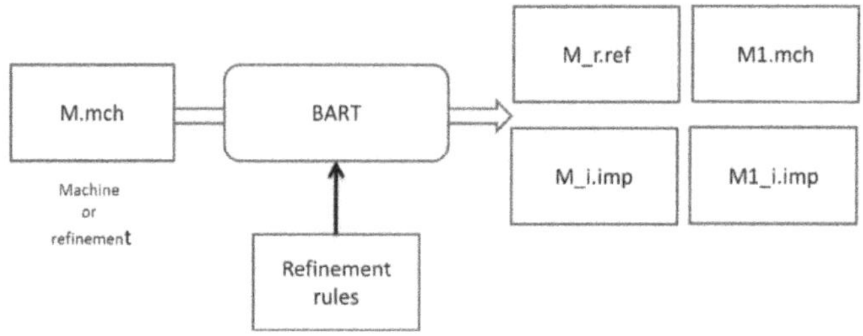

Figure 5.1. *Implementation of BART*

Data and algorithms are progressively modified so that they can eventually be implemented. The user only influences the transformation by occasionally providing new refinement rules, in the cases where the tool becomes blocked. Atelier B is a qualified tool. However, the same is not the case for BART because the validity of the models produced needs to be tested by a mathematical demonstration. If the tool and/or the refinement rules are faulty, then the demonstration cannot be carried out.

Automatic refinement made the semi-automatic generation of 225,000 of the 265,000 lines of B code for the alarm control unit possible, which means final Ada software of 186,000 lines. This is the biggest software package developed in B to date.

Alongside these developments, new applications were created, such as the tool vital embedded settings generator (VESG), which relieves the automatic train protection (ATP) of certain calculations, and produces optimized data describing the paths taken, destination Alstom CC-ATP (carbon controller) Urbalis. The role of the VESG is to produce the file of data that will be brought onboard and that contains information on the tracks.

VESG handles XML files in input, which describe the tracks. These files are generated by the Alstom teams using other dedicated tools. They contain information on various significant elements present on the tracks: switches, signals, slopes, speed limits, etc.

VESG reads these files and then carries out a certain number of precalculations on the information that they contain. Finally, it generates a binary file, which contains the result of these treatments, in a format that can be read by the onboard program. This data file is then loaded onto the trains, which circulate on the same tracks. The energy control program uses this file to find out about the environment of the train in relation to its current position, and thus decide how to proceed as a function of this information, particularly in relation to whether it should activate emergency braking.

To reduce the costs of unitary tests for such SSIL4 software[2], this non-onboard software has been redeveloped in B. The B model [ABR 96] generates approximately 30,000 proof obligations, which are handled using, in particular, many proof rules that are integrated into the tooling of the proof. The VESG regularly undergoes slight modifications, linked to the new types of elements that need to be taken into account on the tracks.

However, in 2010, a larger-scale change took place. Before this, Alstom used a particular tool to manage slopes on the tracks. After information had been generated by this tool, it was then integrated into the XML files for the VESG. In 2010, the decision was taken to merge this tool with the VESG. Thus, the VESG now also manages the more complex calculations on the information regarding slopes.

	Model/code lines
Abstract B model	17,845
Concrete B model	58,046
ADA written manually	5,634
ADA generated automatically	47,685

Table 5.1. *Development metrics*

	Load
Abstract B model	16%
Concrete B model	26%
Proof	38%
ADA and debugging	13%
Validation of added rules	7%

Table 5.2. *Distribution of the development load*

5.2. Control-command systems for controlling platform doors

Toward the end of the 1990s, an extension of the B method became available [ABR 96]. This was known as the B system or event-B, and this

2 There are five software safety integrity level (SSIL) levels from 0 to 4. For more detailed information, see the standard CENELEC EN 50128 [CEN 01, CEN 11].

made it possible to analyze, study and specify not only software, but also systems, in the wider sense of the term. Event-B makes it possible to use "B-like" formalization and proof for systems, which contain a software component alongside an electronic component and equipment.

In this way, a proved definition of system architecture is obtained, or more generally, the proven development of system studies that are carried out before the specification and design of the software. This extension makes it possible to carry out failure studies from the outset in the development of a large-scale system.

The specification of safety-critical software or of systems requires the same approach: use the abstraction, refinement and proof in order to mathematically show that a collection of models is coherent. First, the internal coherence of each model is verified (the behavior described is in line with properties expressed).

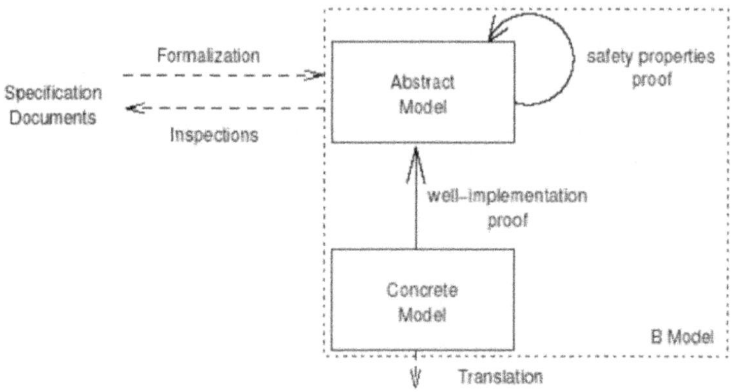

Figure 5.2. *Formal development cycle in B*

Then, we need to establish that each refinement does not contradict its abstraction (the model containing fewer details). Finally, the entire collection of models has been proved, the most concrete part of the model is considered by transitivity to conform to the highest-level specification and the model can then be translated into the chosen target language, as described in Figure 5.2.

Both approaches (modeling the system and modeling the software) are based on set theory, first-order predicate logic and calculation of generalized substitutions. The main difference between them is the modeling paradigm and the way in which the models are structured.

For modeling software, behavior is described in terms of operations, which represent the program functions, executed in sequence. The modeling language varies depending on whether we are in the specification or implementation phase (no sequence in specification, no parallel action in implementation, no loop in specification, only implementable types in implementation, etc.).

```
EVENTS
  route_reservation =
    ANY rr WHERE
      rr:RR-resrt &
      rtbl~[{rr}] /\ resbl = {}
    THEN
      resrt:=resrt \/ {rr} ||
      resbl:=resbl \/ rtbl~[{rr}] ||
      rsrtbl :=rsrtbl \/ (rtbl|>{rr})
    END;

  route_freeing =
    ANY rr WHERE
      rr:resrt-ran(rsrtbl)
    THEN
      resrt:=resrt-{rr}
    END;

  FRONT_MOVE_1 =
    ANY rr WHERE
      rr:resrt &
      fst(rr):resbl-OCC &
      rsrtbl(fst(rr))=rr
    THEN
      OCC:=OCC \/ {fst(rr)}
    END;

  FRONT_MOVE_2 =
    ANY bb,nn WHERE
      bb:OCC &
      nn=nxt(rsrtbl(bb)) &
      bb:dom(nn) &
      nn(bb)/:OCC
    THEN
      OCC:=OCC\/{nn(bb)}
    END;

  BACK_MOVE_1 =
    ANY bb,nn WHERE
      bb:OCC &
      nn=nxt(rsrtbl(bb)) &
     (bb:dom(nn) => nn(bb):OCC) &

     (bb:ran(nn) &
      nn~(bb):dom(rsrtbl)
     =>
      rsrtbl(nn~(bb))/= rsrtbl(bb)
     )
    THEN
      OCC:=OCC-{bb} ||
      rsrtbl:={bb}<<|rsrtbl ||
      resbl:=resbl-{bb}
    END;
```

Figure 5.3. *Example of an event-B model*

The implementation language is called B0. An implementation may import other models (abstract machines) and delegate the implementation of variables to them. In this way, the specification of the program is divided into smaller components, which is a more manageable way to handle the complexity. The design (refinement, decomposition through importation) is verified by proof, as the process happens, and not when the development is complete.

For system modeling, behavior is described in terms of atomic events which modify the state variables of the system. A model is a complete view of a closed system (including, for example, the process that needs to be controlled, the control device and the environment). The modeling language is homogeneous throughout the modeling process (there is no longer any specification language for the implementation).

The event-B language is substantially different to B, in particular because it has been simplified and disambiguated. The B system approach is particularly well-suited for the representation of asynchronous behaviors, such as those of interruption-based software.

For several years now, the RATP in France has used platform doors on metro platforms to avoid passengers falling onto the track. A system of this kind is in use for the driverless SAET-METEOR metro. It also makes it possible to significantly improve train availability. In order to improve the service quality and passenger safety, RATP undertook introducing this type of protection on several Parisian lines, some of which were not automated. The transition from manually operated to automatic metros should take place gradually, with staggered replacement of the rolling stock.

Figure 5.4. *Platform door L13*

Before launching the rollout of a new system of platform doors over a whole line, RATP initiated a project, which aimed to produce a demonstrator for three stations of Line 13 [LEC 07, LEC 08, SAB 00], with an evaluation period of 8 months. The control-command system in charge of the opening and closing of the doors needed to have an SIL safety level[3] 3 as described in the standard CENELEC EN 50128 (CEN 50129 [CEN 03]).

3 SIL (safety integrity level), which can have four possible values, from 1 to 4.

This control apparatus must detect the arrival, complete standstill at the platform and the departure of trains, without having a direct connection with them (in fact SAET-METEOR is able to communicate directly with the platform door through dedicated communication means). Once the train is at a standstill at the platform, the control device must be able to detect the opening and closing of the train door, and to emit orders to open and shut the platform doors. These orders must be safely emitted (opening at the wrong time could lead to the injury or death of a passenger) and the control device must be designed, tested and validated in line with the railway standards (CENELEC EN 50126 [CEN 00], 50128 [CEN 01, CEN 11] and 50129 [CEN 03]).

As the available time before installation and beginning operation was short, a secure architecture, weakly coupled with the sensors used for the detection of trains, was used in order to facilitate acceptation by the authorities[4].

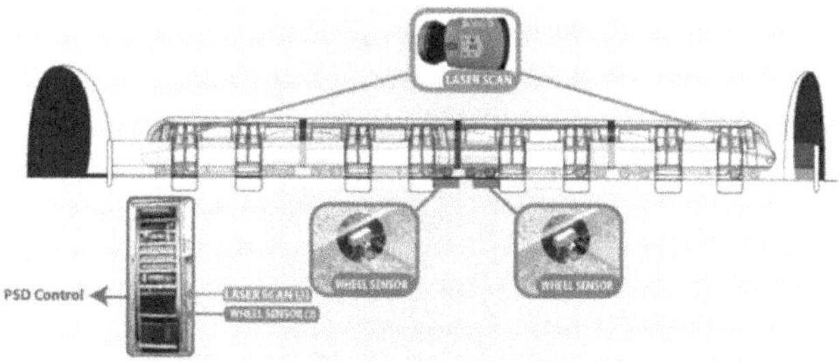

Figure 5.5. *Architecture*

This architecture is based both on a Siemens Simatic S7 safety automaton (level SIL3 according to the standard CEI/IEC 61508 [IEC 98]) and on infrared sensors and standard radars. In this case, safety is ensured by the safety automaton (the automaton has a certificate, which indicates that it is SIL3) and by the redundancy and diversification of the means of measurement, and not by the intrinsic safety of the sensors. This approach provides a solution that is less expensive and easier to maintain.

4 Authorization and opening for operation of a rail system is conducted through a state organization, which is in charge of examining the safety file (DS) for the urban sector, the STRMG (technical service for ski lifts and guided transport). For more information about the STRMG, see http://www.strmtg.equipement.gouv.fr/.

The development process, which should ensure the safety and reliability of the planned system, is constructed around the B method (and event-B) see [SAB 08]. This makes it possible to ensure traceability between the various phases of the project, and in this way to reduce validation effort. Before any development activity, a first phase of system analysis was carried out in order to evaluate the "completeness" and the non-ambiguity of the written specification.

The B method was used to:

– verify that for the platform door/control device system the functional and safety constraints were verified (there was no possibility of establishing forbidden connections between the train and the platform or between the train and the track);

– identify dangerous system behaviors.

A solution based on laser range finders, which was for a time considered, was abandoned in favor of a solution based on the recognition of the arrival and departure sequence of a train in station through sensors of different types. Hyper-frequencies, infrared and laser sensors were used in order to improve the resistance of the system to physical disturbances. The redundancy of the sensors using various technologies improved the confidence level of the measures. These sensors were put in position on the platforms and turned to face the tracks so that they could measure the position and speed of the trains, and also the movements of the train doors.

The system specifications and software were formalized in B [ABR 96] by the development team. Only the nominal behavior of the sensors (excluding any disturbance) was taken into account. The B models developed during the initial functional analysis (independent of any architecture of the control device for the platform doors) were reused directly. The suggested architecture was then modeled and inserted within these models.

The conformity of the new architecture with the functional specifications for the system was successfully proved, including some signaling rules which were introduced at this point into the model. The control device functions were then precisely modeled (arrival of the train, detection of the train, departure of the train, opening of train doors, closing of train doors, etc.).

A safety study was developed at the same time by the safety team in order to determine, in a detailed manner, how exterior disruptions might influence the behavior of the control device. These disruptions were accorded *a priori* or *a posteriori* frequencies, as a function of the availability of relevant data to the RATP, and a mathematical model, independent of the B model, was developed in order to establish the safety level of the system.

The *a priori* frequencies were verified during the 8 months of trials in true scale (if certain frequencies had not been verified and could have led to a diminished safety level of the control device, the overall architecture would have needed to be reexamined).

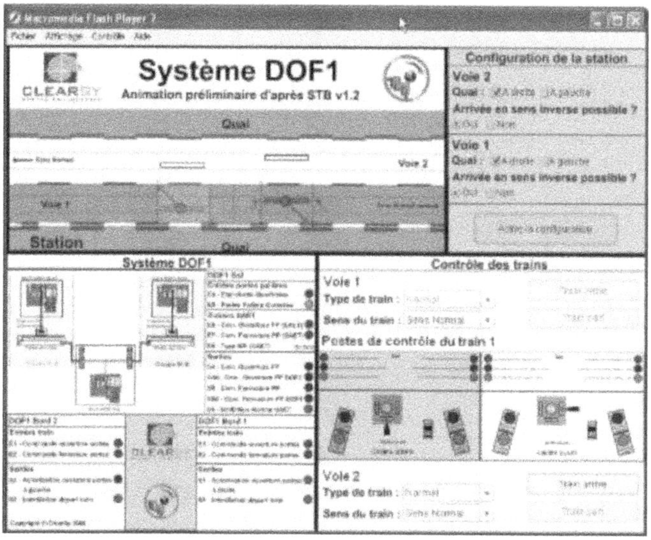

Figure 5.6. *Implementation of Brama*

The formal B model was then animated using the tool Brama in order to verify whether the formal B model had the same behavior as the real system on meaningful scenarios. This model animator was not part of the validation process, because for that to be the case, the tool would need to be qualified to the SSIL3 level, but rather it helped to compare formal models with the real world.

The specification documentation was partially developed starting from B system models, using another tool, Composys. Composys does not have proving capabilities, but rather it is an engineering tool, and it helps the human modeler to add contextual information (comments, description, name of component, etc.) into the B models used to generate the documentation in natural language, which describes the complete system.

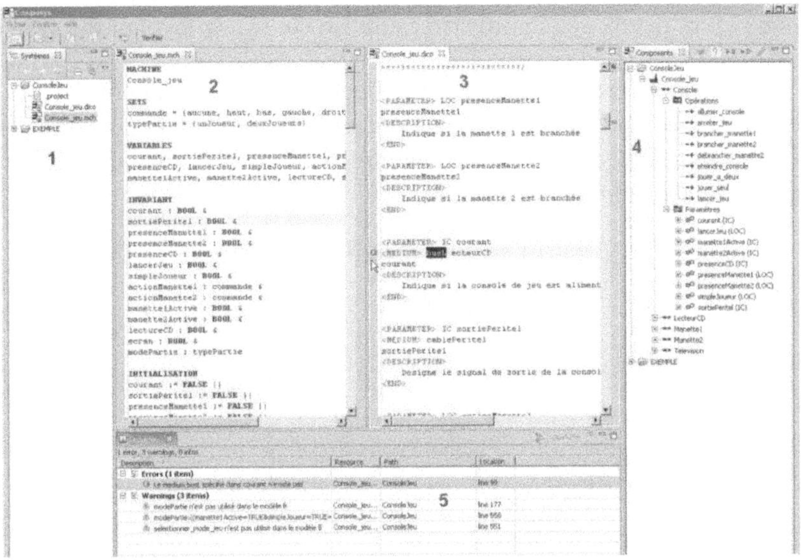

Figure 5.7. *Implementation of Composys*

Due to the fact that events are associated with components and the fact that variables are used by events (in reading/writing), Composys calculates the relationships between the different system components, as a function of how the variables are read or modified. These relationships are then represented by diagrams, which link the various system components with each other, and include the contextual data provided by the modeler. This document allows experts in the domain to validate the formal models, which otherwise are illegible.

The development of the software is finally based on event models developed in this context. The Siemens programmable automaton can be programmed in Ladder (one of the five languages recognized by the standard CEI/IEC 61131-3 [IEC 03]), but, unfortunately, it requires the use of its graphic interface in order to enter the code (if it is not entered in this way, the SIL3 certificate which comes with the automaton is no longer guaranteed).

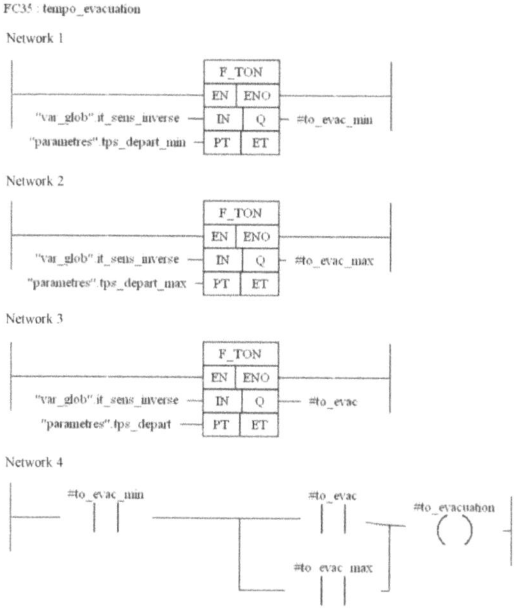

Figure 5.8. *Example of Ladder*

A translation diagram for B into Ladder has been developed. The translation is based on data streams and does not require a large semantic jump. A few optimizations have been contributed to the system in order to guarantee certain temporal constraints (such as keeping to cycle time).

```
OPERATIONS
    bb <-- ope_01 (nn) =
    BEGIN
        IF nn=3
        THEN
            bb := TRUE
        END
    END
```

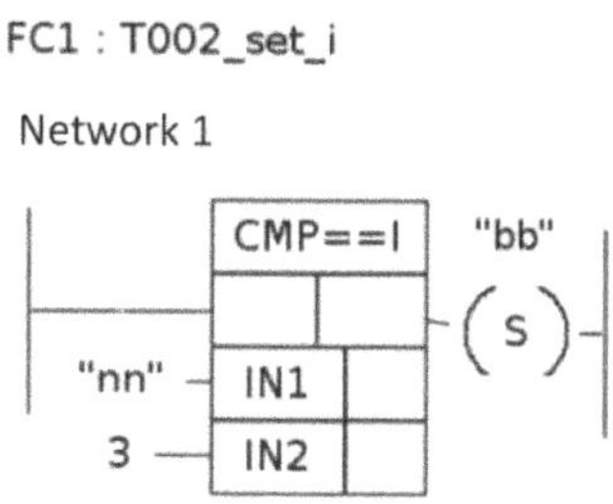

Figure 5.9. *Example of a B model translated into Ladder*

During the validation phase, it was easy to associate an execution path of the Ladder program (a Ladder program is defined by logical equations and is analyzed in terms of execution paths) with an event of the B model. If the source code is generated by a qualified tool (as is the case for metro autopilot-type applications), then unitary tests are not necessary, as this phase has been covered by the proof of the model. In this case, because the code has not been generated by a translator of this kind, extensive unitary testing was carried out.

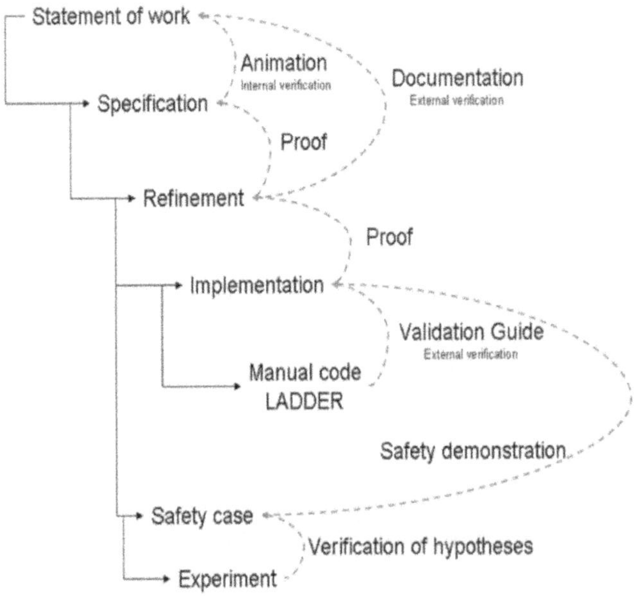

Figure 5.10. *Development and verification process*

Several months after the beginning of the development, a tested and validated functional control device was obtained. The process described in Figure 5.10 made it possible to obtain software tested to 100%, without error with respect to its specification when the test bench was run for the first time. A dedicated test bench was designed in order to simulate major perturbations (the sensors were emulated) and executed for several days, but no faulty behavior was observed.

The integration tests were carried out on a platform on Line 14, which was only used for tests (and which is equipped with the SAET-METEOR). This made it possible to complete configuration of the developed system rapidly in order to verify safety, availability, response time, etc. The choice of technologies for sensors was validated at this point.

Finally, 4 months after the development began, the platform doors were installed on three platforms of Line 13 for an eight-month long trial.

The following metrics were obtained:

– team: a project manager, a developer, a validation engineer, a safety engineer;

– initial system functional specification document: 130 pages;

– safety study: 15 documents of a total of 300 pages;

– development documentation: 30 documents of a total of 600 pages;

– formal B models: 3,300 lines, around 1,000 proof obligations. 90% of these were automatically demonstrated by Atelier B proof tools; it took 2 days to demonstrate the remaining 10%.

At the end of 8 months of trials, around 96,000 trains were checked. No fault or failure was recorded. The assumptions made during the safety study were confirmed and in certain cases refined. The availability of the system complied with the requirements, and after an initial fine-tuning phase, no passenger was prevented from leaving a train (the control device was required to open the doors a minimum of 9,999 times in 10,000 when a passenger train was at a standstill at the platform and the train doors were opening).

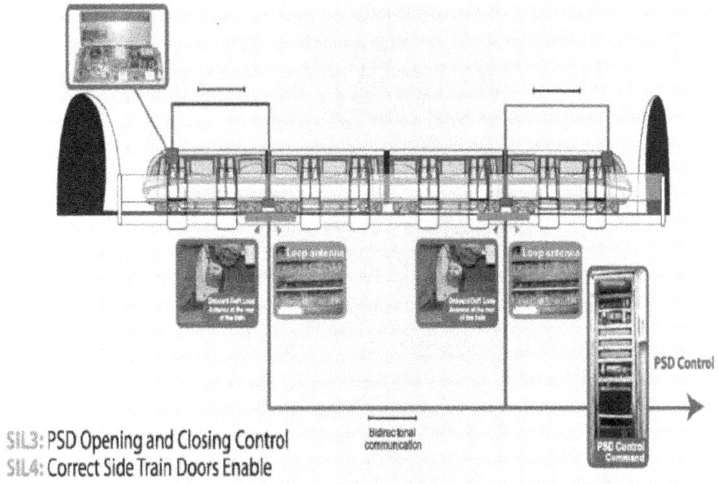

Figure 5.11. *System architecture*

Following these trials, a similar system was developed in the context of the automation of Line 1 of the Paris metro. This system was required to operate in the transition period during which trains driven manually and completely automatic trains were both running. It needed to equip 26 stations and 52 trains. Eventually, there will only be automatic trains on this line, and the system will then be taken down.

The system is partially onboard in trains driven by humans, because the commands for opening and closing doors given by the driver need to be transmitted to a technical station on the platform in order to be registered. These commands are treated and then sent to the platform doors. The installation architecture is shown in Figure 5.11.

This system is at level SIL4 (according to the standard CENELEC EN 50129 [CEN 03] and was based on Siemens S7 SIL3 automata (according to the standard CEI/IEC 61508 [IEC 98]. In this development, the system model was developed in the commercial proposition phase and a system animation was suggested as a technical response element. The system was developed in just under six months. As was the case with the controlling device described earlier, the development cycle used was heavily based on the formal B method [ABR 96]. The developed B models were directly used to demonstrate safety.

Since these two developments took place, a generator of IL code (programming language for automata, on the assembler level) has been developed and is nowadays used alongside a test case generator in order to validate the automatisms for similar applications. This is the first step toward the goal of qualifying the code production tool.

5.3. Safety of microelectronic components

In parallel with its use for safety systems and software in railways, the B method has also been used in microelectronics and in chip cards for safety applications. One example of this is the development of a Java bytecode verifier by Gemplus, and another example is the validation of a secured operating system based on microkernels [SOL 05].

Since event-B became available, new classes of potential applications have appeared. In particular, since the mid-2000s, several microcircuits have been certified to an EAL[5] level of 5+ (common criteria 2.3) and then EAL 6+ (common criteria 3.1)[6].

This certification requires formal modeling of the product's safety policy and proof of conformity between it and the functional specification that must implement it. Another work has also taken place, which has tackled not the *a posteriori* certification of a product, but the specification and construction of a microcircuit that is correct by construction.

This was the system adopted for the Forcoment project[7] (FORmal COdevelopMENT). The aim of this project was to show that an event-B model of a functionality may be transformed into a hardware description that can be directly integrated into a classical electronic circuit development cycle such as that of the STMicroelectronics microcontrollers[8].

The work carried out was consisted of:

– study and determination of abstractions, which could be used to model microelectronic circuits;

– specification of translation diagrams of event-B into the subset of VHDL used by STMicroelectronics, and development of the associated code generator;

– application in true scale on a functionality of buried memory access control and memory protection unit (MPU).

The current process of microcontroller-type circuit development (see Figure 5.12) at STMicroelectronics uses intensive testing for the verification stages, which precede the physical creations of the circuit (welding). These stages take the largest share of the time necessary for this part of the development. The development of test plans relies on the know-how of the engineers in charge of verification and validation.

---

5 Evaluation assurance levels (EALs) are concerned with common criteria, as defined in the standard [ISO 05].

6 See the site of the *Agence Nationale de la Sécurité des Systèmes d'Information* (National Agency for Information System Safety): http://www.ssi.gouv.fr.

7 See http://www.methode-b.com/php/projet-forcoment-fr.php.

8 For more information, see http://www.st.com/.

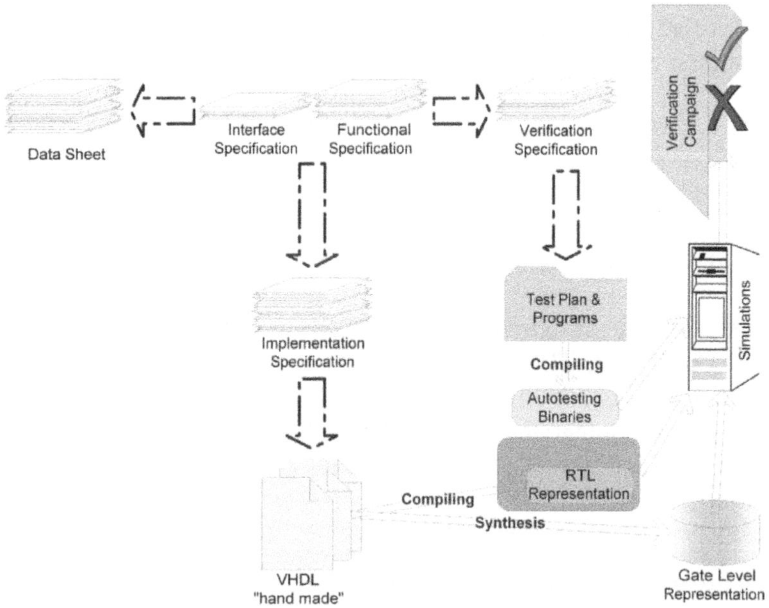

Figure 5.12. *The first stages of the development cycle of a microcircuit functionality*

For this project, we wished to adapt the use of formal development in successive stages favored by the B language ABR 96], which has been proved to be highly successful in the railway sector, to the field of microelectronics.

In fact, in microelectronics, formal methods are really only used after the event, to carry out several verification activities, both on the source code and on its transformations into networks of logical ports, which is the final representation before entry into the manufacturing chain. However, the most costly functional errors are often introduced during the earlier phases in the cycle, well before the source code is written, and in particular in functional specifications, in general and detailed design specifications, known as implantation specifications.

In practical terms, there are no verification tools for all these "paper" representations, and only the vigilance of proofreaders makes it possible to find the "seeds of error" which become "forests of malfunction" once they have been sown in silicon.

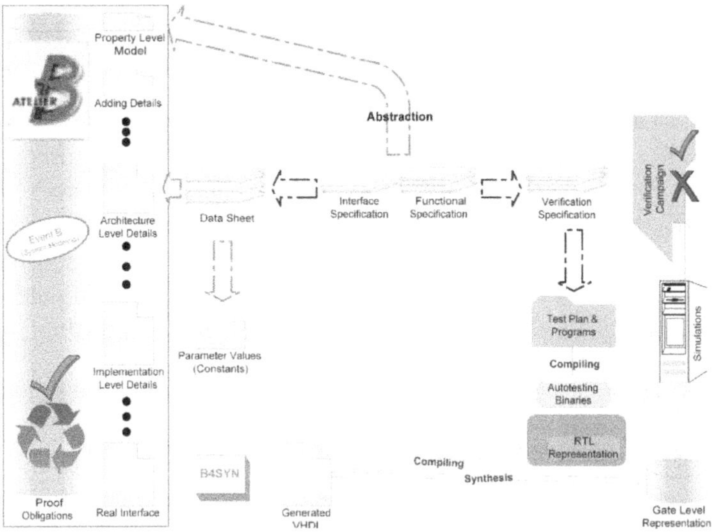

Figure 5.13. *Alternative development cycle, developed and trialed during the project*

During the Forcoment project, an alternative development cycle was constructed (see Figure 5.13), which integrated formal, and therefore exhaustive, verification of the VHDL code with respect to the functional and interface specifications, all the while remaining compatible with the rest of the development stream. This development cycle is based on formal modeling of the functionality in event-B, which aimed to produce correct construction of digital and analogical functions, which were outside the reach of the techniques used because they are simply integrated into the development through their digital interfaces.

This new cycle begins with the writing of a very simple event-B model, which contains a few events representative of an abstraction of the functionality. The operation details linked to its burial in a microcircuit are introduced gradually.

The model to which these details have been added is known as "refined". The process that makes it possible to transition from one model to another, to which details have been added, by explaining the conditions through which it conforms to the first model, is known as refinement. Refinement and verification of conformity conditions are carried out, at each development step, by using basic mathematics such as sets and their operations, predicate logic, or even relations and functions. These concepts are closer to the binary logic of a circuit than it might appear at first glance.

The most detailed event-B model is finally transformed into a VHDL module, using a code generator developed especially for this purpose, called B4SYN (B for synthesis). The VHDL module produced by B4SYN is then injected into the part of the traditional stream that follows. The test campaign carried out on a VHDL module from the traditional stream was a success on the module produced by B4SYN. This made it possible to validate the new stream [BEN 09a, BEN 09b].

Although this new stream is experimental, it can cover a large number of errors with total assurance. However, it would require the integration of the solutions sketched out and explored during the project before it could be extended to the composition of functionalities and before being employed for industrial use.

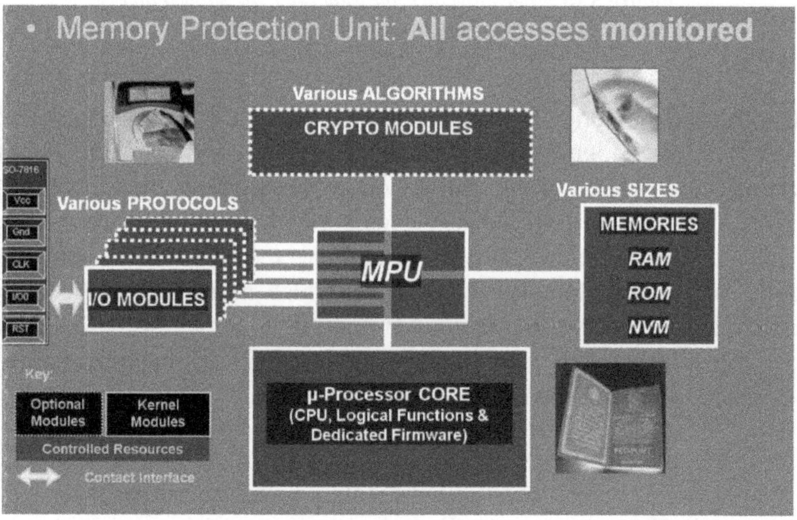

Figure 5.14. *Position of the MPU in the secured microcontroller*

The development cycle described above was used on a study case, a buried memory access controller and memory protection unit (MPU) (see Figure 5.14).

With the metrics collected during the developments associated with this module, both within the traditional stream and in the new experimental stream, we can create a first comparison (see Table 5.3).

Criteria	Classical Flow	Experimental Flow
Effort *person.days*	~145	~145 (~200 translator)
Volume *commented source lines*	~3 600 VHDL	~7 500 B ~3 500 VHDL
Proof *number of items*	-	~1 600 obligations ~ 600 with ~4000 cmds
Structure *module number*	~15 tightly linked	4 loosely linked (only 1 generated module)
Simulation *RTL & gate level*	~30 patterns Ok	~30 patterns Ok (better debug signals)
Size *equivalent nand gates*	~5 Kgates	

Table 5.3. *Comparative effort between traditional development and formal development*

Although this comparison is in no way calibrated, it can nonetheless be seen that the VHDL modules from both of the streams represent an equivalent development effort. Even more interesting is the fact that these modules give rise, after synthesis, to an almost identical number of ports. This allows us to think that the formal proof developed in this way has absolutely no impact on the freedom of design required for the optimization of microcircuits, which are among the most demanding in terms of surface, and which traditionally require "hand-made" development techniques. In addition, the "hand-made" item obtained by the new stream is guaranteed to completely comply with its specification and design through a computerized mathematical proof, which may be subjected to an audit.

5.4. Conclusion

Although formal modeling in B was initially used in railways for the development of autopilot metro systems, today this method is used in a wider system context, which means that it can also now be employed within other sectors.

This switching to other sectors has led to the improvement of the support tool for the method following contributions taken from work in this wider context such as:

– an automatic refinement tool;

– support of the "event-B" language for modeling systems;

– generation of Ladder code and instruction list for programmable automata;

– generation of test cases for automata programs;

– generation of VHDL code for microcircuits;

– generation of memory optimized C code for light onboard applications.

5.5. Glossary

AQL *atelier de qualification logiciel* (a software qualification workshop)

ATP automatic train protection

BART B automatic refinement tool

CC carbon controller

CENELEC[9] *Comité Européen de Normalisation ELECtrotechnique* (European Committee for Electrotechnical Standardization)

IEC[10] International Electrotechnical Commission

EAL evaluation assurance level

MPU memory protection unit

RATP[11] *Régie Autonome des Transports Parisiens* (Autonomous Operator of Parisian Transport)

9 For more information, see http://www.cenelec.eu/Cenelec/Homepage.htm.

10 See http://www.iec.ch/.

11 See http://www.ratf.fr.

SSIL	software safety integrity level
VESG	vital embedded settings generator

5.6. Bibliography

[ABR 96] ABRIAL J.R., *The B-Book*, Cambridge University Press, 1996.

[BAD 05] BADEAU F., AMELOT A., "Using B as a high level programming language in an industrial project", *Formal Specification and Development in Z and B*, LNCS, vol. 3455, Springer-Verlag, pp. 334–354, 2005.

[BEH 93] BEHM P., "Application d'une méthode formelle aux logiciels sécuritaires ferroviaires", *Atelier Logiciel Temps Réel, 6ème Journées Internationales du Génie Logiciel*, 1993.

[BEH 96] BEHM P., "Développement formel des logiciels sécuritaires de METEOR", in HABRIAS H. (ed.), *Proceedings of 1st Conference on the B Method, Putting into Practice Methods and Tools for Information System Design*, Nantes Computer Science Research Institute (IRIN), pp. 3–10, November 1996.

[BEH 99] BEHM P., BENOIT P., MEYNADIER J.M., "METEOR: a successful application of B in a large project", *Integrated Formal Methods*, LNCS, Springer Verlag, vol. 1708, pp. 369–387, 1999.

[BEN 09a] BENVENISTE M., "A proved 'correct by construction' realistic digital circuit", *Recent Innovation and Applications in B, FM Week*, Eindhoven, 3 November 2009.

[BEN 09b] BENVENISTE M., "A proved 'correct by construction' Memory Protection Unit", *SmartEvent'09*, Sophia Antipolis, 22–25 September 2009.

[BOU 12] BOULANGER J.-L. (ed.), *Industrial Use of Formal Method Formal Verification,* ISTE, London, and John Wiley & Sons, New York, 2012.

[CEN 00] CENELEC, EN 50126, Applications Ferroviaires. Spécification et démonstration de la fiabilité, de la disponibilité, de la maintenabilité et de la sécurité (FMDS), January 2000.

[CEN 01] CENELEC, EN 50128, Railway applications – communications, signalling and processing systems – software for railway control and protection systems, May 2001.

[CEN 11] CENELEC, EN 50128, Railway applications – communications, signalling and processing systems – software for railway control and protection systems, July 2011.

[CEN 03] CENELEC, EN 50129, Applications ferroviaires: systèmes de signalisation, de télécommunications et de traitement systèmes électroniques de sécurité pour la signalisation, European Standard, 2003.

[IEC 03] IEC, IEC 61131: Programmable Controllers, International Standard, May 2003.

[IEC 98] IEC, IEC 61508: Sécurité fonctionnelle des systèmes électriques électroniques programmables relatifs à la sécurité, International Standard, 1998.

[ISO 05] ISO/IEC 15408, Information technology – security techniques – evaluation criteria for IT security (three parts), 2005.

[LEC 07] LECOMTE T., THIERRY SERVAT, POUZANCRE G., *et al.*, "Formal methods in safety-critical railway systems", *SBMF '07*, Ouro Preto, Brazil, 2007.

[LEC 08] LECOMTE T., "Safe and reliable metro platform screen doors control/command systems" *FM '08*, Turku, Finland, 2008.

[LEU 10] LEUSCHEL M., "Validation of railway properties with ProB", *Workshop on B Dissemination*, Natal, Brazil, 8 November 2010.

[SAB 00] SABATIER D., LARTIGUE P., "The use of the B formal method for the design and the validation of the transaction mechanism for smart card applications", *Formal Methods in System Design*, vol. 17, no. 3, pp. 245–272, 2000.

[SAB 08] SABATIER D., PATIN F., POUZANCRE G., *et al.*, "Utilisation de la méthode formelle B pour un système SIL3: la commande des portes palières sur la ligne 13 du métro Parisien", *LambdaMu'15,* 28 November 2008.

[SOL 05] SOLA R., COUDERT S., GABRIELE S., *et al.*, "Microkernel API formal modelisation", *SAME 2005 Forum*, Nice, France, October 2005.

6

Formalization of Digital Circuits Using the B Method

6.1. Introduction

The goal of this chapter is to show how it is possible to combine the advantages of the B method in order to design a secure[1] digital circuit that may be easily developed and does not need a design test. The circuit design may be based on the libraries of well-known circuit design language like VHDL.

Our goal is to make use of the B method to produce the electronic or numeric circuits. At the beginning, the circuit specifications are written in the abstract machine. The refinement direction is determined by the basic elements which are used to construct the desired circuit. So the designer can orient the development to the required level. This level can be found as a basic library in B. We demonstrate how VHDL packages can be translated as B circuit components in order to give the designer a high-level view. Using this approach, we can develop a circuit in which each part of the specification has proved to be correct. From the B model it is possible to generate the VHDL code.

Chapter written by Jean-Louis BOULANGER.

1 Secure in this chapter means more than correct; the design performs what the client wants, and furthermore it guarantees not to achieve the unwanted cases.

6.2. B method and VHDL

The B method due to J.R Abrial [ABR 96] is a formal method for the incremental development of specifications and their refinements down to an implementation. It is a model-based approach similar to Z [SPI 92] and VDM [CLI 90]. The software design in B starts from mathematical specifications. Gradually, through many refinement steps ([MOR 90]), the designer tries to obtain a complete and executable specification. This process must be monotonic, that is any refinement has to be proved coherent according to the previous steps of refinement. The abstract machine [ABR 92] is the basic element of a B development. It encapsulates some state data and offers some operations. The description of an abstract machine is composed of three parts:

– the declarative part which describes the states and their properties;

– the execution part which introduces operations;

– composition clauses.

In the B development, the proofs accompany the construction of software. Each time an abstract machine is defined or modified, there are proof obligations related to its mathematical consistency; if the machine is a refinement or an implementation, there are also proof obligations of its correctness with respect to the previous steps of the development chain. The B tool allows us to automatically generate the proof obligations (POs) for each abstract machine. Generally speaking, the POs will be increasingly complex as concrete details are introduced. Then, these POs are discarded either automatically for the simple ones, or in cooperation with the designer for the complex ones. So, at the last refinement, called the implementation, we obtain secure software which does not need to be tested. At this low-level stage, it may be easily translated to a programming language. AtelierB or BToolKit is provided with C, C++ or ADA automatic translators. However, it is possible to extend this code generation to the VHDL language. In this case, we obtain the possibility of co-design between the B method and the VHDL.

VHDL (VHSIC – very high speed integrated circuits – hardware description language) ([IEE 93, AIR 98]) has been an IEEE Standard since 1987. It is "a formal notation intended for use in all phases of the creation of electronic systems [...] it supports the development, verification, synthesis, and testing of hardware designs, the communication of hardware design data..."[2]. VHDL is a programming language used to express the hardware components with a high level of abstraction. It is a good utility to describe the integrated circuits, or complete system of hardware and software. It can also be used to declare the circuit behavior.

Section 6.3 is devoted to showing the cross-fertilization between the circuit design methodology and the B method concepts. At first, a simple circuit design, the NOT port, is chosen to show how the B concepts may be used to produce a simple circuit. Then, an example of a multiplexer design is used to show how a complex circuit may be designed. After that, the methodology of the circuit design is presented. In sections 6.4 and 6.5, the standard VHDL package, the STD_LOGIC_1164, is transposed in the form of a B library[3] as an example to be used as a set of B elementary components. In the same way, other VHDL packages can be translated as B circuit components in order to give to the designer a high-level view. Using this approach, we can develop a circuit in which each part of the specification is proved to be correct. A B circuit may be easily improved and it may be integrated with the other elements in the environment to satisfy safety conditions. Section 6.6 summarizes this work and shows its advantages and disadvantages. This paper continues the previous work described in [BOU 99] and in [BOU 01].

6.3. Modeling digital circuits

This section describes and models some synchronized basic components which will be then reused. A synchronized circuit is viewed as a box, within which one (or more) input line is entering, and out of which one (or more) output line is emerging. A synchronized circuit is supposed to be synchronized by a clock. Then, an example of a more complicated circuit is used to show how many components may be connected. In both examples, the same methodology is used. This methodology is presented as a table at the end of this section. Using VHDL terminology, a module is called an entity and one entity is coded in one B abstract machine. All the inputs and outputs are called ports.

---

2 Preface to the *IEEE Standard VHDL Language Reference Manual*.

3 A B library is a B project; a B project is a collection of abstract machines.

6.3.1. *Modeling methodology*

In this section, our aim is to give a general method for modeling a circuit without knowing the details of the desired circuit. At first the analogy of development between the B method and the numeric circuits design is presented. In B the initial specifications of the desired circuit are written in the abstract machine using mathematical expressions. The abstract machine is refined to obtain the first refinement machine. Abstract machine refinement is performed by determining the data types or by adding algorithms that satisfy a part of the specifications.

Circuits synthesis	B Method
Functional specifications	Abstract machine
Architecture specification and behavior details	Refinements
Validation "'functional to material'"	Proof
Physical description	Implementation machine
Port	Global variable
Connection	Invariant of relation between variables
Signal propagation	Operation call (transmission of values)
Reusing	Importation + renaming

Table 6.1. *Analogy between VHDL and the B method*

The B tools generate the necessary proofs to demonstrate that the refinement is correct. Many of these proofs are automatically proved. The others may be proved in cooperation with the designer. The refinement step may be repeated many times. More and more the components of the circuit become precise as well as its behavior. The result of the last step of the refinement is called the implementation machine, in which the behavior of the circuit is deterministic.

The implementation may be TRUTH TABLES; these tables are concise but are not suitable for describing large-scale circuits; at the same time they need a lot of proof. In our methodology, we represented each port of the circuit by a local variable, so that the connection between the ports is represented as a fixed relation between the global variables. These relations are represented in the INVARIANT clause which contains all the relations that must be satisfied in a machine and in its refinements. In the B method, the OPERATIONS clause represents the dynamic part of a machine in which the values of the global variables may be changed. So signal propagation is done by an operation call. The B method gives us the possibility to reuse other machines. So many already-defined machines may be reused as components of more complex ones (IMPORTS clause). An already defined, machine may also be renamed and reused by adding other operations to produce a more developed circuit. Using this method, 80% of the required proofs are proved automatically, and the others need cooperation with the designer. Sometimes, little changes of the source machines are necessary to create the desired proofs. This enables the designer to correct the possible errors in the design.

The general method described in this section provides the capability to define some B abstract machines that model the behavior of some circuits. However, we want to model some realistic VHDL components and we need some B abstract machines that correspond to VHDL standard library such as STD_LOGIC_1164. [DUC 99] introduces the STD_LOGIC_1164 library and its equivalent in B.

6.3.2. *Modeling a basic logic gate, NOT*

The NOT component is the simplest logic gate. It has one input and one output. The output is the negation of the input.

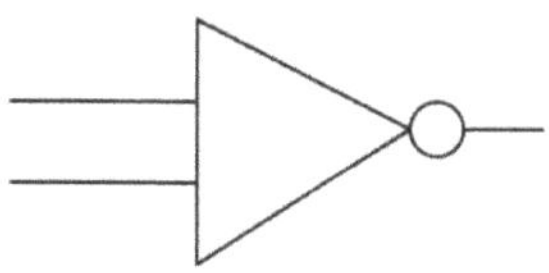

Figure 6.1. *NOT gate*

The NOT gate is described by a graphical specification (see Figure 6.1), but we can complete these specifications with a Boolean expression that describes the behavior:

$$(\text{in} = 0 \Rightarrow \text{out} = 1) \wedge (\text{in} = 1 \Rightarrow \text{out} = 0)$$

The input/output values are Boolean, and they may have the values TRUE or FALSE. We can use the last expression to write a B abstract machine. This abstract machine contains the abstract specifications of the desired circuit (or software):

```
MACHINE             B_Not_0
DEFINITIONS         Compute_(xx,yy) == (((xx = TRUE) => (yy = FALSE))
& ((xx = FALSE) => (yy = TRUE)))
VARIABLES           in, out
INVARIANT           in: BOOL & out: BOOL & Compute_(in, out)
INITIALIZATION      in, out:(in: BOOL & out: BOOL & Compute_(in, out))
OPERATIONS
        In (val) =  PRE    val: BOOL  THEN in, out:(in: BOOL & in = val & out:
BOOL  & Compute_(in, out))  END;
        val ←Out = val:= out
END
```

In this abstract machine, the input and the output are represented by the global variables "in" and "out". These variables can be assigned by all of the defined operations. Each output is attached to a read operation and each input is attached to a store operation. The environment of the circuit will use these operations to know the circuit output or to change the input;

Thus, we choose "in" and "out" as names for these operations. The behavior of the port is described using the Compute_ definition4, which gives us the possibility to express systematically the definition of the function. In the declarative part, the state is described with the set theoretic model and the first-order logic. The INVARIANT clause states the static laws, in our case the properties, that the data must obey regardless of the operation that is applied to it. This abstract machine is automatically proved by the B tool; two proof obligations are generated for the INITIALIZATION clause and two others for the in operation. This abstract machine is not deterministic since we use the operator list_var: (predicate) in the INITIALIZATION and OPERATION clauses. This operator indicates that the list of variables becomes such that the predicate is true. We can generalize this method for any combinatory logical circuit, for the complex ones as well as for the simple ones. We build a library that contains the standard ports, structure which is based on the last machine form.

Given a circuit (and its abstract and logical specification), we used the following modifications:

– the additions of the operations associated to the supplementary ports; the circuits have more than one port in general, so we use in_1;..;in_n to

4 A definition may be seen as a function, but the associated code will be expanded.

mention the n in ports of the circuit and out_1;..; out_m to mention the m out ports;

– the modification of the Compute_ definition corresponding to the logical specification.

The following table lists the definitions used in the B components that we defined before. The calculations are just Boolean evaluations of predicates. During the use of these definitions, the formal parameters xx, yy, … , zz are instantiated by the names of global variables being associated with the ports of the circuit.

Name	Port	Compute_
AND	2 in	Bool ((xx = TRUE) & (yy = TRUE))
AND	3 in	Bool ((xx = TRUE) & (yy = TRUE) & (zz = TRUE))
NAND	2 in	Bool (not((xx = TRUE) & (yy = TRUE)))
NOR	2 in	Bool (not((xx = TRUE) or (yy = TRUE)))
OR	2 in	Bool ((xx = TRUE) or (yy = TRUE))
OR	3 in	Bool ((xx = TRUE) or (yy = TRUE) or (zz = TRUE))

Table 6.2. *Some basics circuits defined by a Boolean equation*

This method may be used for any logical circuit, for the complex ones as well as for the simple ones. We build a library that contains all standard gates, a structure which is based on the method described further. Using the B tool, the coherence of these B abstract machines is proved.

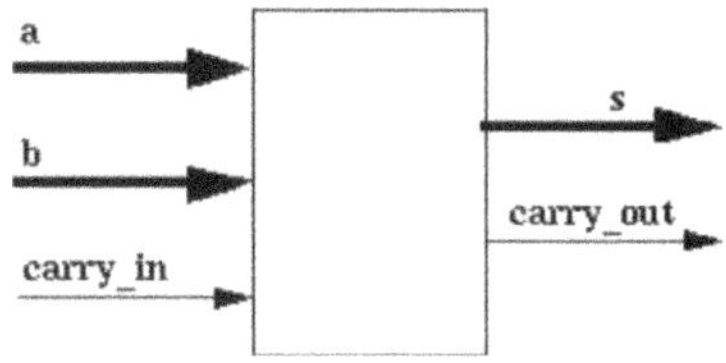

Figure 6.2. *n-bit adder representation*

6.3.3. *Modeling an additioner*

A 4-bit full-adder circuit is used in this section as an example to show how to reuse components previously modeled in order to obtain complex integrated circuits. Based on the logical specification of a component, we can supply an assembly of many simple components to achieve the desired function. This is called the synthesis of a numeric circuit. The n-bit full adder is a circuit with three inputs (2 n-vector and 1 bit) and two outputs (1 n-vector and 1 bit). The n-bit full adder is described by a graphical specification (see Figure 6.2), but we can complete these specifications with a Boolean expression that described the behavior:

> Adder(a, b, carryin, sum, carryout) == $2(n+1)^{BV(carryout)}$+V(sum)=V(a)+V(b) +BV($carry_{in}$)
> With V : vector --> Integer
> and BV : bit --> Integer

The input/output values are Booleans. They may have the values TRUE or FALSE. We can use the last expression to write a B abstract machine. This abstract machine contains the abstract specifications of the desired circuit (or software):

```
MACHINE        B_ADD_4bits_2_0
SEES           B_type_0
DEFINITIONS    COMPUTE_(AA,BB,CIN,SUM,COUT) == SUM + 16*COUT
= AA + BB + CIN
VARIABLES      AA,BB,CIN,COUT,SS
INVARIANT
          IS_A_DECIMAL_16_(AA)
&         IS_A_DECIMAL_16_(BB)
&         IS_A_DECIMAL_16_(SUM)
&         IS_A_DECIMAL_1_(CIN)
&         IS_A_DECIMAL_1_(COUT)
&         COMPUTE_(AA,BB,CIN,SUM,COUT)
INITIALISATION AA, BB, CIN,SUM, COUT := 0,0,0,0,0
OPERATIONS
AA(yy) =
PRE IS_A_DECIMAL_16_(yy)
THEN
 AA, SUM, COUT :(      IS_A_DECIMAL_16_(AA)
                &      AA = yy
                &      IS_A_DECIMAL_16_(SUM)
                &      IS_A_DECIMAL_1_(COUT)
                &      COMPUTE_(AA,BB,CIN,SUM,COUT))
END;
...
xx <-- out_COUT =  xx := COUT;
xx <-- out_SS = xx := SS;
END
```

In our methodology, we represented, in the abstract machine, each port of the circuit by a local variable (AA, BB, SUM, CIN, COUT) so that the connection between the ports is represented as a fixed relation between the global variables. These relations are represented in the INVARIANT clause which contains all the relations that must be satisfied in a machine and in its refinements. The behavior of the port is described using the Compute_ definition[5], which gives us the possibility to express systematically the definition of the function. The INVARIANT clause states the static laws, in our case the properties, that the data must obey whatever the operation applied to it. These variables can be assigned by all of the defined operations. Each output is attached to a read operation and each input is attached to a store operation.

The environment of the circuit will use these operations either in order to know the circuit output or to change the input. So, we choose In and Out as names for these operations. This abstract machine is not deterministic since we use the operator list_var:(predicate) in the OPERATION clauses. This operator indicates that the list of variables becomes such that the predicate is true. We can generalize this method for any combinatory logical circuit, for the complex ones as well as for the simple ones. Given a circuit (and its abstract and logical specification), we used the following modifications:

– the additions of the operations associated to the supplementary ports; the circuits have more than one port in general, so we use in_1;..; in_n to mention the n in ports of the circuit and out_1;..;out_m to mention the m out ports;

– the modification of the Compute_ definition corresponding to the logical specification.

The calculations are just Boolean evaluations of predicates. During the use of these definitions, the formal parameters xx, yy, …, zz are instantiated by the names of global variables being associated with the ports of the circuit. This method may be used for any logical circuit, for the complex ones as well as for the simple ones. We build a library that contains all standard gates (OR, AND, NOT, etc.), a structure which is based on the method described below. Using the B tool (Atelier B 3.5), the coherence of these B abstract machines is proved.

5 A definition may be seen as a function, but the associated code will be expanded.

The 4-bit addition can be split up in bit slices. We obtain the well-known carry-ripple adder, also called ripple through carry adder, consisting of n cascaded full adders for an n-bit adder. Each slice performs the addition of the bits Ai, Bi and the carry-in bit Ci (= carry-out bit of the previous slice). Each slice consists of a 1-bit full adder, illustrated below. A 1-bit full adder is a combinational circuit that computes the arithmetic sum of three input bits of the same magnitude (i.e. 1-bit numbers).

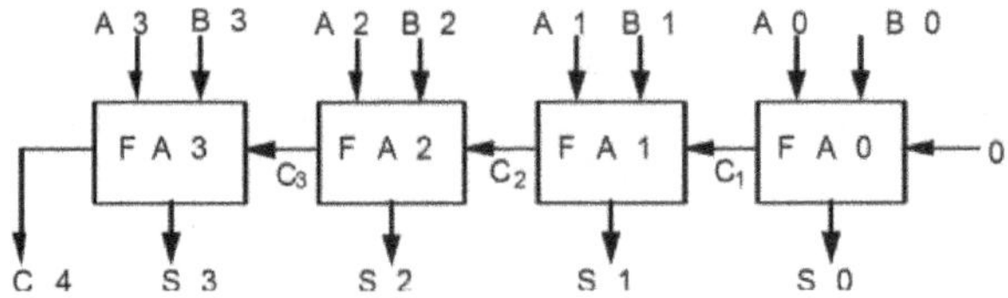

Figure 6.3. *n-bit carry-ripple adder*

The next piece of code shows how we split the 4-bit adder in its implementation. Each slice consists of a 1-bit full adder, illustrated below. As expected in an object-oriented environment, you are able to reuse the single Full_Adder component by instantiating four copies of it (FA0 through FA3). Each copy is instantiated differently in the four port-mapping statements, with actual signal names being substituted for the desired input/output connections.

```
IMPLEMENTATION          B_ADD_4bits_2_n
REFINES                 B_ADD_4bits_2_1
SEES                    B_type_0
IMPORTS                 Fa0.B_FULL_ADD_1bit_0 , Fa1.B_FULL_ADD_1bit_0,
                        Fa2.B_FULL_ADD_1bit_0 ,
                        Fa3.B_FULL_ADD_1bit_0

INVARIANT
        Fa0.AA  = A0
&       Fa0.BB  = B0
&       Fa0.CIN = CIN
&       Fa0.COUT= CI1
&       Fa0.SS  = SS0
...
INITIALISATION
....
OPERATIONS
in_AA(yy) = BEGIN
 A0,A1,A2,A3 ← Decimal16_To_Bit(yy)
```

```
; Fa0.in_AA(A0) ; Fa1.in_AA(A1)
; Fa2.in_AA(A2) ; Fa3.in_AA(A3)
; Fa0.in_CIN(CIN); CI1 ← Fa0.out_COUT; Fa1.in_CIN(CI1)
; CI2 ← Fa1.out_COUT ; Fa2.in_CIN(CI2)
; CI3 ← Fa2.out_COUT ; Fa3.in_CIN(CI3)
; COUT ← Fa3.out_COUT
; SS0 ← Fa0.out_SS; SS1 ← Fa1.out_SS
; SS2 ← Fa2.out_SS; SS3 ← Fa3.out_SS
END
...
END
```

A 1-bit full adder (Figure 6.4) is a combinational circuit that computes the arithmetic sum of three input bits of the same magnitude (i.e. 1-bit numbers).

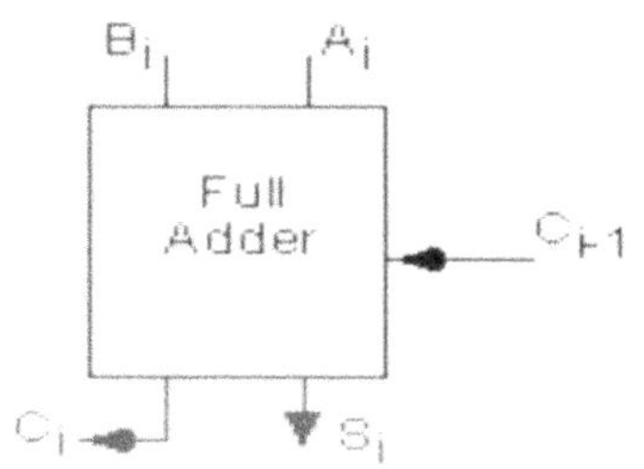

Figure 6.4. *Full-adder representation*

This describes the functionality of the 1-bit adder.

```
sum <= a xor b xor ci;

co  <= ((a or b) and ci) or (a and b);
```

Calculate the sum of the 1-BIT adder:

```
sum <=  (not a and not b and cin) or (not a and b and not cin) or (a and not b and
not cin) or (a and b and cin);
```

Calculate the carry out of the 1-BIT adder:

```
cout <= (not a and b and cin) or  (a and not b and cin) or (a and b and not cin) or
(a and b and cin);
```

```
MACHINE         B_FULL_ADD_1bit_0
SEES            IEEE.B_STD_LOGIC_1164_0 , B_STD_ENTRIE
DEFINITIONS
...
 Sum_(inA, inB, Cin, Sum) ==
     (Sum = bool_to_bit( bool((
( not(Val_(inA))) &
   (  ( not(Val_(inB))   & (    (Val_(Cin))))
   or  (     (Val_(inB))   & (not(Val_(Cin))))))
or  (  (    Val_(inA))
 & (   ( not(Val_(inB)) & not(Val_(Cin)))
    or  (     (Val_(inB)) &      (Val_(Cin))))))))
;      Carry_Expr_(inA, inB, Cin, Cout) ==
     (      (      (Val_(inA)) & not(Val_(inB)) & Val_(Cin)) or
             (not(Val_(inA)) &      (Val_(inB)) & Val_(Cin)) or
            (     (Val_(inA)) &      (Val_(inB))                   )
      )
;      Carry_(inA, inB, Cin, Cout) == (Cout = bool_to_bit(bool(Carry_Expr_(inA,
inB, Cin, Cout))))
;      Compute_(inA, inB, Cin, Sum, Cout) ==    (Sum_  (inA, inB, Cin, Sum) &
Carry_(inA, inB, Cin, Cout))
...
OPERATIONS
in_AA(yy) =
PRE   yy : BIT THEN
AA, COUT, SS  :(                AA : BIT
                  & AA = yy
                  & COUT    : BIT
                  & SS : BIT
                  & Compute_(yy,BB,CIN,SS, COUT))
END
...
END
```

A circuit that implements a full adder is given in Figure 6.5.

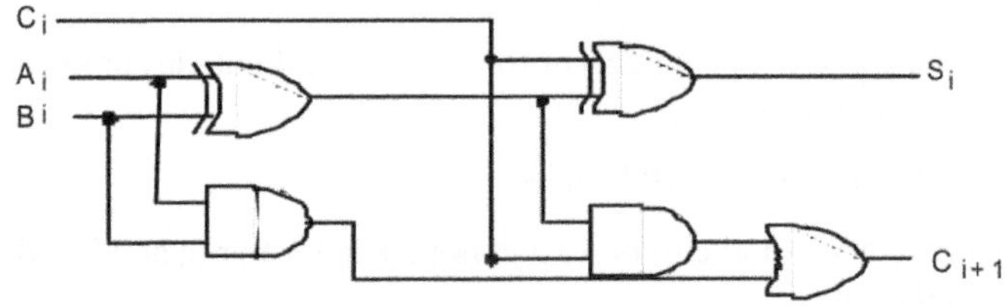

Figure 6.5. *Logic diagram of a full adder*

It is assumed that the behavioral models of each component are provided elsewhere, that is, there are entity-architecture pairs describing a half adder and a two-input OR gate. In Figure 6.5, you can see the internal structure of the full adder. Two half adders (HA) and an OR gate are required to implement a full adder.

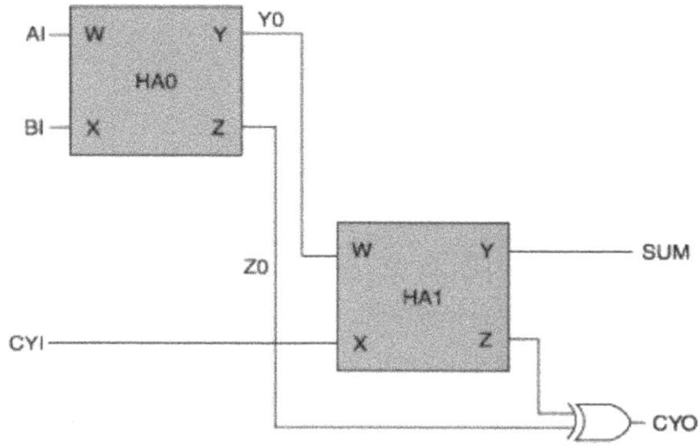

Figure 6.6. *The full adder implementation*

The full adder in Figure 6.6 is described using three instantiation statements. The instance names must be unique.

```
IMPLEMENTATION     B_Full_ADD_1bit_n
REFINES            B_Full_ADD_1bit_0
IMPORTS            add1.B_Half_ADD_1bit_0, add2.B_Half_ADD_1bit_0,
Or.B_Or_0
...
INVARIANT
      AA = add1.AA
&     BB = add1.BB
&     add1.SS = add2.AA
&     CIN = add2.BB
&     add1.COUT    =    Or.in1
&     add2.COUT    =    Or.in2
&     COUT         =    Or.out
&     SS           =    add2.SS
...
OPERATIONS
in_AA(yy) =
VAR xx IN
      AA := yy
```

```
;         add1.in_AA(AA)
;         xx <-- add1.out_SS
;         add2.in_AA(xx)
;         xx <-- add1.out_COUT
;         OU1.In_1(xx)
;         xx <-- add2.out_COUT
;         OU1.In_2(xx)
;         COUT <-- Or.Out
;         SS <-- add2.out_SS
END;
...
END
```

The last piece of the design is the Half_Adder entity, which is instantiated twice in each Full_Adder entity. A half adder is the simplest form of an adder circuit.

```
MACHINE         B_Half_ADD_1bit_0
SEES            IEEE.B_STD_LOGIC_1164_0, B_STD_ENTRIE
DEFINITIONS
     Val_(xx)      ==     (bit_to_bool(xx) = TRUE)
;    Compute_(inA, inB, Som, Cout) ==
   (Som  = bool_to_bit(
         bool ((not(Val_(inA)) &    (Val_(inB)))or
                (   (Val_(inA)) & not(Val_(inB)))))
&    Cout  = bool_to_bit(bool (Val_(inA) & Val_(inB)))
)
CONCRETE_VARIABLES      AA,      BB,      COUT,      SS
INVARIANT     AA : BIT & BB : BIT & COUT : BIT & SS : BIT &
Compute_(AA, BB, SS, COUT)
...
OPERATIONS
...
in_BB(yy) =
PRE  yy : BIT THEN
      BB, COUT, SS :( BB : BIT & COUT : BIT & SS : BIT &  BB = yy &
Compute_(AA,BB,SS,COUT))
END;
...
END
```

The implementation of the multiplexer is made of two AND gates called A1 and A2, one OR gate called O3 and one NOT gate called NN which are instantiate in IMPORTS clause. The link between all ports (multiplexer ports, AND ports, etc.) is done in the INVARIANT clause. All operations introduce the multiplexer behavior, in fact (as we will see later) for each operation; we define the data propagation between ports.

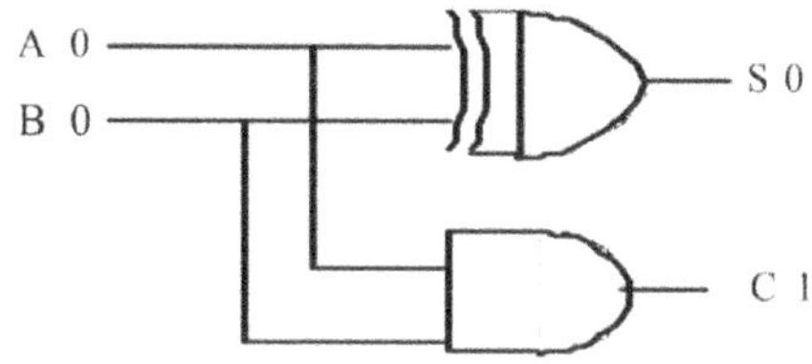

Figure 6.7. *Logic diagram of a half adder*

The last piece of the design is the Half_Adder entity (see Figure 6.7), which is instantiated twice in each Full_Adder entity. A half adder is the simplest form of an adder circuit. The more significant sum bit is called carry-out (cout) because it carries an overflow to the next higher bit position. It has two operand bits x0 and y0 (for bit position 0) that are added to form a sum bit (s0) and a carry bit (cout), we can write s0 = not(x0)y0 + x0 not(y0) and cout = x0y0. The full-adder module can be constructed of two half adders.

```
IMPLEMENTATION              B_Half_ADD_1bit_n
REFINES                 B_Half_ADD_1bit_0
IMPORTS                 xor.B_XOR, and.B_And_0
SEES                    BASIC_IO, IEEE.B_STD_LOGIC_1164_0,
B_STD_ENTRIE
INVARIANT
        AA  =   xor.in1 &   BB  =   xor.in2 &   SS  =   xor.out
&       AA  =   and.in1&    BB  =   and.in2 &   COUT =  and.out
…
OPERATIONS
in_BB(yy) =
BEGIN
        BB := yy;xor.In_2(BB)
;       SS ← xor.Out
;       and.In_2(BB)
;       COUT   ← and.Out
END;
xx ← out_COUT = xx := COUT;
…
END
```

The design method of starting with the topmost level and adding new levels of increasing detail is called top-down design (see Figure 6.8).

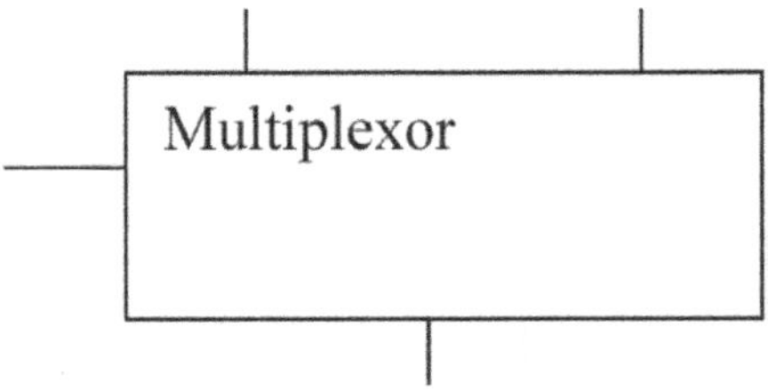

Figure 6.8. *Graphical symbol of a two input multiplexer*

6.3.4. *Modeling of complex circuit: a multiplexer*

A multiplexer circuit is used in this section as an example to show how to reuse previously modeled components in order to obtain complex integrated circuits. On the basis of the logical specification of a component, we can supply an assembly of many simple components to achieve the desired function. This is called the synthesis of a numeric circuit. The multiplexer with n inputs is a circuit with n principal inputs and one output. The output value is equal to the value of the input of the number i; i is determined by other inputs. In our example (n = 2), the input called Select gives the possibility to choose one of the two inputs a and b.

The output out equals in_1 if the selector Select is FALSE and in_2 if it has the value TRUE. We write this:

((Select = FALSE) => (out = in_1)) ∧

((Select = TRUE) => (out = in_2))

To describe the abstract machine for the multiplexer, we can use one that is similar to the NOT gate presented above. Four local variables may be used to represent the inputs/output: Select, in_1, in_2 and out. So we have three input operations and one output one. The principal difference between the two machines is the definition of the compute_ function:

MACHINE

```
   B_Mux_0
DEFINITIONS
Compute_(xx,yy,zz,res) ==
   bool( ((xx=FALSE)=>(res=yy))
                 &((xx=TRUE)=>(res=zz)))
VARIABLES
   Select, in_1 , in_2 , out
INVARIANT
   Select : BOOL &
   in_1 : BOOL & in_2 :BOOL & out : BOOL &
   Compute_(Select,in_1,in_2,out)
INITIALISATION
   Select , in_1 , in_2 , out
   :(
   Select : BOOL & in_1 : BOOL & in_2 :BOOL &
   out : BOOL &
   Compute_(Select,in_1,in_2,out)
   )
OPERATIONS
In_1 (val) =
      in_1 , out :(
            in_1 : BOOL & in_1 = val &
            out: BOOL & Compute_(Select,in_1,in_2,out))
In_2 (val) =
      in_2 , out :(
            in_2 : BOOL & in_2 = val
            & out : BOOL &
            Compute_(Select,in_1,in_2,out) )
Gate (val) =
      Select , out :(
            Select : BOOL & Select = val &
            out : BOOL & Compute_(Select,in_1,in_2,out) )
val <-- Out = val := out
END
```

As in the B_Not_0 abstract machine, the Boolean expression under the INITIALISATION clause and INVARIANT clause is the same. We have four operations. This abstract machine is fully proved by the B tool. The previous B specification can be refined by just modifying the previous Boolean expression defined in the definition Compute_. We rewrite the previous Boolean expression that describes the two multiplexers:

$$out = (in\_1 \wedge (Select)) \vee (in\_2 \wedge Select)$$

```
REFINEMENT
        B_Mux_1
REFINES
        B_Mux_0
DEFINITIONS
Compute_(xx,yy,zz,res) ==
        bool((not(xx=TRUE) & (yy=TRUE)) or (            (xx=TRUE) & (zz=TRUE)))
VARIABLES
select, in_1 ,in_2, out
INVARIANT
Select : BOOL & in_1 : BOOL & in_2 :BOOL & out : BOOL & Compute_(Select,in_1,in_2,out)
INITIALISATION
...
OPERATIONS
In_1 (val) = . . .
In_2 (val) = . . .
Gate (val) = . . .
val <-- Out =. . .
END
```

Figure 6.9 introduces a synthesis for the previous two input multiplexer. The simple circuit machines are used to refine the complex ones. In this example, four machines are used in the refinement of the multiplexer. The relations between the components are described under the INVARIANT clause[6].

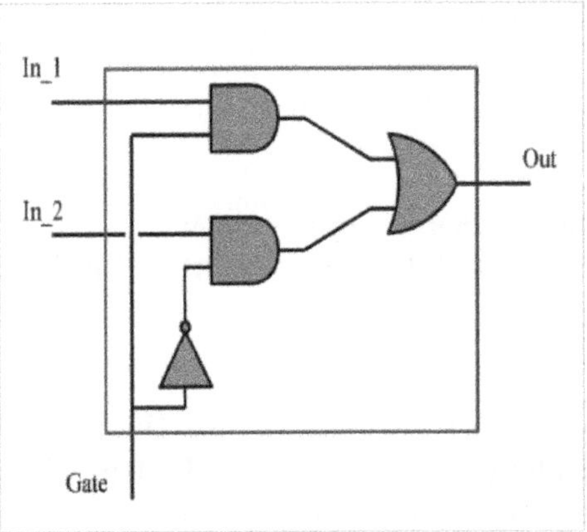

Figure 6.9. *Implementation of two input multiplexer*

6 This refinement of the multiplexer is the last step of all the refinement steps, so it is called IMPLEMENTATION.

The next abstract machine is an implementation of the synthesis defined in Figure 6.10. This abstract machine is just a systematic translation which may be done automatically.

```
IMPLEMENTATION
        B_Mux_n
REFINES
        B_Mux_1
IMPORTS
        A1.B_And_0,
        A2.B_And_0,
        O3.B_Or_0,
        NN.B_Not_0
INVARIANT
        select = A2.in2 & select = NN.in &
        NN.out= A1.in2 & in_1 = A1.in1 &
        in_2 = A2.in1 & A1.out = O3.in1 & A2.out= O3.in2 & out = O3.out

INITIALISATION
VAR xx, yy, zz IN
        NN.In(FALSE)
        ; xx <-- NN.Out
        ; A1.In_1(TRUE)
        ; A1.In_2(xx)
        ; yy <-- A1.Out
        ; A2.In_1(TRUE)
        ; A2.In_2(FALSE)
        ; zz <-- A2.Out
        ; O3.In_1(yy)
        ; O3.In_2(zz)
        ; out <-- O3.Out
END

OPERATIONS

        In_1 (val) = . . .
        In_2 (val) = . . .
        Gate (val) = . . .
        val <-- Out =
                val := out
END
```

The implementation of the multiplexer is made of two And gates called A1 and A2, one OR gate called O3 and one NOT gate called NN which are instantiate in IMPORTS clause. The link between all ports (multiplexer ports, AND ports, etc.) is made in the INVARIANT clause. All operations introduce the multiplexer behavior, in fact (as we will see later), for each operation; we define the data propagation between ports:

```
Gate (val) =
VAR xx, yy, zz IN
        NN.In(val)
        ; xx <-- NN.Out
        ; A1.In_2(xx)
        ; yy <-- A1.Out
        ; A2.In_2(val)
        ; zz <-- A2.Out
        ; O3.In_1(yy)
        ; O3.In_2(zz)
        ; out <-- O3.Out
END
```

The POs generated by the B tool are fully proved and guarantee that this implementation verifies the logic property. We have defined a complete library for the simple logic elements which may be used for more complex ones. Other complex examples, such a 4-bit ADD, are described by B method from the same point of view; all examples are fully proved.

6.4. VHDL libraries

VIIDL is one of the most important tools for describing the electronic circuits. It depends on the conception of modules. The hierarchy enables the programmer to write the program as units. Some of these units are elementary expressions which can be directly compiled. The others may be decomposed into many units. This mechanism makes teamwork easier, especially when the complexity of the module increases. A special library is built for each programmer using the correct units which have been compiled. The programmer may use his own libraries, the libraries of his colleagues and the general libraries. A part of our project is to find correspondence of VHDL general libraries in B. The following section introduces one of the most widely used VHDL libraries, the STD_LOGIC_1164 library and its equivalent in B.

6.4.1. *The STD_LOGIC_1164 library*

The STD_LOGIC_1164 is standardized by the IEEE. This package defines a standard for designers to describe the interconnection data types used in VHDL modeling. It was created to facilitate the portability of VHDL code synthesis. There are nine values in this logic; each of these values may be assigned to a variable or to a signal. These values form the extended bit type[7].

U	Uninitialized
X	Forcing unknown
0	Forcing 0
1	Forcing 1
Z	High impedance
W	Weak unknown
L	Weak 0
H	Weak 1
–	Don't care port

Table 6.3. *Values of extended bit type*

An extension of the classic logic is built to treat these nine values in the VHDL package called STD_LOGIC_1164 instead of two values in the classic one. So the elements of STD_LOGIC_1164 package are:

– a principal type that contains nine values, many subtypes which contain some of these values. And complex types which contain vectors of these types;

– the basic logic operations over the previous types;

– and many functions to cast[8] a type to another;

– many other functions to solve the problem of the signals which have many different resources;

– two functions to determine the direction of the change of a signal if it is with rising_edge or falling_edge;

7 Usually, one of only two different values is used to represent values of bit type.
8 Change the type to another.

– three functions to decide whether or not a signal is determined (if its value is U, X, Z, W or _);

– the STD_LOGIC_1164 package contains also many attributes, which are adjectives that may give the language components.

6.4.2. *The B components for STD_LOGIC_1164*

The B counterpart of the VHDL STD_LOGIC_1164 library mostly consists of two machines (see Figure 6.10). The first machine, called B_STD_LOGIC_1164_0[9], contains all the definitions of types and the operations which concern the extended bit. The second machine, B_STD_LOGIC_1164_VECTOR_0, depends on the first to define the vectors and the corresponding operations. We also created a machine, B_Signal_0, to process the signals.

– B_STD_LOGIC_1164_0: in this machine, we define the principal type STD_ULOGIC as a set of values, and its subtypes as subsets of this set. We define the subset as CONSTANTS[10]. Under the clause PROPERTIES[11], we declare the elements of these types. This method of declaration decreases the number of the necessary proofs which are needed to verify the consistency of the machine because the expressions under PROPERTIES clause are added as axioms. The VHDL functions are represented under the OPERATIONS[12] clause in B. Each operation is a call of a mathematic function. For each element of the domains, we define the correspondent element in the co-domain using tables. We define these tables as constants which have their values under the PROPERTIES clause. In order to be close to the definitions of VHDL, we define some functions as compositions of other functions (NAND using NOT, AND). In order to determine the type of the parameters, we use the substitution PRE pred THEN body END, which enables us to verify the type of the input variables.

The type of the output is decided indirectly in the operation in the first affectation (:=). Each operation consists of a mathematic function call, so the

9 In B tools, the abstract machine is written in a file with the *mch* extension, the refinement with the *ref* one and the implementation with the *imp* one.
10 The constant conception in B includes names which have a fixed value without determining its type.
11 Some characteristics of the constants may be noted under the PROPERTIES clause.
12 The operation in B may be considered as a procedure in the imperative languages.

result is included in the co-domain of that function. As opposed to VHDL, the B method does not accept overloading: VHDL accepts several functions with the same name but with different signatures, and the desired function is decided only during the execution depending on the number and the type of its parameters. So in the B machines of the STD_LOGIC_1164, we have chosen many B operations with different names and introduced the type of parameters in these operations as a part of their names. For example, six functions in VHDL have the name TO_X01. One has an input variable of type BIT, another has an extended bit variable as input and the others have extended bit vector variables as input.

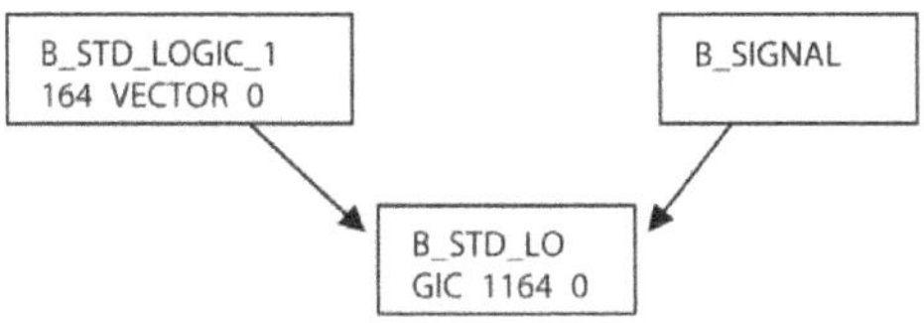

Figure 6.10. *STD_Logic in B*

So we have in these machine two operations: From_std_ulogic_to_X01 and From_BIT_to_X01. The print operation was inserted to test the value of a variable of std_ulogic type. The implementation of this operation depends on the designers needs, so we used the substitution skip[13].

```
in VHDL
    Type std_ulogic IS ('U','X','0','1','Z','W','L','H',' ')
in B
    SETS
    STD_ULOGIC={ UU,XX,OO,II,ZZ,WW,LL,HH,DD}
in VHDL
    SUBTYPE std_logic IS resolved std_ulogic
in B
    CONSTANTS STD_LOGIC
    PROPERTIES
       STD_LOGIC <: STD_ULOGIC
    & STD_LOGIC=STD_ULOGIC {DD}
in VHDL
    SUBTYPE X01 is resolved std_ulogic RANGE 'X' TO '1'
in B
    CONSTANTS
```

13 The substitution skip means that it will be replaced by other substitutions during the refinement steps.

```
    XOI
    PROPERTIES
    XOI <: STD_ULOGIC & XOI = {XX,OO,II}
in VHDL
    SUBTYPE UX01 is resolved std_ulogic RANGE 'U' TO '1'
in B
    CONSTANTS
    UXOI
    PROPERTIES
    UXOI <: STD_ULOGIC & UXOI = {UU,XX,OO,II}
in VHDL
    CONSTANT
    not_table:std_table:stdlogic_1d:= ('U','X','1','0','X','X','1','0','X')
    FUNCTION ``NOT" (l:std_ulogic) RETURN UX01 IS
    BEGIN
    RETURN (not_table(l))
    END ``NOT";
in B
    CONSTANTS NOT_STD
    PROPERTIES
    NOT_STD :STD_ULOGIC > UXOI
    &NOT_STD = { UU |-> UU, XX |-> XX, OO|->II , II|->OO, ZZ|->XX,
    WW|->XX, LL|->II, HH|->OO, DD|-> XX }
    OPERATION
    out ← Not(in)
    PRE
        in :STD_ULOGIC
    THEN
    out := NOT_STD(in)
    END
```

– B_STD_LOGIC_1164_VECTOR_0: in order to deal with the vectors, we wrote a machine which can use the previous one. Using the SEES clause, this machine can read all the constants of the seen machine B_STD_LOGIC_1164_0 (i.e. the tables of the functions). It contains a general function called Apply which takes four parameters op, in1, in2, out.

It applies the operation op, which is a table function in the previous machine, over all the elements of the input vectors in1, in2 and gives as output the vector out. We define the vector as a structure of two elements, the first being a function. Its domain is the maximum size of the vector and its co-domain is the value of the vector (elements from STD_LOGIC or STD_ULOGIC). The second element is the size of the vector. We collect all the vectors used in a set with a maximum size (MAX_VECTOR). Under the OPERATIONS clause, we find the correspondent operations of vector functions in the STD_LOGIC_1164 package. As in the last machine, we can find here a print operation to lay out the desired vector.

```
in VHDL
    TYPE std_ulogic_vector IS ARRAY ( NATURAL RANGE <> ) OF std_ulogic;
in B
    CONSTANTS
          STD_LOGIC_VECTOR,
          STD_ULOGIC_VECTOR ,Max_Element
    PROPERTIES
          Max_Element:NAT1 &
          STD_LOGIC_VECTOR =
          struct (
                    vector: 1..Max_Element >STD_LOGIC,
                    vector_size:NAT1
          )
    &     card(STD_LOGIC_VECTOR)<MAX_VECTOR
    &     !xx.((xx:STD_LOGIC_VECTOR) =>
                    xx'vector_size<Max_Element)
    . . .
in VHDL
    FUNCTION "and" ( l,r : std_logic_vector ) RETURN s      td_logic_vector IS
    ALIAS lv : std_logic_vector ( 1 TO l'LENGTH ) IS l;
    ALIAS rv : std_logic_vector ( 1 TO r'LENGTH ) IS r;
    VARIABLE result : std_logic_vector ( 1 TO l'LENGTH );
    BEGIN
    IF ( l'LENGTH /= r'LENGTH ) THEN
    ASSERT FALSE
    REPORT "arguments of overloaded 'and' operator are not of the same length"
    SEVERITY FAILURE;
    ELSEFOR i IN result'RANGE LOOP
    result(i) := and_table (lv(i), rv(i));
    END LOOP;
    END IF;
    RETURN result;
    END "and";
in B
    DEFINITIONS
    APPLY(op,in1,in2,out) ==
    ANY vv
    WHERE
    vv : STD_LOGIC_VECTOR &
```

```
!xx.((xx:1 .. max(in1'vector_size,in2'vector_size))
=>((vv'vector)(xx)= op((in1'vector)(xx),(in2'vector)(xx))))
THEN out := vv
END
OPERATIONS
out < And(in1,in2)=
PRE
in1 : STD_LOGIC_VECTOR & in2 : STD_LOGIC_VECTOR & in1'vector_size
=in2'vector_size
THEN
    APPLY(AND_STD,in1,in2,out)
END;
```

– B_Signal_0: most of the operations in the previous two abstract machines are included in order to find correspondents to the logic function or to the type converting functions. But there are other functions in the STD_LOGIC_1164 package which are related with the electrical signals. So we need to simulate a signal in order to give a concrete implementation to these functions. The B_Signal_0 abstract machine may be used to solve this problem and could be used as a base to translate other VHDL packages. Here, the signal is expressed in this machine as a structure of two elements; the first is a value of std_logic type (or std_ulogic) and the second is a pointer to another structure of the same type. In order to determine the beginning of the list, we define the null list called nil.

```
ABSTRACT_CONSTANTS
        SIGNAL_ULOGIC , SIGNAL_nil , F_SIGNAL
PROPERTIES
        SIGNAL_ULOGIC = struct ( value : STD_ULOGIC,
                                 next : SIGNAL_ULOGIC)
&       card(SIGNAL) < MAX_SIGNAL
&       SIGNAL_nil : SIGNAL_ULOGIC
&       F_SIGNAL : SIGNAL_ULOGIC --> SIGNAL_ULOGIC
&       F_SIGNAL(SIGNAL_nil)= rec(value :DD,
        next:SIGNAL_nil)
```

With these definitions, it is easy to define an operation which corresponds to the RISING_EDGE functions which return a TRUE value if the signal value changes from a low level to a high one. Using the same conceptions, the FALLING_EDGE function is defined to treat the signal in the other direction. As in the other abstract machines, we defined here the print operation to lay out the value of the signal in a precise time.

in VHDL

```
FUNCTION rising_edge (SIGNAL s : std_ulogic) RETURN BOOLEAN IS
BEGIN
RETURN (s'EVENT AND (To_X01(s) = '1')
AND (To_X01(s'LAST_VALUE) = '0'));
END;
```

in B

```
out <-- rising_edge (in) =
PRE
      in : SIGNAL_ULOGIC
THEN
      out :( out : BOOL & out = bool((in'value = II)
               & ( (F_SIGNAL(in'next))'value = OO)))
END;
```

The last three B abstract machines give the principal characteristics of the VHDL STD_LOGIC_1164 package. These abstract machines are fully proved. To be closed to the standard package, we tried to write the B correspondents with the same element names and definitions. But because of the differences between the two languages, many points must be taken care of.

The correspondence between the STD_LOGIC_1164 package parts and the B machine parts is not direct, so we cannot transmit some comments which give some details about the international programs of all parts of the STD_LOGIC_1164 package.

The last versions of the STD_LOGIC_1164 contain many attribute instructions. Each attribute instruction associates a characteristic with a type or with an object. For example, attribute REFLEXIVE of resolved:function is TRUE[14]. These attributes may be used in the package or in the libraries that depend on this package. In our machines, each time we need these attributes, we use expressions that give the necessary characteristics. For the future when we translate the machines that depend on the STD_LOGIC_1164 package, we ought to find the necessary expressions each time we use these attributes.

In VHDL, we can use general expressions as: TYPE STD_LOGIC_VECTOR is ARRAY (NATURAL RANGE <>) of std_ulogic, the B method does not give the same capacity. So, for our

14 It means the attribute REFLEXIVE is satisfied in resolved which is a function.

example, we ought to determine the limits of the vector range. We do so in the B_STD_LOGIC_1164_VECTOR_0 machine. In the To_bit function, which converts a given value from extended bit type to a normal bit type, we give the value xmap to the undetermined values (U; Z; W; X;). In the function To_bit, the xmap is initialized to O. It may be redefined in the future only by changing the function To_bit. To have the same modification in B, we must change the PROPERTIES clause which is, in the B_std_logic_1164_0.mch, independent of the To_bit functions.

In many functions in STD_LOGIC_1164, we find the instruction: ALIAS lv : std_logic_vector (1 TO 1 0 LENGTH) IS l. We use this instruction to arrange its input vector so that their elements occupy the first positions in the local function array. This arrangement facilitates vector treatments in the function. In B components presented above, we proposed that the vectors are normally[15] represented.

The VHDL language gives the programmer the possibility to prepare an error messages that may be displayed if there is an error during the execution. In STD_LOGIC_1164, we have many of these messages. For example, IF (l'LENGTH /= r'LENGTH) THEN ASSERT FALSE REPORT “arguments of overloaded ‘nand’ operator are not of the same length” SEVERITY FAILURE.

6.4.3. *The multiplexer*

We present in this section, how the designer may use the methodology proposed in the previous section to design a circuit based on the VHDL library. This example is an extension of an example of the multiplexer proposed earlier in the first section. Instead of two Boolean values in the first example, TRUE and FALSE, we use an extended bit with the nine values. In the new proposed example, we describe a multiplexer with three inputs. The output depends on the value of the input Select_a; it takes the value of In_a if Select_a equals OO or LL (the low level), it takes the value of In_b if Select_a equals II or HH (the high level); otherwise it takes the value XX (undetermined).

The following mathematic expression may be summarizing by the definition:

15 The element of the order i in the vector occupies the position of the order i in the array.

((Select_a = OO ∨ Select_a = LL) => (out = in_a))^

((Select_a = II ∨ Select_a = HH) => (out = in_b))^

((Select_a = UU ∨ Select_a = XX ∨ Select_a = ZZ∨

Select_a = WW ∨ Select_a = DD) => (out = XX))

```
MACHINE
        B_Mux_STD_0
SEES
        B_STD_LOGIC_1164_0
DEFINITIONS
Compute_(xx,yy,zz,res) ==
( ((xx = UU) => (res = XX))
& ((xx = XX) => (res = XX))
& ((xx = OO) => (res = yy))
& ((xx = II) => (res = zz))
& ((xx = ZZ) => (res = XX))
& ((xx = WW) => (res = XX))
& ((xx = LL) => (res = yy))
& ((xx = HH) => (res = zz))
& ((xx = DD) => (res = XX)) )
. . .
END
```

Comparing the specifications of the multiplexer in the two examples, we find the following differences:

– in the new machine, the SEES clause is used to enable us to use the variables of the B_STD_LOGIC_1164_0 machine;

– the type of the four local variables is changed from the Boolean type to the STD_ULOGIC type defined in the B_STD_LOGIC_1164_0 abstract machine;

– the definition of the function Compute_ is redefines and extended to cover the nine values of the extended bit. The following B abstract machine contains the specification of this multiplexer[16].

16 In this machine *xx* is a variable, but *XX* is one of the values of the type *STD_ULOGIC*.

6.5. VHDL to B

Semi-automatic translation of similar circuit specification to the B abstract machine is another way of working. In the first step, we define the properties of the new components. The second step is graphical; it introduces the components synthesis by composition of basic components. So, at the last refinement, the implementation, we obtain a safe piece of software; it may be easily converted to another programming. We want to define a tool that creates the possibility of an automatic transformation of the implementation to VHDL language. In this case, we obtain the possibility of co-design between the B method and the VHDL (see Figure 6.11).

From VHDL component, the "entity" part provides a list of procedure and the "architecture" part provides a description of principal properties and introduces the implementation. But we want to add some useful properties (safety, liveness, etc.) and we add some annotation (commentary) in the VHDL description.

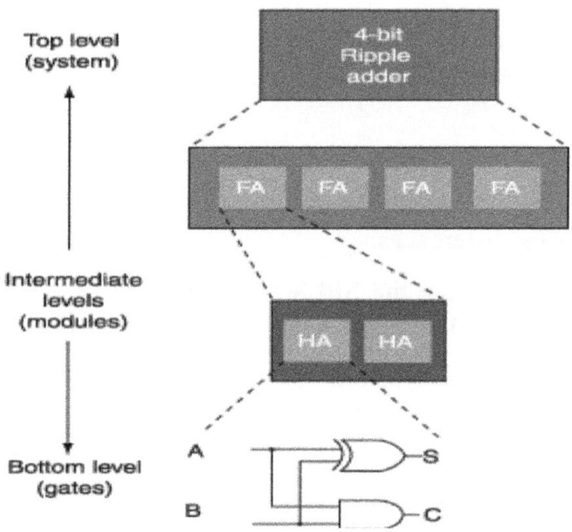

Figure 6.11. *A multilevel design hierarchy detailing components of a full adder is used in VHDL designs*

6.6. Conclusions

6.6.1. *Some limitations*

To develop an electronic circuit in B requires understanding the refinement calculus, that is, a certain adaptation time for a circuit designer. The most recent imperative languages like VHDL include facilities as manipulations of a vector without explicit length or functions with various signatures. Because the B method does not include such features, these differences induce difficulties in transforming VHDL to B. One solution to the problem of vector length is used in the B_STD_LOGIC_1164_VECTOR_0 by passing the length as a parameter and by using the universal quantifier (∀). To design circuits, a large quantity of proofs may be generated and must be proved automatically or in cooperation with the designer. The size of these proofs depends on the quality of the program, the capacity of the prover, the designer, and the tool we use. For very large circuits, the number of the necessary proofs could be extremely large.

When the circuit is designed in B, we can prove that it satisfies the required specifications but we do not yet have any tools to create the real circuits directly from the B specification. But with the B method, it is possible to represent the circuits as close as is needed to the physical level. In [BOU 99], authors refined the B_NOT_0 abstract machine based on abstract machines of CMOS transistors. To simulate a signal propagation, the conception of the time must be represented some delay. Its possible to modelise it by a pair (signal, date). For more complicated cases when it is necessary to treat many signals in the same time, a list of structures may be used to represent each signal. Each structure consists of a value and a date. A global clock may be used to control the harmony between all the signals of the circuit.

6.6.2. *Advantages*

The most important characteristic of the B method is that it produces a secure circuit. The circuit which is obtained in the implementation satisfies the specifications in the abstract machine 100%. It is possible to add the required safety conditions under the INVARIANT clause in the abstract machine. So the circuit design is completely correct. The error may occur only when we describe the specifications or if the physical circuit does not correspond to the proposed model. The cost and the time of the test are gained. To develop a circuit that was proved before, it is enough to prove only the new characteristics. It is not necessary to reprove all the old ones. So the designer may use all the circuits that are designed before; he or she can make some changes and then prove a small part related to the new characteristics. The B tools can automatically decide which parts of the model are changed or added in order to be reproved. This characteristic is quite important for the necessary modifications of the integrated circuit development. The B method is used in many domains. Often the systems to design are composite, both mechanical and electronic, software and hardware. For example, to design a circuit to control a robot which satisfies some needs and conditions of mechanics and electronics. It may be easier to design using the adequate B libraries that we have specified for digital circuits at the same time as mechanical libraries.

6.6.3. *Future work*

We intend to create a simple and complex example to show the refinement development of a circuit design from the abstract specification to the physical level. In such an example, we intend to show the refinement by introducing an algorithm[17]. Also, we intend to create several libraries in B equivalent to the VHDL libraries, in order to facilitate the circuit design in B. Furthermore, this facilitates the transformation operation from B to VHDL. We try to find a common rule which may be used to automatize the translation. Also, we may solve this problem by creating a physical library in B that contains the characteristics of the basic electronic elements or by retranslating the results of a circuit development from B to VHDL. Semi-automatic translation of similar circuit specification to B abstract machine is another way of work. In the first step, we define the properties of the new components. The second step is graphical; it introduces the components synthesis by composition of basic components. So, at the last refinement, the implementation, we obtain a secure software; it may be easily converted to another programming. We want to define a tool that provides the possibility of an automatic transformation of the implementation to VHDL language. In this case, we obtain the possibility of co-design between the B method and the VHDL.

17 In this chapter, we concentrated on the modeling methodology; so one refinement step is used to find the multiplexer components.

In summary, in this chapter, we presented a part of our work for creating B libraries which correspond to some VHDL packages, such as the STD_LOGIC_1164 package. This project enables us to take advantage of the power of the B method to develop a secure circuit. We write the specification of a desired circuit, and then gradually refine our specifications for the implementation of this circuit which depends on the desired libraries. The AtelierB or the Btoolkit enables us to generate the necessary proofs to verify that each description of our circuit is consistent and each step of the refinement satisfies the conditions of the previous one. This implies that it satisfies the specifications in the first description. These proofs may be generated automatically or in cooperation with the designer. In the end, we obtain a circuit that satisfies our needs. The development from the abstract specifications to a complete circuit description does not need an expert in circuits but a B expert. B lacks some programming language characteristics such as the type casting and the generality quality. But on the other hand, one of the B designing advantages is that a change of an old circuit needs proofs corresponding only to the new modifications. Also, we can reach the desired specifications using a mix between electric and electronic libraries.

6.6.4. *To finish*

When the circuit is designed in B, we can prove that it satisfies the required specifications but we do not yet have any tools to create the real circuits directly from the B specification. But with the B method, it is possible to represent the circuits as close as is needed to the physical level.

In [BOU 99], the authors refined the abstract machine that model the NOT gate based on abstract machines of CMOS transistors. To simulate a signal propagation, the conception of the time must be represented by some delay. Its possible to model it by a pair (signal, date). For more complicated cases when it is necessary to treat many signals at the same time, a list of structures may be used to represent each signal. Each structure consists of a value and a date. A global clock may be used to control the harmony between all the signals of the circuit.

The most important characteristic of the B method is that it produces a secure circuit. The circuit which is obtained in the implementation completely satisfies the specifications in the abstract machine. It is possible to add the required safety conditions under the INVARIANT clause in the abstract machine. So the circuit design is completely correct. The error may occur only when we describe the specifications or if the physical circuit does not correspond to the proposed model. The cost and the time of the test are gained. To develop a circuit that was proved before, it is enough to prove only the new characteristics. It is not necessary to reprove all the old ones. So the designer may use all the circuits that are designed before; he or she can make some changes and then prove a small part related to the new characteristics.

6.7. Bibliography

[ABR 92] ABRIAL J.-R., "On constructing large software systems: in algorithms, software, architecture", *Information Processing 92, IFIP 12th World Computer Congress*, vol. A-12, pp. 103–112, 7–11, September 1992.

[ABR 96] ABRIAL J.-R., *The B Book: Assigning Programs to Meanings*, Cambridge University Press, August 1996.

[AIR 98] AIRIAU R., BERGÉ J.-M., OLIVE V., *et al.*, *VHDL Langage, modélisation, synthèse.* Collection Technique et scientifique des télécommunications, Romandes Polytechnic and University Press, 1998.

[BOU 99] BOULANGER J.-L., MARIANO G., Modélisation formelle de circuits numériques par la méthode B, Technical Report 1999-25-RT, 1999.

[BOU 01] BOULANGER J.-L., ALJER A., MARIANO G., "Conception sûr de circuit basée sur la notion de propriété", *14 ème journée internationales Génie Logiciel & ingénierie de systèmes et leurs applications, du 4 au 6 décembre 2001, ICSSEA 2001*, 2001.

[BOU 02] BOULANGER J.-L., MARIANO G., "Formalization of digital circuits using the B method", *3rd European Systems Engineering Conference*, Toulouse, 21–24 May 2002.

[CLI 90] CLIFF B.J. *Systematic Software Development Using VDM*, 2nd ed., Prentice-Hall International, Englewood Cliffs, NJ, 1990.

[DUC 99] DUCASSÉ M., ROZÉ L., "Proof obligations of the B formal method: local proofs ensure global consistency", *Proceedings of the LOPSTR'99*, LNCS, Springer-Verlag, pp. 10–29, September 1999.

[IEE 93] IEEE, *Standard VHDL Reference Manual*, IEEE, 1993.

[KER 98] KERN C., MARK R., *Greenstreet: Formal Verification in Hardware Design*, Romandes Polytechnic and University Press, 1998.

[MOR 90] MORGAN C., *Deriving Programs from Specifications,* Prentice-Hall International, 1990.

[NIC 99] NICOLI F., Vérification formelle de descriptions VHDL comportamentales, PhD Thesis, Provence University, July 1999.

[NIC 00] NICOLAIDIS M., ZAIDAN N., CALIN T., *et al.*, "ISIS: a fail-safe interface realised in mart power technology", *IEEE*, pp. 191–197, 2000.

[SPI 92] SPIVEY J.M., *The Z Notation: A Reference Manual*, 2nd ed., Prentice Hall International Series in Computer Science, 1992.

[STE 98] STERIA B., *Manuel de Référence*, September 1998.

7

Pragmatic Use of B: The Power of Formal Methods without the Bulk

7.1. Introduction

Many observers and industrial actors still see the B method [ABR 96] and formal models [BOU 11, BOU 12a, BOU 12b] as forming an overly restrictive approach which is difficult to implement. A considerable number of them still presume that these methods are only suitable for use by personnel with rare and highly specific capabilities.

The various industrial projects carried out at Systerel over the last few years have led us to refine this crude, but widespread, vision.

The aim of this chapter is to show that practices widely used in classic developments can also be applied in the context of formal processes, facilitating their implementation and acceptability.

7.2. Prototyping for formal models

In the context of modern industry, it is rare to find development projects for systems, equipment or software which do not include the creation of one or more prototypes in the earliest stages.

These prototypes provide users with a clearer understanding of the product being created, specificities related to its use, relevance of certain

---

Chapter written by Christophe METAYER, François BUSTANY and Mathieu CLABAUT.

technical choices, performances expected of the product and a number of other aspects which need to be taken into consideration early in the process. In addition to functional aspects, prototypes offer considerable benefits for the formal modeling phase. For this reason, we use an initial prototype of formal models in our projects before starting work on a full software model.

In the case under consideration in this chapter, the prototyping process concerns a software development using B, from the formal specification stage to the generation of a binary file, including proof activities. At this stage in the project, only certain representative functions of the final program are established. The purpose of the prototype is not, therefore, to evaluate the functions of the program. Indeed, when studying the functional aspects of a system, it is generally best to use a language or tools which reduce development time, for example Java or script languages like Python.

Our prototype of a B software model is intended for use in studying the qualities of the future model based on the different aspects discussed further.

By looking as far ahead as the binary file stage, we obtain an initial idea of the execution time of the produced code. At this stage, it is difficult to gain a precise evaluation of the execution time, as not all functions will have been implanted; however, we can compare this time to that taken by a "manually" produced executable file. This allows us to check for execution delays linked to architectural or data-structuring choices.

By developing a prototype, we are also able to verify that modeling choices, particularly those related to data structures, do not generate excessive levels of complexity in the model, making it difficult to re-read, control and maintain.

Modeling choices also have a significant impact on proof activities. Poor choices can increase the number of proof obligations (POs), or produce highly complex POs. In order to validate modeling choices in relation to these proof issues, the prototyping phase includes a proof aspect. This allows us to check that the program will be provable within reasonable time delays. Certain ideas may be abandoned if they are seen to generate excessively complex proof requirements.

The gains in productivity due to prototyping are hard to measure; however, the reduction in risks which might generate extra development costs is, in our opinion, more than enough to justify the added workload.

7.3. Inspiration from agile methods

Developments with the help of the B method are essentially related to safety-critical software. The standards which cover the development of these programs impose a task sequence following the classic V cycle and require development and validation to be carried out by independent teams. Development teams often carry out no test activities. The first versions supplied to the validation team are therefore often of poor quality and require significant communications between the teams. In addition, the validation team only has access to the program from the moment of the first validations, limiting their efficiency in the early stages. In cases of dysfunction, the validation team will require considerable time to determine whether this is due to a software anomaly or if the test itself is incorrect.

The following paragraphs aim to provide some elements of response to these issues concerning the relationships and responsibilities of the development and validation teams.

7.4. Simultaneous development and validation

While working on a project presenting a certain number of technical challenges, we decided to create a validation team from the outset. Firstly, this team produced a functional prototype of the program, before creating a set of validation tools. The team then developed testing activities based on this prototype, which facilitated validation of the operational principles of the system at a very early stage in the software development process.

This phase also enabled the validation team to gain experience related to this particular system, meaning that the required knowledge and abilities had already been acquired before the start of the validation phase, facilitating communications with the development team. The validation team was able to provide rapid analysis of anomalies and assist the developers in this respect.

Furthermore, the validation toolset was operational before the end of the development phase, giving the development team access to testing methods throughout the development process.

It was therefore possible to carry out testing throughout the coding stage: once the development was sufficiently advanced to produce an executable file, the code was able to be tested. In this respect, the development followed certain principles used in agile development methods.

Furthermore, the development and validation teams had access to the same tools, leading to easier communications when treating anomalies; the developers were able to work with testing methods themselves and to make use of debugging tools.

Note that this approach does not provide any additional coverage in terms of standards regulating safety developments. However, it is easy to establish and appears to be relevant. Although the associated gains are hard to quantify, the benefits of early establishment of the validation team are evident. Note, in passing, that this approach does not depend on the use of formal methods, and can be used with both classic and formal techniques.

7.5. Performances of software developed in B

B is known and used in relation to safety requirements. It is not known for its response to performance issues. Our experiences have shown that, contrary to popular belief, the performance of programs written in B can be at least as good as that of software produced "by hand".

The poor image of B in terms of performance is most likely due to confusion with other formal methods which do present performance issues.

These other methods are based on a high-level formalism which is often quite distant from the final program, generally obtained using code generators. The greater the gap between the formalism and the generated code, the more complex the code generator, and this situation often produces code which is very difficult to re-read and hard to compare to the initial program. Debugging the projects of this type is an extremely complicated process. The approach also has repercussions on code performance, as it is hard for complex generators to take account of optimization issues. There is thus a risk of obtaining inefficient programs, and the associated models must be modified to conform to the constraints imposed by the code generator. The B approach is very different from these methods.

The B method relies upon an abstract language in order to model software in an abstract manner. However, the method is based on the use of refinements, applied successively until we reach a level known as B0.

Level B0 only permits data structures and instructions which may be implemented using any classic programming language (C, Ada, Java and so on). We then use a translation tool to carry out the required syntactic transformation.

Software B facilitates precise mastery of generated code in exactly the same way as manual development. There is therefore no reason for the resulting performances to be inferior to those obtained using other methods, and experience has shown that very good results may be obtained using this approach.

The main benefits of B for software stem from the fact that we are able to implement techniques which are not usually possible in a manual development context, due to the fact that all of the transformation steps involved are guaranteed by proof.

In safety software, for example, it is standard practice to avoid replicating information: information may only be kept in one single form, otherwise it becomes difficult to ensure the coherency of multiple representations of the same information. In B, this coherency is ensured by proof.

To illustrate this point, let us consider object lists and the associated actions:

– creation and deletion of lists;

– adding or removing an element from a given list.

No particular constraints are imposed, and an object may be present in several lists at the same time.

We begin by choosing a first data structure which facilitates the addition or removal of list elements: a two-dimensional table in which each line contains the elements of the corresponding list.

Table 7.1 shows a current state in which three of five possible lists are made up of different elements. List 1 contains objects 5, 26 and 13; list 2 contains objects 1 and 9, and list 3 contains objects 26, 4, 2 and 7.

List number						
1	5	26	13			
2	1	9				
3	26	4	2	7		
4						
5						

Table 7.1. *Example of a list*

This data structure is suitable for displaying all elements in a list, and it is relatively easy to add elements. The removal of an element may require us to shift the remaining elements.

Now imagine that an algorithm requires us to know all of the lists in which a given segment appears. Using the previous data structure, we would need to go through all of our lists and all of our elements to obtain this information.

If this information is frequently required in a program, we may use a second data structure, representing the same information but in a different way.

We can thus create lists in which the first element is an object number and the following elements are the numbers of the lists in which the object appears.

Object number						
1	2					
2	3					
4	3					
5	1					
7	3					
9	2					
13	1					
26	1	3				

Table 7.2. *Example of a redundant list*

Table 7.2 shows this structure, which duplicates information from the list shown in Table 7.1.

However, this approach introduces an additional difficulty related to the maintenance of coherency between the two data structures.

Information duplication is generally avoided as it results in a loss of control. Coherency cannot be guaranteed by classic testing activities: while we are able to create test plans for functional specifications, we cannot currently create test plans in the presence of constraints linked to data structures.

In other words, if we introduce a coherency requirement for two data structures, validators will be unable to identify which tests to carry out.

When using B, coherency is followed as guaranteed by proof. Information replication therefore poses no particular difficulties and is widely used.

B therefore allows us to create more sophisticated programs and complex optimizations (cache management, information replication, circular buffers, etc.). This produces software with much better performance levels, the correctness of which is guaranteed by proof.

Once again, contrary to popular belief, we see that the use of formal methods does not necessarily entail extra costs in terms of execution time; on the contrary, these methods offer optimization possibilities which would be difficult to exploit without the use of proof.

7.6. Use of infinity: separating algorithmic thinking and programming issues

The notion of infinity is more usually relegated to the domain of philosophy and, more generally, research, rather than engineering, as infinite concepts are not usually handled by engineers; however, the subject has come to be of increasing importance.

The use of infinity is not without consequences, and raises questions concerning testing using infinite structures, or model checking for these structures, which is problematic given the combinatorial explosion phenomena which come into play when using significant quantities of data.

Experiments have shown that the use of data structures involving infinite structures facilitates both model writing and proof. These structures also offer the possibility of more high-performance implementations.

As an illustration, let us consider the use of a list of ordered elements. This is a classic problem in computing, but also in algorithmics (e.g. in connection with a list of contiguous track sections).

Using standard approaches, these lists are coded by finite index functions, starting from zero and with a size limited by an upper bound. This approach is well suited to tables produced by programming languages.

Figure 7.1 shows a graphical description of the ordered list 23, 12, 4, 9.

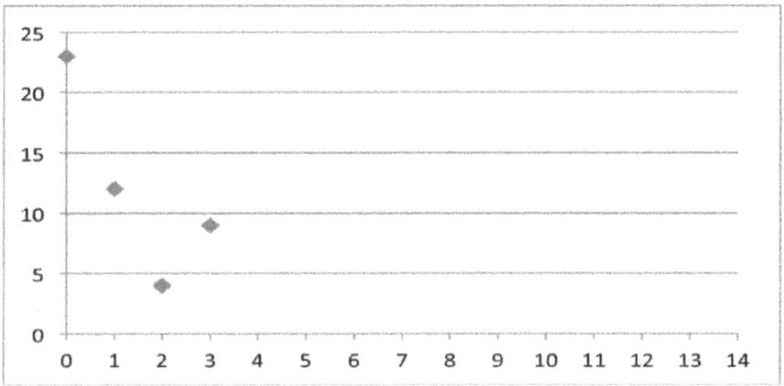

Figure 7.1. *Description of an ordered list*

The structure used in Figure 7.1 is well suited for the addition of elements at the end of the list. In our example, if we wish to add the element 2, we simply need to modify the index function, associating index value 4 with element 2.

However, the situation becomes more difficult if we wish to add (or remove) an element at the beginning of the list, in which case all of the elements in the list must be re-indexed.

The problem with this data structure lies in the fact that the index function begins at zero, and the structure is asymmetric: we can easily add or remove elements from one side of the structure, while an addition or removal on the other side of the structure will require us to shift the index.

This type of data structure means that operations need to be specified on a case-by-case basis depending on the side of the structure involved. It makes the model more complicated and creates additional work in terms of proof.

We used a slightly different data structure in one of our projects in an attempt to avoid this problem, based on the use of an index function starting with any given integer *a* (positive or negative) instead of zero.

As before, the number of indexed elements is bounded, and the function indexes elements using integers contained between an index value *a* and a higher index value *b*.

Figure 7.2 shows the index function for the same series of numbers used in the previous example.

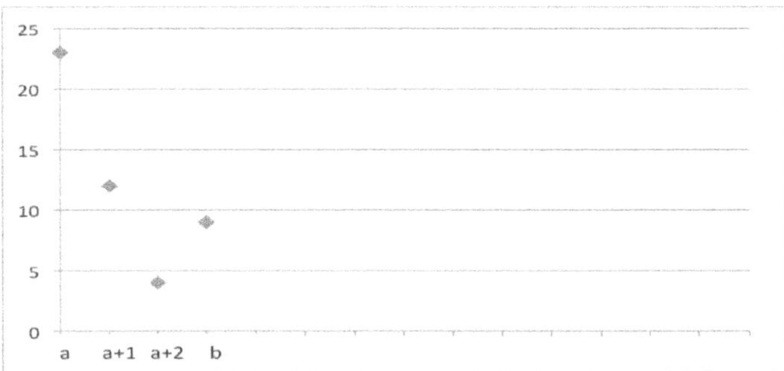

Figure 7.2. *Second representation*

This new structure homogenizes index management, and the addition or removal of an element essentially consists of modifying index *a* or *b*, removing the shifting issue.

This structure is relevant when we consider that there are no constraints on bounds *a* and b, except for the fact that the distance between *a* and *b* must be less than a given constant. This is only possible using natural integers, which constitute an infinite set. Evidently, through the refinement process, the final produced code operates using finite integers, implementing a circular buffer algorithm; however, abstract modeling using infinity is simpler to handle and facilitates reasoning.

This experiment shows that the use of abstract objects, specifically infinity, is not only viable in industrial projects, but also contributes to the simplification of engineering tasks. Engineers begin by concentrating on list management (the modeling phase) then implementation (programming phases); in other cases, it is possible to reuse existing implementation plans, the correct realization of which is guaranteed by refinement proof.

The separation of algorithmic considerations and programming issues is a key pathway to follow in attempting to optimize engineering activities.

7.7. Industrial implementation of event-B

Currently, it is rare for more than a few individuals within any given company to have a clear idea of the way a system operates. This information is difficult to transmit, and is generally only obtained through experience and practice. The accumulation of ideas over time means that the reasons leading to a particular organization may become hidden from view. This loss of knowledge leads to immobility and resistance to change: as users no longer know why things are done in a particular way, we become unaware of the potential consequences of change, generating reluctance to challenge tried and tested practices.

The progressive use of different model-based approaches (model-led engineering) represents a challenge to this mindset, but the approximate nature of the semantics involved and the difficulty of guaranteeing coherency between viewpoints mean that any successes have been rather limited.

This situation has led us to make increasing use of event-B, initially in the context of studies with a limited industrial impact (initial phases, modeling for verification or specification consolidation purposes), then more broadly in the system design phases of critical industrial projects.

Experience has demonstrated the power of this technique in identifying essential concepts for system safety, the exact point at which these concepts become useful in the system design process and their precise contribution to the safe operation of a system.

This advantage of event-B is due to a reasoning approach with considerable differences to that usually employed in mastering system complexity.

In traditional methods, engineers use the full specification of a system, which often already presents a high (sometimes excessive) level of detail, and apply a progressive decomposition process to obtain sub-system specifications which are simple enough to be easily mastered. However, even when this method is successful, the engineers will not have the necessary information to ensure that these sub-systems will constitute a safe system when interconnected or reconstructed, as the approach does not give consideration to this aspect.

Using event-B, the first stage involves abstraction of the system specification, i.e. identification of the abstract data making up the system and the abstract events leading to the evolution of this data over time. This is followed by a refinement and proof process, involving the progressive information of data, concepts, trigger conditions and other details; each of these details is only introduced as and when they become necessary to the proof activity, i.e. for demonstration of a specific system property.

In other words, event-B guides engineers through a detailed reasoning process. Initially, it leads users to gain a sufficiently general view for understanding system behaviors, before going into greater detail, focusing on the elements which contribute to expected system behaviors. The key to this approach is the mathematical demonstration of the effective role of these elements in system safety.

System complexity is therefore mastered by a process based on abstraction followed by proved refinement, rather than by a decomposition process in which there is no guarantee that elementary properties will be reconstructed into the desired expected general property.

In the specific context of our project, we were able to benefit from circumstances which are rare in an industrial setting:

– the ability to reconsider earlier system specification and design phases;

– the ability to continue or modify later production processes.

This experience also highlighted another interesting point concerning the final design of a system design. Through building and proving a system model in event-B, we were able to identify certain design principles which are essential both in demonstrating system safety and in facilitating development and validation. One example of this is the ability of a train movement management function to keep trains within safe boundaries in all circumstances, rather than having to guarantee safety in specific cases where trains move outside of these boundaries.

The use of event-B thus enabled us to influence system design, with the aim of mastering system behavior and demonstrating safety, rather than dealing with these aspects *a posteriori*. We were also able to avoid situations in which a solid safety demonstration cannot be established; situations of this kind involve backtracking in the design process, which cannot be avoided due to the safety levels of the systems involved.

7.8. B method for software and event-B

The B method for software can be used to improve practices based on event-B, and vice-versa.

Lessons may be learned from the implementation of both methods, and certain practices can be transferred from one method to the other.

For example, event-B has had an influence on practices using B method for software in the field of animation. Model animation, with graphical representations, was carried out very early in event-B; the transfer of these practices to the B method for software has proved fruitful.

This is the reason behind the inclusion of graphical interfaces in the validation approaches of software developed with the B method. These interfaces represent the state of piloted systems and the state of software; together, they constitute a simulator which facilitates rapid analysis of anomalies.

Inversely, the use of prototyping in B could be transferred to event-B for system modeling. In this case, an initial prototyping phase would be added for the event-B model of the system in order to study data structures and their impact on proof.

This phase is likely to provide inspiration in optimizing refinement and proof activities, enabling us to concentrate on the progressive construction of the system and eliminating pure modeling and proof issues as far as possible.

7.9. Conclusion

These perspectives are the result of over 15 years' experience in the industrial use of B and show a variety of aspects of this method.

Firstly, we have seen that the application of B is based on a range of practices widely used in industry, particularly the software industry, and that these practices contribute to facilitating its implementation, and consequently its wide acceptation, by removing typical issues related to the representative aspects of B models, their ability to be proved or the performance of the resulting code.

More importantly, we have shown how this type of method provides engineers with another means of specifying and designing complex systems, offering possibilities which are not present in other approaches:

– reasoning using abstract notions which are sufficiently concise to be handled with ease;

– decoupling of the algorithmic and coding activities during the design phase, offering an increased ease of reasoning and greater efficiency;

– optimization of verification and validation efforts, using refinement proof to guarantee progressive and organized transformation from "what" to "how" and on toward an "optimized how".

The use of formal methods such as B allows engineers to focus on their primary role in specifying and designing systems or programs, using powerful reasoning tools, without needing to devote time and effort to later, purely coding-related stages.

7.10. Glossary

IDE	Integrated development environment
PO	Proof obligation
V&V	Verification and validation

7.11. Bibliography

[ABR 96] ABRIAL J.-R., *The B-Book*, Cambridge University Press, 1996.

[ABR 06] ABRIAL J.-R., BUTLER M.J., HALLERSTEDE S., *et al.*, "An open extensible tool environment for event-B", *ICFEM,* Macao, pp. 588–605, November 1–3, 2006.

[BOU 11] BOULANGER J.-L. (ed.), *Static Analysis of Software*, ISTE, London, and John Wiley & Sons, New York, 2011.

[BOU 12a] BOULANGER J.-L. (ed.), *Industrial Use of Formal Method: Formal Verification*, ISTE, London, and John Wiley & Sons, New York, 2012.

[BOU 12b] BOULANGER J.-L. (ed.), *Formal Methods: Industrial Use from Model to the Code*, ISTE, London, and John Wiley & Sons, New York, 2012.

8

BRILLANT/BCaml — A Free Tools Platform for the B Method

8.1. What is BRILLANT/BCaml?

BRILLANT [BRI 14, COL 10] is a collaborative tool collection associated with the B formal language. The collection is centered around one particular tool known as BCaml. In this chapter, BRILLANT will often be used to refer to this tool in the context of the collection, while BCaml will be used when referring to specific aspects of the tool itself.

The initial and main purpose of BCaml is the implementation of the B method using recent methodologies, languages and technologies. This goal involves not only the implantation of the method, but also feedback from use of the B method in real-world contexts and the possibility of experimentation upon the method itself, for example in interfacing with other formalisms or through extensions of the B language. The project was launched in 1997 when work began on formalizing the grammar.

This central objective was broken down into two key aspects:

– the provision of open access tools, in a spirit of scientific and academic collaboration and sharing;

– the choice of the most appropriate methods for each tool-based aspect of the B method.

Chapter written by Samuel COLIN and Dorian PETIT.

The first aspect means that the tools were made available through an open-source collaborative development platform. In addition to ensuring availability, this system enables the creation of different versions through modification, reporting and documentation of known bugs, communications between developers, etc. This way of working is known as a "forge", although the term was not used in this context when work on BCaml began.

The second main goal will be discussed in detail in section 8.3. Certain general choices were made as needs arose:

– OCaml [LER 11] was selected as the basic language due to its symbolic handling capacities;

– the Lex and Yacc tools (the OCaml versions) were selected for language analysis, essentially because they are based on a mature, tried-and-tested language analysis technology;

– the XML [CON 00] exchange format was chosen based on the possibilities it offers and the obligations it involves in terms of information structures;

– Coq [COQ 08] is a proof assistant chosen for experiments on proof in connection with the B method. It was selected partly due to its rich theorem library, and partly to its close connections with OCaml.

The current organization of BRILLANT will be presented in section 8.2.

8.2. Organization

Figure 8.1 shows the overall organization of the tools included in the BRILLANT platform.

This organization is the result of the development history of BCaml and of the natural organization of tools used with the B method, discussed below in roughly chronological order, as seen from the publication dates of the documents cited below.

The first project associated with BRILLANT was the implementation of a syntax analyzer for the B language. This project highlighted the academic interest of this type of tool, as it was closely followed by two studies: one on B typing [BOD 02] (see the box under the syntax analyzer in Figure 8.1) and the other on the refinement of B specifications using relational databases [LAL 00].

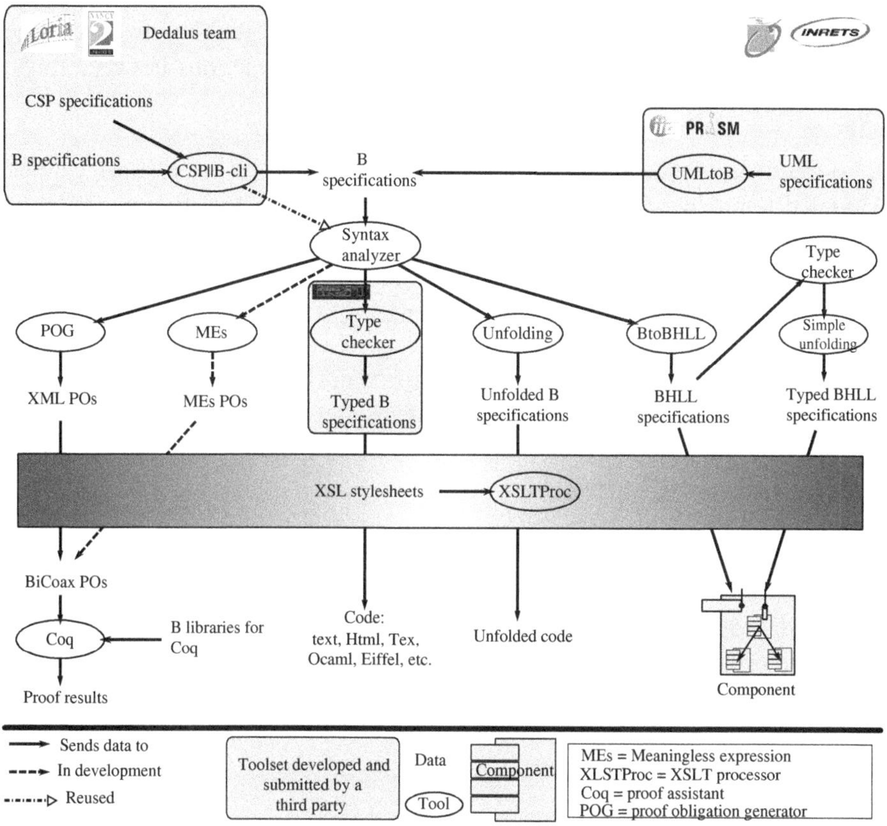

Figure 8.1. *Organization of BRILLANT/BCaml+BiCoax*

This encouragement from the academic community led us to take an interest in the code generation process, which naturally led on to consideration of B component deployment issues [PET 03b] and the modularity of the language [PET 03a].

As the B method is based on proof, we need to deal with proof obligations (POs) and their demonstration. As part of the developments described above, we implemented a proof obligation generator (POG). This section of the B tool chain also includes a proof tool based on PhoX [ROC 04].

The only metalanguage used in the platform was Objective Caml [LER 11]. We did not wish to be dependent, or oblige other collaborators to depend on a single development language. These considerations led us to define and use an Extensible Markup Language (XML)-based format for B [COL 05] to facilitate interactions between tools, whatever the languages used in development.

A number of academic publications exist on the passage from Unified Modeled Language (UML) to B, and the creation of a tool to convert UML specifications with Object Constraint Language (OCL) constraints to B by PRiSM [MAR 02] was a logical step. This tool is also included in the BRILLANT platform (see the box on the top right of Figure 8.1).

Later, the low levels of maintenance carried out on the PhoX proof assistant led us to reconsider the "proof" aspect of the tool, translating the B libraries described in PhoX syntax to Coq. This resulted in the production of a tool known as BiCoax [COL 09].

The most recent tool to use BRILLANT is a specification verification assistant, Communicating Sequential Processes (CSP)||B [NGU 10] (see the box on the top left of Figure 8.1). This tool reuses the syntax analyzer from BCaml to process the B aspect of CSP||B specifications.

The functions of some of these tools will be discussed in greater detail in section 8.3.

8.3. Functions

We will not describe the functions of all of these tools here; instead, we will limit ourselves to those which correspond to the usual development chain using B (from B specifications to proof). Details involving other tools may be found in the references given in section 8.2.

8.3.1. *The historic kernel*

The BCaml syntax analyzer is based on the use of the OCaml version of Lex and Yacc. Therefore, we created a grammar which is compatible with Yacc, and consequently LALR(1). This grammar was initially based on a

Backus-Naur Form (BNF) grammar provided by B-Core, described in the Atelier B reference manual, but with modifications to ensure LALR(1) compatibility. The only aspects from the reference manual to be retained for the current version were operator priorities and associations. The resulting B language grammar is free from shift/reduce and reduce/reduce conflicts.

This grammar is compatible with any B component described in accordance with the Atelier B reference manual. It constitutes an overset of the manual in its own right, as it takes into account constructions for which little documentation is available. An example of this is `f(x)(y) := E`, which is a little-used form of the construction `f(x) := E` whose interpretation can prove confusing. The proposed grammar also offers alternative notations for ambiguous operations in the grammar, such as >*< for Cartesian products and the backslash \ for set difference.

Finally, the full parser is able to take into account so-called definitions due to a preprocessing and expansion phase, carried out prior to the parsing process itself. Note that Menhir [POT 05] may be used instead of OCamlYacc without needing to change source files for the purposes of grammatical experimentation.

The typechecker is based on the type inference algorithm described succinctly in [BOD 02]. The tool is able to obtain type information and can distinguish between simple relationships, partial functions and total functions.

While this tool is an integral part of BCaml, it is shallowly integrated: its functions depend on modifications to the abstract syntax tree (AST) used by BCaml, hence the tool embeds a modified copy of the functions needed for manipulating the AST. Work is currently underway to develop:

– a tool based on the same algorithm, but with full integration into the current AST. While, in principle, this constitutes the fusion of two development branches, in practice, the absence of historical background in the checking branch means that this development may be considered as a redevelopment based on the published algorithm, with visual comparison in relation to the code in the verification branch;

– full documentation for the type inference algorithm in [BOD 02], which only provides a description for those predicates and expressions that are most relevant to the algorithm itself.

At the time of writing, the new version of the typechecker is compilable but remains incomplete. The algorithm documentation has been completed up to the B component level.

The *POG* is a direct implementation of the proof obligation generation method described in the B-Book [ABR 96]. It is based on a weakest pre-condition calculus, a translation library from B substitutions to generalized substitutions, and PO generation functions that follow the formulas described in the B-Book to the letter [ABR 96]. The generated files are predicates that respect the XML format defined for BCaml, and can therefore be translated *a priori* for any proof or model-checking tool able to operate using predicates and expressions as defined in the B language.

The *XML format* connects tools together, and all of the tools mentioned above generate XML files. The XML structure used for these files closely follows the abstract B syntax used in BCaml; however, work is currently underway to define XML schemas and/or Document Type definition (DTD)s for the standardization of the format.

8.3.2. *Code manipulation*

One of the key objectives of B is the generation of code to create executable files, and BCaml includes code manipulation functions for this purpose.

The *component unfolder* (bunfold) is an implementation of the unfolding algorithm developed by [BEH 00]. Unfolding brings together several levels of refinement of a component, even several components, to enable treatments which would not have been possible in their initial form. This operation is carried out by the B component unfolder as part of the code generation process.

BHLL is the next step in the code generation process. The tool, based on the work of [PET 03a], allows us to re-express a set of B components in a modular form, which is better suited for code generation. There is no "official" documentation covering the translation of a B model into any given programming language, nor for transforming the semantics of B modules to fit the modular character of the target language. BHLL is an experimental project which aims to tackle these issues.

Code generation is the final stage of code manipulation, situated just after the enrichment of the B component with typing information. This stage, together with the previous stages, produces a component described in the B implementation sublanguage, which is supposedly close to a programming language. The result is supplied in XML format. From these two observations, we see that code can be generated via the application of eXtensible Stylesheet Language (XSL) style sheets to XML files. Therefore, code generation in BCaml comes down to the description of rules for translating XML into the language chosen in XSL style sheets format. This way, components can be translated into Spark/Ada and into Eiffel, for instance.

8.3.3. *Proving B specifications*

It is currently possible to prove B specifications using the BiCoax tool included in BRILLANT. This implementation takes the form of a shallow embedding of the semantics of B expressions and predicates in Coq.

The initial objective of the tool was the mechanization of the different theorems presented in the B-Book with the aim of ensuring their consistency. This goal has been attained, as implementation highlighted certain errors which are now described in an ERRATA file supplied with BiCoax.

The other objective, which is also a consequence of this implementation, was to create a proof tool for B. This aim has been partially fulfilled, as the implementation covers all B constructions except for parts of the integer definitions and the sequence and tree aspects. BiCoax can, therefore, be used as an interactive proof tool for relatively simple B models which do not use these specific constructions, for example for teaching purposes. However, the tool is not designed for automatic use.

8.4. Perspectives

A certain number of developments are currently underway in relation to the tool platform:

– the XML Application Programming Interface (API) currently used by BCaml is no longer maintained, and produces incorrect results when using characters which are problematic for XML in B character strings. Therefore, we have begun to use Xmlm as an alternative, with the aim of completely replacing the current XML API in the long run;

– continuing to focus on the XML API, these modifications have led us to consider stabilization, and possibly even standardization, of the XML format used for BCaml.

Slightly further down the road, our aims focus on completing BCaml as a "classic" B development chain. We also wish to implement another POG approach that would follow the Atelier B reference manual rather than the B-Book; as the differences between the two are minor, the changes needed should cause relatively few disruptions. Along the same lines, we intend to add to the POG for ill-defined expressions [BUR 00].

Integration work is currently underway for a tool allowing generation of a B component based on an SysML specification with added goal models [LAL 10], with the aim of providing still better coverage of the production chain using the B method.

Longer term perspectives exist in relation to BiCoax:

– the tool requires additions in order to cover the end of the third chapter of the B-Book, i.e. the missing section on integers, sequences and trees. However, the section on trees may be limited to the congruous aspects, given that this part of the B language is very rarely used in practice;

– enrichment of BiCoax using proof tactics would offer interesting possibilities. Certain tactics offered by Coq are highly efficient in cases where the logic involved respects certain properties. When the operators form a ring structure, for example, as in the case of set structures, a generic tactic exists to allow equation-based reasoning. It would then be possible to compare the efficiency of Coq tactics with that of other proof tools for B.

In the same vein, POs could also be translated into different formats in order to exploit the capacities of *multiple* provers and/or *model-checkers*, as in [MEN 12].

Finally, future perspectives will depend on requirements and on those involved in developing tools, and we wish to encourage all interested parties to contribute to the platform, where they will receive a warm welcome from the existing community of passionate and enthusiastic developers.

In conclusion, we thank Georges Mariano for his remarks on this chapter. We also wish to thank all past, present and future contributors to the BRILLANT project for their efforts and enthusiastic contributions.

8.5. Bibliography

[ABR 96] ABRIAL J.-R., *The B Book – Assigning Programs to Meanings*, Cambridge University Press, August 1996.

[BEH 00] BEHNIA S., Test de modèles formels en B: cadre théorique et critères de couvertures, PhD Thesis, National Polytechnic Institute of Toulouse, October 2000.

[BOD 02] BODEVEIX J.-P., FILALI M., "Type synthesis in B and the translation of B to PVS", in BERT D., BOWEN J.P., HENSON M.C., *et al.*, (eds.), *ZB'2002 – Formal Specification and Development in Z and B*, of *Lecture Notes in Computer Science,* Springer-Verlag, vol. 2272, pp. 350–369, January 2002.

[BRI 14] BRILLANT. Available at gna.org/projects/brillant, 2014.

[BUR 00] BURDY L., Traitement des expressions dépourvues de sens de la théorie des ensembles: Application à la méthode B, PhD Thesis, CEDRIC-CNAM, 2000.

[COL 05] COLIN S., PETIT D., ROCHETEAU J., *et al.,* "BRILLANT : an open source and XML-based platform for rigourous software development", *Software Engineering and Formal Methods (SEFM)*, September 2005.

[COL 09] COLIN S., MARIANO G., "BiCoax, a proof tool traceable to the BBook", *From Research to Teaching Formal Methods – The B Method (TFM B'2009)*, June 2009.

[COL 10] COLIN S., PETIT D., MARIANO G., *et al.,* "BRILLANT: an open source platform for B", *Workshop on Tool Building in Formal Methods (held in conjunction with ABZ2010)*, February 2010.

[CON 00] CONSORTIUM WORLD WIDE WEB, Extensible markup language (XML) 1.0, 2nd ed. – W3C Recommendation, 2000. Available at www.w3.org/TR/2000/WD-xml-2e-20000814

[COQ 08] THE COQ DEVELOPMENT TEAM, The Coq proof assistant reference manual – Version V8.2, 2008. Available at coq.inria.fr/doc-eng.html

[LAL 00] LALEAU R., MAMMAR A., "A generic process to refine a B specification into a relational database implementation", YORK D.C.S. (ed.), *ZB'2000 – International Conference of B and Z Users*, Lecture Notes in Computer Science, Springer-Verlag, Helsington, York, United Kingdom, vol. 1878, pp. 22–41, August 2000.

[LAL 10] LALEAU R., SEMMAK F., MATOUSSI A., *et al.*, "A first attempt to combine SysML requirements diagrams and B", *ISSE NASA journal (Innovations in Systems and Software Engineering)*, Springer, vol. 6, nos. 1–2, pp. 47–54, March 2010.

[LER 11] LEROY X., DOLIGEZ D., FRISH A., *et al.*, The objective caml system, Report, Software and documentation, INRIA, 2011. Available at caml.inria.fr/

[MAR 02] MARCANO-KAMENOFF R., Spécification formelle à objets en UML/OCL et B: Une approche transformationnelle, PhD Thesis, University of Versailles – PRiSM, December 2002.

[MEN 12] MENTRÉ D., MARCHÉ C., FILLIÂTRE J.-C., *et al.*, "Discharging proof obligations from Atelier B using multiple automated provers", *ABZ Conference*, Pisa, Italy, June 2012.

[NGU 10] NGUYEN H.N., JACQUOT J.-P., "A tool for checking CSP||B specifications", *Workshop on Tool Building in Formal Methods - Held in conjunction with the 2nd International ABZ Conference*, Orford, Québec, Canada, 2010.

[PET 03a] PETIT D., Génération automatique de composants logiciels sûrs à partir de spécifications formelles B, PhD Thesis, University of Valenciennes and Hainaut-Cambrai, December 2003.

[PET 03b] PETIT D., MARIANO G., POIRRIEZ V., *et al.*, "Automatic annotated code generation from B formal specifications", in TARNAI G., SCHNIEDER E., (eds.), *Symposium on Formal Methods for Railway Operation and Control Systems*, IEEE, 2003.

[POT 05] POTTIER F., RÉGIS-GIANAS Y., Menhir, December 2005. Available at gallium.inria.fr/fpottier/menhir/.

[ROC 04] ROCHETEAU J., COLIN S., MARIANO G., *et al.*, "Évaluation de l'extensibilité de PhoX: B/PhoX un assistant de preuves pour B", in MÉNISSIER-MORAIN V. (ed.), *Journées Francophones des Langages Applicatifs (JFLA 2004)*, INRIA, pp. 37–54, 2004.

9

Translating B and Event-B Machines to Java and JML

9.1. Introduction

There are currently two dominant approaches for formally engineering software systems: those that use a refinement calculus methodology [MOR 90] and those that are based on the ideas of design-by-contract [MEY 92]. In the refinement calculus approaches (notably B [ABR 96] and Event-B [ABR 10a]) systems are first modeled in an abstract way. Next, the model is proven to satisfy certain safety and security properties, and then transformed to code via a series of property preserving refinement steps. The bulk of the development effort goes into discharging refinement proof obligations, thus ensuring that a model and its refinement are models of the same system. Often, code is automatically generated from a final concrete model [EDM 10, EDM 11, MER 11]. In design-by-contract approaches (notably JML [BUR 05, CHA 06] and Spec# [BAR 04]), contracts between software modules are specified in first-order logic, and tools that support the approach are used to verify that implementations satisfy those contracts. Implementations are hand-coded, and producing and verifying these implementations constitute most of the development effort.

Although the underlying goal of refinement calculus and design-by-contract approaches is similar – they both aim to produce formally verified implementations of mathematical specifications – the approaches are

Chapter written by Néstor CATAÑO, Víctor RIVERA, Camilo RUEDA and Tim WAHLS.

quite different, and in our view, largely complementary. Refinement calculus approaches provide excellent tool support for analyzing and verifying properties of abstract models, while design-by-contract approaches typically have little to offer in this regard. However, refining an abstract model to an implementation-level one is a laborious process that typically requires numerous refinement steps, each associated with many proof obligations. While refinement calculus approaches often incorporate tools for generating code from concrete models, the code generated by previous tools is typically simplistic – making unsophisticated use of the data structures built-in to the programming language and no use of structures provided by Application Programming Interfaces (APIs) or other libraries. Design-by-contract approaches are best used to specify the behavior of classes and methods, and often use notations based on a particular programming language – JML is based on Java, and Spec# is based on C#. JML provides specifications for many of the standard Java APIs, allowing a JML developer to make full use of the data structures (and other functionalities) provided by these APIs.

For example, consider producing an implementation from an Event-B model that uses mathematical functions. Previous Event-B code generation tools [EDM 10, EDM 11, MER 11] typically cannot directly generate implementations for such models, requiring the developer to refine any models that use functions into models that use arrays. These concrete models can then be translated to implementations that use arrays. Now, consider specifying the same system in JML and implementing it in Java. JML provides a complete specification of the Java library `HashMap` class that can naturally be used to implement finite functions, so a class that is specified in terms of mathematical functions can be implemented using `HashMaps`, and the implementation can be verified against the specification. This produces a cleaner and more efficient implementation, at the price of making the verification proof more difficult (as states specified via functions must be related to implementation states represented using `HashMaps`). A closely related option is to provide custom APIs (with full formal specifications) that directly implement mathematical objects such as sets, functions and relations that are often used in formal specifications for use in both specifications and implementations. This idea is implemented in JML via the class specifications and implementations in the `org.jmlspecs.models` package, and we have used it largely in the work described in the rest of this chapter.

More generally, we believe that refinement calculus based approaches are best used in the earliest stages of software development – when the system is first being modeled at an abstract level and when properties of the model are being verified. As development proceeds and models become more implementation-oriented, the ability to make effective use of features and APIs provided by the implementation language becomes increasingly important. The refinement calculus approach of producing models that are programming language neutral up until the final refinement (into programming language code) requires these concrete models to use only features that are common to all target languages (i.e. arrays). A refinement calculus model could be translated into a design-by-contract notation by hand, but this process would be tedious and error prone, and any mistake in the translation would invalidate the entire sequence of (otherwise) correctness preserving refinement steps. These observations are the motivations for the two tools described in this chapter: B2Jml [CAT 12], which translates B machines to JML specifications, and EventB2Java [RIV 14], which translates Event-B machines and associated contexts to JML annotated Java implementations. Automating these translations eliminates the tedium just mentioned, and reduces the likelihood of translation errors. Even better, such errors can be entirely eliminated by proving the soundness of an automated translation, as we have done for EventB2Java [CAT 13]. As a final motivation for our approach, we note that software developers with the mathematical sophistication needed for developing, verifying and refining refinement calculus models are likely to be in short supply. Transitioning to a design-by-contract approach such as JML (which requires less mathematical expertise to use) allows developers with less mathematical sophistication to make meaningful contributions much earlier in the development process.

Our software development methodology begins with an abstract model of the system, expressed in B or Event-B as dictated by the nature of the system and the preferences of the developers. The model is verified using standard B/Event-B tools [BUT 06, BOU 03, CLE 08], and transformed via a (likely to be short) sequence of refinement steps to the point where specific programming language data structures and APIs are of use. Next, the model is translated using B2Jml or EventB2Java as indicated by the initial choice of notations. If B2Jml is used, developers then implement the JML specification in Java and prove the correctness of the implementation with respect to the specification, with the likely use of a tool such as OpenJML [COK 11]. If

EventB2Java is used, developers have the choice of just using the generated Java implementation or providing a hand-coded implementation of the JML specification just as they would use with B2Jml. Developers may opt not to use the generated implementation for reasons such as efficiency, the desire to use APIs to supply particular aspects of the implementation, or data persistence (in other words, to store data in a database or file rather than in memory).

We initially developed our methodology while working on the B2Jml [CAT 12] tool. One particularly difficult issue with the translation is the complex ways in which B machines can be related via the INCLUDES, IMPORTS and SEES keywords, and in fact we do not yet have a satisfactory way to translate these relationships. This issue motivated us to consider translating Event-B as Event-B machines are related only via refinement – a particularly simple form of including one machine within another. More importantly, using Event-B allowed us to extend our methodology to the development of reactive systems, and to consider issues such as concurrency and atomicity. In particular, we have used EventB2Java to generate critical components of several Android applications [PER 12, RIV 12]. Our initial work in this area consisted of translating Event-B machines and associated contexts to JML specifications, thus mirroring our work on translating B machines. As we were performing this work, we realized that the generated specifications followed a simple pattern that was amenable to direct translation to Java implementations, with heavy reliance on customized JML-specified Java implementations of Event-B mathematical objects (sets, functions and relations). This observation led directly to the development of EventB2Java.

In the remainder of this chapter, we provide a brief introduction to B, Event-B and JML. Then we present the B2Jml and EventB2Java tools, including descriptions of the translation performed by each tool, some notes on the implementation of each tool, and a small case study in applying each tool. We conclude with some remarks on our experiences in applying our methodology and directions for future work.

9.2. Background

In this section, we give a broad view of the B and Event-B formal methods, and a brief introduction to JML. The expression "formal method" refers to a direct technique for constructing *dependable* systems. The system is dependable when there is evidence that its benefits outweigh its risks. A direct technique is one that focuses dependability on the system satisfying some *critical* properties, rather than on the functions or tasks it should perform. A formal method provides ways to integrate these properties into the system design and to mathematically prove system compliance with them.

9.2.1. *The B method*

The B method [ABR 96] is a formal methodology to specify, build and implement software systems. Each stage in this process is associated with *proofs* of compliance to designer supplied properties. The B method addresses all aspects of the software lifecycle: technical specification, system construction by successive refinements, layered architecture and code generation. The B method approach is model-oriented. This means that each stage in the B software development provides a model of the system at a certain level of abstraction. Each model in B, called a *machine*, defines a state-space of the system together with *operations* representing state transitions. Machines are essentially abstract data types with state. A B machine consists of variables, invariant properties constraining their values (i.e. the state-space) and operations. The model of a large system comprises several machines composed of various ways. It is constructed in a modular fashion by stepwise refinements. Refinement machines progressively define more details for a specification. B model specification is based on first-order logic, set theory, abstract machine theory and refinement theory.

Figure 9.1 shows an example of a B machine. It is a much simplified version of a social network (SN) model where a collection of people organize content items in their pages.

Variables $persons$ and $contents$ model the users and data, respectively, of the SN. Variable $owner$ tracks the ownership of each data item, and $pages$ represents content items stored in user pages. The invariant section gives types to these variables. The underlying logic is untyped and typing information for variables appears in the invariant as set membership predicates. The foundations are based on Zermelo set theory with an axiom of choice, an axiom of infinity and an axiomatic definition of the Cartesian product (see [ABR 96]).

MACHINE $snAbstr$
SETS
PERSON; CONTENTS;
VARIABLES
$persons, contents, owner, pages$
INVARIANTS
$persons \subseteq PERSON \wedge$
$contents \subseteq CONTENTS \wedge$
$owner \in contents \twoheadrightarrow persons \wedge$
$pages \in contents \leftrightarrow persons$
INITIALIZATION
$persons := \varnothing \;||$
$contents := \varnothing \;||$
$owner := \varnothing \;||$
$pages := \varnothing$

OPERATIONS
$create\_account(c1, p1) =$
PRE
$c1 \in \text{CONTENTS} \wedge$
$c1 \notin contents \wedge$
$p1 \in \text{PERSON} - persons$
THEN
$contents := contents \cup \{c1\} \;||$
$persons := persons \cup \{p1\} \;||$
$owner := owner \cup \{c1 \mapsto p1\} \;||$
$pages := pages \cup \{c1 \mapsto p1\}$
END

Figure 9.1. *A machine in the B language*

Variables $persons$ and $contents$, are typed as subsets of uninterpreted *carrier* sets. Variable $owner$ is a total surjection (denoted by $\twoheadrightarrow$) from contents to persons, thus establishing that each content item in the SN belongs to a single user and that each user must own at least one content item. Variable $pages$ is a relation (denoted by $\leftrightarrow$) giving, for each content item, those users who have it in their pages. The invariant can also include non-typing properties, expressed in set theory and predicate logic, such as the assertion that any owned content must also belong to the page of the owner.

Operations are defined as "generalized substitutions". A number of constructs mimic the usual assignment notation, such as $x := y + 1$ for x becomes equal to the current value of y plus one, or loose specifications such as $x :\in S$, for x becomes equal to some unspecified element of the set S. The semantics of the operations is given by the weakest pre-condition. Operation *create_account(c1,p1)* opens an account for user $p1$ with the initial content $c1$. This content item is added to the set of items $contents$ in the SN, and $p1$ is added to $persons$. Relations in B are sets of pairs, and a pair (a, b) is written as $a \mapsto b$. Thus, substitution $owner := owner \cup \{c1 \mapsto p1\}$ adds pair $(c1, p1)$ to the $owner$ relation.

Models in B must be proven correct. Correctness is defined by compliance with *proof obligations* that are generated from the model. For example, machines generate proof obligations to show that (1) the state after the initialization satisfies all invariants and (2) that the state transition computed by each operation maintains each invariant property. B method tools such as Atelier B [CLE 08] help the user discharge these proof obligations, either automatically or with some interaction.

9.2.2. *The Event-B method*

The B method was conceived for modeling software systems in isolation. For designing whole systems (software plus hardware devices), Abrial developed the Event-B method [ABR 10a]. Event-B combines B with *action systems* [BAC 91], a formalism describing the behavior of a system by the (atomic) actions that the system carries out. An action system describes the state-space of a system and the possible actions that can be executed in it. The purpose of the Event-B method is thus to extend B to an action system that can model in a single framework both the system and the way that it reacts to its environment.

As in B, the state-space of the system is defined by a collection of variables. Atomic actions, called *events*, are "triggered" as the system reacts to its environment. The effect of each action is a transition in the state-space. An Event-B model is comprised of a static and a dynamic part. The static part defines the context of the system (constants and uninterpreted sets and their properties) and the state-space (variables, their types and properties). The dynamic part defines all possible events, including the event computing the initial state. An event is comprised of a *guard* and an *action*. The guard represents conditions that must hold in a state for the event to trigger. The action computes new values for state variables, thus performing an observable state transition. If the system reaches a state where no event guard holds, it halts and is said to have *deadlocked*. There is no requirement that the system should halt, and indeed, most Event-B models represent systems that run forever. Additionally, the system may reach a state where the guards of more than one event hold. In this situation, the system is said to be *non-deterministic*: Event-B semantics allow any of the events whose guards are satisfied to be triggered.

Figure 9.2 presents a simplified Event-B model of the SN system described in section 9.2.1. The initialization (not shown) is as in Figure 9.1. Two events are shown: one that is triggered when any user uploads a new-content item (the *upload* event), and the other triggered when a content item is hidden from some user page (the *hide* event). The construct:

$$\text{ANY } x \text{ WHERE } G(x,v) \text{ THEN } v := A(x,v) \text{ END}$$

specifies a *non-deterministic* event which can be triggered in a state where the guard $G(x,v)$ holds for some value x. When the event is triggered, a value for x is non-deterministically chosen and the event action $v := A(x,v)$ is executed with x bound to that value. The correctness condition of the event requires that, for any x chosen, the new value(s) of the state variable(s) computed by the action of the event maintain the invariant properties of the machine. The semantics of events thus models a system that is controlled by interactions from the environment (i.e. user actions) that may occur at any time.

```
CONTEXT snctx
SETS
    PERSON
    CONTENTS
END

MACHINE snEvB SEES snctx
VARIABLES
    persons, contents, owner, pages
INVARIANTS
    persons ⊆ PERSON
    contents ⊆ CONTENTS
    owner ∈ contents ↠ persons
    pages ∈ contents ↔ persons

EVENTS
event upload
    ANY
        c1 p1
    WHERE
        c1 ∈ CONTENTS
        c1 ∉ contents
        p1 ∈ persons
    THEN
        contents := contents ∪ {c1}
        owner(c1) := p1
        pages := pages ∪ {c1 ↦ p1}
    END

event hide
    ANY
        c1 p1
    WHERE
        c1 ∈ contents
        p1 ∈ persons
        c1 ↦ p1 ∈ pages
        owner(c1) = p1
    THEN
        pages := pages \{c1 ↦ p1}
    END
```

Figure 9.2. *A simplified social networking machine in the Event-B language*

There are some minor syntactic differences between the B and Event-B languages. For example, in Event-B the "\" symbol is used for set difference.

The example in Figure 9.2 uses the Rodin [ABR 10b] tool notation, where predicates on different lines are implicitly conjoined and actions on different lines are executed simultaneously.

9.2.3. *JML*

JML is an interface specification language for Java – it is designed for specifying the behavior of Java classes, and is included directly in Java source files using special comment markers `//@` and `/*@ */`. JML's type system includes all built-in Java types and additional types representing mathematical sets, sequences, functions and relations, which are represented as JML specified Java classes in the `org.jmlspecs.models` package. Similarly, JML expressions are a superset of Java expressions, with the addition of notations such as `==>` for logical implication, `\exists` for existential quantification, and `\forall` for universal quantification.

JML class specifications can include invariants (assertions that must be satisfied in every visible state of the class), `initially` clauses (specifying conditions that the post-state of every class constructor must satisfy), and history constraints (which are similar to invariants, with the additional ability to relate pre- and post-states of a method). Concrete JML specifications can be written directly over the fields of the Java class, while more abstract ones can use specification-only `model` and `ghost` fields. Ghost fields are not related to the concrete state of the class and can be declared `final`, while model fields are related to implementation fields via a `represents` clause, which acts much like a gluing invariant in B refinement.

JML provides pre-post style specifications for Java methods, using keywords `requires` for pre-conditions, `ensures` for post-conditions, and `assignable` for frame conditions (a list of locations whose values can change from the pre-state to the post-state of a method). In an `ensures` clause, the keyword `\old` is used to indicate expressions that must be evaluated in the pre-state of the method – all other expressions are evaluated in the post-state. The `\old` keyword can also be used in history constraints, providing a convenient way to specify (for example) that the post-state value of a field is always equal to the pre-state value, thus making the field a constant.

Figure 9.3 presents a simple example of a JML specified Java abstract class. This class defines bounded mathematical relations over the integers, each represented by a `JMLEqualsSet` of pairs. Note that this specification is for purposes of example only – the built-in class `JMLEqualsEqualsRelation` contains a much more complete implementation (and JML specification) of mathematical relations. The history constraint (keyword `constraint`) specifies that the post-state value of the relation for each method always contains the pre-state value, thus preventing any pair from being removed from the relation. The invariant specifies that the maximum size of any relation is 10 pairs, and the `initially` clause specifies that a newly created `BoundedRelation` is always the empty set.

The specification of the add method uses two specification cases: the first specifying that a pair is added to the relation if it is not at capacity, and the second specifying that attempting to add to a `BoundedRelation` that is already at capacity has no effect. An assignable clause of `\nothing` prevents any location from being modified from the pre- to the post-state. The specification of the `apply` method demonstrates the syntax of existentially quantified assertions in JML, and the use of `exceptional_behavior` specification cases to specify when exceptions are to be thrown – in this case, when the user attempts to apply a key that does not occur in the relation. Note that if the same key maps to multiple values in a relation, the specification of the `apply` method allows it to return any of those values.

9.3. Translating B to JML

The descriptions of B2Jml in this section (of both the translation that it performs and of the tool itself) are adapted from [CAT 12].

9.3.1. *The translation*

We present the translation from B to JML using the B2Jml operator, which takes B syntax as input and returns corresponding JML syntax. We define B2Jml inductively via rewriting rules. Then we describe (in section 9.3.2) the B2Jml tool that implements these translation rules.

```
//@ model import org.jmlspecs.models.JMLEqualsSet;
//@ model import org.jmlspecs.models.JMLEqualsEqualsPair;

public abstract class BoundedRelation {
  //@ public model JMLEqualsSet<
       JMLEqualsEqualsPair<Integer, Integer>> elems;
  public static int MAXSIZE = 10;

  //@ public constraint \old(elems).isSubset(elems);
  //@ public invariant elems.int_size() <= MAXSIZE;
  //@ public initially elems.isEmpty();

  /*@ public normal_behavior
     requires elems.int_size() < MAXSIZE;
     assignable elems;
     ensures elems.equals(\old(elems).insert(
       new JMLEqualsEqualsPair(key, value)));
  also requires elems.int_size() == MAXSIZE;
     assignable \nothing;
     ensures true; */
  public abstract void add(Integer key, Integer value);

  /*@ public normal_behavior
     requires (\exists JMLEqualsEqualsPair<Integer,
       Integer> p; elems.has(p); p.key.equals(key));
     assignable \nothing;
     ensures (\exists JMLEqualsEqualsPair<Integer,
       Integer> p; elems.has(p); p.key.equals(key) &&
                  \result.equals(p.value));
  also public exceptional_behavior
     requires !(\exists JMLEqualsEqualsPair<Integer,
       Integer> p; elems.has(p); p.key.equals(key));
     assignable \nothing;
     signals (IllegalArgumentException) true; */
  public abstract Integer apply(Integer key);
}
```

Figure 9.3. *A JML specification of an abstract class representing bounded relations*

9.3.1.1. *Translating machines to classes*

An entire B machine is translated to a JML-annotated Java abstract class via rule M for B2Jml below. For simplicity, rule M considers machines with a single-carrier set, constant, property, variable, assertion and non-initialization operation – extending the rule to handle 0 or many of each of these components is straightforward, but requires minor additional mechanics. Rule M makes heavy use of other rules for B2Jml, many of which are presented subsequently.

B2Jml(SETS s) = S B2Jml(INVARIANT I) = I
B2Jml(CONSTANTS c) = C B2Jml(ASSERTIONS A) = A
B2Jml(PROPERTIES P) = P B2Jml(INITIALISATION B) = B
B2Jml(VARIABLES v) = V B2Jml(OPERATIONS $op = Q$) = Q

――――――――――――――――――――――――――――――――――――――― (M)

B2Jml(MACHINE M
SETS s
CONSTANTS c
PROPERTIES P
VARIABLES v
INVARIANT I
ASSERTIONS A
INITIALISATION B
OPERATIONS $op = Q$
END) =

```
publicabstractclass M {
  S C V P I A B

  Q
}
```

As we have no information about the elements of carrier sets, they are translated as final sets of integers. We use a JML `ghost` variable, because JML `model` variables are not allowed to be `final`.

――――――――――――――――――――――――――――――――――――――― (Set)

B2Jml(SETS s)
=

```
/*@ publicfinal ghost
  JMLEqualsSet<Integer> s; */
```

Constants are similarly translated as `final ghost` variables. We use the TypeOf operator to translate an inferred B type to the corresponding JML type.

Some of the rules defining TypeOf are presented at the end of this section.

$$\frac{\mathsf{TypeOf}(c) = \texttt{Type}}{\mathsf{B2Jml}(\mathsf{CONSTANTS}\ c)}\ (\mathsf{Cons})$$

$$=$$

```
//@ public static final ghost Type c;
```

Machine variables are translated to JML `model` variables, again with the assistance of TypeOf.

$$\frac{\mathsf{TypeOf}(v) = \texttt{Type}}{\mathsf{B2Jml}(\mathsf{VARIABLES}\ v)}\ (\mathsf{Var})$$

$$=$$

```
//@ public model Type v;
```

Rule Inv translates B invariants to JML invariants, as both act as constraints on states of the system being specified. Similarly, the rule for translating B PROPERTIES clauses (not shown) produces a static JML invariant constraining the values of `ghost` variables translated from constants. As both B ASSERTIONS and JML redundant invariants are implied by ordinary invariants, the rule for translating ASSERTIONS (not shown) produces a JML `invariant_redundantly` clause. The Pred operator translates a B expression to an equivalent JML expression. Several of the rules defining Pred are presented at the end of this section.

$$\frac{\mathsf{Pred}(I) = \mathsf{I}}{\mathsf{B2Jml}(\mathsf{INVARIANT}\ I) = \texttt{//@ public invariant}\ \mathsf{I};}\ (\mathsf{Inv})$$

A B INITIALIZATION clause is translated to a JML `initially` clause. JML `initially` clauses are implicitly conjoined with the post-condition of each class constructor, ensuring that any instance of a class resulting from the translation performed by B2Jml is initialized in a manner consistent with the machine initialization.

$$\frac{\mathsf{Pred}(E) = \mathsf{E}}{\mathsf{B2Jml}(\mathsf{INITIALISATION}\ v := E) =}\ (\mathsf{Init})$$

```
//@ initially v.equals(E);
```

9.3.1.2. *Translating operations to methods*

As shown in rule OP-PRE, a B operation defined using a PRE substitution is translated to a Java method with a heavyweight JML specification. The specification has two cases: (1) a `normal_behavior` case that specifies the behavior of the method when the pre-condition of the B operation is satisfied, and (2) an `exceptional_behavior` case that forces the method to signal an exception when the B operation would abort. The effective pre-condition of a JML method with multiple specification cases is the disjunction of the pre-conditions of each specification case, so method specifications generated by this translation rule have an effective pre-condition of true. Rules defining the Mod operator (which collects the set of variables updated by a substitution) are defined at the end of this section[1].

$$\frac{\mathsf{Pred}(P) = \mathtt{P} \quad \mathsf{Mod}(S) = \mathtt{A} \quad \mathsf{B2Jml}(S) = \mathtt{S}}{\mathsf{B2Jml}(\mathsf{OPERATIONS}\ op = \mathsf{PRE}\ P\ \mathsf{THEN}\ S\ \mathsf{END})}\ (\text{OP-Pre})$$

$$=$$

```
/*@ public normal_behavior
      requires P; assignable A;
      ensures S;
    also public exceptional_behavior
      requires !P; assignable \nothing;
      signals(Exception) true; @*/
    publicabstractvoid op();
```

Translating a B operation defined using a substitution other than PRE is simpler, as only one JML specification case is required.

$$\frac{\mathsf{B2Jml}(Q) = \mathtt{Q} \quad \mathsf{Mod}(Q) = \mathtt{A}}{\mathsf{B2Jml}(\mathsf{OPERATIONS}\ op = \ Q)}\ (\text{OP-NP})$$

$$=$$

```
/*@ public normal_behavior
      requires true; assignable A;
      ensures Q;@*/
    publicabstractvoid op();
```

1 The Mod operator is based on a similar operator defined within the Chase tool [CAT 03].

We have also defined rules (not shown) for B operations with input parameters, and for B operations with single and multiple output parameters. These rules use the TypeOf operator to translate B types to JML types. In the case of a B operation with multiple output parameters, the return type of the resulting Java method is `Object []`.

Rules OP-Pre and OP-NP use the B2Jml operator to translate B substitutions nested within operations. We present definitions of several of these translation rules below.

Rule Sel translates a guarded substitution to a JML implication (==>). Rule When generalizes Sel to consider two guards.

$$\frac{\mathsf{Pred}(P) = \mathtt{P} \quad \mathsf{B2Jml}(S) = \mathtt{S}}{\mathsf{B2Jml}(\mathsf{SELECT}\ P\ \mathsf{THEN}\ S\ \mathsf{END}) = \atop \mathtt{\backslash old(P)\ ==>\ S}}\ (\mathsf{Sel})$$

$$\frac{\mathsf{Pred}(P) = \mathtt{P} \quad \mathsf{B2Jml}(S) = \mathtt{S} \atop \mathsf{Pred}(Q) = \mathtt{Q} \quad \mathsf{B2Jml}(T) = \mathtt{T}}{\mathsf{B2Jml}(\mathsf{SELECT}\ P\ \mathsf{THEN}\ S\ \mathsf{WHEN}\ Q\ \mathsf{THEN}\ T\ \mathsf{END}) = \atop \mathtt{(\backslash old(P)\ ==>\ S)\ \&\&\ (\backslash old(Q)\ ==>\ T)}}\ (\mathsf{When})$$

Rule Choice translates bounded choice substitutions, whose meaning is the meaning of any of the nested substitutions.

$$\frac{\mathsf{B2Jml}(S) = \mathtt{S} \quad \mathsf{B2Jml}(T) = \mathtt{T}}{\mathsf{B2Jml}(\mathsf{CHOICE}\ S\ \mathsf{OR}\ T\ \mathsf{END}) = \mathtt{S}\ ||\ \mathtt{T}}\ (\mathsf{Choice})$$

An ANY substitution is used to bind a variable x to any value that satisfies a predicate P. If no value of x satisfies P, the substitution is equivalent to SKIP. This semantics is realized in the JML translation by rule Any.

$$\frac{\mathsf{Pred}(P) = \mathtt{P} \quad \mathsf{B2Jml}(S) = \mathtt{S} \quad \mathsf{TypeOf}(x) = \mathtt{Type}}{\mathsf{B2Jml}(\mathsf{ANY}\ x\ \mathsf{WHERE}\ P\ \mathsf{THEN}\ S\ \mathsf{END}) = \atop \mathtt{(\backslash exists\ Type\ x;\ \backslash old(P)\ \&\&\ S)\ ||\ (\backslash forall\ Type\ x;\ !\backslash old(P))}}\ (\mathsf{Any})$$

Simple assignments are translated via rule Asg below. If variable v is of a primitive (numeric or boolean type), == would be used rather than the `equals` method.

$$\frac{\mathsf{Pred}(E) = \mathtt{E}}{\mathsf{B2Jml}(v := E) = \mathtt{v.equals(\backslash old(E))}} \text{ (Asg)}$$

Simultaneous substitutions are translated as the conjunction of the translation of the contained substitutions (rule Sim). Note that rules Sim and Asg together correctly translate $x := y \mid\mid y := x$ to `x.equals(\old(y)) && y.equals(\old(x))`.

$$\frac{\mathsf{B2Jml}(S) = \mathtt{S} \quad \mathsf{B2Jml}(SS) = \mathtt{SS}}{\mathsf{B2Jml}(S \mid\mid SS) = \mathtt{S\ \&\&\ SS}} \text{ (Sim)}$$

The language used in B expressions is essentially predicate logic and set theory. In our translation, we represent sets, binary relations and binary functions by the JML library model classes `JMLEqualsSet`, `JML-Equals-To-Equals-Relation`, and `JML-Equals-To-Equals-Map`, respectively. These classes test membership using the `equals` method of the class that the elements belong to, rather than the Java == operator. B expressions are translated to JML by means of the Pred operator. We present several examples of rules defining the Pred operator below, where s_i's are sets and r is a relation.

$$\frac{\mathsf{Pred}(s_1) = \mathtt{s1} \quad \mathsf{Pred}(s_2) = \mathtt{s2}}{\mathsf{Pred}(s_1 \subseteq s_2) = \mathtt{s1.isSubset(s2)}} \text{ (Subset)}$$

$$\frac{\mathsf{Pred}(x) = \mathtt{x} \quad \mathsf{Pred}(s) = \mathtt{s}}{\mathsf{Pred}(x : s) = \mathtt{s.has(x)}} \text{ (Has)}$$

$$\frac{\mathsf{Pred}(r) = \mathtt{r} \quad \mathsf{Pred}(s) = \mathtt{s}}{\mathsf{Pred}(r[s]) = \mathtt{r.image(s)}} \text{ (Apply)}$$

TypeOf maps a B set type to the JML model class `JML-Equals-Set`, a relation type to `JML-Equals-To-Equals-Relation`, and a function type to `JML-Equals-To-Equals-Map`. As the types of B variables are specified implicitly (by stating membership in some possibly deferred set), the type must be inferred from its usage within the machine. This type of inference was already implemented in ABTools (the framework within which our translation tool is implemented), so in the implementation we simply translate from the representation of B types used by ABTools to the corresponding JML types. We use library code to capture additional properties of B types. For instance, given the B expression:

$$d \in \mathcal{P}(\mathsf{NAT}) \ \wedge \ r \in \mathcal{P}(\mathsf{NAT}) \ \wedge \ f \in d \rightarrow r$$

which states that f is a total function from d to r, the type of f is translated as `JMLEqualsToEqualsMap<Integer, Integer>` and the following is generated as part of the class invariant:

```
(new Total<Integer, Integer>(d, r)).has(f)
```

Library class `org.jmlspecs.b2jml.util.Total` represents the set of all total functions from the specified domain to the specified range, so the `has` method returns true if and only if `f` is a total function from `d` to `r`.

The Mod operator collects the set of variables assigned by a substitution. Mod was used in rules OP-Pre and OP-NP to construct the `assignable` clause, which specifies the frame condition – which locations can change from the pre-state to the post-state of a method. The most interesting rule for Mod is for assignment substitutions as shown in rule ModAsg below.

$$\frac{}{\mathsf{Mod}(v := E) = \{\mathtt{v}\}} \ (\mathsf{ModAsg})$$

Variables introduced by a B VAR substitution are local to the substitution and should not appear in an `assignable` clause.

$$\frac{\mathsf{Mod}(S) = \mathtt{A}}{\mathsf{Mod}(\mathsf{VAR}\ x\ \mathsf{IN}\ S\ \mathsf{END}) = \mathtt{A\ -\ \{x\}}} \ (\mathsf{ModVar})$$

The rules for Mod for other B substitutions simply collect the variables that are assigned within those substitutions, and so are not presented here.

9.3.2. *The B2Jml tool*

We have implemented the translation described in section 9.3.1 as the B2Jml tool. More precisely, B2Jml is implemented as a processing option within the ABTools [BOU 03] suite. Additional options within ABTools can be used to generate refinement proof obligations from B machines, and to translate B machines to ASCII, LaTeX, HTML and XML formats. ABTools also includes some preliminary support for generating C and Java implementations from implementation machines. ABTools uses the ANTLR [PAR 07] parser generator, and all processing options (including B2Jml) are implemented as ANTLR tree walkers. Full source code for ABTools and B2Jml is available at [BOU 13], and more information and installation instructions for B2Jml can be found at: http://poporo.uma.pt/favas/B2JML.html.

The B2Jml, Pred and Mod operators are realized as a single ANTLR tree walker. As this walker traverses the abstract syntax tree that ABTools has constructed for a B model, it generates the appropriate JML syntax for the type of node being visited, and collects the variables modified by each B operation as a side effect. Utility classes implement the B operators on functions, relations and sequences that do not directly correspond to methods of the JML model classes, as well as providing support for B typing via classes such as `org.-jmlspecs.-b2jml.-util.-Total` as previously described.

9.3.3. *Case study: translating the B social networking model to JML*

We have validated the B2Jml tool by using it to translate the social networking model that was briefly described in section 9.2. This model consists of an abstract machine that defines the social networking core and five refinements that add features such as edit and view permissions, a notion of principal content items for users and a wall for users to post comments on. This model was not written with translation by B2Jml in mind, and makes use of a wide range of B substitutions and operations on sets and relations. The refinement machines do not become closer to an implementation machine as they might in a typical B development – rather, each adds new features and functionality.

As an example of the kind of events that are included in this model, Figure 9.4 presents the *create_account* and *comment_wall* events from the fourth refinement machine. In this machine, variable *wallcontents* is the set of content items that appear on walls, *wall* is a relation from *wallcontents* to *persons* that determines which contents can be seen by which people, *wallaccess* is a relation from *persons* to *persons* determining who has rights to see someone else's wall, and *wallowner* is a function from *wallcontents* to *persons* that determines the owner of each content item. The *create_account* event is a refinement of the corresponding event from the most abstract machine (presented in Figure 9.1) that sets the new machine variables added in intervening refinements appropriately. The *comment_wall* event allows a person *ow* to post a comment *cmt* to someone's wall if they have access to that wall.

$create\_account(c1, p1) =$
PRE
$\quad c1 \notin wallcontents$
THEN
$\quad contents := contents \cup \{c1\} \parallel$
$\quad persons := persons \cup \{p1\} \parallel$
$\quad owner := owner \cup \{c1 \mapsto p1\} \parallel$
$\quad pages := pages \cup \{c1 \mapsto p1\} \parallel$
$\quad viewp := viewp \cup \{c1 \mapsto p1\} \parallel$
$\quad editp := editp \cup \{c1 \mapsto p1\} \parallel$
$\quad principal := principal \cup \{c1\} \parallel$
$\quad required := required \cup \{c1\} \parallel$
$\quad wallaccess :=$
$\qquad wallaccess \cup \{p1 \mapsto p1\}$
END

$comment\_wall(ow, cmt) =$
SELECT
$\quad ow : dom(wallaccess) \wedge$
$\quad cmt \notin (contents \cup wallcontents)$
THEN
$\quad wallcontents :=$
$\qquad wallcontents \cup \{cmt\} \parallel$
$\quad wall := wall \cup$
$\qquad (\{cmt\} * wallaccess[\{ow\}]) \parallel$
$\quad wallowner :=$
$\qquad wallowner \cup \{cmt \mapsto ow\}$
END

Figure 9.4. *The create_account and comment_wall events from the fourth refinement machine*

Figure 9.5 contains the JML translation resulting from running the B2Jml tool on the *comment_wall* event from Figure 9.4. As specified by the translation rules in section 9.3, the SELECT substitution is translated as an implication, and the simultaneous assignments are translated as a conjunction of calls to `equals` methods specifying the post-state values of class fields (that were translated from machine variables). `ModelUtils` is a library class that contains static helper methods such as `toSet` (which converts a relation or map to a set of pairs) and `maplet` (which creates a pair from two values).

```
/*@public normal_behavior
   requires true;
   assignable wallcontents, wall, wallowner;
   ensures (\old(wallaccess.domain().has(ow) &&
       !contents.union(wallcontents).has(cmt)) ==>
        (wallcontents.equals(\old(wallcontents.union(
          ModelUtils.toSet(cmt))) &&
         wall.equals(\old(wall.union(
          ModelUtils.cartesian(ModelUtils.toSet(cmt),
          wallaccess.image(ModelUtils.toSet(ow))))) &&
         wallowner.equals(\old(wallowner.union(
          ModelUtils.toRel(ModelUtils.maplet(cmt,ow))))))
        ); */
public abstract void comment_wall(Integer ow, Integer cmt);
```

Figure 9.5. *The JML translation of the comment_wall event from Figure 9.4 as produced by the B2Jml tool*

As a further validation step, we syntax and type-checked the JML translations of all six B models using OpenJml [COK 11]. This process uncovered a few errors in B2Jml, largely related to the type inference performed by ABTools. After correcting these errors, we translated the JML translation of the fourth refinement machine to a constraint program using the jmle tool [KRA 06, CAT 09]. jmle translates JML specifications to Java classes in which the functionality of each method is implemented by a constraint program generated from that method's specification. These constraint programs are executed using the Java constraint kit (JCK) [ABD 02], so all parts of the system are implemented in Java. Thus, the class generated by jmle is a pure Java implementation of the JML specification (which is in turn a model of the B machine in this case), although significantly larger and slower than a hand-coded implementation.

Our next step was to implement JUnit test cases for the translation of the fourth refinement machine. We initially tried using the fifth (last) refinement, but that model contains a constant definition that jmle cannot execute. The test cases for each method were used to check that the behavior of the Java translation matches that of the original B event, confirming (albeit in a somewhat indirect manner) that the translation performed by B2Jml is correct for the given inputs. An example of a test case for the `comment_wall` method (as translated from the corresponding event) is presented in Figure 9.6. Because the translation of a B machine is an abstract Java class, we also needed to implement a simple implementation class that inherits from that class and overrides all of the abstract methods. These overriding methods provide no additional functionality – they are needed only for correct compilation, and in fact they have no specifications and their bodies are empty. The `testNet` variable in Figure 9.6 is an instance of this class. We did add simple accessor methods for the fields of the class so that the test cases could check the correctness of the states resulting from executing the translated methods. The `create_account` method called here is translated from the corresponding B event in Figure 9.4 and is used to create a state that satisfies the guard of the *comment_wall* event.

```
@Test
public void testCommentWall() {
    testNet.create_account(0, 3);
    testNet.comment_wall(3, 1);
    Assert.assertTrue(testNet.getWallContents().has(1));
    Assert.assertTrue(testNet.getWall().has(1,3));
    Assert.assertTrue(testNet.getWallOwner().has(1,3));
}
```

Figure 9.6. *A sample JUnit test case for the translation of the comment_wall event*

Using jmle to execute the JML specifications generated by B2Jml revealed some additional errors in the implementation of B2Jml. Most notably, the parameters to the B; (relational composition) operator were being passed to the `compose` method of class `JMLEqualsToEqualsRelation` (used as the type of B relations in the translation) in reverse order. More significantly, using B2Jml and jmle together in this manner revealed several areas in which the B model was incomplete. For example, one case in the translation of the delete event could not be tested, because no combination of uses of other events in the model could create a state that satisfied the guard of the SELECT substitution in that event. This incompleteness can easily be remedied by adding an appropriate event to the B model. The test cases written for the classes generated by B2Jml and jmle can be applied to a hand-coded implementation of the B model directly, providing an easy check of the correctness of such a model. More generally, using B2Jml and jmle together provides a quick method for generating a prototype from a B model written at a high level of abstraction, which is useful in the development of the model itself and of code that will interact with the final implementation of the model.

$$\frac{\begin{array}{l}\text{EB2Prog(sets } s) = \mathtt{S}\\ \text{EB2Prog(constants } c) = \mathtt{C}\\ \text{EB2Jml(axioms } X(s,c)) = \mathtt{X}\\ \text{EB2Jml(theorems } T(s,c)) = \mathtt{T}\\ \text{EB2Java(variables } v) = \mathtt{V}\\ \text{EB2Jml(invariants } I(s,c,v)) = \mathtt{I}\\ \text{EB2Prog(events } e) = \mathtt{E}\\ \text{EB2Jml(event } initialisation \text{ then } A(s,c,v) \text{ end)} = \mathtt{I1}\\ \text{EB2Java(event } initialisation \text{ then } A(s,c,v) \text{ end)} = \mathtt{I2}\end{array}}{\begin{array}{l}\text{EB2Prog(machine } M \text{ sees } C\\ \quad\quad \text{variables } v\\ \quad\quad \text{invariants } I(s,c,v)\\ \quad\quad \text{event } initialisation \text{ then } A(s,c,v) \text{ end}\\ \quad\quad \text{events } e\\ \quad\quad \text{end)} =\end{array}} \text{(M)}$$

```
E
publicclass M{
  X T I

  S C V

  /*@ requirestrue;
      assignable \everything;
      ensures I1;*/
  public M(){
    I2
    //Javacodethatcreatesspawnsallevents
  }
}
```

Figure 9.7. *The translation of machine M, and the context C that M* sees

9.4. Translating Event-B to JML and Java

The translation from Event-B to JML-annotated Java programs presented in this section and the description of the EventB2Java tool are based on the work introduced in [RIV 14]. The translation (presented in section 9.4.1) uses a collection of translation operators (primarily EB2Prog) that are defined via syntactic rules as in section 9.3. The EventB2Java tool[2] (presented in section 9.4.2) implements the EB2Prog rules. When using this tool, we can opt to discharge all proof oblitations of the Event-B model (e.g. in Rodin) before translating it, or translate the Event-B model with undischarged proof obligations for developmental or experimental purposes. We assume that all proof obligations are discharged before generation of specifications and code that are intended for "production" use, and so do not consider Event-B constructs such as witnesses or variants that are useful only for verification purposes in the translation.[3]

9.4.1. *The translation*

The translation is realized through syntactic rules, and implemented with the aid of an EB2Prog operator that translates an Event-B machine and any context that it sees to a JML-specified Java class implementation. EB2Prog relies on the operators EB2Java and EB2Jml to generate Java code and JML specifications, respectively. For example, EB2Java translates machine variables as Java class attributes, and EB2Jml translates Event-B machine invariants as JML class invariants. In turn, these two operators rely on helper operators TypeOf, Mod and Pred, which are analogous to the operators of the same names introduced in section 9.3. Several rules make use of classes `BSet` and `BRelation`, which implement sets and relations in Java. More detail on these classes is presented in section 9.4.2.2.

Figure 9.7 presents Rule M, which translates a machine M that sees context C (not shown). An Event-B machine is translated as a JML-specified Java class, and the translation of the machine incorporates the translation of each context that the machine sees. Therefore, the Java class includes the translation of carrier sets, constants, axioms and theorems (declared in the contexts), and variables and invariants (declared in the machine). In Event-B, all components of a refined machine are included in a refinement machine, either explicitly (variables, initializations, guards and actions of a refining event defined using refines) or implicitly (invariants, guards and actions of a refining event defined using extends). Hence, a refinement machine can be

2 Available at http://poporo.uma.pt/Projects/favas/EventB2Java.html

3 A witness contains the value of a disappearing abstract event variable, and a variant is an expression that should be decreased by all convergent events.

translated in exactly the same manner as an abstract machine, as long as all included components from refined machines are included and translated.

The distinguished machine *initialization* event is translated as the constructor of the class obtained via translation of the machine. The constructor includes a JML post-condition that specifies the initial values of the class attributes. As shown in Rule Any below, each non-*initialization* event is translated as a Java class that extends class `Thread`. As each of these classes needs access to the translations of the machine variables, they each have a reference to the same instance of class `M` (see object reference `m` in rule Any below).

In Event-B, an event can only execute when its guard is satisfied, and events execute atomically – which is, only one event can be executing at any point in time. To facilitate modeling this behavior, the subclass of `Thread` that is generated for each event *evt* includes three methods: a `guard_-evt` method that tests if the guard of the event *evt* holds, a `run_-evt` method that models the execution of *evt*, and a `run()` method that implements Lamport's Bakery algorithm for the critical section [LAM 74]. For efficiency (and to better match the semantics of Event-B), we allow multiple `guard_-evt` methods (for different events) to execute concurrently. The actions of an event are only executed if its guard is satisfied and no other event is executing, and so those actions may not be executed even when the corresponding `guard_-evt` method has been called and returns `true`.

In rule Any, expression `GuardValue<Type>.-next()` returns a value of type `Type` that satisfies the guard event. Variables bounded by an any construct are translated as parameters of the `run_-evt` and `guard_-evt` methods. As described in section 9.3, the helper operator Mod calculates the set of variables assigned by the actions of the event, which are then listed in the `assignable` clause of the JML specification. Operator Pred translates an Event-B predicate or expression to its JML counterpart. The JML specification of `run_evt` uses two specification cases. In the first case, the translation of the guard is satisfied and the post-state of the method must satisfy the translation of the actions. In the second case, the translation of the guard is not satisfied, and the method is not allowed to modify any fields, ensuring that the post-state is the same as the pre-state. This matches the semantics of Event-B: if the guard of an event is not satisfied, the event cannot execute and hence cannot modify the system state. Since the effective pre-condition of a JML method with multiple specification cases (separated by `also` in JML) is the disjunction of the pre-conditions of each case, the pre-condition of a `run_evt` method is always `true`. Hence, even though we translate guards as pre-conditions, no method in the translation result has a pre-condition. Rather, the translation of the guard determines which behavior the method must exhibit.

$$\frac{\begin{array}{ll}\mathsf{EB2Jml}(A(s,c,v,x)) = \mathtt{A} & \mathsf{EB2Java}(A(s,c,v,x)) = \mathtt{B} \\ \mathsf{TypeOf}(x) = \mathtt{Type} & \mathsf{Pred}(G(s,c,v,x)) = \mathtt{G} \\ \mathsf{Mod}(A(s,c,v,x)) = \mathtt{D} & \end{array}}{\begin{array}{c}\mathsf{EB2Prog}(\mathsf{event}\ evt\ \mathsf{any}\ x\ \mathsf{where}\ G(s,c,v,x) \\ \mathsf{then}\ A(s,c,v,x)\ \mathsf{end}) =\end{array}}\ (\mathsf{Any})$$

```
publicclass evt extends Thread{
  /*@spec_public*/ private Mm;   privateint eventId;

  /*@ requirestrue;   assignable \everything;
      ensures this.m==m && this.eventId==i;*/
  public evt(Mm, int i){ this.m=m;   this.event=i; }

  /*@ requirestrue;   assignable \nothing;
      ensures \result<==>G;*/
  privateboolean guard_evt(Typex){ returnG; }

  /*@ requires guard_evt(x);
      assignable D;
      ensures A;
        also
      requires !guard_evt(x);
      assignable \nothing;
      ensures true;*/
  private void run_evt(Typex){ if (guard_evt(x)){B} }

  publicvoid run(){
    while(true){
      ...
      Typex=GuardValue<Type>.next();
      if (guard_evt(x)){
        m.util.lock(event);
        run_evt(x);
        m.util.unlock(event);
      }
      ...
    }
  }

}
```

In Event-B, every event must maintain the machine invariant. In JML, invariants state properties that must hold in every visible system state, specifically after the execution of the class constructor and after a method is invoked. This is semantically equivalent to conjoining the invariant to the post-condition of each method and the constructor. Since the $initialisation$ event translates to the post-condition of the class constructor, and the actions of every other type of event translate to the post-condition of an *atomic* `run_evt` method, we translate Event-B invariants as JML invariants.

$$\frac{\text{Pred}(I(s,c,v)) = \texttt{I}}{\begin{array}{l}\text{EB2Jml(invariants } I(s,c,v)) = \\ \texttt{//@ publicinvariant I;}\end{array}}\ (\text{Inv})$$

As axioms are often used to specify properties of constants, they are translated as `invariants`. In Event-B, theorems should be provable from axioms, matching the semantics of the `invariant_redundantly` clause in JML.

$$\frac{\text{Pred}(X(s,c)) = \texttt{X}}{\begin{array}{l}\text{EB2Jml(axioms } X(s,c)) = \\ \texttt{//@ publicinvariant X;}\end{array}}\ (\text{Axiom})$$

$$\frac{\text{Pred}(T(s,c)) = \texttt{T}}{\begin{array}{l}\text{EB2Jml(theorems } T(s,c)) = \\ \texttt{//@ publicinvariant\_redundantly T;}\end{array}}\ (\text{Thm})$$

Carrier sets are translated as class attributes with the addition of a JML history `constraint` that prevents any change in their values. As no information about the type of the carrier sets is available, they are simply translated as sets of integers.

$$\frac{\text{EB2Jml(sets } s) = \texttt{SS} \quad \text{EB2Java(sets } s) = \texttt{SC}}{\begin{array}{l}\text{EB2Prog(sets } s) = \\ \texttt{SS} \\ \texttt{SC}\end{array}}\ (\text{Set})$$

$$\overline{\qquad\qquad\qquad\qquad\qquad\qquad\qquad\qquad}\ (\text{Set})$$

EB2Java(sets s) =
```
publicstaticfinal BSet<Integer>s=
  new BSet<Integer>(new Range(
    Integer.MIN_VALUE,Integer.MAX_VALUE));
```

$$\overline{\qquad\qquad\qquad\qquad\qquad\qquad\qquad\qquad}\ (\text{Set})$$

EB2Jml(sets s) =
```
//@ publicconstraint s.equals(\old(s));
```

Translation of constants follows the same pattern, except that the values of constants are constrained by axioms. In particular, we omit the rule for EB2Prog that translates constants, as it simply calls EB2Jml and EB2Java and combines the results as above. The helper operator TypeOf translates the type of an Event-B variable or constant to the Java representation of that type. `Value<Type>.-next()` returns a value of type `Type` that satisfies the axioms defined in the context the machine sees.

$$\overline{\qquad\qquad\qquad\qquad\qquad\qquad\qquad\qquad}\ (\text{Cons})$$

EB2Jml(constants c) =
```
//@ publicconstraint c.equals(\old(c));
```

TypeOf(c) = `Type`   `v=Value<Type>.next()`
$$\overline{\qquad\qquad\qquad\qquad\qquad\qquad\qquad\qquad}\ (\text{Cons})$$
EB2Java(constants c) =
```
publicstaticfinal Typec=v;
```

Machine variables are translated as class attributes. The JML keyword `spec_public` makes a `protected` or `private` attribute or method `public` to any JML specification.

TypeOf(v) = `Type`
$$\overline{\qquad\qquad\qquad\qquad\qquad\qquad\qquad\qquad}\ (\text{Var})$$
EB2Java(variables v) =
```
/*@ spec_public */private Typev;
```

Deterministic and non-deterministic assignments are translated as follows[4]. The symbol: | represents non-deterministic assignment.

4 Note that EventB2Java does not yet support non-deterministic assignments.

Non-deterministic assignments generalize deterministic assignments (formed with the aid of $:=$), e.g. $v := v + w$ can be expressed as $v :| v' = v + w$. Note that machine variables are referenced from class `evt` via the field `m` (of type `M`), which requires the use of mutator methods in the generated Java code.

$$\frac{\mathsf{Pred}(E(s,c,v)) = \mathtt{E}}{\mathsf{EB2Jml}(v\ := E\ ) = \mathtt{m.v.equals(\backslash old(E));}}\ \text{(Asg)}$$

$$\frac{\mathsf{Pred}(E(s,c,v)) = \mathtt{E}}{\mathsf{EB2Java}(v\ := E) = \mathtt{m.setV(E);}}\ \text{(Asg)}$$

$$\frac{\mathsf{Pred}(P(s,c,v,v')) = \mathtt{P}\quad \mathsf{TypeOf}(v) = \mathtt{Type}}{\begin{array}{c}\mathsf{EB2Jml}(v :| P) = \\ (\mathtt{\backslash exists\ Type\ v';\ \backslash old(P)\ \&\&\ m.v.equals(v'))}\end{array}}\ \text{(NAsg)}$$

Multiple actions in the body of an event are translated individually and the results are conjoined, e.g. a pair of simultaneous actions $x := y$ and $y := x$ is translated to the JML post-condition `x == \old(y) && y == \old(x)` for variables x and y of type integer. This translation correctly models simultaneous actions as required by the semantics of Event-B. In the Java translation, simultaneous assignments are implemented by first calculating the value of each right hand side of the assignment into a temporary variable.

9.4.2. *The EventB2Java tool*

The EventB2Java tool is a Rodin [ABR 10b] plug-in that implements the translation described in section 9.4.1. Rodin is an open-source Eclipse IDE for Event-B that provides a set of tools for working with Event-B models, e.g. an editor, a proof generator and several provers. Rodin provides an API for the data model and persistence layer that allows plug-ins to work with Event-B components. The data model is composed of a series of Java interfaces for manipulating these components, and the persistence layer (called the Rodin database) uses `XML` files to store them. It is intended to abstract the concrete persistence implementation from the data model. EventB2Java uses the Rodin API to collect all components of the machine to be translated, e.g. carrier sets, constants, axioms, variables, invariants and events, as well as all the necessary information (such as the gluing invariant) from the refined machines. All this information is stored in the Rodin database. EventB2Java parses expressions and statements as abstract syntax trees using the AST library provided by Rodin. The Rodin API also provides a library to traverse trees (a tree walker) and to attach information to tree nodes. The bulk of the implementation of EventB2Java is realized through the extension of the walker to generate Java code and JML specifications. Since Event-B includes mathematical types that are not built-in to Java or JML, we implemented them as Java classes (see section 9.4.2.2). The implementation allows EventB2Java to support the static part of Event-B's syntax. We also implemented a utility class that constructs and stores variable types in Java from the model in Event-B.

As described in section 9.4.1, EventB2Java translates Event-B events to subclasses of class `Thread`. Event actions are executed sequentially for the event in the critical section. In Event-B, non-mutually exclusive event guards allow the interleaving of the execution of events whereas mutually exclusive guards force events to run sequentially. EventB2Java translates the latter case without overriding the `run()` method, forcing the implementation to run sequentially. As such, EventB2Java can generate both multi-threaded and sequential Java implementations of Event-B models.

The EventB2Java tool is available at http://poporo.uma.pt/Projects/favas/EventB2Java.html. This web site includes detailed instructions on how to install and use the tool. The EventB2Java plug-in's update site is http://poporo.uma.pt/Projects/EventB2JavaUpdate, and EventB2Java has been tested on Rodin version 2.8.

9.4.2.1. *EventB2Java tool usage*

In a typical interaction with EventB2Java, a user right-clicks an Event-B machine in the Explorer panel of Rodin and selects "translate to multi-threaded Java" or "translate to sequential Java". EventB2Java generates an Eclipse project that includes the JML-annotated Java implementation of the machine and the libraries needed to execute the Java code. This Eclipse project is available in the "resource" perspective of Rodin. The Eclipse project includes a folder that contains the generated code, and an "eventb_-prelude" sub-folder that contains the libraries implementing sets and relations in Java (see section 9.4.2.2).

9.4.2.2. *Java implementation of Event-B mathematical notations in EventB2Java*

The Event-B modeling language is composed of five mathematical languages (see Chapter 9 of [ABR 10a]):

– a Propositional Language,

– a Predicate Language,

– an Equality Language,

– a Set-Theoretic Language, and

– Boolean and Arithmetic Languages.

Each language defines a series of constructs to model systems. To provide support for the translation from Event-B, we have implemented a series of JML-specified Java classes; other Event-B constructs are supported natively in Java. These classes are: `BOOL`, `INT`, `NAT`, `NAT1`, `Enumerated`, `Pair`, `BSet`, `BRelation` and `ID` (implementing, respectively, booleans, integers, natural numbers with and without 0, the enumerated type, pairs of elements, sets, relations, and the identity relation). `BSet` is implemented as a subclass of the standard Java class `TreeSet`, and `BRelation` as a set of pairs. We had previously implemented versions of these classes for the translation from B to JML as described in section 9.3.

Some of the constructs of the Propositional Language are supported natively in Java. The negation $\neg$ translates as `!`, the conjunction $\wedge$ as `&&`, the disjunction $\vee$ as `||`. Other constructs such as $\Rightarrow$ and $\Leftrightarrow$ are implemented as methods of the class `BOOL`. The Predicate Language introduces constructs for universal and existential quantification. Universal and existential quantified predicates $\forall\ x \cdot (P)$ and $\exists\ x \cdot (P)$ are translated as the JML universal and existential quantified expressions `(\forall T x; P)` and `(\exists T x; P)`, respectively, where `P` is the JML translation of P. The Predicate Language also includes a construct $e \mapsto f$ that maps an expression e of type E into an expression f of type F. EventB2Java translates this construct as an instance of `Pair<E,F>`.

The Event-B Equality Language introduces equality predicates $E = F$ for expressions E and F, translated as `E.equals(F)`, if `E` and `F` are object references, or `E == F`, if they are of a primitive type. The Set-Theoretic

Language introduces sets and relations in Event-B. Set operations include membership ($\in$), cartesian product ($\times$), power set ($\mathbb{P}$), inclusion ($\subseteq$), union ($\cup$), intersection ($\cap$) and difference ($\setminus$). These operations are all implemented as methods of the class `BSet`. Relations in Event-B include operations for domain restriction ($\lhd$), range restriction ($\rhd$), etc. All these operations are implemented as methods of the class `BRelation`. Relations also include notations for surjective relations $\leftrightarrow\!\!\!\!\!\twoheadrightarrow$, total surjective relations $\twoheadleftrightarrow$, functions, etc. EventB2Java translates all these as instances of `BRelation` with JML invariants that constrain the domain and the range of the relation, e.g. a total function is a relation in which each element in the domain is mapped to a single element in the range.

The Boolean and Arithmetic Languages define the set BOOL, containing elements TRUE and FALSE, $\mathbb{Z}$, containing the integer numbers, $\mathbb{N}$, containing the natural numbers (0 inclusive), and $\mathbb{N}_1$, containing the natural numbers (0 exclusive). EventB2Java includes implementations of these constructs in Java, namely, classes `BOOL`, `INT`, `NAT`, and `NAT1`. The Arithmetic Language defines constructs over numbers. Operators such as $\leq$, $\geq$, etc. are directly mapped into Java operators <=, >=, etc. The construct a .. b, which defines an interval between a and b, is implemented as an apropriate instance of the class `Enumerated`.

9.4.2.3. *Support for Event-B model decomposition*

When modeling systems with Event-B, we usually start with the design of a single closed machine that includes both the modeling of the system and the surrounding environment. The machine is then refined into a more concrete model of the system. Abstract machines usually include few events and variables, while (elaborated) refinements include many more of each. This complicates both defining additional refinements and discharging proof obligations in Rodin. Thus, a machine decomposition mechanism that helps the user understand, which variables and events are actually involved in a given refinement step is needed. This raises the question of whether code generation for decomposed machines is feasible. In [ABR 07], Abrial and Hallerstede propose a technique for machine decomposition based on shared variables in which each decomposed machine simulates the behavior of other decomposed machines through the use of *external* events. In [BUT 09], Butler proposes a technique for machine decomposition by shared events in which decomposed machines include copies of all variables used by events.

This latter technique is implemented in Code Generation [EDM 10]. Both machine decomposition techniques produce independent machines that include local copies of shared variables, or local events that simulate the effect of other decomposed machines acting on the shared variables. As such, the decomposed machines are independent, and the EventB2Java tool can generate Java implementations for them in a straightforward manner.

9.4.2.4. *Support for code customization*

The JML specifications generated by EventB2Java enable users to write bespoke Java implementations of the machine that was translated by EventB2Java. Thus, the user may customize part or all of the generated implementation, and then use an existing JML tool such as OpenJML [COK 11] to verify the customized implementation against the JML specification generated by the EventB2Java tool. Of course, this only guarantees that the implementation is a refinement of the Event-B model if the translation from Event-B to JML is sound. A soundness proof of this translation is presented in [CAT 13]. The soundness proof ensures that any state transition step of the JML semantics of the translation of some Event-B construct into JML can be simulated by a state transition step of the Event-B semantics of that construct. All steps in the proof are modeled in Event-B and implemented in Rodin. The soundness condition just described is stated as a theorem and proved interactively in Rodin.

9.4.3. *Case Study: translating the Event-B social networking model to Java and JML*

We have validated the EventB2Java tool by using it to translate an Event-B model for a social-event planner. This model is an Event-B adaptation of the B social network (SN) model that was described in sections 9.2.1 and 9.3.3. The social-event planner model adds the ability for users in the SN to define social-events (e.g. parties, meetings), to share contents among the invited people (e.g. comments, pictures), to invite people in the SN to a social-event, to grant permission to invite more users, and for an invitee to reply to the social-event (e.g. yes, no, maybe). The social-event planner Event-B model consists of an abstract machine and five refinements that model the SN (these first six machines are the adaption from the B SN). We then added three refinements that define the features of the social-event planner explained above. We could have translated the adaptation of the SN in Event-B to Java using the EventB2Java tool and then added the features of the social-event planner in Java, but this approach would not ensure that the social-event planner is a refinement of the original SN model. Hence, we used Event-B to define the core functionality of the social-event planner, discharged the refinement proof obligations, used EventB2Java to generate Java code for the model, and then hand-coded the graphical interface and other non-core features in Java.

Figure 9.8 presents the $create\_account$ and $create\_social\_event$ events from the sixth refinement machine ($social\_events$), which is the first refinement to include features of the social-event planner. The $create\_account$ event is an adaptation of the $create\_account$ operation in the SN B model (see Figure 9.4). This machine "sees" context c (not shown here) that defines carrier set EVENTS (possible social-events within the SN), and extends carrier sets PERSON and CONTENTS (as before, the potential persons and content items in the SN). The Event-B variable $persons$ contains the actual people in the network, $contents$ defines the actual contents in the network (e.g. a comment or picture), and $owner$ maps a content item to the person who owns it. This variable is defined as a function, so a content item is owned by one person. Variable $pages$ represents the content items stored in person's pages. Variables $editp$ and $viewp$ represent view and edit permissions on content items. Variables $principal$ and $required$ store principal and required content items. Variable $wallaccess$ maps users to users, determining who has access to someone else's wall. Finally, $sevent$ is the set of the actual Social-Events in the SN, and $eventowner$ maps an existing social-event to its owner. The $create\_account$ event defines the behavior of the network when a new user creates an account. The new user $p1$ is added to the network with a new principal and required content item $c1$. Additionally, $p1$ owns $c1$, $c1$ is one of the pages of $p1$, and $p1$ has view and edit permissions on $c1$. Hence, the pair $\{c1 \mapsto p1\}$ is added to each of the corresponding variables. The $create\_social\_event$ event in Figure 9.8 specifies the behavior of the network when a user (pe) (who is already present in the network) creates a social-event (se). The event adds a new social-event and associates it with its owner.

After discharging all proof obligations for the Event-B model, we translated it to Java using EventB2Java. The EventB2Java tool generates one Java class (not shown here) containing the translation of the carrier sets, constants and variables (with their respective initializations), and the Event-B invariant. The tool also generates a Java `Thread` implementation for each machine event, as specified by the rules in section 9.4. Figure 9.9 presents the translation of the event *create_social_event* in Figure 9.8 to Java[5], where `m` is a reference to the machine class implementation and `eventId` is the event identifier. Methods `guard_create_social_event` and `run_create_social_event` implement the behavior of *create_social_event* in Java. The first method checks the event guard, and the second method may execute when that guards hold. Whether `run_create_social_event` executes when `guard_create_social_event` holds is determined by the `run()` method of `create_social_event` in coordination with the respective `run()` methods of all existing events. The implementation of `run()` methods respects Event-B semantics for the execution of events: the guards of two or more events can be evaluated concurrently, whereas only one event can execute (its critical section) at any point. This ensures that events execute monotonically.

create_account
 any $c1\ p1$
 where
  grd1 $p1 \in \text{PERSON} \setminus persons$
  grd2 $c1 \in \text{CONTENT} \setminus contents$
 then
  act1 $contents := contents \cup \{c1\}$
  act2 $persons := persons \cup \{p1\}$
  act3 $owner := owner \cup \{c1 \mapsto p1\}$
  act4 $pages := pages \cup \{c1 \mapsto p1\}$
  act5 $viewp := viewp \cup \{c1 \mapsto p1\}$
  act6 $editp := editp \cup \{c1 \mapsto p1\}$
  act7 $principal := principal \cup \{c1\}$
  act8 $required := required \cup \{c1\}$
  act9 $wallaccess := wallaccess \cup \{p1 \mapsto p1\}$
 end
end

create_social_event
 any $pe\ se$
 where
  grd1 $pe \in persons$
  grd2 $se \notin sevents$
 then
  act1 $events := sevents \cup \{se\}$
  act2 $eventowner(se) := pe$
 end
end

Figure 9.8. *The create_account and create_social_event events from the social_events refinement of the Social-Event Planner Event-B model*

5 The actual code generated by EventB2Java uses getters and mutators for variables defined in machine implementation `m`.

```
public class create_social_event extends Thread{
 private social_events m; private int eventId;

 /*@ requires true; assignable \everything;
     ensures this.m == m && this.eventId == i; */
 public create_social_event(socialevents m, int i) {
    this.m = m; this.eventId = i;
 }

 /*@ requires true; assignable \nothing;
     ensures \result <==> (machine.get_persons().has(pe)
      && !machine.get_sevents().has(se)); @*/
 private boolean guard_create_social_event(Integer pe, Integer se) {
  return (machine.get_persons().has(pe)
    && !machine.get_sevents().has(se));
 }

 /*@ requires guard_create_social_event(pe,se);
     assignable m.sevents, m.eventowner;
     ensures m.get_sevents().equals(\old((m.get_sevents()
         .union(new BSet<Integer>(se)))))
       && m.get_eventowner().equals(\old((m.get_eventowner()
         .override(new BRelation<Integer,Integer>(
          new Pair<Integer,Integer>(se,pe))))));
    also
     requires !guard_create_social_event(pe,se);
     assignable \nothing;
     ensures true; @*/
 private void run_create_social_event(Integer pe, Integer se){
  if(guard_create_social_event(pe,se)) {
   BSet<Integer> sevents_tmp = m.get_sevents();
   BRelation<Integer,Integer> eventowner_tmp = m.get_eventowner();

   m.set_sevents((sevents_tmp.union(new BSet<Integer>(se))));
   m.set_eventowner((eventowner_tmp.override(
          new BRelation<Integer,Integer>(new Pair<Integer,
                                              Integer>(se,pe)))));
  }
 }

 public void run() { ... }
}
```

Figure 9.9. *Translation of event create_social_event*

Variables contents_tmp, pages_tmp, etc., hold temporary values of variables contents, pages, etc., respectively. EventB2Java uses these temporary values to implement simultaneous assignment in Java.

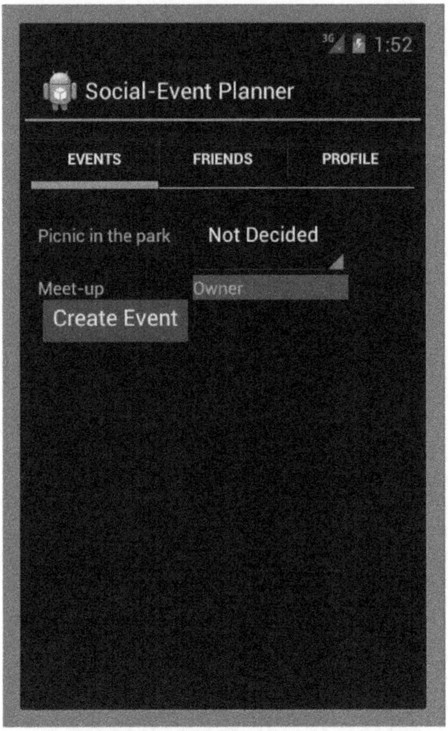

Figure 9.10. *Part of the user interface for the social-event planner*

As a validation step of the translation performed by EventB2Java, we syntax and type-checked the generated Java code and JML specifications using Eclipse and the OpenJML tool. This process revealed some errors in EventB2Java related to the translation of Event-B types to Java. It also uncovered an error in the translation of Event-B invariants involving relations and functions to JML invariants. After correcting these issues in the EventB2Java tool, we generated JML-specified Java code for all nine machines in the social-event planer. Next, we extended this core functionality to realize a usable version of the social-event planner as an Android application. The application uses the model-view-controller (MVC) design pattern, with the code generated by EventB2Java as the *model*. The *controller* (hand-implemented in Java) uses the generated getter and setter methods to communicate with the *model*. The *view* was developed using the Android API. Figure 9.10 shows the screen of the Android interface that lists social-events for one user.

We have further validated the EventB2Java tool by applying it to the Event-B models available at: http://poporo.uma.pt/Projects/favas/EventB2Java.html. See [RIV 14] for further details on this work. In addition, we used EventB2Java to generate Java code for an Event-B model of Tokeneer (a security-critical access control system), and then implemented a suite of JUnit Tests for the generated code. Even though we had discharged all proof obligations for the model before translation, the tests uncovered some issues with the behavior of the system. To address these problems, we made improvements to the Event-B model, translated it to Java and re-ran the JUnit tests, repeating these steps until all tests passed successfully. This experiment provides a high degree of confidence in the system since the model is correct (all proof obligations were discharged), and the generated code behaves as expected (all JUnit tests passed). See http://poporo.uma.pt/Tokeneer.html for more information on this experiment.

9.5. Future work and conclusion

One potential weakness of our approach is that the JML specifications produced by both tools make extensive use of custom library classes representing B and Event-B mathematical types, as do the Java implementations produced by EventB2Java. It could be argued that understanding the behavior of these library classes is just as difficult as learning the mathematical notations of B and Event-B. While we have not studied this issue systematically, our experience suggests that it is not a serious problem in practice. Students who have worked with the JML specifications produced by B2Jml and EventB2Java have not had undue difficulty in understanding them, even when those students had no previous experience with B. We attribute this in part to the fact that B mathematical operators are translated to Java methods with meaningful names, and that the JML specifications and Java implementations of those methods are available for reference. Additionally, students who built Android applications around Java code generated by EventB2Java had no apparent difficulties in understanding and using that code. A master's student was able to implement a car racing game in Android [PER 12] following the MVC design pattern. The model code was automatically generated from an Event-B machine using an earlier version of EventB2Java, while the view and controller parts were manually implemented. A first year PhD student repeated a similar experiment with a social-event planner application for Android [RIV 12]. In our view, EventB2Java allows people from different backgrounds to use formal (e.g. Event-B and refinement calculus) and less-formal (e.g. design of interfaces) techniques together.

One important area for future work is proving the soundness of our translations – this is critical for ensuring that the resulting implementation is in fact a refinement of the original model. We have produced an initial version of this proof for the JML translation performed by EventB2Java [CAT 13], but do not yet have a corresponding proof for B2Jml. The EventB2Java soundness proof was accomplished by embedding the translation and the semantics of JML and Event-B in Event-B itself, stating the soundness result as a theorem, and proving that theorem using the interactive prover in Rodin. Because of this embedding step, this proof shows the soundness of an Event-B axiomatization of the translation algorithm, rather than the algorithm itself. As such, we are considering alternate approaches that could be applied directly to our formulation of the translation algorithm as rewriting rules. Ideally, such an approach could also be used to prove the soundness of the translation performed by B2Jml.

We would also like to perform larger scale case studies in order to validate and refine our approach. In the case of B2Jml, we have not (yet) used the tool to develop a larger scale system, and so have limited experience in verifying hand-coded implementations against JML specifications produced by the tool. Such a study would give us significantly more insight into how to use refinement calculus and design-by-contract approaches together in practice, and would help in uncovering any remaining inconsistencies in the translation algorithm or errors in its implementation. We have considerably more experience using EventB2Java in system development – one author regularly has students in his classes use EventB2Java to generate code for parts of Android applications – but largely in the context of smaller, "academic" applications. Applying EventB2Java in the development of an industrial scale would surely yield additional insights into its usability and effectiveness, particularly in cases where the implementation is hand-coded and verified against the generated JML specification.

The B2Jml and EventB2Java tools represent our efforts to bridge the refinement calculus and design-by-contract approaches to formal software development – in particular, to take advantage of the strengths and avoid the weaknesses of each approach. Using B or Event-B in the early stages of the process gives developers excellent support for modeling software systems in an abstract manner, and particularly for verifying safety, security and correctness properties of those models. Transitioning to JML/Java at an appropriate point (as determined by the developers themselves, rather than being dictated by the tools being used) allows developers to take full advantage of data structures and APIs in the implementation language, and permits engineers with less mathematical expertise to contribute earlier in the development process. The EventB2Java tool is particularly noteworthy for its ability to generate executable code directly from abstract Event-B models, while still providing the option to produce a hand-coded Java implementation and verify it against a JML specification. We believe that tool support of this nature is a necessary pre-condition for combining formal method approaches in practice – hand translation is very time-consuming and introduces so many opportunities for human error. Our research efforts going forward are intended to ensure the soundness of the tools that we have developed, and to refine our tools to enhance their usefulness in practice.

9.6. Bibliography

[ABD 02] ABDENNADHER S., KRÄMER E., SAFT M., *et al.*, "JACK: a Java constraint kit", HANUS M. (ed.), *Electronic Notes in Theoretical Computer Science*, Elsevier, vol. 64, 2002.

[ABR 96] ABRIAL J.R., *The B-Book: Assigning Programs to Meanings*, Cambridge University Press, New York, NY, 1996.

[ABR 07] ABRIAL J.-R., HALLERSTEDE S., "Refinement, decomposition and instantiation of discrete models: application to Event-B", *Fundamentae Informatica*, vol. 77, nos. 1–2, pp. 1–24, 2007.

[ABR 10a] ABRIAL J.-R., *Modeling in Event-B: System and Software Design*, Cambridge University Press, New York, NY, 2010.

[ABR 10b] ABRIAL J.-R., BUTLER M., HALLERSTEDE S., *et al.*, "Rodin: an open toolset for modeling and reasoning in Event-B", *STTT*, vol. 12, no. 6, pp. 447–466, 2010.

[BAC 91] BACK R., SERE K., "Stepwise refinement of action systems", *Structured Programming*, vol. 12, pp. 17–30, 1991.

[BAR 04] BARNETT M., LEINO K. R.M., SCHULTE W., "The Spec# programming system: an overview", *CASSIS*, of *LNCS*, Springer, Marseille, France, vol. 3362, pp. 49–69, 2004.

[BOU 03] BOULANGER J.-L., "ABTools: another B Tool", *Proceedings of Application of Concurrency to System Design (ACSD)*, Guimaraes, Portugal, 2003.

[BOU 13] BOULANGER J.-L., The ABTools Suite, 2013. Available at http://-sourceforge.-net/-projects/-abtools/.

[BUR 05] BURDY L., CHEON Y., COK D., *et al.*, "An overview of JML tools and applications", *International Journal on STTT*, vol. 7, no. 3, pp. 212–232, 2005.

[BUT 06] BUTLER M.J., JONES C.B., ROMANOVSKY A., *et al.* (eds.), *Rigorous Development of Complex Fault-Tolerant Systems [FP6 IST-511599 RODIN project]*, LNCS, Springer, 2006.

[BUT 09] BUTLER M., "Decomposition structures for Event-B", *Proceedings of the 7th International Conference on Integrated Formal Methods, (IFM '09)*, Berlin, Heidelberg, pp. 20–38, 2009.

[CAT 03] CATAÑO N., HUISMAN M., "Chase: a static checker for JML's assignable clause", in ZUCK L.D., ATTIE P.C., CORTESI A., *et al.* (eds.), *VMCAI*, of LNCS, New York, NY, Springer-Verlag, vol. 2575, pp. 26–40, 9–11 January 2003.

[CAT 09] CATAÑO N., WAHLS T., "Executing JML specifications of Java card applications: a case study", *24th ACM SAC, Software Engineering Track*, Waikiki Beach, Honolulu, Hawaii, 8–12 March 2009.

[CAT 12] CATAÑO N., WAHLS T., RUEDA C., *et al.*, "Translating B machines to JML specifications", *27th ACM Symposium on Applied Computing, Software Verification and Testing track (SAC-SVT)*, Trento, Italy, 26–30 March 2012.

[CAT 13] CATAÑO N., RUEDA C., WAHLS T., "A machine-checked proof for a translation of Event-B machines to JML", *ArXiv e-prints*, September 2013.

[CHA 06] CHALIN P., KINIRY J., LEAVENS G., *et al.*, "Beyond assertions: advanced specification and verification with JML and ESC/Java2", *Proceedings of FMCO*, LNCS, Springer Verlag, vol. 4111, 2006.

[CLE 08] CLEARSY, ATELIER B., The industrial tool to efficiently deploy the b method, Clearsy, 2008.

[COK 11] COK D.R., "OpenJML: JML for Java 7 by extending OpenJDK", *NASA Formal Methods Symposium*, pp. 472–479, 2011.

[EDM 10] EDMUNDS A., BUTLER M., "Tool support for Event-B code generation", *WS-TBFM2010*, Québec, Canada, 2010.

[EDM 11] EDMUNDS A., BUTLER M., "Tasking Event-B: an extension to Event-B for generating concurrent code", *PLACES 2011*, 2011.

[KRA 06] KRAUSE B., WAHLS T., "JMLE: a tool for executing JML specifications via constraint programming", in BRIM L. (ed.), *Proceedings of FMICS*, Lecture Notes in Computer Science, Springer-Verlag, vol. 4346, pp. 293–296, August 2006.

[LAM 74] LAMPORT L., "A new solution of Dijkstra's concurrent programming problem", *Commun. ACM*, vol. 17, no. 8, pp. 453–455, August 1974.

[MER 11] MÉRY D., SINGH N.K., "Automatic code generation from Event-B models", *Proceedings of the Second SoICT*, SoICT '11, 2011.

[MEY 92] MEYER B., "Applying "Design by contract", *Computer*, vol. 25, no. 10, pp. 40–51, October 1992.

[MOR 90] MORGAN C., *Programming from Specifications*, Prentice-Hall, Inc., Upper Saddle River, NJ, 1990.

[PAR 07] PARR T., *The Definitive ANTLR Reference: Building Domain-Specific Languages*, Pragmatic Bookshelf, 2007.

[PER 12] PERCHY S., CATAÑO N., The racing car game, 2012. Available at http://cic.javerianacali.edu.co/ysperchy/formal-game.

[RIV 12] RIVERA V., CATAÑO N., The social-event planner, 2012. Available at http://poporo.uma.pt/Projects/favas/Social-EventPlanner.html.

[RIV 14] RIVERA V., CATAÑO N., "Translating Event-B to JML-specified Java programs", *Accepted for the 2014 ACM Symposium on Applied Computing, Software Verification and Testing track (SAC-SVT)*, 2014.

10

Event B

Event B [ABR 10a, CAN 07a] is a modeling language which can describe state-based models and required safety properties. The main objective is to provide a technique for incremental and proof-based development of the reactive systems. It integrates set-theoretical notations and a first-order predicate calculus, models called machines; it includes the concept of refinement expressing the simulation of one machine by another machine. An Event B machine models a reactive system, i.e. a system driven by its environment and its stimuli. An important property of these machines is that its events preserve the invariant properties defining a set of reachable states. The Event B method has been developed from the classical B method [ABR 96] and it offers a general framework for developing the correct construction systems by using an incremental approach for designing the models by refinement. Refinement [BAC 79, DIJ 76, BAC 98, BAC 89] is a relationship relating two models such that one model is simulating the other model. Refinement is also called simulation and preserves properties of the abstract model in the refined or concrete model. When an abstract model is refined by a concrete model, the concrete model simulates the abstract model and any safety property of the abstract model is also a safety property of the concrete model. In particular, the concrete model preserves the invariant properties of the abstract model. Event B aims to express models of systems characterized by invariants and by a list of safety properties. We can consider liveness properties as in UNITY [CHA 88] or TLA$^+$ [LAM 02, LAM 94] but in a restricted way.

Chapter written by Dominique MÉRY and Neeraj Kumar SINGH.

10.1. Introduction

This chapter is organized into eight sections. Section 10.2 gives results on the modeling and verification of systems using transition systems. The goal is to provide the basic fundamental and conceptual theories, which support Event B approach. In particular, we explain how invariant properties and safety properties are defined in the framework of a transition system, which may model a program, an algorithm or a distributed system. Section 10.3 details the Event B language and related concepts such as events, contexts, machines and refinement. We give an explanation of proof obligations (POs) generated for checking the consistency of the Event B structure. Then, in sections 10.4 and 10.5, we develop three case studies, in order to illustrate the incremental and proof-based modeling using Event B. We emphasize the notion of proof-based patterns applied for the Event B method. Section 10.6 describes available tools for supporting the Event B modeling language and we conclude this chapter with the current and future trends for this method.

10.2. Modeling and verification of a system

10.2.1. *Modeling*

A relational abstract model $\mathcal{AM}$ ($\mathcal{AM}_{\text{P}}$ of a program P or $\mathcal{AM}_{\text{P}}$ of a system P) is defined by a set of states Σ, a set of initial states $Init_{\text{P}}$, a set of terminal states $Term_{\text{P}}$ and a binary relation $\mathcal{R}$ over Σ. The set of terminal states may be empty and, in this case, the program does not terminate; this feature can be used for modeling programs or procedures of operating systems which are not terminating and cannot terminate at all. We will use a system rather than a program, since we can describe elements, which are more general than computer programs but also the formalism is usable for describing distributed applications.

A system is characterized by a set of traces generated from the abstract model as follows:

$s_0 \underset{R}{\longrightarrow} s_1 \underset{R}{\longrightarrow} s_2 \underset{R}{\longrightarrow} s_3 \underset{R}{\longrightarrow} \ldots \underset{R}{\longrightarrow} s_i \underset{R}{\longrightarrow} \ldots$ is a trace generated by the abstract model.

The observation of a system can be summarized by the analysis of its traces; Θ_{S} is a set of all traces of S. The expression of properties requires an assertion language or a formulas language: $\mathcal{L}$ is an assertion language. A simple choice is to consider the language of assertions defined by $\mathcal{P}(\Sigma)$ (power set of Σ) and $\varphi(s)$ (or $s \in \varphi$), which means that φ is true in the state s. The assertion language allows us to express properties, however it may be possible that the language is not expressive enough. We assume that the language is sufficiently expressive (following Stephen Cook) and this means that the required properties for completeness can be expressed in the language.

Properties of a system S are, in particular, safety properties and liveness properties. Safety properties are, for instance, the partial correctness of a system S with respect to its specifications, the absence of runtime errors; liveness properties are, for instance, the termination of a program P with respect to its specifications or the total correctness of P with respect to its specifications. We could also consider program properties as performance but this leads to the models for expressing the non-functional properties. Properties are expressed in a language $\mathcal{L}$ and its components can be combined using logical connectives or instantiation of variables; the implication relation upto the equivalent relation defines a partial ordering over a set of formulas.

We assume that a system S is modeled by a set of states Σ_{S}, denoted by Σ, where $\Sigma \stackrel{def}{=} \text{VARIABLES} \longrightarrow \text{VALEURS}$. The expression $s \in A$ is equivalent to $s[\![\varphi(x)]\!]$, where x is a list whose elements are variables VARIABLES; this means that $s \in A$ is equivalent to $\varphi(x)$ is true in s. The meaning of a formula or a predicate can be given using an inductive process on $s[\![\varphi(x)]\!]$.

EXAMPLE 10.1.–

1) $s[\![x]\!]$ is the value of s in x, i.e. $s(x)$ or the value of x in s.

2) $s[\![\varphi(x) \wedge \psi(x)]\!] \stackrel{def}{=} s[\![\varphi(x)]\!]$ and $s[\![\psi(x)]\!]$.

3) $s[\![x = 6 \wedge y = x + 8]\!] \stackrel{def}{=} s[\![x]\!] = 6$ and $s[\![y]\!] = s[\![x]\!] + 8$.

We use the notations for simplifying the indication of a state: for instance, $s[\![x]\!]$ is the value of x in s and the name of the variable x and its value will not be distinguished; $s'[\![x]\!]$ is the value of x in s' and will be denoted by x'. Consequently, $s[\![x = 6]\!] \wedge s'[\![y = x + 8]\!]$ is simplified into $x = 6 \wedge y' = x' + 8$. The consequence is that we can write the transition between two states as a relation relating the state of variables in s and the state of variables in s'.

Let s, s' be two states of the set $\text{VARIABLES} \longrightarrow \text{VALS}$.
$s \underset{R}{\longrightarrow} s'$ is rewritten as a relation $\mathrm{R}(x, x')$ where x and x' are values of x.

We have introduced primed variables borrowed from the Temporal Logic of Actions of Lamport [LAM 94] and x' is the value after the transition under consideration and x is the value before the transition under consideration. The expression $\exists y.\mathrm{R}(x, y)$ defines the condition for transition or the guard. We are interested in particular expressions like $cond(x) \wedge x' = f(x)$ where *cond* is a condition over x and f is a function. We can express induction principles using relations over unprimed and primed variables. Initial conditions are defined by a predicate characterizing the initial values of variables. We propose to define more generally a relational model of a system. A set of states is Σ for a given system and we identify this set with a set of possible values of flexible variables x. We use the same notation but VALS will be a set of possible values of x.

DEFINITION 10.1.– *Relational model of a system*

A relational model $\mathcal{MS}$ for a system $\mathcal{S}$, is a structure

$$(Th(s, c), x, \text{VALS}, \text{INIT}(x), \{r_0, \ldots, r_n\}),$$

where

– $Th(s, c)$ *is a theory defining sets, constants and static properties of these elements.*

– x *is a list of flexible variables.*

– VALS *is a set of possible values for* x.

– $\text{INIT}(x)$ *defines a set of initial values of* x.

– $\{r_0, \ldots, r_n\}$ *is a finite set of binary relations relating the prevalues* x *and the postvalues* x'.

A relational model $\mathcal{MS} = (Th(s, c), x, \text{VALS}, \text{INIT}(x), \{r_0, \ldots, r_n\})$ for a system $\mathcal{S}$ is a structure for studying a system defined by a model. We assume that the r_0 is the relation $Id[\text{VALS}]$, identity over VALS.

DEFINITION 10.2.– *Let* $(Th(s, c), x, \text{VALS}, \text{INIT}(x), \{r_0, \ldots, r_n\})$ *be a relational model for a system* $\mathcal{S}$. *The relation* NEXT *attached to this model, is defined by the disjunction of relations* r_i: $\text{NEXT} \stackrel{def}{=} r_0 \vee \ldots \vee r_n$.

Modeling a system leads to identifying state variables x, a predicate defining the initial conditions of x and a relation NEXT expressing how the values of variables before and after are related. Induction principles are formulated in these relational models and here, we introduce the definition as follows:

Let $(Th(s,c), x, \text{VALS}\ , \text{INIT}(x), \{r_0, \ldots, r_n\})$ be a relational model of a system $\mathcal{S}$. The theory $Th(s,c)$ is defined in an assertion language, which can express properties. An example is the set theory of the B language. When we consider a property φ, we use this set-theoretical language of B. For any variable x, we define the following values:

– x is the current value of x.

– x' is the next value of x.

10.2.2. *Safety properties*

The safety property states that *nothing bad will happen [LAM 80]*. For instance, the value of x is *always* between 0 and 67; the sum of the current values of x and y is the current value of z. The assertion language is supposed to be $(\mathcal{P}(\Sigma), \subseteq)$ and we suppose that the satisfaction relation is defined using the membership relation.

DEFINITION 10.3.– *A property φ is a safety property for a system* S, *when*

$$\forall s, s' \in \Sigma. s \in Init_S \wedge s \xrightarrow[R]{\star} s' \Rightarrow s' \in \varphi.$$

The expression $\xrightarrow[R]{\star}$ stands for the reflexive transitive closure of the relation $\xrightarrow[R]{}$. The safety property uses a universal quantification over states. For proving a safety property, we can either check a property for each possible state, if the set of states is finite, or, find an induction principle. In the case of an exhaustive checking, we can use an algorithm for computing the set of reachable states from the initial nodes: the *model checking* [MCM 93, HOL 97, CLA 00]. It helps to find the counter-examples and is a complementary approach to use the induction principle following in the next property.

THEOREM 10.1.– Induction principle

A property φ is a safety property for a program P if, and only if, there exists a property INV satisfying

$$\begin{cases} (1)\ Init_{\mathrm{P}} \subseteq INV \\ (2)\ INV \subseteq \varphi \\ (3)\ \forall s, s' \in \Sigma_{\mathrm{P}}.s \in INV \wedge s \underset{R}{\longrightarrow} s' \Rightarrow s' \in INV \end{cases}$$

The property INV is called a program invariant and it is a special safety property stronger than the other safety properties of a program. The justification of this principle is simple.

PROOF.–
$\langle 1\rangle 1$. SUPPOSE THAT: There exists a property INV such that

$$\begin{cases} (1)\ Init_{\mathrm{P}} \subseteq INV \\ (2)\ INV \subseteq \varphi \\ (3)\ \forall s, s' \in \Sigma_{\mathrm{P}}.s \in INV \wedge s \underset{R}{\longrightarrow} s' \Rightarrow s' \in INV \end{cases}$$

PROVE THAT: φ is a safety property for the program P.

PROOF.– Let two states s, s' such that $s \in Init_{\mathrm{P}} \wedge s \overset{\star}{\underset{R}{\longrightarrow}} s'$. We can construct a sequence of states $s = s_0 \underset{R}{\longrightarrow} s_1 \underset{R}{\longrightarrow} s_2 \underset{R}{\longrightarrow} s_3 \underset{R}{\longrightarrow} \ldots \underset{R}{\longrightarrow} s_i = s'$. from assumption (1), we derive that INV holds at s. By using (3) for any state of the trace, we derive that INV holds at $s_1, s_2, \ldots s_i$. Then, we apply (2) for the state s' and we derive that s' satisfies φ. □

$\langle 1\rangle 2$. SUPPOSE THAT: $\forall s, s' \in \Sigma.s \in Init_{\mathrm{P}} \wedge s \overset{\star}{\underset{R}{\longrightarrow}} s' \Rightarrow s' \in \varphi$
PROVE THAT: There exists a property INV such that

$$\begin{cases} (1)\ Init_{\mathrm{P}} \subseteq INV \\ (2)\ INV \subseteq \varphi \\ (3)\ \forall s, s' \in \Sigma_{\mathrm{P}}.s \in INV \wedge s \underset{R}{\longrightarrow} s' \Rightarrow s' \in INV \end{cases}$$

PROVE THAT: φ is a safety property for the program P

PROOF.– We define the following property $INV \overset{def}{=} \exists s \in \Sigma.s \in Init_{\mathrm{P}} \wedge s \overset{\star}{\underset{R}{\longrightarrow}} s'$. INV states that the state s' is a reachable state from some initial state of P. $\mathcal{R}^\star$ is the reflexive transitive closure of $\mathcal{R}$. The three properties are simple to check for INV. INV is called the strongest invariant of the program P. □

$\langle 1 \rangle 3$. Q.E.D.

PROOF.– By steps $\langle 1 \rangle 1$ and $\langle 1 \rangle 2$, we infer the conclusion. □

□

The property explains Floyd's invariance proof method also known as Floyd–Hoare's methods [FLO 67, HOA 69], initially sketched by Turing in 1949 [TUR 49]. The property gives a general form for the induction and then we can rephrase it according to the required invariance properties (partial correctness and absence of deadlocks, etc.). P. and R. Cousot [COU 00, COU 79, COU 92, COU 78] give a complete synthesis on the different possible induction principles. We apply these results to the case of relational models of a system and we obtain an expression of a safety property as follows:

DEFINITION 10.4.– *Let* $(Th(s,c), x, \text{VALS}, \text{INIT}(x), \{r_0, \ldots, r_n\})$ *be a relational model for a system* $\mathcal{S}$*. A property* φ *is a safety property for a system* $\mathcal{S}$*, when* $\forall y, x \in \Sigma . Init(y) \wedge \text{NEXT}^\star(y,x) \Rightarrow \varphi(x)$.

From the induction principle of the previous section, we can derive the following property.

THEOREM 10.2.– (Induction principle for a relational model)

Let $(Th(s,c), x, \text{VALS}, \text{INIT}(x), \{r_0, \ldots, r_n\})$ be a relational model for a system $\mathcal{S}$.

A property $\varphi(x)$ is a safety property for $\mathcal{S}$ if, and only if, there exists a property $i(x)$ such that

$$\begin{cases} (1)\ \forall x \in \text{VALS} . Init(x) \Rightarrow i(x) \\ (2)\ \forall x \in \text{VALS} . i(x) \Rightarrow \varphi(x) \\ (3)\ \forall x, x' \in \text{VALS} . i(x) \wedge \text{NEXT}(x,x') \Rightarrow i(x') \end{cases}$$

PROOF.– Derived from the proof of the property 10.2. □

If we transform properties, we obtain a form closer to what we will use in the next sections and closer to the concept of *abstract systems* or *abstract machines* of Event B.

THEOREM 10.3.– The two sentences are equivalent:

1) There exists a state property $\mathrm{I}(x)$ such that

$$\forall x, x' \in \text{VALS} : \begin{cases} (1) & \text{INIT}(x) \Rightarrow \mathrm{I}(x) \\ (2) & \mathrm{I}(x) \Rightarrow \mathrm{P}(x) \\ (3) & \mathrm{I}(x) \wedge \text{NEXT}(x, x') \Rightarrow \mathrm{I}(x') \end{cases}$$

2) There exists a state property $\mathrm{I}(x)$ such that:

$$\forall x, x' \in \text{VALS} : \begin{cases} (1) & \text{INIT}(x) \Rightarrow \mathrm{I}(x) \\ (2) & \mathrm{I}(x) \Rightarrow \mathrm{P}(x) \\ (3) & \forall i \in \{0, \ldots, n\} : \mathrm{I}(x) \wedge x \; r_i \; x' \Rightarrow \mathrm{I}(x') \end{cases}$$

PROOF.– The proof is obvious by applying the following rule: $\forall i \in \{0, \ldots, n\} : A \wedge x \; r_i \; x' \Rightarrow B \equiv (A \wedge (\exists i \in \{0, \ldots, n\} : x \; r_i \; x')) \Rightarrow B$ and the definition of $\text{NEXT}(x, x')$. □

We have given an explanation of the induction rule used in Floyd's method [FLO 67, TUR 49, HOA 69] which states that the invariance properties are necessary for deriving the safety properties. The invariance properties are stronger than safety properties. The invariance properties are also the special case of safety properties. There is a confusion in the literature where we claim that *always true* and *invariant* are two equivalent concepts: an invariant is an inductive property.

The Event B method uses these two kinds of properties: the clause INVARIANTS for invariants and in earlier versions of Rodin, the clause THEOREMS for safety properties. Current versions distinguish both classes by a feature stating that the predicate is either an invariant or a safety property (theorem). An invariant is obviously a safety property. Now, we summarize the Event B language and the incremental and proof-based development of event-based models.

10.3. Event B: a modeling language

Event B is both a language and a method. Its concepts are limited and allow the user to manage a simple palette of tools: axioms, theorems, theories, events, machine, context and refinement. We shortly describe these elements, but it is clear that examples constitute the best way to learn and understand how to use tools.

The construction of an Event B model is based on concepts like sets, constants, axioms, theorems, variables, invariants and events; these syntactic constructions are organized into two kinds of structures:

– Contexts express axiomatic static properties of the models. Contexts may contain carrier sets, constants, axioms and theorems. Axioms describe properties of carrier sets and constants. Theorems derive properties that can be proved from the axioms. POs associated with contexts are straightforward: the stated theorems must be proved, which follow from the predefined axioms and theorems. Additionally, a context may be indirectly seen by machines. Namely, a context C can be seen by a machine M indirectly if the machine M explicitly sees a context, which is an extension of the context C.

– Machines express dynamic behavioral properties of the models, which may contain variables, invariants, theorems, events and variants. Variables v represents the state of the machine. Variables, like constants, correspond to simple mathematical objects: sets, binary relations, functions, numbers, etc. They are constrained by invariants $I(v)$. Invariants are supposed to hold whenever variable values change.

When a machine is organizing events, it modifies the state variables and uses static information defined in context. These basic structure mechanisms are extended by the refinement mechanism which provides a mechanism for relating an abstract model and a concrete model by adding new events or by adding new variables. This mechanism allows us to gradually develop Event-B models and to validate each decision step using the proof tools. The refinement relationship should be expressed as follows: a model M is refined by a model P, when P simulates M. The final concrete model is close to the behavior of a real system that is executing events using real source code. We give details now regarding the definition of events, refinement and guidelines for developing complex system models.

– The consistency of a context or a machine in Event B is achieved by proving *proof obligation* generated by tools [CLE 02, ABR 10b] and sound with respect to the results of section 10.2. If these POs are discharged, then the structure (context or machine) is correct at least with respect to the typing. Indeed, the main tricky point is the statement and the proof of the invariant property of a machine, but the refinement is a technique for facilitating the proof process and the discovery of invariants.

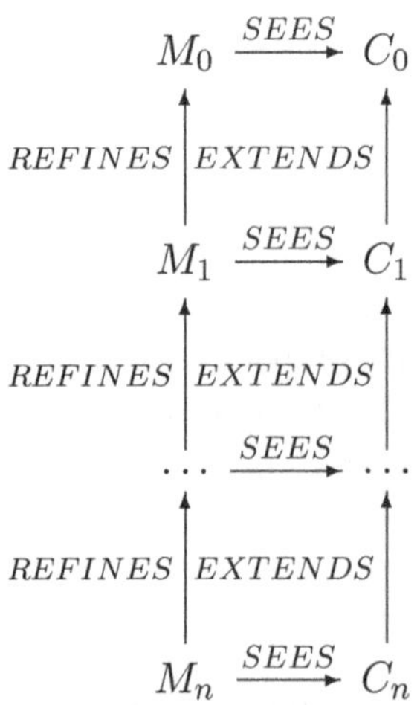

In the next section, we summarize each structure (context, machine) used for constructing models for a given system using relations as EXTENDS, SEES, REFINES among the structures. We summarize the general form of an Event B development in the diagram. The main advice is to use the refinement of machines and events as much as possible.

10.3.1. *Basic elements of an Event B model*

We start by defining the events that are at the heart of this method and that react to a condition called a guard. An event is characterized by a parameter (t), a condition (also called a guard G) and an action (a relation P). One of the three parts may not be in the event and a special event called $skip$ corresponds to the absence of the three parts. $skip$ means that the variables are stuttering. Intuitively, the observation of an event is made in the case where the guard is true but the fact that the guard is true does not allow us to conclude that the event is or will be observed. Each event can be defined by a relationship before–after denoted by $BA(x, x')$.

An event is characterized by its guard, which is determined at the modeling phase and it can only be triggered if the guard is true. We will detail proof obligations generated for a given event e and explain the meaning of these proof obligations. In our chapter, we want to emphasize the role of refinement, which is defined on events. The general form of an event is as follows:

```
EVENT e
  ANY  t
  WHERE
    G(c, s, t, x)
  THEN
    x :|(P(c, s, t, x, x'))
  END
```

– c and s designate constants and visible sets by an event e are defined in the context of clause SEES.

– x is the state variable or a list of state variables.

– $G(c, s, t, x)$ is the guard or the enableness condition of e.

– $P(c, s, t, x, x')$ is the predicate stating the relation between the pre value of x, denoted as x, and the post value of x, denoted as x'.

– $BA(e)(c, s, x, x')$ is the *before-after* relation for the event e defined by $\exists t.G(c, s, t, x) \wedge P(c, s, t, x, x')$.

For each event e, POs are named according to the following format: $e/inv/ < type >$ where $< type >$ is either INV, or FIS, or GRD, or SIM, or THM, or $WFIS$, or WD, etc. and correspond to generated POs for ensuring invariance, guard strengthening, simulation, safety and well-definedness, etc. We do not list the complete list of possible names and refer to the book of J.-R. Abrial [ABR 10a] for a full version, as well as to the Rodin platform [ABR 10b]. Now we analyze how the POs are generated.

10.3.2. *Invariance properties in Event B*

The invariant $I(x)$ of a model is an invariant property for all events of a system, including the initial event. If e is an event of the model, then the condition of preservation of this invariant by this event is: $I(x) \wedge BA(e)(c, s, x, x') \Rightarrow I(x') \ (INV)$. $I(x)$ is written as a list of predicates labeled $inv_1 \ldots inv_n$ and interpreted as a conjunction. The condition on the initial conditions is as follows: $Init(x, s, c) \Rightarrow I(x) \ (INIT)$.

When an event e defines the predicate before–after $BA(e)(c, s, x, x')$, the feasibility of this event means that under hypothesis defined by the invariant $I(x)$ and guard grd(e), of the event, there is still x' such that $BA(e)(c, s, x, x')$. In other words, it means that this event, when observed, will not induce unwanted behaviors and we give a condition for each event: $I(x) \wedge \mathsf{grd}(e) \Rightarrow \exists x' \cdot BA(e)(c, s, x, x') \quad (FIS)$.

Safety properties are derived by the proof that the system invariant implies safety property $A(x)$ and, moreover, we add the context $C(s, c)$ of this proof. The context of this proof is given by the properties $C(s, c)$, where sets s and constant c are defined in the model: $C(s, c) \wedge I(x) \Rightarrow A(s, c, x) \quad (THM)$.

To conclude this point on POs, they are derived from the theorem 10.2 and we can therefore conclude the following property.

THEOREM 10.4.– Let $Th(s, c)$ be a theory defined by sets s, constants c and axioms $C(s, c)$ and let E be a finite list of events modifying x in the context define by the theory $Th(s, c)$. We assume the following points:

– VALS is a set of possible values for x.

– $\{r_0, \ldots, r_n\}$ is a set of relations $BA(e)(s, c, x, x')$ defined for event e of E and one of the events is the event $skip$.

– INIT(x) is the predicate defining the initial conditions of x.

If the POs (INIT) and (INV) are valid, then the relational model $(Th(s, c), x, \text{VALS}, \text{INIT}(x), \{r_0, \ldots, r_n\})$ satisifies the invariant $I(x)$ and the safety properties $A(s, c, x)$.

We now give the various POs generated from the general form given above. We assume that the context of theory is $C(s, c)$ and we use the notation $C(s, c) \vdash P$ to express the proof obligation P in $C(s, c)$ context. So, we have the following reformulation:

– *INIT/I/INV*: $C(s, c), INIT(c, s, x) \vdash I(c, s, x)$

– *e/I/INV*: $C(s, c), I(c, s, x), G(c, s, t, x), P(c, s, t, x, x') \vdash I(c, s, x')$

– *e/act/FIS*: $C(s, c), I(c, s, x), G(c, s, t, x) \vdash \exists x'.P(c, s, t, x, x')$

We have instantiated the induction principle to ensure invariance of I. The POs generator also performs important simplifications for facilitating the proof checking process by the provers.

10.3.3. *Refinement of events*

```
EVENT e
  ANY t
  WHERE
    G(c, s, t, x)
  THEN
    x :|(P(c, s, t, x, x'))
  END
```

```
EVENT f
  REFINES e
  ANY u
  WHERE
    H(c, s, u, y)
  WITNESSES
    t : W1(c, s, t, u, y)
    x' : W2(c, s, t, x', y)
  THEN
    y :|(Q(c, s, t, y, y'))
  END
```

In the above schema, $t : W1(c, s, t, u, y)$ is a proof witness to connect the current parameter u and the parameter t of the event e, $x' : W2(c, s, t, x', y)$ is a proof witness to connect the variable y and the next value of x. The event f refines the event e, when the observation of f at the concrete level, implies that the event e at the abstract level also appears. More formally, the refinement of e by f is defined by the formula: I $I(c, s, x) \quad \wedge \quad J(c, s, x, y) \quad \wedge \quad BA(f)(c, s, y, y') \quad \Rightarrow \quad \exists x'.(BA(e)(c, s, x, x') \quad \wedge \quad J(c, s, x', y'))$ where $J(c, s, x, y)$ is the invariant of the concrete level ensuring the relationship between concrete and abstract variables. We schematize refinement as follows:

abstract level	$I(x) \xrightarrow{e} I(x')$	$machine\ M : x, I(x)$
		$REFINES \uparrow$
concrete level	$J(x, y) \xrightarrow{f} J(x', y')$	$machine\ N : y, J(x, y)$

Note that the role of predicates $W1$ and $W2$ is to provide values to prove existential properties induced by parameters but also by reference to the abstract level. Without these hints, the user should propose possible values while using the interactive proof tools. The refinement of f by e also takes into account the case where f is a new event at the concrete level and in this case f refines $skip$ that does not change the variable x. We will give the above formulation as generated POs.

$$\text{– e/act/SIM: } \begin{pmatrix} C(s,c), \\ I(c,s,x), J(c,s,x,y), H(c,s,t,y), \\ Q(c,s,t,y,y'), \\ W1(c,s,t,u,y), W2(c,s,t,x',y) \end{pmatrix} \vdash P(c,s,t,x,x')$$

$$\text{– e/grd/FIS: } \begin{pmatrix} C(s,c), \\ I(c,s,x), J(c,s,x,y), \\ H(c,s,t,y), W1(c,s,t,u,y) \end{pmatrix} \vdash G(c,s,t,x)$$

We have given the clear definitions of generated POs to verify the refinement of an event by others. What remains is to define the structures of machines and contexts.

10.3.4. *Structures for Event B models*

The Event B modeling language provides a framework for supporting our methodology as applied to the development of sequential programs. Abrial [ABR 03b] has demonstrated the possibility of developing sequential programs using Event B. The modeling process deals with various languages, as seen by considering the triptych of Bjoerner [BJO 06a, BJO 06b, BJO 06c, BJØ 07]: $\mathcal{D}, \mathcal{S} \longrightarrow \mathcal{R}$. Here, the domain $\mathcal{D}$ deals with properties, axioms, sets, constants, functions, relations and theories. The system model $\mathcal{S}$ expresses a model or a refinement-based chain of models of the system. Finally, $\mathcal{R}$ expresses requirements for the system to be designed. Considering the Event B modeling language, we notice that the language can express *safety* properties, which are either *invariants* or *theorems* in a machine corresponding to the system. Recall that two main structures are available in Event B.

– Contexts express static information about the model.

– Machines express dynamic information about the model, invariants, safety properties and events.

10.3.4.1. *Contexts*

The first structure is called a context (see Figure 10.1), and it provides the definition of the sets, constants, axioms for sets and constants, and theorems that can be derived from the axioms of the context $\mathcal{D}$. The context $\mathcal{AD}$ is a previous context that has already been defined, and it extends the current context. A context is validated when sets $S_1, \ldots, S_n$, constants $C_1, \ldots, C_m$

and axioms $ax_1, \ldots, ax_p$ are well-formed and when all theorems $th_1, \ldots, th_q$ are proved.

CONTEXT $\mathcal{D}$
EXTENDS $\mathcal{AD}$
SETS
  $S_1, \ldots S_n$
CONSTANTS
  $C_1, \ldots, C_m$
AXIOMS
  $ax_1 : P_1(S_1, \ldots S_n, C_1, \ldots, C_m)$
  $\ldots$
  $ax_p : P_p(S_1, \ldots S_n, C_1, \ldots, C_m)$
THEOREMS
  $th_1 : Q_1(S_1, \ldots S_n, C_1, \ldots, C_m)$
  $\ldots$
  $th_q : Q_q(S_1, \ldots S_n, C_1, \ldots, C_m)$

MACHINE $\mathcal{M}$
REFINES $\mathcal{AM}$
SEES $\mathcal{D}$
VARIABLES x
INVARIANTS
  $inv_1 : I_1(x, S_1, \ldots S_n, C_1, \ldots, C_m)$
  $\ldots$
  $inv_r : I_r(x, S_1, \ldots S_n, C_1, \ldots, C_m)$
THEOREMS
  $th_1 : SAFE_1(x, S_1, \ldots S_n, C_1, \ldots, C_m)$
  $\ldots$
  $th_s : SAFE_s(x, S_1, \ldots S_n, C_1, \ldots, C_m)$
EVENTS
  EVENT initialisation
    BEGIN
      $x :|(P(x'))$
    END
  $\ldots$
  EVENT e
    ANY t
    WHERE
      $G(x, t)$
    THEN
      $x :|(P(x, x', t))$
    END
  $\ldots$END

Figure 10.1. *Context and Machine*

A context clearly states the static properties of the (system) model under construction. The *extends* construct enables reuse by extending a previously defined context.

The proof process is based on the management of sequents, with an associated environment for proof called $\Gamma(\mathcal{D})$. The proof environment includes axioms, properties and theorems already proved. An environment is initially provided, but the intention is to add new theorems. This means that we intend to prove the following properties in the sequent calculus style:

for any j in $\{1..q\}, \Gamma(\mathcal{D}) \vdash th_j : Q_j(S_1, \ldots S_n, C_1, \ldots, C_m)$.

Theorems for the context are proved using the RODIN tool, but it is clear that the process for constructing the domain $\mathcal{D}$ is crucial to modeling the system, from consideration of the triptych of Bjoerner [BJO 06a, BJO 06b, BJO 06c, BJØ 07] and variations of this methodology.

The possibility of reusing former definitions is crucial, but we do not consider this point in this chapter. Instead, we *simulate* the reuse of theories by manipulating the contexts directly. Among the requirements, we can list the theorems of the context, and we can, in fact, interpret the triptych as follows: for any

$$j \text{ in } \{1..q\}, \mathcal{D} \longrightarrow th_j : Q_j(S_1, \ldots S_n, C_1, \ldots, C_m).$$

Here, it appears that the system is not mentioned, and this is the case for static properties. Therefore, we have an interpretation of the triptych for the static information, which can be reused later for any system.

10.3.4.2. *Machines*

The dynamic part of a model is expressed using the notion of the *machine* (see Figure 10.1). A machine is either a basic machine or a refinement of an abstract machine. A machine models a state via a list of variables x that are assumed to be modifiable by events listed in the machine. The view is assumed to be closed with respect to events. Each event maintains an assertion called an *invariant*, which is a conjunction of logical statements called inv_j. Each reached state satisfies properties of the theorem part called safety properties. POs are given in section 10.6, and they are generated and checkable by the RODIN framework. The validation of the machine M leads to the validation of the safety and invariance properties.

We can obtain a variation of the triptych ($\Gamma(\mathcal{D}, M)$ is an associated environment for proof) as follows:

– For any j in $\{1..r\}$, $\Gamma(\mathcal{D}, M) \vdash INITIALISATION(x') \Rightarrow I_j(x', S_1, \ldots S_n, C_1, \ldots, C_m)$

– For any j in $\{1..r\}$, for any event e of M, $\Gamma(\mathcal{D}, M) \vdash (\bigwedge_{j \in \{1..r\}} I_j(x, S_1, \ldots S_n, C_1, \ldots, C_m)) \wedge BA(e)(x, x') \Rightarrow I_j(x', S_1, \ldots, S_n, C_1, \ldots, C_m)$

– For any k in $\{1..s\}$, $\Gamma(\mathcal{D}, M) \vdash (\bigwedge_{j \in \{1..r\}} I_j(x, S_1, \ldots, S_n, C_1, \ldots, C_m)) \Rightarrow SAFE_k(x, S_1, \ldots S_n, C_1, \ldots, C_m)$

We use temporal operators for expressing the safety and invariant properties.

– For any j in $\{1..r\}$, $\mathcal{D}, M \longrightarrow \Box I_j(x, S_1, \ldots S_n, C_1, \ldots, C_m)$.

– For any k in $\{1..s\}$, $\mathcal{D}, M \longrightarrow \Box SAFE_k(x, S_1, \ldots S_n, C_1, \ldots, C_m)$.

We summarize the requirements expressed by the machine M as follows:

$$\mathcal{D}, M \longrightarrow \Box \left(\begin{array}{c} \left(\bigwedge_{j \in \{1..r\}} I_j(x, S_1, \ldots S_n, C_1, \ldots, C_m) \right) \\ \left(\bigwedge_{k \in \{1..s\}} SAFE_k(x, S_1, \ldots S_n, C_1, \ldots, C_m) \right) \end{array} \right)$$

We will use the notation $\mathcal{I}(M)$ to stand for the invariant of the machine M and $\mathcal{SAFE}(M)$ to stand for the safety properties of the machine M. We have shown that requirements $\mathcal{R}$ are first expressed using the *always* temporal operator. To specify total correctness properties, we should extend the scope of the requirements language by adding *eventuality* properties. Eventuality properties will be defined in section 10.4, which will be specific to our methodology.

10.4. Formal development of a sequential algorithm

In this section, we discuss two simple case studies to illustrate how we can develop sequential algorithms using the Event B method following two development techniques. From previous works, we quote case studies developed by J.-R. Abrial [ABR 03b] and his transformation rules used from Event B models to obtain sequential algorithms; however, we have also proposed a method [MÉR 09b, MÉR 09a] providing a framework to guide refinement steps, relying on an interpretation of an event as a procedure call. The second approach allows us to produce recursive algorithms from an Event B model and to express an invariant in a simple way. Transformation techniques can be applied on the resulting recursive algorithms and are used to produce iterative algorithms implemented in a real programming language like Spec# [MÉR 13]. We illustrate these two techniques by two very simple examples: the problem *computing the sum of a vector of integer values* $v_1, \ldots, v_n$ and the problem *searching for an item x in a table t.*

10.4.1. *Derivation of an algorithm for computing the sum of a sequence of values by refinement and transformation of the model into an algorithm*

10.4.1.1. *Description of the problem*

At first, we state the sum s of the sequence v in the Event B language; the mathematical expression is easy: $s = \sum_{k=1}^{k=n} v(k)$. As the notation for the summation of a finite sequence is not available in Event B, we have to *define* this notion in a context *summation0*, which will contain inputs and specific notations of the problem.

Inputs of the problem n and v are defined as a non zero natural number ($axm1$ and $axm2$) and a total function defined on $1..n$ and ranging over $\mathbb{N}$ ($axm3$). We have to define the underlying theory of the problem.

Second, we introduce a sequence u of values defining partial summations: $\sum_{k=1}^{k=i} v(k)$, which is inductively defined:

– u is a total function from $\mathbb{N}$ into $\mathbb{N}$ (axiom $axm4$).

- Initially, the summation starts by 0 and $u(0) = 0$ (axiom $axm5$).

– When i is smaller than n, the value $u(i)$ is defined from $u(i-1)$ and $v(i)$ (axiom $axm6$).

– When i is greater than n, the value of $u(i)$ is $u(n)$ (axiom $axm7$).

Axioms are given in the context *summation0* and constitutes a theory which will be used for proving properties of models.

CONTEXT $summation0$
CONSTANTS
n, v, u
AXIOMS
$axm1 : n \in \mathbb{N}$
$axm2 : n \neq 0$
$axm3 : v \in 1 .. n \rightarrow \mathbb{N}$
$axm4 : u \in \mathbb{N} \rightarrow \mathbb{N}$
$axm5 : u(0) = 0$
$axm6 : \forall i \cdot i \in \mathbb{N} \land i > 0 \land i \leq n \Rightarrow u(i) = u(i-1) + v(i)$
$axm7 : \forall i \cdot i \in \mathbb{N} \land i > n \Rightarrow u(i) = u(n)$
THEOREMS
$thm1 : \forall i \cdot i \in \mathbb{N} \Rightarrow u(i) \geq 0$
END

In the above context, it is noted that the clause THEOREMS is used and its use allows us to derive properties for mathematical data defined by their axioms. In the current tool Rodin, the authors merge axioms and theorems in the clause AXIOMS. However, among the list of statements, the tool identifies the two different sets of statements for axioms and theorems. We use a notation that allows a better expression of these theories. Finally, each axiom is validated by a set of generated POs to ensure consistency of definitions. It is the same for theorems that must be proved from an environment defined by the axioms with the rules of proof assistant. So we have defined the mathematical framework of the problem and we will now define the problem of summation of the sequence v.

10.4.1.2. *Specification of the problem to solve*

The problem is to calculate the value of sum of elements of the sequence v. We define a machine *summation1,* which is a model expressing through the event summation, the expression of the *postcondition* $sum = u(n)$. In fact, new value of the variable sum amount is $u(n)$, when the event summation1 has been observed. The initial value of sum is any initialization. Finally, the variable sum must satisfy the simple invariant $inv1 : sum \in \mathbb{N}$. The event summation1 is simply an assignment of value $u(n)$ to sum.

```
MACHINE summation1
SEES summation0
VARIABLES
  sum
INVARIANTS
  inv1 : sum ∈ ℕ
EVENT INITIALISATION
  BEGIN
    act1 : sum :∈ ℕ
  END
EVENT summation1
  BEGIN
  act1 : sum := u(n)
  END
END
```

We can state an expression as a HOARE triple HOARE: $\{n > 0 \wedge v \in 1..n \rightarrow \mathbb{N}\} SUMMATION \{sum = u(n)\}$ where $SOMMATION$ is the algorithmic solution. The visible data or inputs are in the context *summation0*. The problem is then to find an algorithm $SUMMATION$ computing the value $u(n)$ and storing it in the variable sum. C. Morgan [MOR 90] uses the same method and we are only simulating his refinement calculus, with the objective to construct an algorithmic solution from a pre- and post specification.

We have described the domain of the problem and we have formulated what we want to calculate. The next step is the development of *calculation method,* which requires an *idea of solution* using refinement.

10.4.1.3. *Refining for computing*

We have defined the specification of the problem *calculating the sum of elements of the sequence v* and now we must find an algorithmic method for computing the value $u(n)$. In the previous machine, we state *what to compute* and now we define *how to compute*. The assignment $sum := u(n)$ is an expression for combining a variable sum and a constant $u(n)$. A well-known trivial and inefficient solution is to store the values of sequence u in a table t and to translate the assignment as $sum := t(n)$ where t verifies the property $\forall k.k \in dom(t) \Rightarrow t(k) = u(k)$ and this property forms an invariant $inv8$. The idea is to use the variable t ($t \in 0 \; nupto \nrightarrow \mathbb{N}$) to control the calculation and its progression. The progression is ensured by the event step2 that decreases the value $n - i$ and thus ensures the convergence of the process.

MACHINE $summation2$
  REFINES $summation1$
SEES $summation0$
VARIABLES
  sum, t, i
INVARIANTS
  $inv1 : i \in \mathbb{N}$
  $inv2 : i \geq 0$
  $inv3 : i \leq n$
  $inv4 : t \in 0 \,..\, n \nrightarrow \mathbb{N}$
  $inv5 : dom(t) = 0 \,..\, i$
  $inv6 : n \notin dom(t) \Rightarrow i < n$
  $inv7 : dom(t) \subseteq dom(u)$
  $inv8 : \forall k \cdot \begin{pmatrix} k \in dom(t) \\ \Rightarrow \\ t(k) = u(k) \end{pmatrix}$
  $inv9 : dom(u) = \mathbb{N}$

EVENT INITIALISATION
  BEGIN
    $act1 : sum :\in \mathbb{N}$
    $act2 : t := \{0 \mapsto 0\}$
    $act3 : i := 0$
  END
EVENT summation2
  REFINES summation1
  WHEN
    $grd1 : n \in dom(t)$
  THEN
    $act1 : sum := t(n)$
  END
EVENT step2
  WHEN
    $grd11 : n \notin dom(t)$
  THEN
    $act11 : t(i+1) := t(i) + v(i+1)$
    $act12 : i := i + 1$
  END
END

The model $summation2$ describes a process that gradually fills t and therefore retains all intermediate results. POs are fairly easy, to some extent, to prove through proof assistant. We summarize a proof statistics table at the end of development. It is quite clear that the variable t is in fact a witness or a track of intermediate values and this variable can be hidden in this model, when it will be refined. Before hiding this variable, we will put aside the value to maintain $t(i)$.

10.4.1.4. *Focus on a value to keep*

The next refinement $summation3$ leads to the introduction of a new variable $psum$ that will hold the value $t(i)$. It thus makes a *superposition* [CHA 88] on the model. The idea is that this model refines or simulates the previous model $summation2$; it also means that the properties of the refined model are verified by the new model $summation3$ as long as all the POs are discharged.

```
MACHINE summation3
  REFINES summation2
SEES summation0
VARIABLES
  sum, i, t, psum
INVARIANTS
  inv1 : psum ∈ ℕ
  inv2 : psum = u(i)
EVENT INITIALISATION
  BEGIN
  act1 : sum :∈ ℕ
  act2 : i := 0
  act3 : t := {0 ↦ 0}
  act4 : psum := 0
  END
```

```
EVENT summation3
  REFINES summation2
  WHEN
    grd1 : n ∈ dom(t)
    grd2 : i = n
  THEN
    act1 : sum := psum
  END
EVENT step3  REFINES step2
  WHEN
    grd1 : n ∉ dom(t)
    grd2 : i < n
  THEN
    act1 : t(i + 1) := t(i) + v(i + 1)
    act2 : i := i + 1
    act3 : psum := psum + v(i + 1)
  END
END
```

This model is very expressive and provides extensive information to ensure that the model is correct with respect to the specification expressed in the model $summation1$. It is even clear that this model $summation3$ is expensive in terms of use of variables. Refinement allows us to select only useful variables for calculation. In the following, we will make the more algorithmic model and keep the model sufficient concrete for calculating variables.

10.4.1.5. *Obtaining an algorithmic model*

In this last step, we refine the model $summation3$ by a model $summation4$ and we hide the variable t in the abstract model $summation3$. Thus, the model $summation4$ includes variables sum, $psum$ and i and it should also be noted that it satisfies safety properties called theorems in the model $summation4$. The properties are proved from the properties of the previous refined models. Here, we have a model with an initialization and two events:

– The event summation4 is observed, when the value of i is n and, in this case, the variable $psum$ contains the value $u(n)$. The invariant ensures that the value of $psum$ is $u(n)$.

– The event step4 is observed, when the value of i is smaller than n. It means that, while this value is smaller than n, the event can be observed and the traces generated from these events correspond to an iterative construct.

```
MACHINE summation4
  REFINES summation3
SEES summation0
VARIABLES
  sum, i, psum
THEOREMS
  inv1 : psum = u(i)
  inv2 : i ≤ n
EVENT INITIALISATION
  BEGIN
    act1 : sum :∈ ℕ
    act2 : i := 0
    act3 : psum := 0
  END
```

```
EVENT summation4  REFINES summation3
  WHEN
    grd1 : i = n
  THEN
    act1 : sum := psum
  END
EVENT step4  REFINES step3
  WHEN
    grd1 : i < n
  THEN
    act1 : i := i + 1
    act2 : psum := psum + v(i + 1)
  END
END
```

J.-R. Abrial [ABR 10a] proposes rules for progressively transforming models into algorithm. These rules are simple and we are considering them in our example.

Fusion of two events for deriving an iteration

Consider the two events which can be merged to obtain an algorithmic expression:

– If P is an invariant for S, then the two events can be merged into one event:

```
WHEN
  P
  Q
THEN
  S
END
```

```
WHEN
  P
  ¬Q
THEN
  T
END
```

```
WHEN
  P
THEN
  WHILE Q DO
    S
  OD;
  T;
END
```

– If P is not in the events, then there is no guard.

Merging two events for deriving a conditional statement.

Consider the two events which can be merged to obtain an algorithmic expression:

– If the condition on P is weaker then we can introduce a conditional statement:

```
WHEN
  P
  Q
THEN
  S
END
```

```
WHEN
  P
  ¬Q
THEN
  T
END
```

```
WHEN
  P
THEN
  IF  Q  THEN
    S
  ELSE;
    T;
  FI;
END
```

These two transformations are correct, since they preserve the generated traces. In our case, we can apply the first transformation on the model $summation4$. Let the three events of $summation4$:

```
EVENT summation4
  REFINES summation3
  WHEN
    grd1 : i = n
  THEN
    act1 : sum := psum
  END
```

```
EVENT pas3
  REFINES pas3
  WHEN
    grd1 : i < n
  THEN
    act1 : i := i + 1
    act2 : psum := psum + v(i + 1)
  END
```

```
EVENT INITIALISATION
  BEGIN
    act1 : sum :∈ ℕ
    act2 : i := 0
    act3 : psum := 0
  END
```

```
BEGIN
act1 : sum :∈ ℕ;
act2 : i := 0;
act3 : psum := 0;
WHILE   grd1 : i < n   DO
      act2 : psum := psum + v(i + 1)
      act1 : i := i + 1
OD;
act1 : sum := psum
END
```

The algorithm is obtained by merging the two events summation4 and step4 in an iteration and by sequential composition of the initialization.

$$\left\{\begin{pmatrix} n > 0 \\ \wedge v \in 1 \,..\, n \rightarrow \mathbb{N} \end{pmatrix}\right\}$$

```
BEGIN
sum :∈ ℕ;
i := 0;
psum := 0;
WHILE   i < n   DO
   psum := psum + v(i + 1)
   i := i + 1
OD;
sum := psum
END
```

$$\{sum = u(n)\}$$

Examples which have been treated with this method, can be found on the website dedicated to the Rodin project. In the publications [ABR 10a, ABR 03b], J.-R. Abrial has addressed both this technique and examples in more or less complicated way. Before concluding this study, it is important to give statistics on the number of POs and the difficulties of proofs, which are proved manually with the help of proof assistant. Table 10.1 indicates that 78.2% of POs are proved automatic but 21.7%, made by interaction with a proof assistant, are not complicated, as long as we use the progressive refinement.

Model	Total	Auto	Manual	% Auto	% Manual
summation0	5	0	5	0%	100%
summation1	4	3	1	75%	25%
summation2	23	21	2	87%	13%
summation3	7	5	2	71%	29%
summation4	7	7	0	100%	0%
Total	46	36	10	78.2%	21.7%

Table 10.1. *Table for statistics for the development of summation*

10.4.2. *Development of a sequential algorithm using the proof-based pattern call-as-event*

If we consider the problem to solve, we recall that we try to write a PROCEDURE correctly with respect to the pre/post specification:

PROCEDURE PROCEDURE(x; VAR y)
PRECONDITION $P(x)$
POSTCONDITION $Q(x, y)$

For the second development of a sequential algorithm, we use the proof-based pattern:

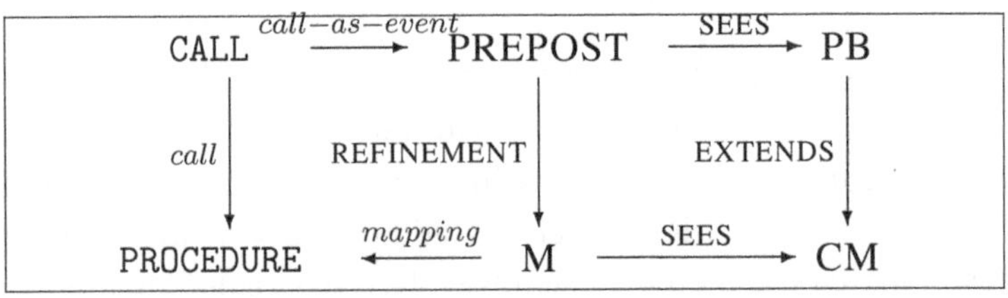

The schema is explained as follows:

– CALL is the call of PROCEDURE.

– PREPOST is the machine containing the events stating the pre- and post-conditions of CALL and PROCEDURE, and M is the refinement machine of PREPOST, with events including control points defined in CM.

– The *call-as-event* transformation produces a model PREPOST and a context PB from `CALL`.

– The *mapping* transformation allows us to derive an algorithmic procedure that can be mechanized.

– `PROCEDURE` is a node corresponding to a procedure derived from the refinement model M. `CALL` is an instantiation of `PROCEDURE` using parameters x and y.

– M is a refinement model of PREPOST, which is transformed into `PROCEDURE` by applying structuring rules. It may contain events corresponding to the calls of other procedures.

We consider the problem *searching a value v in a table t*. The specification is stated as follows:

PROCEDURE `search`$(x, t, n;$ VAR $i, ok)$
PRECONDITION $x \in A \wedge n > 0 \wedge t \in 1\,..\,n \rightarrow A$
POSTCONDITION $\begin{pmatrix} (\forall k \cdot k \in 1\,..\,n \Rightarrow t(k) \neq x) \Rightarrow ok = no \\ (\exists k \cdot k \in 1\,..\,n \wedge t(k) = x) \Rightarrow ok = yes \end{pmatrix}$

We try to identify the following elements of the pattern for our problem:

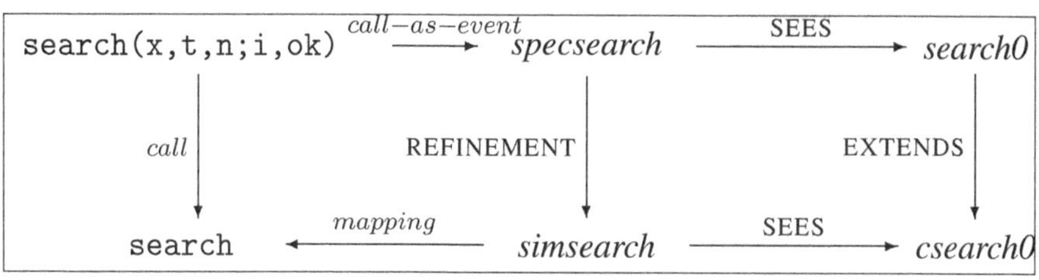

```
CONTEXT search0
SETS
  A
  REPLIES
CONSTANTS
  x, t, n, yes, no
AXIOMS
  axm1 : n ∈ ℕ1
  axm2 : x ∈ A
  axm3 : t ∈ 1 .. n → A
  axm4 : REPLIES = {yes, no}
  axm5 : yes ≠ no
END
```

Describing the context of the problem PB is given by a context $search0$ that easily defines the structure of search t. We also need to define a set of possible results. This context is actually used to correctly describe the pre-condition of the search $search0$. We can now define the specification itself by writing the machine $specsearch$ which will include events simulating the call `search`.

The machine $specsearch$ includes an initialization event and two events: find that models the procedure search, when it finds an element x in the table t, and unfind which models the procedure `search`, when it finds no element x in the table t. In fact, the two events give a definition of *what* but not of *how*, and these events are a simple way to describe the expected behavior. To define in a more operational way, we will *refine*. Thus, these two events are only two instances of calling this procedure.

```
MACHINE specsearch
SEES search0
VARIABLES
  i, ok
INVARIANTS
  inv1 : ok ∈ REPLIES
  inv2 : i ∈ 1 .. n

EVENT INITIALISATION
  BEGIN
  act1 : i :∈ 1 .. n
  act2 : ok := no
  END
```

```
EVENT find
  ANY
    j
  WHERE
    grd1 : j ∈ 1 .. n
    grd2 : t(j) = x
  THEN
    act1 : ok := yes
    act2 : i := j
  END
EVENT unfind
  WHEN
    grd1 : ∀k·k ∈ 1 .. n ⇒ t(k) ≠ x
  THEN
    skip
  END
END
```

To solve our problem from an operational point of view, we have to analyze the problem by considering several cases and we introduce a new variable c, which models the control of the search process. We use a new context $csearch0$ that extends $search0$ defining possible control points:

CONTEXT $csearch0$
EXTENDS $search0$
SETS
  $LOCS$
CONSTANTS
  $start, end, call1$
AXIOMS
  $axm1 : partition(LOCS, \{start\}, \{end\}, \{call1\})$
END

MACHINE $simsearch$
  REFINES $specsearch$
SEES $csearch0$
VARIABLES
  i, ok, c
INVARIANTS
  $inv1 : c \in LOCS$
  $inv2 : c = call1 \Rightarrow n \neq 1 \wedge ok = no$
  $inv3 : c = call1 \Rightarrow t(n) \neq x$
  $inv4 : c = end \wedge ok = yes \Rightarrow t(i) = x$
  $inv5 : c = end \wedge ok = no \Rightarrow (\forall g \cdot g \in 1 \,..\, n \Rightarrow t(g) \neq x)$
  $inv6 : c = start \Rightarrow ok = no$
...

The invariant describes what is happening during the computation:

– When the control point is at the *end* and when the variable *ok* is yes, then $t(i) = x$.

– When the control point is at the *end* and when the variable *ok* is no, then i contains any value and x does not occur in t.

To perform this calculation, two cases are introduced: either n is equal to 1 or n is not equal to 1. Consider the case where n is 1. In this case, we refine find by findone, to explain how the value of x can be found in an array with only one value, if it is indeed in this table, and we refine unfind by notfoundone in case the value of x is not in t (i.e. $t(1) \neq x$). We consider the two subcases and the translation into an algorithmic notation of these two events is immediate. Each event (findone and notfindone) is translated in the form of a conditional statement. We can also use EB2ALL [MÉR 11b] tool to translate the full model and get a C, C++, C# or Java program.

EVENT INITIALISATION
BEGIN
$act1 : i :\in 1 .. n$
$act2 : ok := no$
$act3 : c := start$
END
EVENT findone
REFINES find
ANY
j
WHERE
$grd1 : j \in 1 .. n$
$grd2 : t(j) = x$
$grd3 : c = start$
$grd4 : n = 1$
$grd5 : t(n) = x$
THEN
$act1 : ok := yes$
$act2 : i := 1$
$act4 : c := end$
END

EVENT nofindone
REFINES unfind
WHEN
$grd1 : \forall k \cdot k \in 1 .. n \Rightarrow t(k) \neq x$
$grd2 : n = 1$
$grd3 : t(n) \neq x$
$grd4 : c = start$
THEN
$act1 : c := end$
END

For the second case, we assume that n is not equal to 1 and we will refine both events find and unfind, for simulating a recursive search. We have events in parts related to the recursive analysis and these events are controlled using c:

– foundlastone *finds* the x in the last cell of the table t and sets the variable ok to yes. The control variable c gets the value end and the search is completed.

– notfoundlastone does find the value of x in the last cell of the table t and the *searching* process should continue on the remaining unvisited cells of the table t between 1 and $n-1$. The control is switching to $call1$ by updating c.

– The two next events are observed when $c = call1$, depending on whether there is a value. Each of these events simulates the procedure `search` between 1 and $n-1$. Obviously, it does not say how the searching process is done and we translate these two events by recursive calls. This point simplifies invariants and proofs; reference may be referring to the document [MÉR 09b, MÉR 09a] introducing this technique to refer to the calculation of the shortest path and thus to find that the invariant is fairly easy to find even if it is complex in its final form.

```
EVENT foundlastone
  REFINES find
  WHEN
    grd1 : n ≠ 1
    grd2 : t(n) = x
    grd3 : c = start
  WITNESSES
    j : j = n
  THEN
    act1 : c := end
    act2 : i := n
    act3 : ok := yes
  END
EVENT notfoundlastone
  WHEN
    grd1 : c = start
    grd2 : n ≠ 1
    grd3 : t(n) ≠ x
  THEN
    act1 : c := call1
  END
```

```
EVENT foundrec
  REFINES find
  ANY
    k
  WHERE
    grd1 : k ∈ 1 .. n − 1
    grd2 : c = call1
    grd3 : t(k) = x
  WITNESSES
  j : j = k
  THEN
    act1 : c := end
    act2 : i := k
    act3 : ok := yes
  END
EVENT notfounrec
  REFINES unfind
  WHEN
    grd1 : ∀l·l ∈ 1 .. n − 1 ⇒ t(l) ≠ x
    grd2 : c = call1
  THEN
    act1 : c := end
  END
END
```

We have to derive an algorithm from the list of events in the last model.

```
Procedure  search(x, t, n; i, ok)
BEGIN
  i :∈ 1 .. n; ok := no;
  IF  n = 1 ∧ t(n) = x   THEN
    ok := yes;   i := 1
  ELSE  IF  n = 1 ∧ t(n) ≠ x   THEN
    skip
  ELSE  IF  n ≠ 1 ∧ t(n) = x   THEN
    ok := yes;   i := n;
  ELSE  search(x, t, n − 1, i, ok);
  FI
END
```

The procedure (or algorithm) is generated by transformations of events into fragments of codes and these fragments are organized according to the variable *c*.

As we have already pointed out, this technique simplifies the construction of the invariant and also simplifies its proof. We [MÉR 09b, MÉR 09a] have made a list of classic calculation examples of the binomial coefficients, calculating the shortest path, the primitive recursive functions, the CYK algorithm analysis syntax. The tool EB2ALL [MÉR 11b] could be used to translate these models into C, C++, C# or Java. These two techniques of development simulate the method of C. Morgan [MOR 90] but the difference lies in the systematization of the refinement as simple as possible. Do not develop the model too quickly but introduce machines or intermediate models that will simplify the work of proof. Finally, note that this model has used the clause WITNESSES in the event foundrec in the form of $j : j = k$, this clause allows the prover to help for instantiating an existential quantifier that expresses in the abstract event refined by foundrec, it must be given a value j to observe the abstract event. This device allows us to retain information in the proof of the abstract model. In the balance sheet of POs, Table 10.2 describes automatic and interactive proofs, where three interactive proofs require some simple interactions.

10.5. Development of a distributed algorithm

10.5.1. *Modeling distributed algorithms*

We will illustrate a technique for developing distributed algorithms using the Event B method. This technique relies on a model of distributed computing called Visidia [MOS 14] and the objective is to produce an algorithm. We consider the problem of spanning tree of a graph and we consider a proof-based pattern integrating the refinement and allowing us to develop Visidia algorithms, which can be simulated on the platform Visidia [MOS 14]. The pattern of development is characterized by the following diagram:

Model	Total	Auto	Manual	% Auto	% Manual
search0	0	0	0	0%	0%
csearch0	0	0	0	0%	0%
specsearch	5	5	0	100%	0%
simsearch	52	49	3	94.2%	5.8%
Total	57	54	3	94.7%	5.3%

Table 10.2. *Table with statistics for proof effort in the development of the* `search` *procedure*

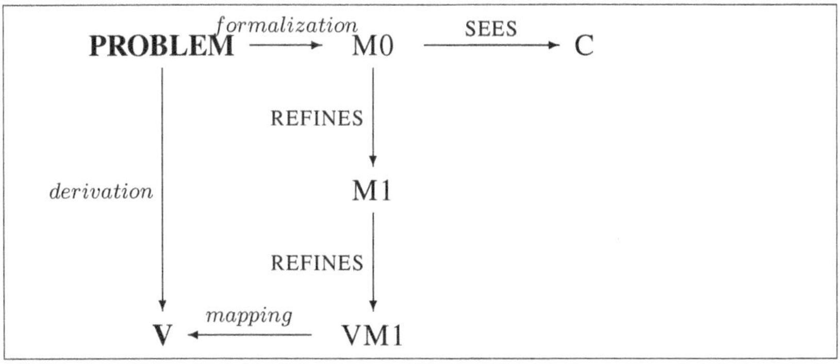

– The context *C* details the required properties of graphs, as distributed algorithms often use properties of graphs.

– The machine *M0* describes the problem to solve by giving an abstract event-based expression, for instance, the leader election in a network is expressed by the emergence of a node, which knows that it is the leader and the other nodes know that they are not leader but a leader can be elected. The existence of a solution obviously depends on the properties of the supporting graph of the distributed computing.

– Refinement of *M0* by *M1* expresses how a Visidia model performs a computation; a model in Visidia is a list of relabeling rules for graph, that simulates the execution of a distributed computing by localizing the computations at node or even between two neighbors. The model is very simple and relatively abstract, but is supported by a simulation tool.

– The next refinement simplifies the model *M1*, a model where no relabeling rule appears.

– *V* is a Visidia model derived from *VM1*; *mapping* ensures the translation of *VM1* into VISIDIA [MOS 14].

The leader election is simply defined by rules applied on two neighbors nodes:

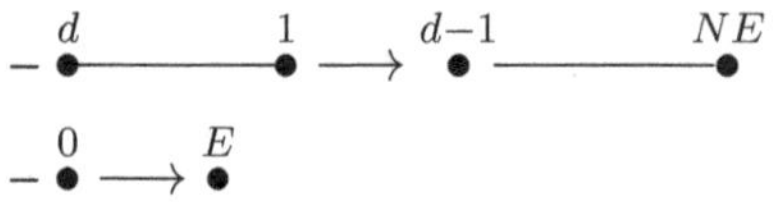

Each node is labeled by the number of neighbors and the application of rules is non-deterministic. The leader is a unique node, where all neighboring nodes request for this node to be a leader. We have developed the leader election protocol for IEEE 1394 [ABR 03a] on this principle, but up to a more concrete level, without resolving the issue of probabilities inherent in this type of algorithm. In Figure 10.2, we give a leader example in graph labeled with execution rules. Note that these rules calculate the leader in a graph without cycle.

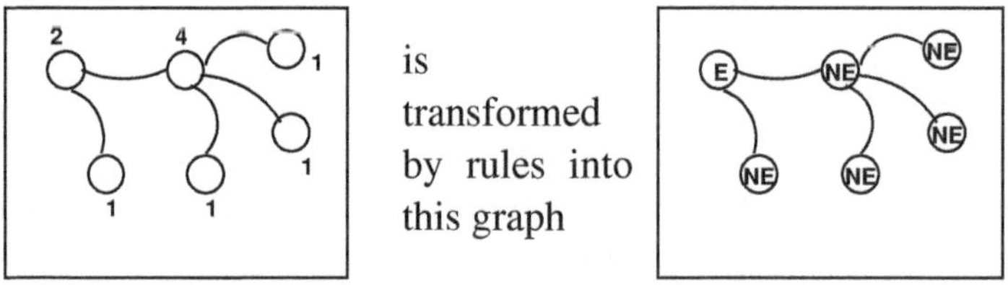

Figure 10.2. *Graph for the leader election*

We introduce rules for computing the spanning tree in the computing model. We present the development of the computation of spanning tree in this model (see Figure 10.3).

We apply the proof-based pattern for solving the problem of computing a spanning tree of a connected graph. The problem is called SPAN.

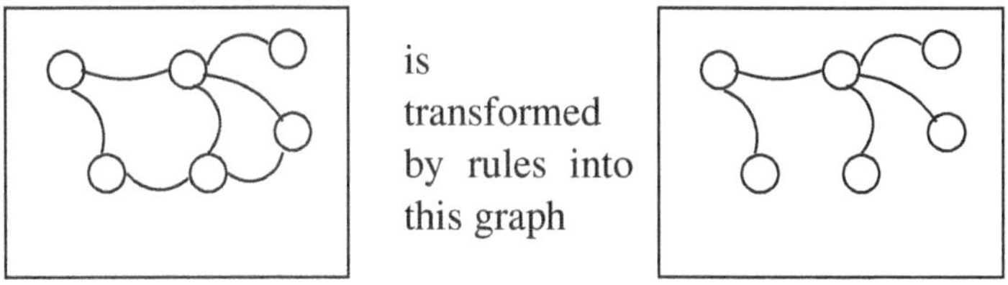

Figure 10.3. *Computing the spanning tree of graph with a model Visidia*

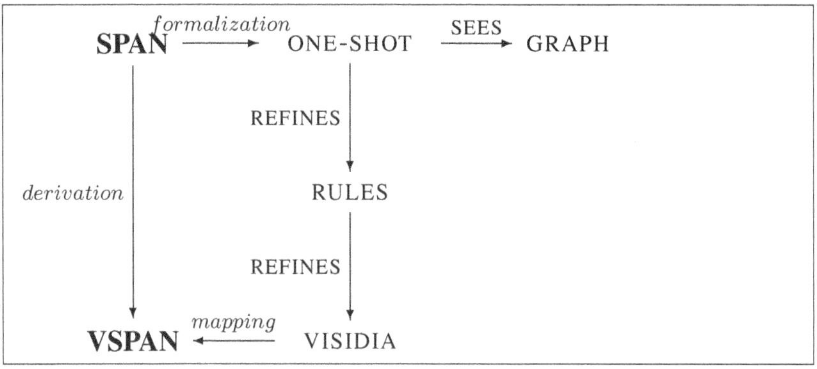

10.5.2. *Elements of a proof-based pattern*

The modeling of graphs is the starting point of this development. The context *graph* defines a graph g as a subset of the set $N \times N$ and adds axioms characterizing that it is symmetrical ($axm2$) and connected ($axm3$).

CONTEXT *graph*
SETS
  N
CONSTANTS
  g, r
AXIOMS
  $axm0 : r \in N$
  $axm1 : g \subseteq N \times N$
  $axm2 : g = g^{-1}$
  $axm3 : \forall s \cdot s \subseteq N \land r \in s \land g[s] \subseteq s \Rightarrow N \subseteq s$
END

Then, we give a predicated expression in an event for computing in one shot of a spanning tree. The machine $one - shot$ has a single-event span that sets the variable $span$ a spanning tree of graph g. The invariant is simply the expression $span$ is a subset of g, but it is a spanning tree as indicated by the expression of the value ar. The important point is to demonstrate that the value at exists. This is proved by showing that this event is feasible and derived from the existence of a spanning tree in the mathematical world.

MACHINE $one - shot$
SEES $graph$
VARIABLES
  $span$
INVARIANTS
  $inv2 : span \subseteq g$
EVENT INITIALISATION
  BEGIN
    $act2 : span := \varnothing$
  END
EVENT span
  ANY
    at
  WHERE
    $grd1 : at \subseteq g$
    $grd2 : at \in N \setminus \{r\} \rightarrow N$
    $grd3 : \forall s \cdot s \subseteq N \wedge r \in s \wedge at^{-1}[s] \subseteq s \Rightarrow N \subseteq s$
  THEN
    $act1 : span := at$
  END
END

Then, we refine this machine by another machine *simulating* the computation of this tree using two variables a and r. The variable a is used to contain nodes already selected during the calculation for the family tree and tr contains the spanning tree in construction. The invariant expresses that r is a forest that is to say that tr is a subset of g without cycle ($inv7$). The invariant $inv6$ expresses that tr is a total function with a domain a without r and tr plays the role of root of this tree.

MACHINE $rules$ REFINES $one-shot$
SEES $graph$
VARIABLES
$span, tr, a$
INVARIANTS
$inv4 : a \subseteq N$
$inv2 : tr \subseteq g$
$inv5 : r \in a$
$inv6 : tr \in a \setminus \{r\} \rightarrow a$
$$inv7 : \forall s \cdot \begin{pmatrix} s \subseteq a \\ \wedge r \in s \\ \wedge tr^{-1}[s] \subseteq s \end{pmatrix} \Rightarrow a \subseteq s$$

Two events span and rule1 model the possible modifications of tr and a. We note that it is important to choose a special node starting the process and a is initialized to the singleton containing r an arbitrary node. The event span detects the end of the process by testing whether a contains all the elements of N and sets $span$ to the value of tr. The role of rule1 is different and it chooses a node y not yet in a but that is reachable from a node of a by the graph g. This condition aims to avoid creating a cycle.

EVENT INITIALISATION
BEGIN
$act4 : span := \varnothing$
$act2 : tr := \varnothing$
$act3 : a := \{r\}$
END
EVENT span
REFINES span
WHEN
$grd1 : a = N$
WITNESSES
$at : at = tr$
THEN
$act1 : span := tr$
END

EVENT rule1
ANY
x, y
WHERE
$grd1 : x \in N$
$grd2 : y \in N$
$grd3 : x \mapsto y \in g$
$grd4 : x \in a$
$grd5 : y \notin a$
THEN
$act2 : a := a \cup \{y\}$
$act1 : tr := tr \cup \{y \mapsto x\}$
ENDEND

The machine $visidia$ refines the machine $rules$ by making it closer to Visidia model. In fact, it is a refinement to make the tree symmetric and to transform events in the rules of model $visidia$. For representing the membership of a, we use the color black. The new variable lb is used to localize this information for each node a and the invariant $inv2$ expresses this relationship property between nodes a and black nodes. Colors of marking are expressed by the set $MARKING$. At the initialization, all nodes are in white except r.

MACHINE $visidia$ REFINES $rules$
SEES $cvisidia$
VARIABLES
  tr, lb
INVARIANTS
  $inv1 : lb \in N \to MARKING$
  $inv2 : \forall i \cdot i \in a \Leftrightarrow lb(i) = BLACK$

The two events span and rule1 refine events with the same name in the model $rules$ and express local conditions in the variable lb.

EVENT INITIALISATION
  BEGIN
    $act2 : tr := \varnothing$
    $act4 : lb := lb0$
  END
EVENT span
  REFINES span
  WHEN
    $grd1 : \forall i \cdot i \in N \Rightarrow lb(i) = BLACK$
  THEN
    $skip$
  END

EVENT rule1
  REFINES rule1
  ANY
    x, y
  WHERE
    $grd3 : x \mapsto y \in g$
    $grd4 : lb(x) = BLACK$
    $grd5 : lb(y) = WHITE$
  THEN
    $act2 : lb(y) := BLACK$
    $act1 : tr := tr \cup \{y \mapsto x\}$
  END
END

The last step is the generation of rules in the distributed programming model Visidia and from the event rule1, we derive only one rule when one of the nodes is black at the initial state.

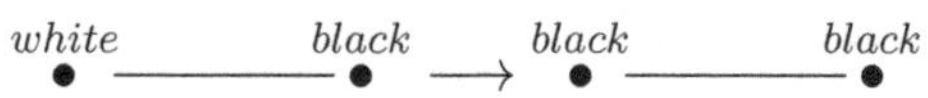

We extract the rule defining the Visidia program from the events of the machine $Visidia$, which contains in its events only localizable information. We can therefore deduce the distributed program that builds a spanning tree. The issue of convergence of this system is inferred from the analysis of decreasing the set $N\ a$ by the event rule1.

10.6. Tools

The Event B method is supported by tools like Atelier B [CLE 02] tool and Rodin [ABR 10b] platform.

10.6.1. *Atelier B*

The Atelier B tool [CLE 02] is freely distributed by the company ClearSy, which is proposed for the four platforms Windows, Linux, MacOS and Solaris; distribution under license and provides access to the documentations and case studies. This platform proposes features in a single frame for the Classical B method and Event B, where Event B syntax is slightly different. The offered features include the generation of POs to support the interactive proof, automatic refinement with Bart [CLE 10] tool and translation tools to C or ADA . The same company continues the free distribution of a platform called B4Free [CLE 04] based on the joint work of J.-R. Abrial and D. Cansell on the Balbulette [ABR 03c]. The idea of Balbulette is to provide an interface with the components of Atelier B as the proof obligation generator (POG), the prover or translators, to facilitate the developer's task in the approach of interactive proof and project management. One of the difficulties in the use of tools such as Atelier B lies in the interactive use of the proof assistant to discharge the POs that could not be handled by the automatic procedures. B4Free offers support during the process of proof and applying rules. This tool was a great success with the academic partners and its features are integrated into the Rodin platform.

10.6.2. *The Rodin platform*

The Rodin platform is supporting the Event B method in the Eclipse environment, and follows the work in the framework tools like Click'n'Prove [CAN]. It is dedicated to Event B but only provides functionality as plugins (translation into programming languages from Event B models or integration methodologies like UML). The Rodin platform was used to develop case studies illustrating this text and we [MÉR 09c, MÉR 10d, MÉR 10b, MÉR 10c] have used complementary tools like ProB [HEI 11], which provides the functionality, such as animation and model checking.

10.7. Conclusion and perspectives

10.7.1. *Applications in case studies*

The applications of this technique are numerous and the development of tools has facilitated these case studies. In our presentation, we have mainly used the Rodin platform but the Atelier B platform can be substituted. The proof assistant is partly provided by the platform and provers have been developed for Rodin in order to show both the Rodin platform and the Atelier B platform, which may also be modeled, and the strength of tools.

Distributed algorithms [ABR 03a] constitute a class of interesting complex algorithmic problems; the development of the leader election in the case of a acyclic undirected network has opened avenues of research for exploring issues of time integration [CAN 07b, REH 09] in development and management inherent and often implicit. Among distributed algorithms, the cryptographic algorithms constituent also an interesting class to measure the impact of refinement in their derivation but measure the expressive power of language Event B face model the Dolev–Yao attacker [BEN 08]. This has led to the development of algorithms for authentication distribution key [BEN 09c, BEN 09b, BEN 09a, BEN 10b, BEN 10a] highlighting basic mechanisms constituting these algorithms. To some extent, the difficulties lie in the understanding of property being modeled. These case studies have led also to the proposed development patterns facilitating introducing time [CAN 07b, REH 09] and patterns of development in the programming model distributed Visidia [MÉR 11a, MÉR 10a]. More recently, the issue of dynamic networks like networks graphs that evolve over time was studied in Event B for the discovery of topology [HOA 09b] or routing dynamic [MÉR 11c].

Regarding sequential algorithms, J.-R. Abrial [ABR 03b] has proposed rules for translating the Event B models into an algorithmic notation. The approach has been outlined in this chapter and actually allows us to (re)develop sequential algorithms. The approach based on the relation *call - event* [MÉR 09b, MÉR 09a] allows a relatively simple development of sequential algorithms facilitating the expression of invariant and highlighting a recursive analysis of the problem.

More conventionally, the Event B method is used to develop systems integrating software components and requiring objective arguments to certify their operation. J.-R. Abrial has designed a model of a mechanical press [ABR 10a] for ensuring the maintenance of security properties. Event B is an effective engineering framework with a formal system and a set of proof-based development patterns [ABR 10a, HOA 09a] and structures, and refinement charts [MÉR 11f]. Among the important studies, there are several case studies like pacemaker modeling [MÉR 10b, MÉR 11e, SIN 11] electric heart model [MÉR 11g, SIN 13, SIN 11] and medical protocols [MÉR 11g, SIN 13, SIN 11]. Modeling related to the security issues such as access control [BEN 07, BEN 10a] have also showed that the Event B language is sufficiently flexible to integrate access control models such as RBAC or ORBAC. Finally, the development of Event B models [MÉR 11h, MÉR 11d] can produce the code using integrated tools in the Rodin platform, which can be further used for assembling the system.

10.7.2. *Conclusion and perspectives*

The Event B method is based on a powerful language based on set theory and first order predicate calculus; it provides simple structures, *machines*, to describe reactive systems. To some extent, it can be described in other languages for reactive systems but refinement is a key concept that allows us to develop incrementally and safely complex models of relatively large systems like a mechanical press or a pacemaker. Furthermore, the tools have matured in both the interface and the proof tools; they require some practice, but with the proof assistant or the ProB animator, each sheds light on developed models and contributes to the validation of models. To conclude our outlook, we believe that the treatment of time, probabilistic aspects of less formal system integration languages, proof-based patterns of development and case studies are points to explore, while for now a development tool [ABR 08] is freely available.

10.8. Bibliography

[ABR 96] ABRIAL J.-R., *The B book – Assigning Programs to Meanings*, Cambridge University Press, 1996.

[ABR 03a] ABRIAL J.-R., CANSELL D., MÉRY D., "A mechanically proved and incremental development of IEEE 1394 tree identify protocol", *Formal Aspects of Computing*, vol. 14, no. 3, pp. 215–227, 2003.

[ABR 03b] ABRIAL J.-R., "Event based sequential program development: application to constructing a pointer program", in ARAKI K., GNESI S., MANDRIOLI D. (eds.), *FME*, Lecture Notes in Computer Science, Springer, vol. 2805, pp. 51–74, 2003.

[ABR 03c] ABRIAL J.-R., CANSELL D., "Click'n prove: interactive proofs within set theory", in BASIN D.A., WOLFF B. (eds.), *TPHOLs*, *Lecture Notes in Computer Science*, Springer, vol. 2758, pp. 1–24, 2003.

[ABR 08] ABRIAL J.-R., BUTLER M.J., HALLERSTEDE S., *et al.*, "A Roadmap for the Rodin Toolset", in BÖRGER E., BUTLER M. J., BOWEN J.P., *et al.*, (eds.), *ABZ*, *Lecture Notes in Computer Science*, Springer, vol. 5238, p. 347, 2008.

[ABR 10a] ABRIAL J.-R., *Modeling in Event-B: System and Software Engineering*, Cambridge University Press, 2010.

[ABR 10b] ABRIAL J.-R., BUTLER M. J., HALLERSTEDE S., *et al.*, "Rodin: an open toolset for modeling and reasoning in Event-B", *STTT*, vol. 12, no. 6, pp. 447–466, 2010.

[BAC 79] BACK R.J.R., "On correct refinement of programs", *Journal of Computer and System Sciences*, vol. 23, no. 1, pp. 49–68, 1979.

[BAC 89] BACK R.-J., KURKI-SUONIO R., "Decentralization of process nets with centralized control", *Distributed Computing*, vol. 3, no. 2, pp. 73–87, 1989.

[BAC 98] BACK R.-J., VON WRIGHT J., *Refinement Calculus A Systematic Introduction*, Graduate Texts in Computer Science, Springer-Verlag, 1998.

[BEN 07] BENAISSA N., CANSELL D., MERY D., "Integration of security policy into system modeling", *The 7th International B Conference – B2007*, Besançon, France, January 2007.

[BEN 08] BENAISSA N., "Modeling attacker's knowledge for cascade cryptographic protocols", in BÖRGER E., BUTLER M., BOWEN J.P., *et al.* (eds.), *First International Conference on Abstract State Machines, B and Z – ABZ 2008*, Lecture Notes in Computer Science, Springer, London, United Kingdom, vol. 5238, pp. 251–264, 2008.

[BEN 09a] BENAISSA N., MÉRY D., "Cryptographic protocols analysis in Event B", *Seventh International Andrei Ershov Memorial Conference "PERSPECTIVES OF SYSTEM INFORMATICS" – PSI 2009*, Lectures Notes in Computer Science, Springer-Verlag, Novosibisrk, Russia, November 2009.

[BEN 09b] BENAISSA N., MÉRY D., "Cryptologic protocols analysis using proof-based patterns", *Seventh International Andrei Ershov Memorial Conference "PERSPECTIVES OF SYSTEM INFORMATICS" – PSI 2009*, Lecture Notes in Computer Science, Springer-Verlag, Novosibirsk, Russia, June 2009.

[BEN 09c] BENAISSA N., MÉRY D., "Développement combiné et prouvé de systèmes transactionnels cryptologiques", *Approches Formelles dans l'Assistance au Développement de Logiciels – AFADL 2009*, Toulouse, France, January 2009.

[BEN 10a] BENAISSA N., La composition des protocoles de sécurité avec la méthode B événementielle, PhD Thesis, Henri Poincaré University, Nancy I, May 2010.

[BEN 10b] BENAISSA N., MÉRY D., "Proof-based design of security protocols", MAYR E.W. (ed.), *5th International Computer Science Symposium in Russia, CSR 2010, Lecture Notes in Computer Science*, KAZAN, Russia, Farid Ablayev, Springer, vol. 6072, pp. 25–36, June 2010.

[BJO 06a] BJORNER D., *Software Engineering 1 Abstraction and Modeling*, Texts in Theoretical Computer Science, EATCS Series, Springer-Verlag, 2006.

[BJO 06b] BJORNER D., *Software Engineering 2 Specification of Systems and Languages*, Texts in Theoretical Computer Science, EATCS Series, Springer-Verlag, 2006.

[BJO 06c] BJORNER D., *Software Engineering 3 Domains, Requirements, and Software Design*, Texts in Theoretical Computer Science, EATCS Series, Springer-Verlag, 2006.

[BJØ 07] BJØRNER D., HENSON M.C. (eds.), *Logics of Specification Languages*, EATCS Textbook in Computer Science, Springer, 2007.

[CAN] CANSELL D., Click'N'Prove. Available at http://plateforme-qsl.loria.fr/click %20n%20prove.php.

[CAN 07a] CANSELL D., MÉRY D., "*The Event-B Modeling Method: Concepts and Case Studies*", pp. 33–140, Springer, 2007. (see [BJØ 07])

[CAN 07b] CANSELL D., MÉRY D., REHM J., "Time constraint patterns for Event B development", in JULLIAND J., KOUCHNARENKO O. (eds.), *7th International Conference of B Users, January 17–19, 2007*, of Lecture Notes in Computer Science, Besançon, France, Springer-Verlag, vol. 4355, pp. 140–154, 2007.

[CHA 88] CHANDY K.M., MISRA J., *Parallel Program Design A Foundation*, Addison-Wesley Publishing Company, 1988.

[CLA 00] CLARKE E.M., GRUNBERG O., PELED D.A., *Model Checking*, The MIT Press, 2000.

[CLE 02] CLEARSY, AIX-EN-PROVENCE (F), ATELIER B., 2002. Available at http://www. atelierb.eu.

[CLE 04] CLEARSY, AIX-EN-PROVENCE (F), B4FREE, 2004. Available at http://www. b4free.com.

[CLE 10] CLEARSY, AIX-EN-PROVENCE (F), BART, 2010. Available at http://www. atelierb.eu.

[COU 78] COUSOT P., Méthodes itératives de construction et d'approximation de points fixes d'opérateurs monotones sur un treillis, analyse sémantique des programmes, PhD Thesis, Université Joseph Fourier, Grenoble, 21 March 1978.

[COU 79] COUSOT P., COUSOT R., "Systematic design of program analysis frameworks", *Proceedings Records of Sixth Proceedings of the Symposium on Principles of Programming Languages*, San Antonio, Texas, pp. 269–282, 1979.

[COU 92] COUSOT P., COUSOT R., "Abstract interpretation frameworks", *Journal of Logic and Computation*, vol. 2, no. 4, pp. 511–547, 1992.

[COU 00] COUSOT P., "Interprétation abstraite", *Technique et science informatique*, vol. 19, no. 1–2–3, pp. 155–164, January 2000.

[DIJ 76] DIJKSTRA E.W., *A Discipline of Programming*, Prentice-Hall, 1976.

[FLO 67] FLOYD R.W., "Assigning meanings to programs", in SCHWARTZ J.T. (ed.), *Proc. Symp. Appl. Math. 19, Mathematical Aspects of Computer Science*, American Mathematical Society,, vol. 19, pp. 19–32, 1967.

[HEI 11] HEINRICH-HEINE-UNIVERSITÄT DÜSSELDORF, The ProB animator and model checker. Available at http://www.stups.uni-duesseldorf.de/ProB, 2000–2011.

[HOA 69] HOARE C.A.R., "An axiomatic basis for computer programming", *Communications of the Association for Computing Machinery*, vol. 12, pp. 576–580, 1969.

[HOA 09a] HOANG T.S., FURST A., ABRIAL J.-R., "Event-B patterns and their tool support", in HUNG D.V., KRISHNAN P. (eds.), *SEFM*, IEEE Computer Society, pp. 210–219, 2009.

[HOA 09b] HOANG T.S., KURUMA H., BASIN D.A., *et al.*, "Developing topology discovery in Event-B", *Sci. Comput. Program.*, vol. 74; no. 11–12, pp. 879–899, 2009.

[HOL 97] HOLZMANN G., "The spin model checker", *IEEE Trans. on software engineering*, vol. 16, no. 5, pp. 1512–1542, May 1997.

[LAM 80] LAMPORT L., "Sometime is sometimes not never: a tutorial on the temporal logic of programs", *Proceedings of the Seventh Annual Symposium on Principles of Programming Languages*, pp. 174–185, 1980.

[LAM 94] LAMPORT L., "A temporal logic of actions", *Transactions On Programming Languages and Systems*, vol. 16, no. 3, pp. 872–923, May 1994.

[LAM 02] LAMPORT L., *Specifying Systems: The TLA$^+$+ Language and Tools for Hardware and Software Engineers*, Addison-Wesley, 2002.

[MCM 93] MCMILLAN K.L., *Symbolic Model Checking*, Kluwer Academic Publishers, 1993.

[MÉR 09a] MÉRY D., "A simple refinement-based method for constructing algorithms", *ACM SIGCSE Bulletin*, vol. 41, no. 2, pp. 51–59, June 2009.

[MÉR 09b] MÉRY D., "Refinement-Bbsed guidelines for algorithmic systems", *International Journal of Software and Informatics*, vol. 3, nos. 2–3, pp. 197–239, September 2009.

[MÉR 09c] MÉRY D., SINGH N.K., Pacemaker's functional behaviors in Event-B, Research report, University of Lorraine, 2009.

[MÉR 10a] MÉRY D., MOSBAH M., TOUNSI M., "Proving distributed algorithms by combining refinement and local computations", in BENDISPOSTO J., LEUSCHEL M., ROGGENBACH M. (eds.), *AVOCS 2010 10th International Workshop on Automated Verification of Critical Systems*, Dusseldorf, Allemagne, Germany, September 2010.

[MÉR 10b] MÉRY D., SINGH N.K., "Functional behavior of a cardiac pacing system", *International Journal of Discrete Event Control Systems (IJDECS)*, Dr. MOHAMED KHALGUI, vol. 1, December 2010.

[MÉR 10c] MÉRY D., SINGH N.K., Technical report on formal development of two-electrode cardiac pacing system, Research report, University of Lorraine, February 2010.

[MÉR 10d] MÉRY D., SINGH N.K., "Trustable formal specification for software certification", in MARGARIA T., STE B. (eds.), *4th International Symposium On Leveraging Applications of Formal Methods – ISOLA 2010*, of Lecture Notes in Computer Science, Heraklion, Crete, Greece, Springer, vol. 6416, pp. 312–326, October 2010.

[MÉR 11a] MÉRY D., MOSBAH M., TOUNSI M., "Refinement-Based Verification of Local Synchronization Algorithms", in BUTLER M., SCHULTE W., (eds.), FM, Lecture Notes in Computer Science, Springer, vol. 6664, p. 338–352, 2011.

[MÉR 11b] MÉRY D., SINGH N.K., EB2C: a tool for Event-B to C conversion support, 2011. Available at http://eb2all.loria.fr.

[MÉR 11c] MÉRY D., SINGH N.K., "Analysis of DSR protocol in Event-B", *13th International Symposium on Stabilization, Safety, and Security of Distributed Systems (SSS 2011)*, 2011.

[MÉR 11d] MÉRY D., SINGH N.K., B2C : A Tool for Event-B to C Conversion Support, http://eb2all.loria.fr., 2011.

[MÉR 11e] MÉRY D., SINGH N.K., "Formal development and automatic code generation: cardiac pacemaker", *International Conference on Computers and Advanced Technology in Education (ICCATE 2011)*, 2011.

[MÉR 11f] MÉRY D., SINGH N.K., "A generic framework: from modeling to code", *ISSE*, vol. 7, no. 4, p. 227–235, 2011.

[MÉR 11g] MÉRY D., SINGH N.K., "Formalisation of the heart based on conduction of electrical impulses and cellular-automata", *International Symposium on Foundations of Health Information Engineering and Systems (FHIES 2011)*, 2011.

[MÉR 11h] MÉRY D., SINGH N.K., "A generic framework: from modeling to code", *Fourth IEEE International workshop UML and Formal Methods (UML&FM'2011), (to be appeared in special issue of ISSE NASA Journal, Innovations in Systems and Software Engineering)*, 2011.

[MÉR 11g] MÉRY D., SINGH N.K., "Medical protocol diagnosis using formal methods", *International Symposium on Foundations of Health Information Engineering and Systems (FHIES 2011)*, 2011.

[MÉR 13] MÉRY D., MONAHAN R., "Transforming Event B models into verified C# implementations", LISITSA A., NEMYTYKH A.P. (eds.), *VPT@CAV*, of *EPiC Series*, EasyChair, vol. 16, pp. 57–73, 2013.

[MOR 90] MORGAN C., *Programming from Specifications*, Prentice Hall International Series in Computer Science, Prentice Hall, 1990.

[MOS 14] MOSBAH M., VISIDIA. Available at http://visidia.labri.fr., 2014.

[REH 09] REHM J., Gestion du temps par le raffinement, PhD Thesis, Henri Poincaré University, Nancy I, December 2009.

[SIN 11] SINGH N.K., Fiabilité et sûreté des systèmes informatiques critiques, Thèse d'université, Université Henri Poincaré Nancy 1, October 2011.

[SIN 13] SINGH N.K., *Using Event-B for Critical Device Software Systems*, Springer, 2013.

[TUR 49] TURING A., "On checking a large routine", *Conference on High-Speed Automatic Calculating Machines*, University Mathematical Laboratory, Cambridge, 1949.

11

B-RAIL: UML to B Transformation in Modeling a Level Crossing

11.1. Introduction

The use of computer science has increased over recent years. The introduction of computers into more or less complex systems must be carried out with care. This development affects both everyday products (domestic electrical appliances, cars, etc.) and industrial products (industrial management systems, medical equipment, financial transactions, rail systems, etc.).

Informal specifications provide a description of what is required of a computer system using natural language. They describe the services and operating conditions expected of an element. In order to produce a system which corresponds to the specified requirements, these requirements are described in a prescriptive model.

The modeling of complex rail systems presents significant difficulties, particularly in cases involving safety functions. In this chapter, we have chosen to consider level crossings (railroad crossings), which constitute a critical sub-system.

In this chapter, we propose a modeling methodology based on the pairing of a semi-formal method, unified modeling language (UML) [OMG 07], and a formal method, the B method [ABR 96], to provide the rigor needed when

---

Chapter written by Jean-Louis BOULANGER.

designing critical systems. UML notation allows us to describe a system in its environment. The impact of faults is formalized in the form of use cases and sequence diagrams. The behavior of the system is described as a class graph, and for each graph, behavior is characterized by a state/transition diagram. At the end, we propose a process for the translation of UML models into B language. This process is currently centered on the use of state/transition diagrams. Work is currently underway to integrate the translation of OCL constraints into B into our process.

The chapter begins with a brief presentation of the issues associated with level crossings, and a rapid presentation of UML notation. We then cover the different stages of our methodology point by point.

11.2. Level crossings: general overview

A level crossing is characterized as the intersection of a road traffic route and a rail route. The zone of intersection between the two traffic zones is known as the "danger zone". Level crossings remain a source of accidents despite the use of protection systems.

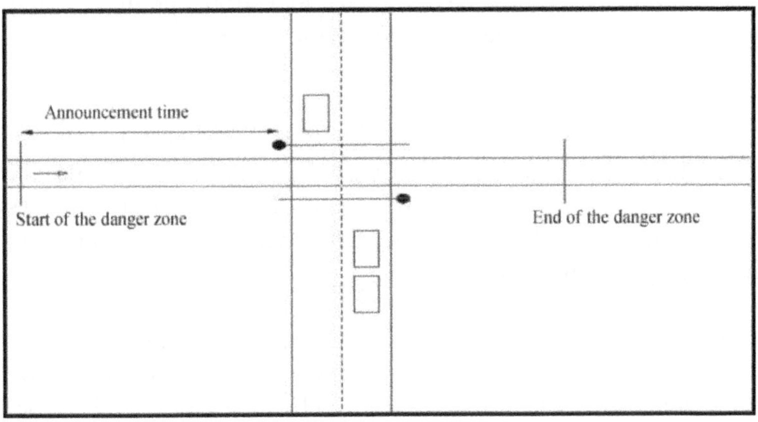

Figure 11.1. *Level crossing*

We have chosen to use the operational specification supplied by [JAN 00] as our initial informal specification. This operational specification presents a description involving "real-time" constraints and distributions for an entirely software-controlled level crossing. We shall begin by considering a single railway line in intersection with a two-way road. The zone prior to the intersection is known as the announcement zone.

A classic level crossing, as shown in Figure 11.1, is equipped with barriers and traffic lights. The light signals consist of a flashing orange light and a red light. When the signals are extinguished, road users (drivers, pedestrians, cyclists, etc.) may cross. The flashing orange signal indicates a request to stop and the red light indicates that the passage is closed and rail traffic takes priority.

The level crossing we wish to model may be controlled by local agents. In this case, these agents will have all of the abilities required to ensure the safety of the level crossing.

In this initial presentation, we do not aim to redefine the functional specification, but rather to present those elements which are relevant for our study. As space does not permit an exhaustive presentation of the specification, readers may wish to refer to [JAN 00] for full details.

11.3. Managing requirements

Examples of requirement management in automotive and rail contexts are presented in [BOU 06, RAM 09] Chapter 2 and [RAM 11] Chapter 3. The purpose of this section is to provide those elements necessary for understanding our specific example.

11.3.1. *Requirements*

The standards applicable in different domains necessitate identification of the requirements of software applications. Note that several terms are used synonymously in published works on the subject, including prescriptions, recommendations, requirements, constraints and properties. The general standard CEI/IEC 61508 [IEC 08] uses the notion of "prescriptions", but the notion of "requirements" is the most widespread.

Two main types of requirement exist, as shown in Figure 11.2: functional and non-functional requirements (safety, reliability, performance, etc.).

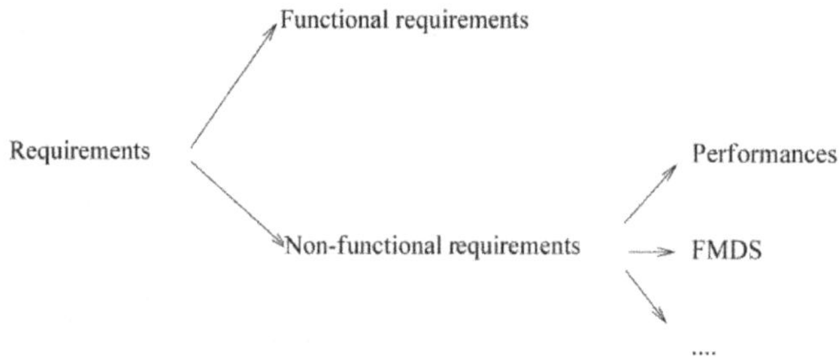

Figure 11.2. *Different requirement types*

Table 11.1 is taken from [STA 94], and shows that over 30% of the causes of failure in system creation are the result of incomplete requirements, omissions in requirements or unrealistic requirements.

Description	%
Incomplete requirement	13.1
Lack of user involvement	12.4
Lack of resources	10.6
Unrealistic expectations	9.9
Lack of executive support	9.3
Changing requirement/specification	8.7
Lack of planning	8.1
Didn't need it any longer	7.5

Table 11.1. *Causes of failure*

[STA 01] identifies the implementation of a requirement management environment as the best way of having a significant impact on the success of a project. The definition of a minimum set of requirements produces a manageable base and may be used as a tool for communication between teams.

The main difficulty therefore lies in defining the notion of requirements. Several projects have attempted to provide a precise definition of requirements and the way in which they should be taken into account.

[HUL 05] gives one of the fullest summaries. For our purposes, we shall use the following definition, developed for use in industrial contexts.

11.3.2. *Recommendations, requirements and properties*

The creation of a contract involves two parties, the client and the supplier. A contract constitutes an agreement by the supplier to produce a system which will satisfy the requirements of the client. The client's demands are generally expressed using a functional specification document.

The importance of these client requirements is variable. Certain demands may be linked to functional requirements, regulatory obligations (general standards, trade standards, etc.) and/or operational safety requirements, notably in the case of safety critical systems.

DEFINITION 11.1.– REQUIREMENT[1].– *A requirement is a stipulation which translates a need and/or constraints (techniques, costs, time delays, etc.). This stipulation may be expressed in a natural, mathematical or other language.*

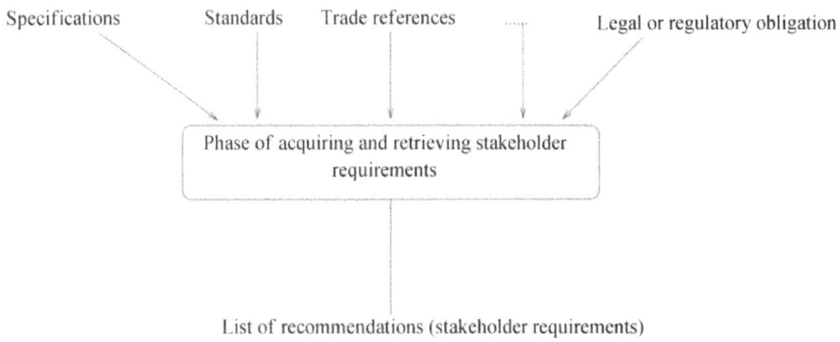

Figure 11.3. *Recommendation acquisition phase (stakeholder requirements)*

For clear identification, each requirement is treated as an element with a unique identification label which characterizes an element of the system to be created.

1 The AFIS, *Association Française d'Ingénierie Système* (French Association of Systems Engineers), includes a workgroup with a specific focus on managing requirements. For more information, see www.afis.fr.

The term “requirement” has several meanings, depending on the level at which it is used: expression of client needs, expression of the service to provide or expression of the effective service provided.

The initial documents for a system (functional specification, standards, trade references, regulations, etc.) contain requirements which must be taken into account when producing a system. The first stage (Figure 11.3) involves highlighting stakeholder requirements. To distinguish these stakeholder requirements, which constitute a form of input into the process, from the requirements generated during later phases, we shall use the term “recommendations”.

DEFINITION 11.2.– RECOMMENDATION.– *A recommendation is a stakeholder requirement which constitutes a “desire”. It may be explicit (e.g. contained in the functional specification or a trade reference document) or implicit.*

This first phase results in the production of a list of recommendations. These are often very badly expressed from a realization perspective, and may be too precise (involving technological choices), too general, not applicable, etc.

Figure 11.4 shows a summary of the user requirement acquisition process.

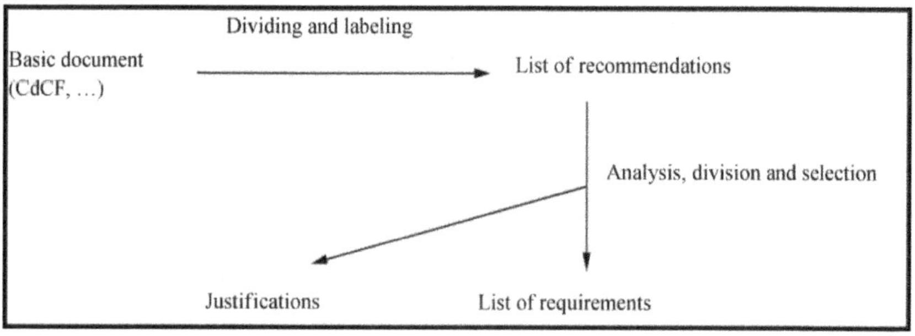

Figure 11.4. *Requirement establishment process*

This acquisition phase is followed by an extraction/elicitation phase, which aims to define requirements to take into account when creating the system. This phase is carried out in collaboration with the client.

A set of criteria needs to be established before defining requirements (recommendations or properties). These criteria are used to qualify requirements. In general terms, requirements must be unambiguous, complete and consistent. From a process perspective, requirements must be identifiable, verifiable and modifiable.

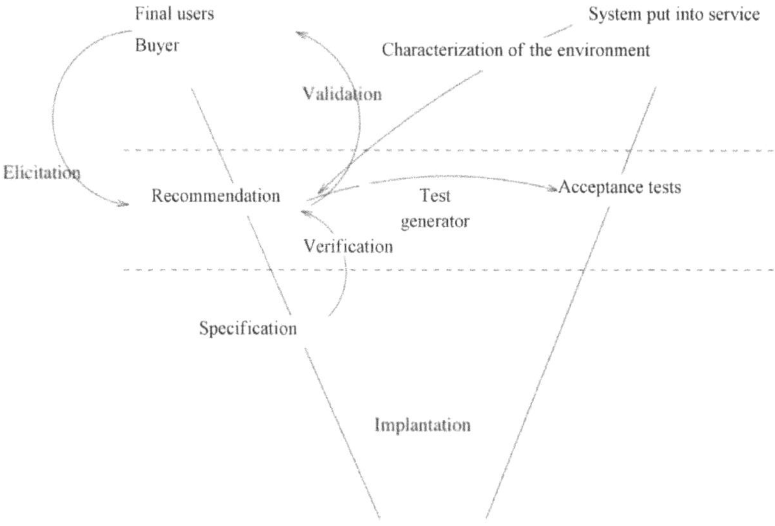

Figure 11.5. *Elicitation, traceability and verification*

As we see from Figure 11.5, a verification process must be established to show that the recommendations expressed by the stakeholder have been taken into account during creation of the system.

Requirements are analyzed and taken into account at each stage of the system creation process. In the context of hardware and/or software design phases, a requirement may be transformed into a property or properties related to specific components.

DEFINITION 11.3.– PROPERTY.– *A property is a characteristic which a component (hardware or software) must verify.*

Properties are generally grouped into two categories: safety properties and liveness properties.

DEFINITION 11.4. – SAFETY PROPERTY.– *A safety property expresses the fact that something bad will not happen during execution.*

Examples of safety properties include the absence of blockages, mutual exclusion, etc., or, in this particular context, the absence of collisions between trains.

DEFINITION 11.5.– LIVENESS PROPERTY.– *A liveness property expresses the fact that something good will always happen during execution.*

The completion of an application, the absence of famine (constant progression of applications) and guaranteed service are all examples of liveness properties.

Any property P may be expressed as the conjunction of a liveness property V and a safety property S.

11.3.3. *Requirements engineering*

In this context, we are not concerned with purely software- or hardware-based applications, but with the development of a complex system. The requirement generation process (identification, traceability, classification, etc.) for a complete system is generally referred to as requirements engineering. This process may or may not make use of tools. In this section, we present the basis of this process and its implementation.

11.3.3.1. *From recommendations to requirements*

As we see from Definition 11.2, client recommendations can be expressed using different formalisms of varying formality levels. Generally, requirements at this level are expressed in natural language and intervention is required to make them useable. This first phase is used to define system requirements.

The aim of the analysis and transformation process (Figure 11.6) is to clarify the recommendation text, highlighting any conflicts (requirements which are contradictory or have different aims), lacunas, unspoken assumptions, etc. This stage involves the removal of descriptive aspects and concentrates the focus on essential aspects.

This first phase leads to the creation of a set of requirements, used as input for the system analysis phase. As we shall see, requirements are linked to analysis levels. Each requirement possesses at least four attributes: a label, a description, a level and a justification.

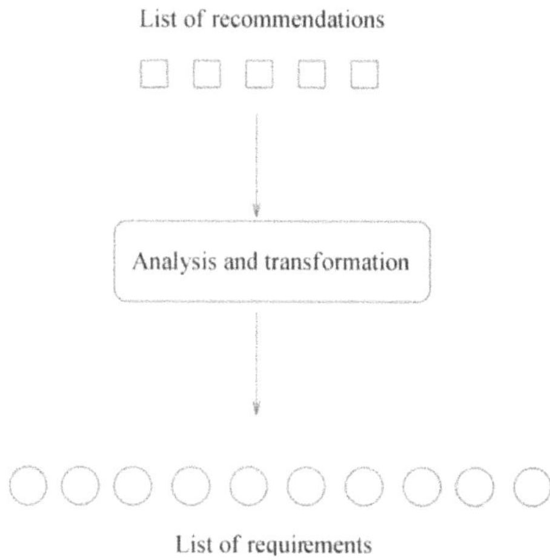

Figure 11.6. *From recommendations to requirements*

We may add other attributes qualifying the requirement to this list: family (functional, RAM, safety, performance, etc.), priority (defined as a function of the project), verifiability (yes/no), verification type (test, simulation, etc.), source (who), state (awaiting treatment, analyzed, rejected, etc.), document type, version, etc. Attributes must be defined at the beginning of the project.

11.3.3.2. *Traceability*

Figure 11.7 shows the ways in which client recommendations may be present throughout the system, and the way in which the process may continue down to the software and hardware elements level.

During the verification phase for level n_i, we must demonstrate that the requirements for this level relate to the higher level, n_{i-1}. This relationship is demonstrated using traceability procedures.

The implementation of traceability requires us to define at least one connection between two objects. In the case of requirements, traceability connections should allow us to show that a requirement at level n_i is connected to a requirement from the previous level n_{i-1}. By following the connection in the opposite direction, we are able to show that no requirements have been forgotten during the realization process.

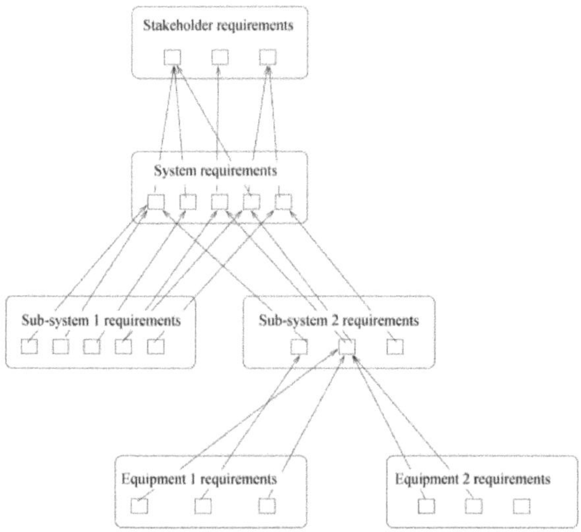

Figure 11.7. *Partial traceability from client requirements to specific equipment requirements*

As we see from Figure 11.8, a requirement (from recommendations to properties) may be subjected to a variety of basic transformations. Two of these cases, the addition and the removal of requirements, are particularly interesting as justification is required in both situations.

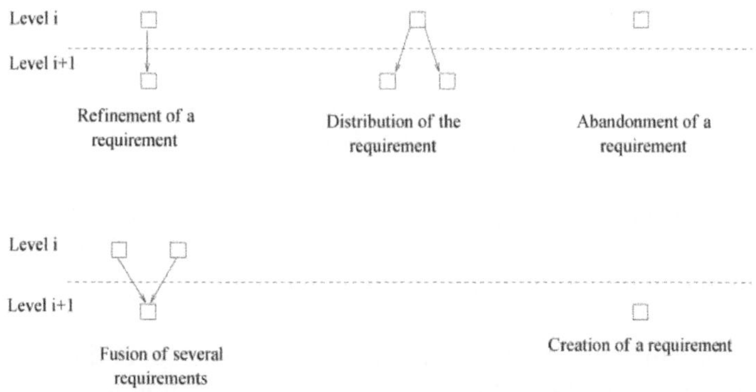

Figure 11.8. *Basic transformations of requirements*

The purpose of traceability is to define links between requirements. As we see from Figure 11.9, the basic connection shows a relationship between two requirements on different, consecutive levels.

This connection defines an “is derived from” type relationship. The inversion of this connection gives an “is taken into account by” type relationship.

1. Link “is taken into account by” 2. “Logical” link between requirements

Figure 11.9. *Connections between requirements*

The “is derived from” connection may not be sufficient to describe more complex relationships between requirements. As we see in part 2 of Figure 11.9, we can also define “logical” relationships (using OR, AND and other operators) between requirements. This type of complex relationship may be used as a means of recording part of the reasoning process.

Requirements are then associated with system functions. A function is a behavior which is expected of the system. This process is repeated for all sub-systems, pieces of equipment, hardware and software aspects.

Figure 11.10 shows a traceability matrix used to connect requirements and functions, and to associate requirements with other, derived requirements.

Part 1 of Figure 11.10 shows the functional relationship and the association of requirements across two levels. Function Fct1 is made up of three sub-functions. As we see from part 2, requirement Rq2 is broken down into two requirements which are associated with two sub-functions of Fct1.

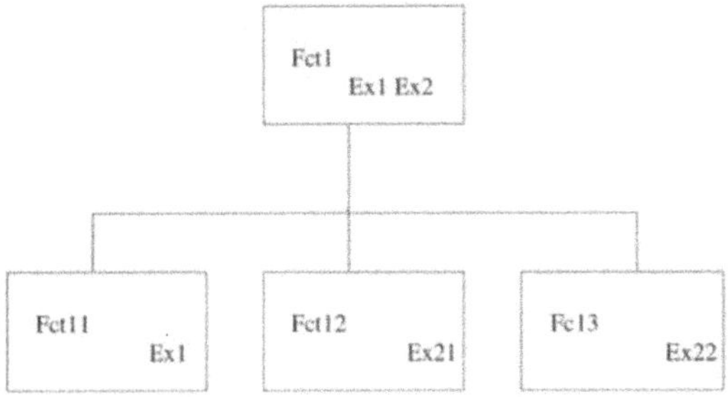

1. Functional tree view

	Ex1	Ex2
Fct11	Ex1	
Fct12		Ex21
fct13		Ex22

2. Traceability matrix

Figure 11.10. *Requirement traceability diagrams*

11.3.3.3. *Verification*

A requirement verification phase is implemented for each stage in the production process. This phase aims to show:

– that the initial requirement has been taken into account: this requires traceability between requirements at the current level and at the preceding (higher) level. Traceability must be verified through the existence and justification of connections;

– that the set of requirements taken as a whole is correct: we must show that our requirements are understandable, unambiguous, verifiable, possible, etc., and that the set of requirements is coherent (free from conflicts).

When considering traceability, we should be able to show that all requirements have been implemented, but also that all implemented aspects are required.

11.3.3.4. *Activities*

Requirements are used to create connections between documents (specifications, design documents, coding files, etc.), but also as test objectives. Different test categories (unit tests, software/software integration, hardware/software integration, functional tests and receipt tests) can be associated with requirements using the verification type attribute. This creates a requirement management process which allows us to connect initial requirements, production choices and validation phases (see Figure 11.11).

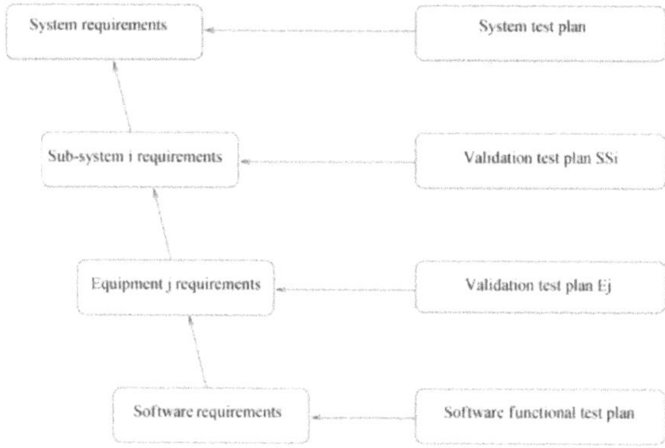

Figure 11.11. *Connections between activities*

During the verification phase, we check requirement coverage levels and the coherency of the established connections. From a project persepctive, the verification of requirement coverage allows us to quantify work which has been carried out and that which remains to be done.

Mastering the evolution of requirements and analyzing the impact of these developments on associated requirements and on products constitute key elements in requirements engineering. This mastery of evolutions represents the main difficulty of requirements engineering.

11.3.3.5. *Implementation*

Requirements management involves the establishment of simple mechanisms, such as:

– identifier management;

– description of requirements;

– definition of a traceability table.

A text edition tool may therefore be sufficient[2] (using tables, identifier management, links between documents, etc.) to process one or more

2 Between 1994 and 1998, the INTERLEAF text processor was used to define and generate all requirements (from the system to the program, written in B) in the context of the dual validation process used by the RATP for the SAET-METEOR system (line 14 of the Paris metro).

documents. In the case of complex systems, the number of documents and the number of stages (see Figure 11.12) create a need for a tool-based requirement management process.

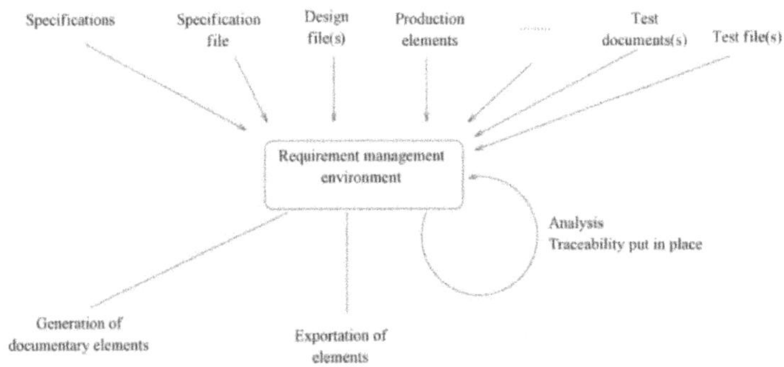

Figure 11.12. *Outline of a requirement management environment*

[CHO 01] presents the common airbus requirements engineering (CARE) approach, designed for use in developing the Airbus A380. This approach is based on the definition of a global methodology, based on the EIA-632 standard [EIA 98], with accompanying tools.

Requirements engineering is supported by tools which are used to acquire requirements and establish traceability, reporting and document generation. Examples of this type of tool include DOORS (distributed by IBM), RTM (Integrated Chipware Inc.), RequisitePro (Rational) and Reqtify (created by Dassault for traceability matrix generation). One of the main issues associated with the use of these tools is their integration into the trade processes used by individual companies.

In the course of the CNRS AS 164 project (June 2003–June 2004), we studied the level of mastery of the requirements management process in the context of rail transport. The interviews carried out during the project showed that clients (the RATP and the SCNF) had begun to provide some or all of their specifications in the form of requirements, and that industrial actors in the field (including SIEMENS, ANSALDO, ALSTOM, ALCATEL and THALES) now include requirements management in their trade processes. Further investigation has shown that all actors in the rail transport domain now make use of more or less extensive requirements engineering processes.

11.3.3.6. *Standardization*

In this section, we shall present two examples of standardization processes concerning the notion of requirements. We do not aim to provide exhaustive coverage of the subject, but to illustrate the approaches currently used in a real-world context.

11.3.3.6.1. User requirements notation: URN

URN is an initiative launched by the International Telecommunication Union (ITU[3]) in 1999 with the aim of standardizing notation for the visual description of requirements for complex applications and systems. Standard Z.150 [ITU 03] is used for the graphical description of both functional and non-functional requirements.

The standard includes two languages:

1) a language used to describe company goals and objectives, alternatives and non-functional requirements, the goal-oriented requirement language (GRL);

2) a language used to describe functional requirements in scenario form, use case maps (UCM).

As this work was carried out at the ITU, these languages display strong links to other standardized languages, such as LOTOS, SDL and the MSCs. These connections have made it easier to create tools for the passage from UCM scenarios to these languages.

It is also possible to envisage combined use of the GRL and UCM notations (for requirement acquisition) and UML notation (via a transformation process) for system specification.

11.3.3.6.2. System modeling language: SysML

UML notation [OMG 07] allows us to model complex systems using multiple formalisms (class graphs, state/transition diagrams, sequence diagrams, use cases, etc.). UML notation is based on a formalization of the meta-model, permitting a definition of the particularization of notation, which is possible via the definition of usage profiles.

3 See www.itu.int.

System modeling language (SysML[4]) may be seen as a usage profile[5]. SysML [SYS 05] takes account of requirement processing [HAU 05] using a new diagram type, the requirement diagram. It uses two notions which are interesting from a requirement management perspective: requirements and test cases.

Connections can then be made via four different aspects: composition, derivation, satisfaction and verification. The requirement stereotype is associated with default attributes: an identifier, source, text description, requirement type, risk and verification method.

SysML can thus be used within a UML model to describe requirements and the results of the derivation process. The ARTISAN[6] tool, for example, offers an implementation of SysML which allows us to take account of requirements within a model.

11.4. UML notation and the B method

11.4.1. *UML notation*

UML is the result of a fusion of dominant object methods (OMT, Booch and Jacobson), standardized by the Object Management Group (OMG[7]) in 1997. It rapidly became the key industrial standard for modeling software applications. UML is used for object-oriented software application modeling: systems are modeled using several types of diagrams, each contributing to the construction of a system [MUL 01]. Further details on the syntax and semantic aspects of the notation may be found in the UML reference guide [OMG 07].

Although UML notation allows us to represent models, it does not define the process used in creating these models. However, in the context of modeling a computer application [BOO 99], the developers of UML notation recommended an iterative and incremental approach, guided by the needs of system users and focused on the software architecture.

4 See www.sysml.org.

5 SysML is based on part of UML 2.0 with additions relating to system and requirement management aspects.

6 See http://www.artisansw.com/.

7 See http://www.omg.org/.

Figure 11.13 shows an example of a UML model of a rail system involving different modelings: use cases, a sequence diagram, a state/transition diagram and a class diagram.

UML is not the source of object concepts, but it provides a more formal definition and adds a methodological dimension which was previously lacking in the object-based approach. The definition and introduction of object constraint language (OCL) within UML represents a significant step forward, allowing us to define constraints, including safety or liveness properties, during the design phase.

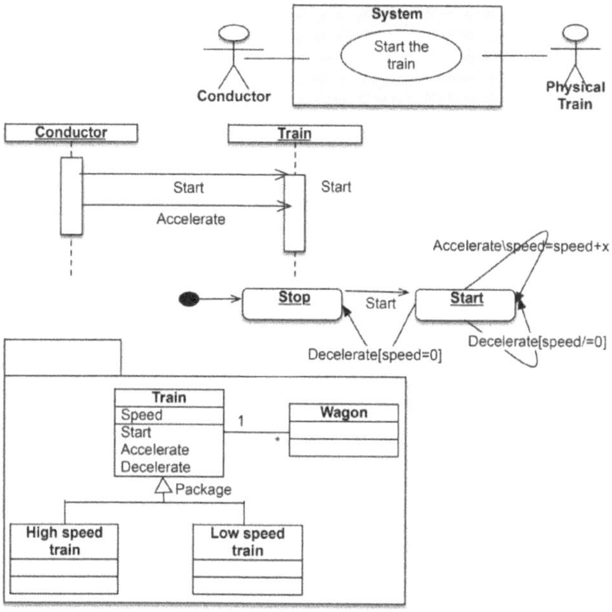

Figure 11.13. *Example of a UML model*

As UML notation does not impose one particular way of working, it may be integrated into any system and/or software development process in a transparent manner. It may therefore be seen as a toolkit to be used for the progressive improvement of working practices, while preserving the specific modes of operation used in different domains. The popularity of UML notation is reinforced by the availability of a significant number of tools, the *integrated development environment* (IDE) software workshops, which allow graphical implementation of the notation and which support the development process through partial code generation, documentation and retro-engineering.

UML is widely supported by the whole computer science community, and is used in all domains, having recently been introduced into the field of critical applications. Note that the standards applicable to critical systems in different domains, including aeronautics (DO178, JAR/FAR), rail transport (CENELEC EN 50126, EN 50128, EN 50129) and programmable electronic systems (CEI/IEC 61508), do not permit the use of object-oriented techniques (memory allocation, dynamic variables, polymorphism, inheritance, determinist execution, etc.).

The use of UML notation raises certain questions [BOU 07, OSS 07], for example concerning the use of notation without semantics, the evaluation of UML-based applications and so on. Several publications, including [FAA 04] and [MOT 05], have aimed to offer responses to these questions.

One pathway used in the development of UML notation concerns the creation of trade profiles, particularly the establishment of profiles enabling the manipulation of system aspects. The SysML profile [OMG 06] facilitates the handling of requirements and test cases. Work is currently underway on incorporating this profile into our methodology; it will not be presented in greater detail here.

11.4.2. *The B method*

Jean-Raymond Abrial's B method [ABR 96] is a model-oriented formal method, like Z and VDM, but which allows incremental development from a specification to code through the notion of refinements, using a single formalism, abstract machine language. During each stage of a B development, proof obligations are generated to guarantee the validity of refinements and the consistency of the abstract machine. The B modeling paradigm is based on the introduction of properties which the model must verify; these properties are then subject to refinement.

In France, the use of formal methods in the rail transport domain, particularly the B method, is increasingly common in the development of critical systems. The programs used for these safety systems (rail signaling systems, automatic piloting, etc.) must respond to extremely strict quality, reliability and robustness criteria.

One of the first applications of formal methods was carried out *a posteriori* on the SACEM system[8] [GUI 90]. More recent projects, such as SAET-METEOR [BEH 93, BEH 96, BEH 97, BOU 06], the VAL (*Véhicule Automatique Léger*, automated light vehicle)[9] system at Charles de Gaulle Airport and the automatic system on line 1 of the Paris metro (brought into service in 2011) have used the B method throughout the development process, from specification to coding.

11.4.3. *Overview*

Rail transport systems are subject to major operational safety constraints, as demonstrated by the CENELEC reference document [CEN 00, CEN 01, CEN 11, CEN 03] which regulates the creation of these systems (in terms of both hardware and software). The notion of requirements and requirement mastery forms a central element of the CENELEC document.

As [ZOW 05] demonstrates, requirements can be explained using a number of different processes (such as interviews, questionnaires, domain analysis, work groups, observations, perspective studies, safety studies, etc.). Appendix A of [MEI 02] presents methodological elements linked to requirements engineering, which is one of the tools proposed by systems engineering, as we see from standard EIA-632 [EIA 98].

We shall now give a step-by-step description of our methodology.

8 The SACEM (*Système d'Aide à la Conduite, à l'Exploitation et à la Maintenance*) driving, usage and maintenance support system, installed in 1988, provides drivers with speed recommendations through a screen installed onboard trains for driving assistance purposes.

9 The first VAL system was inaugurated in Lille, France, in 1983. VAL systems are now used in a variety of locations including Taipei, Toulouse, Rennes and Turin (since January 2006). Worldwide, VAL networks include over 119 km of track and over 830 vehicles are currently in use or under construction. The VAL at Charles de Gaulle Airport combines VAL technology with additional computer equipment based on the B method.

11.5. Step 1: requirement acquisition

This first phase is an important stage in our methodology, and consists of extracting the requirements involved in system design from a specification written in natural language.

11.5.1. *Requirement extraction*

In section 11.3 (and in [BOU 06]), we noted the basic principles involved in requirements engineering. Further details on the subject of requirements may be found in [HUL 05].

The functional specification (or any other input document) is made up of a variety of elements. These include functional requirements, comments, assessments, recommendations, etc. The aim of this first phase is to sort elements and select requirements which correspond to the needs of the user.

This phase also involves the definition of a functional outline of the application in the form of a collection of requirements. Figure 11.3 shows a summary of the user requirement creation process. The input reference document (functional specification, reference, system specification or others) is divided into a set of labeled recommendations.

Label	Description of recommendation
FS1	The chosen case study is a control system for managing a level crossing. This control system is distributed and based on radio communications. The objective of a level crossing is to manage the intersection between a railway line and a road. The railway line is a single line.
FS2	The point of intersection of the road and the railway line is known as the "danger zone". We must avoid situations where a train and a road user enter the danger zone simultaneously in order to avoid collisions.
FS3	The level crossing is equipped with barriers and traffic lights. Two traffic lights are associated with a level crossing: one red, one orange. When the orange light is showing, this indicates that road users (car drivers, cyclists, pedestrians, etc.) should stop at the edge of the level crossing, if possible. The red light indicates that the crossing is closed to road traffic and access is prohibited.
	...

Table 11.2. *Example of recommendations*

The second stage is an analytical process in which recommendations are broken down (or clarified) to produce a set of labeled user requirements. If a recommendation is abandoned, this decision needs to be justified. A textual analysis of our case study gives a collection of recommendations, some of which are shown in Table 11.2.

Label	Description of requirement
UR1	Distributed system based on radio communications
UR2	Level crossing
UR3	The objective of a level crossing is to manage the intersection between a railway line and a road.
UR4	The railway line is a single line.
UR5	The intersection of the road and the railway line is known as the "danger zone".
UR6	We must avoid situations where a train and a road user enter the danger zone simultaneously in order to avoid collisions.
UR7	The level crossing is equipped with barriers.
UR8	The level crossing is equipped with traffic lights.
UR9	Two traffic lights are associated with a level crossing: one red, one orange.
UR10	When the orange light is showing, this indicates that road users (car drivers, cyclists, pedestrians, etc.) should stop at the edge of the level crossing, if possible.
UR11	The red light indicates that the crossing is closed to road traffic and access is prohibited.
	....
UR23	The main components are able to communicate via a radio communications system.
UR24	The transmission times for the radio communications system are not fixed and may vary.
UR25	Messages traveling through the radio communications system may be lost.
	...
UR37	Faults must be taken into account in order to create a "safe" level crossing.
UR38	The main sources of faults are linked to captors and actuators.
	...
UR43	A fault may occur at any time.
	...
UR45	List of potential faults: Traffic light fault Barrier fault Train captor fault Communication fault: delays, lost messages, modified messages, etc.
	...

Table 11.3. *Example of requirements*

The resulting collection of user requirements is shown in Table 11.3.

A traceability matrix (see Table 11.4) is established between the selected user requirements and the initial recommendations. This shows that nothing has been forgotten.

User requirements	Recommendation
UR0 + UR1 + UR2	FS1
UR3 + UR4 + UR5	FS2
UR6 + UR7 + UR8 + UR9 + UR10 + UR11	FS3
...	
UR23 + UR 24 + UR25	FS7
...	

Table 11.4. *Traceability between requirements and recommendations*

This process identified 20 recommendations, which were then broken down into 84 user requirements.

11.5.2. *Risk identification*

The identification of operational risks (step 2 of the process set out in the CENELEC EN 50129 standard, [CEN 03]) may be carried out by analyzing user requirements (UR) and/or using a classic risk analysis process. User requirement UR6 describes a collision between a train and a road user (pedestrian, cyclist, car, etc.) in the danger zone.

Collision thus constitutes the major risk. This requirement may be modeled as part of a UML model via a use case (Figure 11.14). Note that this study only takes account of the level crossing, which represents a single aspect of a rail transport system. In a real case study, we would need to take account of all of the risks involved in rail transport.

This gives us a model which may be used both by the production team and by the team responsible for demonstrating safety. This shared model facilitates early consideration of requirements associated with operational safety and provides better requirement traceability, while avoiding any confusion concerning the specific responsibilities of different groups.

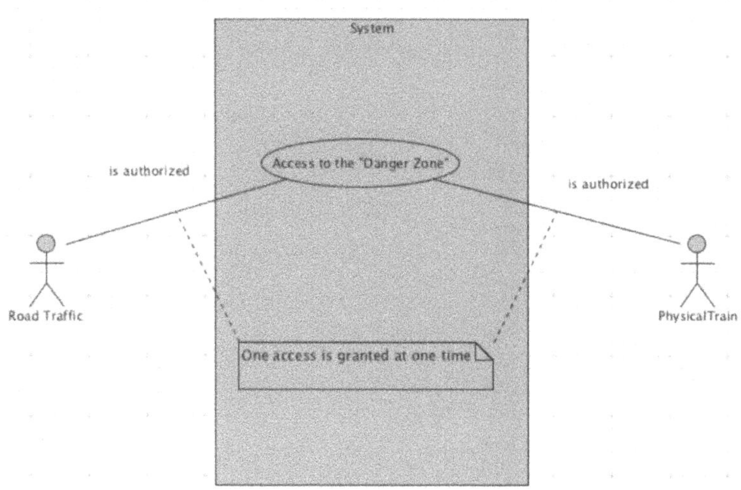

Figure 11.14. *Taking account of the collision risk.*

11.5.3. *Identification of services*

By analyzing user requirements and the collision risk, we are able to identify three services at system level:

– opening of the level crossing for road traffic to circulate (cars, bicycles, pedestrians, etc.);

– closure of the level crossing for rail traffic to circulate;

– message transmission (to and from trains and the operations center).

This view is introduced into the UML in the form of a class diagram (Figure 11.15). This class diagram allows us to visualize system actors and their interactions with the required system.

This diagram may be supplemented by a set of sequence diagrams characterizing the interactions between actors (road traffic, trains and the danger zone). Figure 11.16 shows the sequence of access authorizations for the danger zone.

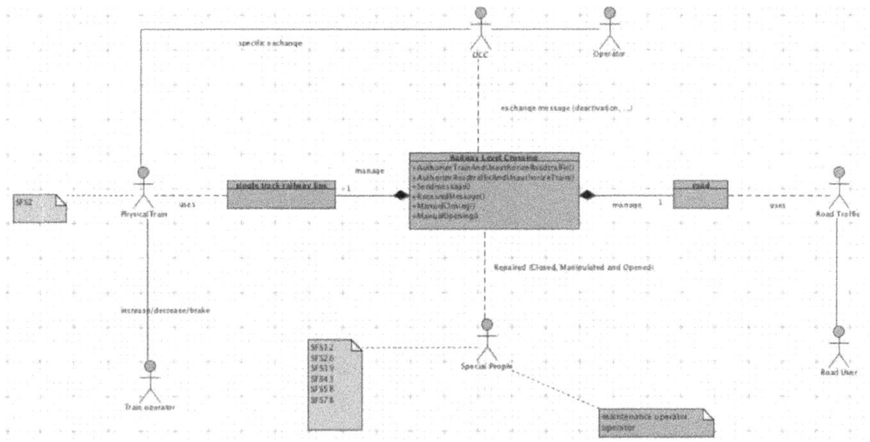

Figure 11.15. *System view*

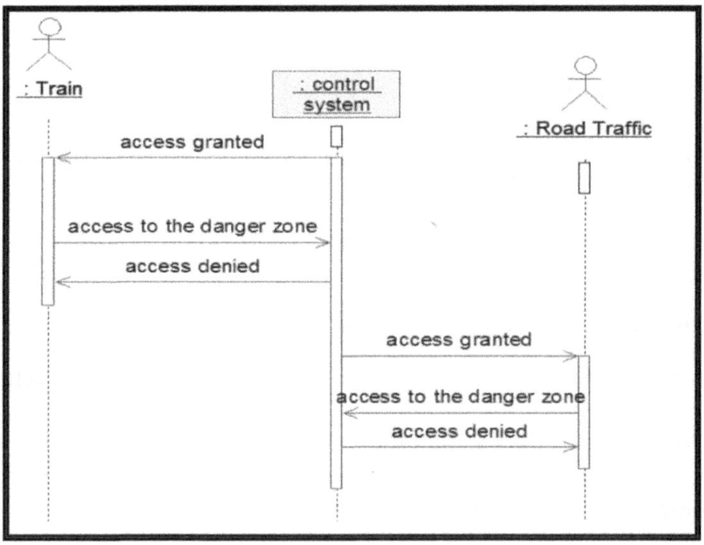

Figure 11.16. *Interaction between elements*

We may add system states, as identified in the requirements, to the sequence diagram in Figure 11.16. The level crossing is either closed (train circulation authorized) or open (road traffic authorized). These states and state changes are modeled in the form of a state/transition diagram (Figure 11.17). At this level, it is interesting to introduce a "hold" state used if a fault occurs (UR43, UR45).

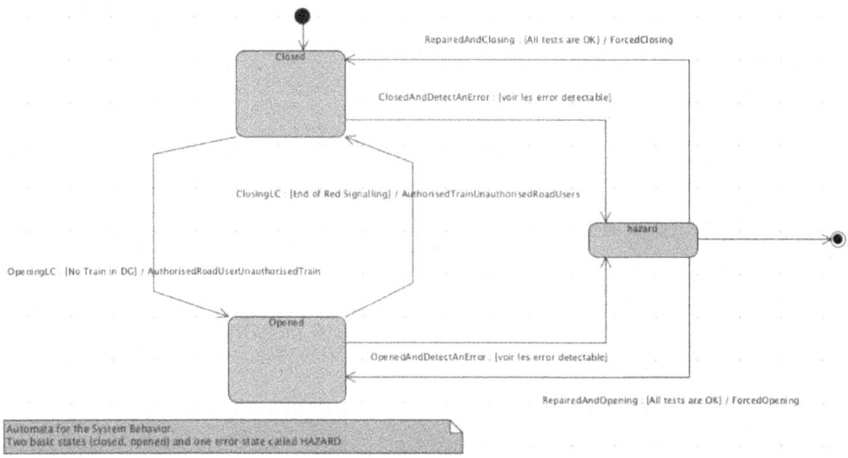

Figure 11.17. *Behavior management at system level*

11.6. Step 2: environment and risk analysis

11.6.1. *Identification of the environment*

The purpose of the second step is to define the perimeter of the application by specifying the environment and the interactions between the environment and the system. This may be done by analyzing user requirements (see Table 11.5).

Our "world" is made up of two families of elements:

– environment: the barriers, lights, captors and the operations center (OP) are considered as elements in interaction with our system;

– sub-system: the local level-crossing control system (LCCS), the train control system (TCS) and the communications system (MCR).

Term	Description
LC	Level crossing
LCCS	Level-crossing control system
TCS	Train control system
MCR	Communications system
OP	Operations center
TL	Traffic lights
Barrier	Barrier protecting access to the LC
Captor	Captor detecting train arrival

Table 11.5. *Our "world"*

Using this description of our "world", we are able to create a diagram which introduces connections between different elements, highlighting the relationships between actors. In our model, we have used operators, train drivers, maintenance personnel and installation personnel (grouped together under the term "special people").

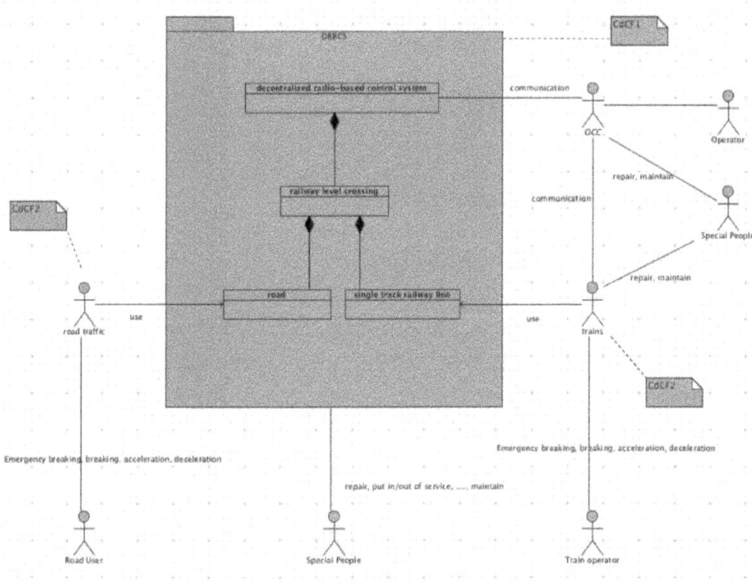

Figure 11.18. *Model of the level-crossing environment*

The behavior of each actor and their interactions with the system may be formalized via use cases, as shown in Figures 11.19 and 11.20.

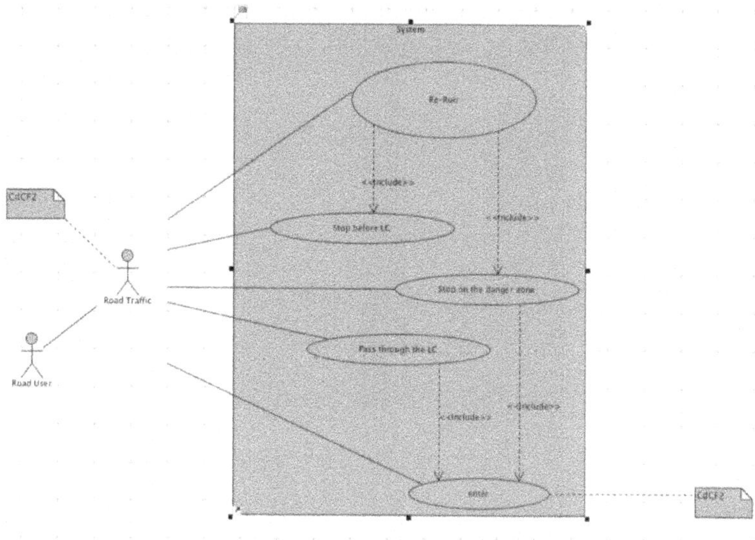

Figure 11.19. *Model of "road user" behavior*

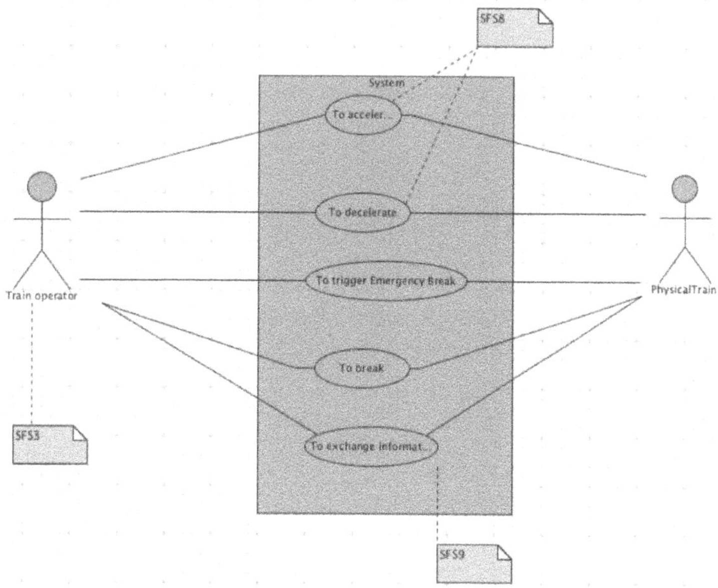

Figure 11.20. *Model of "rail user" behavior*

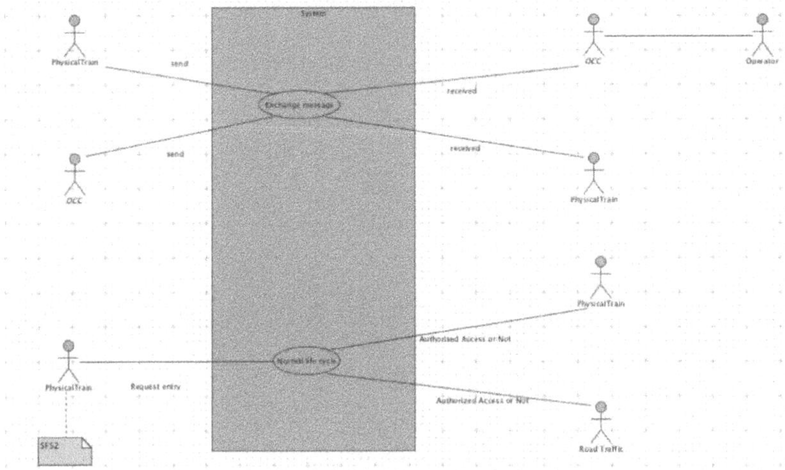

Figure 11.21. *Model of correct behaviors*

Figure 11.21 describes "good" behaviors, i.e. the behaviors expected of the system. This diagram includes interfaces (barriers, etc.) and final actors.

Note the inclusion of requirement traceability in each diagram through the use of specific boxes. This allows us to connect each element to the associated requirements.

11.6.2. *Description of the environment*

Analysis of user requirements should facilitate full identification of the environment. Table 11.6 shows a partial list of the functional requirements used to describe the behavior of the level crossing.

Label	Description of functional requirement	UR
FR1	LC is a distributed system based on radio communications.	1
FR2	LC is equipped with traffic lights.	8, 9,19
FR3	LC is equipped with barriers.	5,17
FR4	When the train has left the danger zone, the LC may be opened for road traffic.	21
FR5	The LC may be opened after confirmation of train passage has been received from the TCS.	62
	…	

Table 11.6. *Functional requirements*

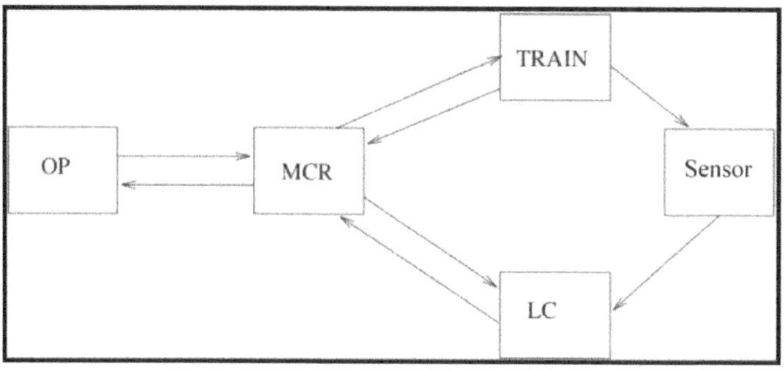

Figure 11.22. *Distributed architecture*

A set of functional requirements, including FR1, highlights the distributed aspect of the architecture. The idea behind this distribution is that the management of a level crossing must be the result of an interaction between the level crossing and the trains which use it. In practice, it is dangerous to keep a level crossing closed as this may lead to user impatience, crossing of the half-barrier, etc.

By analyzing these requirements, we are able to produce an interface diagram (Figure 11.22). Note that the operations center supervises the whole line, and the purpose of the established communication links is to make the transmission of information concerning detective faults possible, in order to trigger curative maintenance operations.

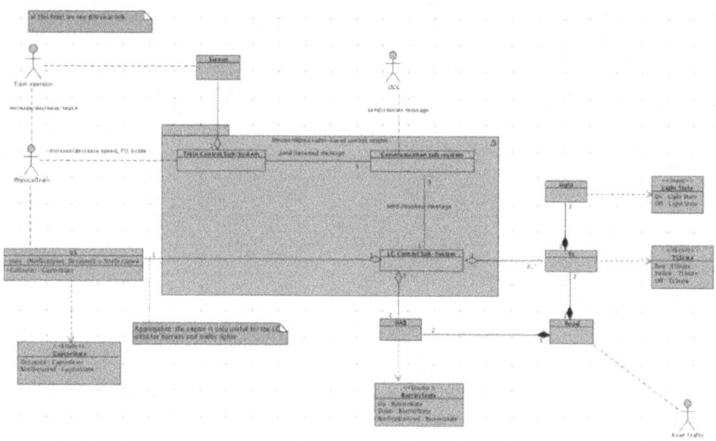

Figure 11.23. *Sub-system view*

Functional requirements analysis needs to be carried out for each element. At the end of this process, we are able to describe sub-system architecture using a class diagram, characterizing interactions between elements of equipment (Figure 11.23). This diagram shows the different components of our "world" (Table 11.6) along with their interactions.

To complete the description of the sub-system, we have modeled the interactions between the environment and the system as a set of use cases (Figures 11.19, 11.20 and 11.21) describing functional requirements and a set of sequence graphs describing the effects of the environment on the system.

11.6.3. *Environmental faults*

In the context of our study, the initial specification contains requirements concerning the existence of faults which need to be taken into account. If this fault list did not exist, we would need to carry out a study at this point in order to create a list of probable faults associated with environmental elements.

The results of the risk identification phase and this first fault list are used as a starting point for a safety study. They provide preliminary risk analysis (PRA), which allows us to identify new requirements, associated with system safety, to add to the list of functional requirements.

Label	Description	UR
F1	Failure of orange light	37, 38, 43, 45
F2	Failure of red light	37, 38, 43, 45
F3	Barrier failure	37, 38, 43, 45
F4	Faulty train captors	37, 38, 43, 45
F5	Faults linked to communication delays	37, 38, 43, 45
F6	Message loss	37, 38, 43, 45
F7	Faults in the system itself	41, 43
F8	Incorrect human behavior	

Table 11.7. *List of faults to take into consideration*

A fault tree may be used to connect the risk of collision with the associated requirements.

The primary risk of collision between a train and another vehicle is derived using fault tree analysis (FTA). FTA allows us to identify the causes of potential problems in a product, process or service, and is mostly used for safety predictions or to analyze the performance of a design.

Fault tree creation is a graphical methodology which provides systematic description of the impacts of faults which may occur during the life of a system (further details may be found in [IEC 90]). The method combines hardware faults with human errors, and gives an overview of potential problems and their relationships, while imposing detailed analysis; this produces concrete results during the design phase.

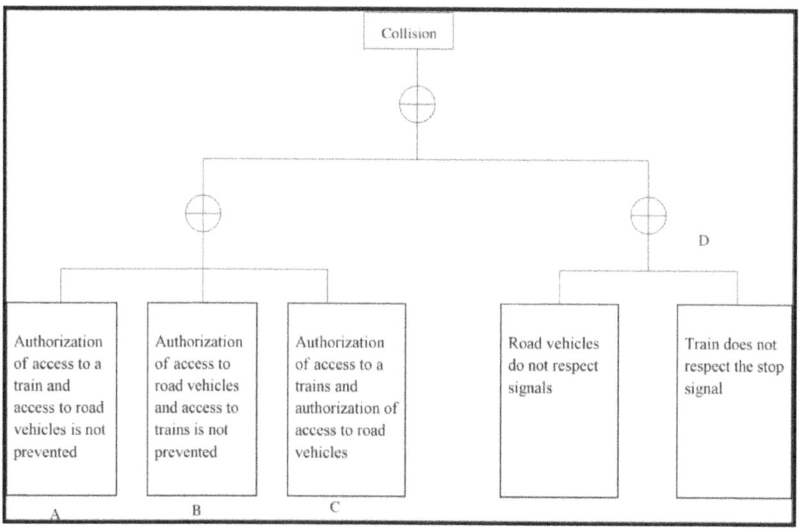

Figure 11.24. *Fault tree*

For safety critical systems, the root node of the tree often represents a catastrophic event taken from the risk list at system level. Figure 11.24 shows an example of the derivation of a collision risk between trains and cars.

As our example is provided for illustrative purposes, we have shown a reduced version of the fault tree (the example only includes OR gates). This first fault tree is broken down into multiple cases. Sub-tree D concerns human errors. Sub-tree C presents the basic property of our software-based system: the system must not allow trains and road traffic simultaneous access to the danger zone. Sub-trees A and B are the result of equipment failures (barriers, traffic lights, communications equipment, train presence captors, etc.). Sub-tree A is shown in Figure 11.25.

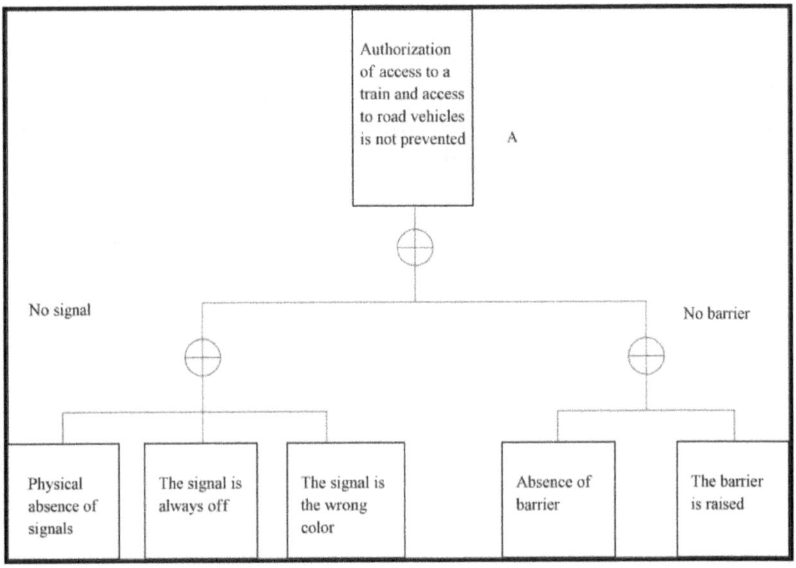

Figure 11.25. *Fault tree for physical equipment*

This type of analysis highlights new requirements, such as the fact that we must verify the existence of physical objects (lights, signals, captors, etc.), and that, when preparing the installation, the incoming captor must be positioned at the point of announcement (i.e. as the train arrives in the sector). The point at which the train is announced is known as the announcement origin. A delay must be respected between the announcement trigger and the moment when the fastest possible train will arrive at the crossing. This delay, known as the announcement period, is a function of the maximum speed of the trains using the level crossing.

The fault tree may be partially modeled within the UML model using a use case diagram, which introduces a "consequences on" link (Figure 11.26).

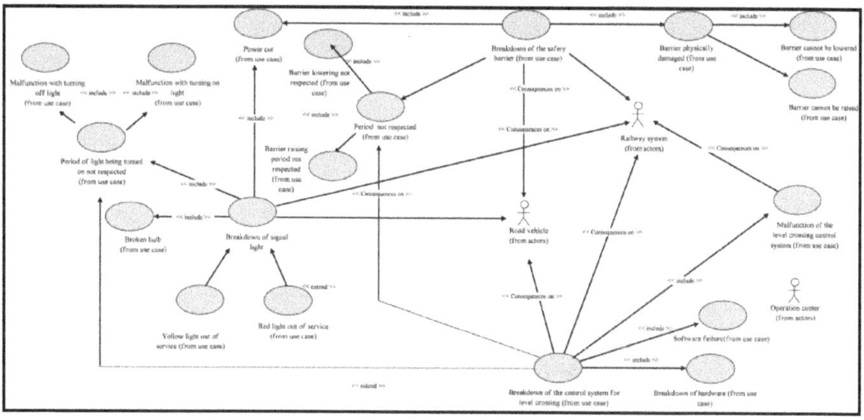

Figure 11.26. *Links between faults*

Our environment model must take account of possible faults. As we see from Table 11.7, captor faults pose considerable difficulties. In our case, the communications between sub-systems are not safe (i.e. not guaranteed).

A system cannot be considered safe if no objectives linked to system safety are taken into account. The degradation of hardware (immobile barriers, faulty lights, etc.) can also lead to degraded situations. In the case of barriers, faults may only be detected if an opening or closure delay is not respected.

As we see from functional requirement UR43, faults may occur at any time, but repairs can only be undertaken if the level crossing is free, i.e. not occupied by a train. Use cases may be used to describe actions which actors may carry out on the system.

Figure 11.26 shows a use case which presents different types of barrier faults, with three trigger events: power loss, full breakdown (barrier out of order) and excessive lowering or raising delays.

Figure 11.28 shows faults linked to traffic lights (burnt-out bulbs, power outage, excessive activation delay, etc.). Traffic light faults may have consequences on road transport and on the rail system as a whole. The level crossing is the first element to be affected, but effects may be felt on the whole line.

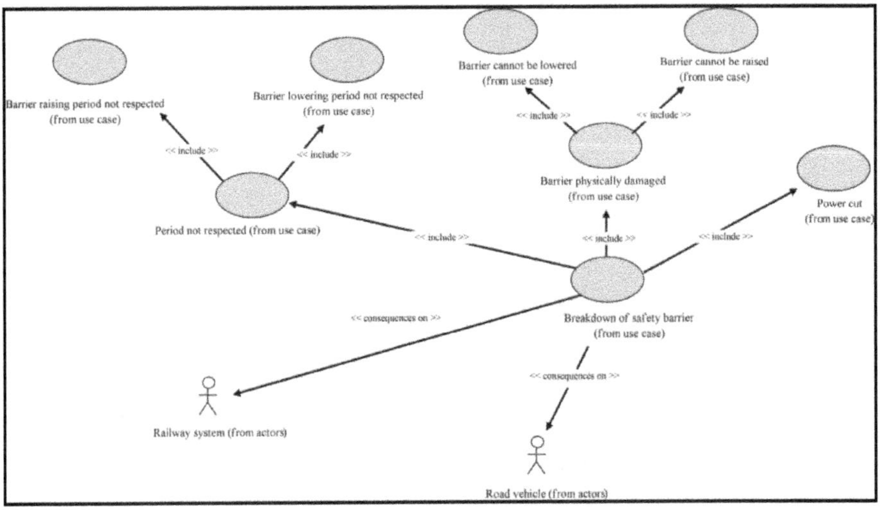

Figure 11.27. *Description of different possible barrier failures*

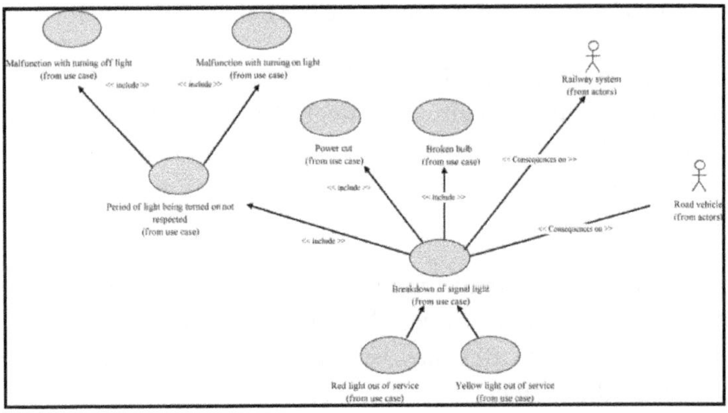

Figure 11.28. *Description of different possible light signal failures*

11.6.4. *Maintenance*

Maintenance aspects (barrier repairs, traffic light repairs, etc.) must be taken into account via a specific phase in which we identify required actions and their effects on the system. These actions may be included in our model in the form of use cases (Figure 11.29), sequence diagrams and as additions to the class diagram.

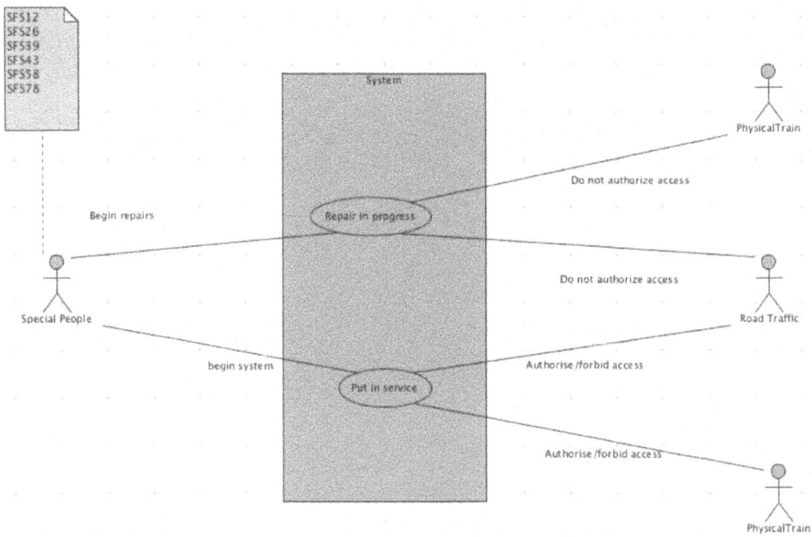

Figure 11.29. *Managing maintenance*

The inclusion of maintenance actions in the model allows us to define their impact on the system and create connections with exported requirements. These connections may continue as per the definition of procedures.

11.6.5. *Impact of the environment on the system*

Sequence graphs are used to describe the impact of an environment on a system. The sequence graph in Figure 11.30 shows the basic operation of a protocol used by trains when passing through a level crossing.

Firstly, the traffic lights are activated in order to stop road traffic. If the zone is not noise-sensitive (e.g. outside of residential areas), a sound signal will also be produced as the lights are activated. After a warning period, the barriers are lowered. If the barriers are lowered without incident (i.e. within the maximum allowable time delay), the system is said to be in safe mode, and the train is allowed to pass through the level crossing.

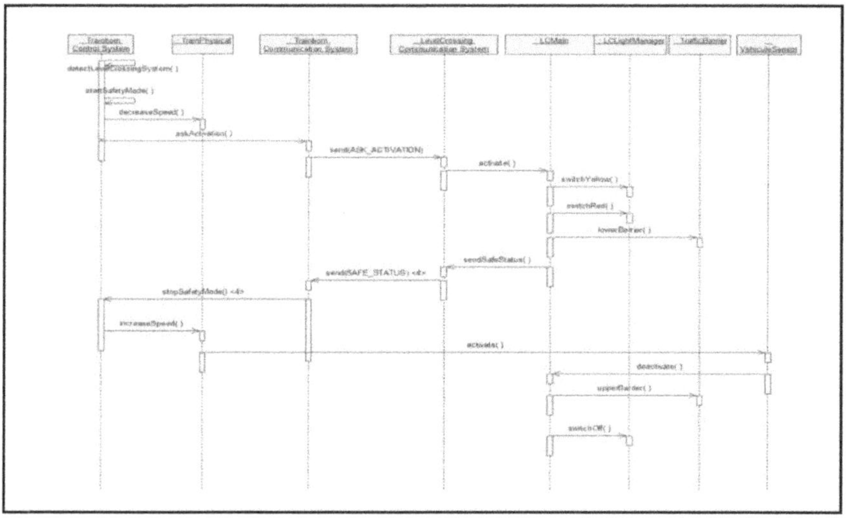

Figure 11.30. *Level-crossing authorization protocol*

Once the train has passed, the barriers are raised and the light signals are extinguished. Any noise signals will also cease. Note that the control system may pass into manual mode at any point, corresponding to human intervention in managing the safety of the level crossing (e.g. by the crossing warden). This may be triggered by a hardware malfunction (barriers not lowering, faulty traffic lights, etc.).

If the train does not receive confirmation that the level crossing is in a safe state, two things may happen:

1) the train brakes and comes to a halt;

2) the driver takes control (Figure 11.31) and continues at restricted speed.

11.6.6. *Results*

Figure 11.32 shows a first architecture of the system and its environment. The control center sub-system, the operation center (OC), is not involved in system safety, and we have chosen not to model it in the context of our case study.

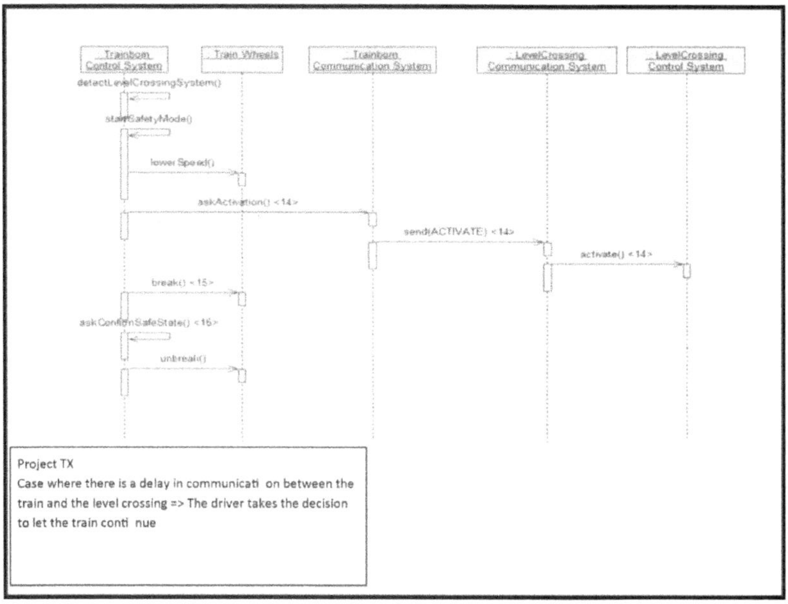

Figure 11.31. *Level-crossing access in manual mode*

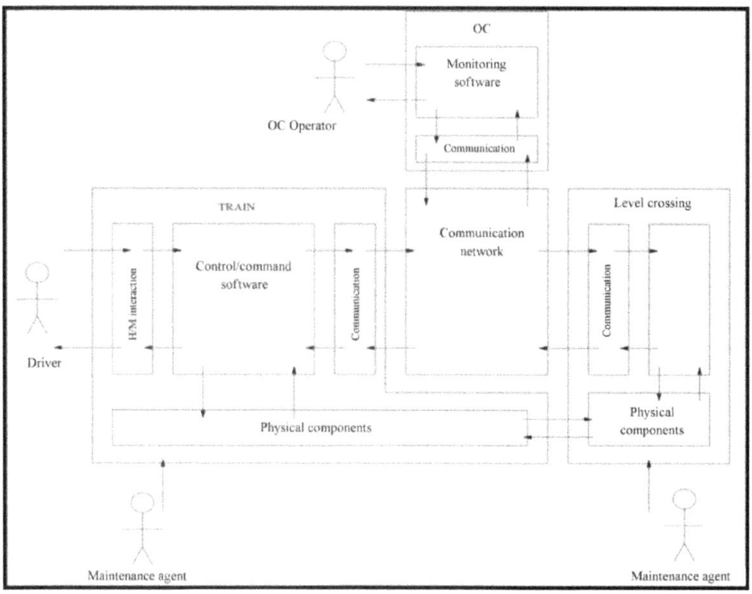

Figure 11.32. *Architecture*

As we stated in section 11.6.1, this synthesis shows different human actors. The implemented safety analyses must therefore include the effects of human actions on system safety (usage procedures, maintenance procedures, etc.).

The architecture shown in Figure 11.32 may be modeled using a component diagram, as shown in Figure 11.33.

11.7. Step 3: component breakdown

11.7.1. *Requirement selection*

In the previous section, we discussed the establishment of a risk analysis process. This process allows us to define functional and safety requirements, which must then be taken into account in sub-systems; while it does not constitute a formalization of the process, it does allow us to justify the choice of requirements.

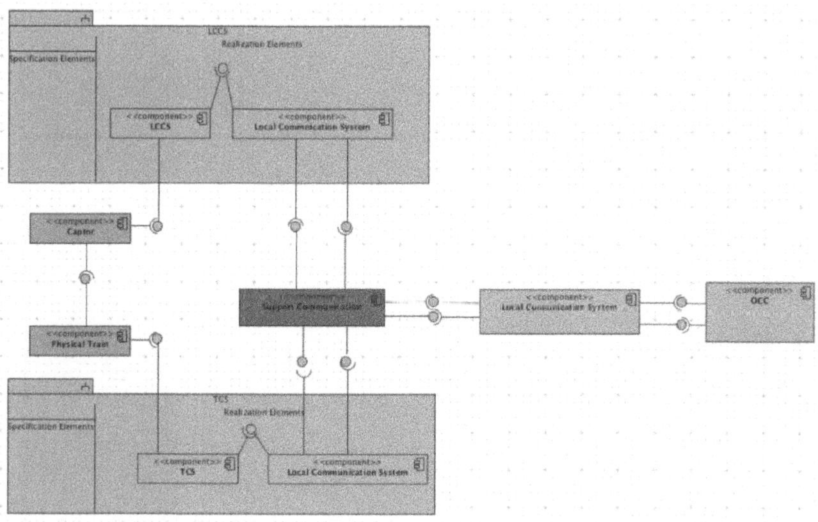

Figure 11.33. *Architecture model*

A list of requirements (Table 11.8) is established for each sub-system, with traceability in relation to the functional requirements (FR) defined earlier. [MAR 04a] and [MAR 04b] have shown how logical properties may be coded in the form of OCL constraints included in different diagrams.

Label	Description of functional requirement	FR
ER1	The objective of the LCCS is to manage access to the danger zone	10
ER2	The LCSS manages traffic lights	2, 12
ER3	The LCCS manages barriers	3, 13
ER4	The LCCS communicates with the TCS over the radio network	1,17, 23
	...	

Table 11.8. *Equipment requirements for the LCCS*

11.7.2. *Architecture*

In the previous sections, we proposed an initial system architecture. Figure 11.34 shows an architecture of the system and its environment.

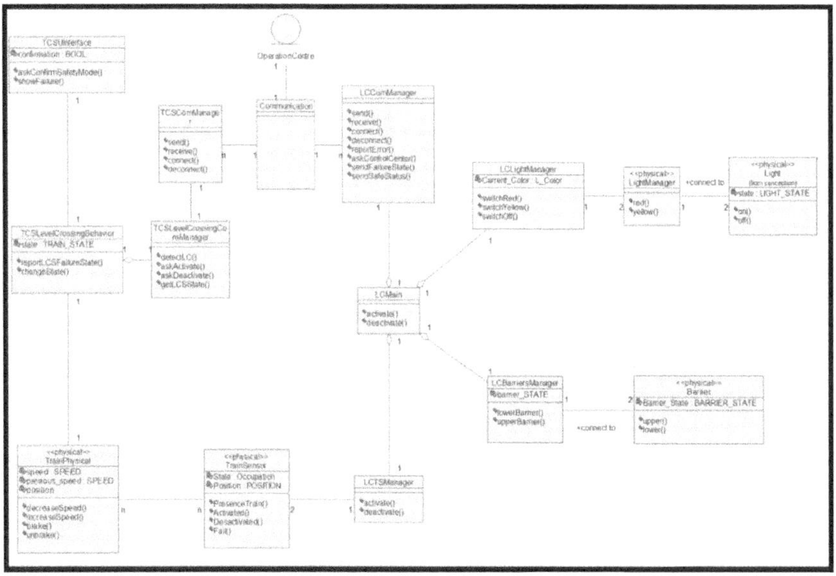

Figure 11.34. *Class graph describing architecture*

The class graph shows physical actors (PhysicalTrain, Captor, TrafficLights, Barrier) and their interactions. To take one example, we see that there is a relationship between the PhysicalTrain class and the Captor class. This relationship means that the associated physical elements interact with each other.

The provision of full environment information (actor list, all interactions, fault lists, etc.) is important. Note that the Captor class offers a "fault" method, indicating that captors may break down.

11.7.3. *Behavior*

In this section, we shall use state diagrams to describe the control system and the onboard TCS.

11.7.3.1. *The level-crossing control system (LCCS)*

The barriers, traffic lights and sound signals are managed by the level-crossing control system. The control sub-system is activated by announcement information triggers. Upon activation of the LCCS, the system carries out an ordered sequence of actions in order to empty the level crossing in time and to guarantee its closure to road traffic.

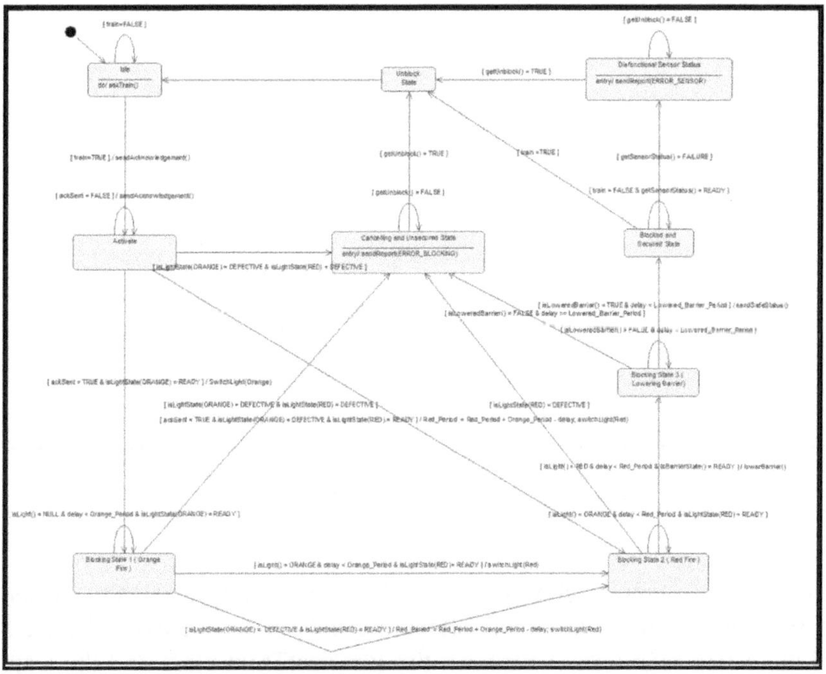

Figure 11.35. *Behavior of the command control program*

Figure 11.35 shows the state/transition diagram characterizing the behavior of the LCCS sub-system. This state/transition diagram is supplemented by use case and sequence diagrams, which characterizes different behavior phases (arrival announcement, passage authorization, prohibition of passage, etc.). These diagrams will not be presented here due to space considerations.

11.7.3.2. *The onboard system (TCS)*

The TCS carries out a series of actions on approaching a level crossing (Figure 11.36). When the train passes the origin point for the announcement to the level crossing, it requests confirmation from the LCCS that barrier lowering has begun.

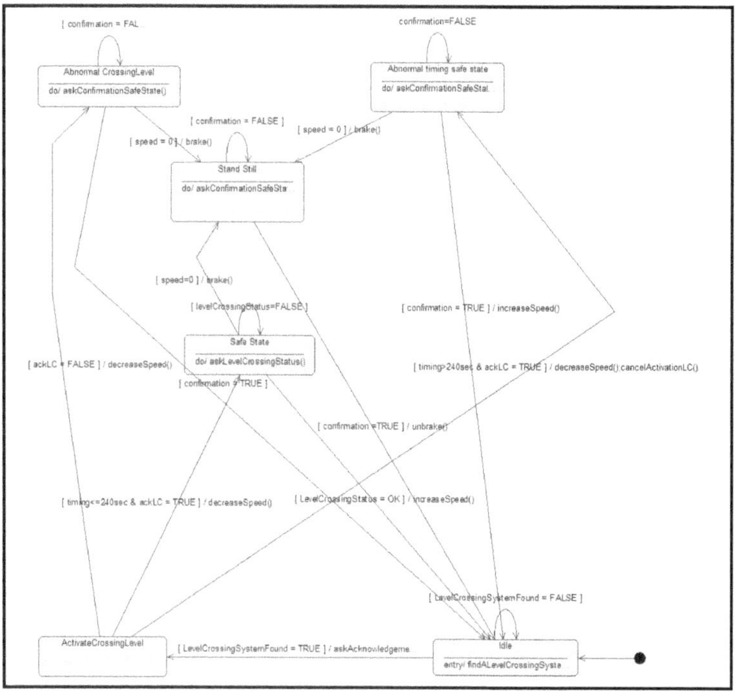

Figure 11.36. *Behavior of onboard software*

On receiving confirmation, the TCS goes into holding mode, and starts braking in order to leave the barriers enough time to close. At the end of this waiting period, the LCCS transmits state information to the TCS. If the level crossing is in safe mode, the TCS cancels the braking order and returns to initial speed. An “end of passage” captor (captor class) detects the fact that the train has passed through the crossing, and triggers the barrier lifting and traffic light deactivation mechanisms.

As we have already seen, use cases and sequence diagrams are used in addition to the state/transition diagram describing the behavior of the TCS in order to specify scenarios for the approach to, passage of and departure from the level crossing.

11.8. Step 4: verification

We now have a model of our case study which can be translated into a B model.

11.8.1. *Introduction*

Several studies have been carried out on the generation of B models [ABR 96] from UML models [OMG 07], including important work by the Dédale team[10] [LED 01, LED 02] and by sial/arlog [MAR 01][11]. The work carried out in the context of the B-RAIL project did not aim to describe a new code generation process; here, we wish to propose a global methodology offering the best possible means of acquiring requirements based on B model generation techniques.

Our current work focuses on finding the best way to combine the results of different work carried out on the subject. We proposed a first process for generating B models from UML models in [BON 03], based on the class diagram and on state/transition diagrams. [JAN 00] added OCL requirements to this process. However, the process for generating a B code from a UML code has yet to be completed, and tools have not yet been developed.

[MAR 04a] showed that time constraints cannot be verified without extending the B language. In our UML model, time constraints take the form

10 More information on the DEDALE team may be found at www.loria.fr/equipes/dedale/home.html.

11 More information on the ARLOG team may be found at www.prism.uvsq.fr/recherche/themes/sial/arlog.

of notes and/or comments; they are therefore not taken into account in generating our B models. Work on this aspect is underway as part of the RT3-TUCS project[12].

11.8.2. *Description of formal models*

In this section, we present the B model obtained by translating our UML model. The abstract machine in Figure 11.37, TCS_LevelCrossingBehavior_0, defines all states in the STATE set, and introduces an operation, change_state, to describe state changes in the level-crossing management sub-system. This component is not determinist, as it uses the substitution list_var:(predicate) to describe the change_state operation. This substitution indicates that the set of variables becomes such that the predicate is true.

```
MACHINE TCS_LevelCrossingBehavior_0
SETS   STATES ={          Idle, SafeState, ActivateCrossingLevel, StandStill,
                          AbnormalTimingSafeState,
AbnormalCrossingLevel}
CONCRETE_VARIABLES current_state
INVARIANT                      current_state : STATES
INITIALISATION                 current_state := Idle
OPERATIONS
change_state =
BEGIN
 current_state :(  current_state :STATES
 &((current_state$0= Idle)=>current_state:{ActivateCrossingLevel,Idle})
 ...
 &((current_state$0= StandStill)
   => current_state/:{SafeState, AbnormalTimingSafeState})
 )
END
END
```

Figure 11.37. *Machine: TCS_LevelCrossingBehavior_0*

12 The RT3-TUCS project is a French inter-regional project (Picardie, Nord Pas de Calais and Alsace) forming part of the RT3 network, begun in February 2006 for a duration of three years.

Figure 11.38 is an extract from the implementation of TCS_LevelCrossingBehavior_n. This implementation conforms to the state/transition diagram shown in Figure 11.35.

```
IMPLEMENTATION      TCS_LevelCrossingBehavior_n

REFINES             TCS_LevelCrossingBehavior_0

INVARIANT

         (current_state  = StandStill) => (brake = TRUE)

 &       (current_state /= StandStill) => (brake = FALSE)

INITIALISATION      current_state := Idle

OPERATIONS

change_state =CASE current_state OF

          EITHER  Idle THEN

          VAR bb IN

               bb <-- detectLevelCrossingSystem;

               IF     ( bb = TRUE ) THEN

               BEGIN

                    current_state := ActivateCrossingLevel

               ;    AskAcknowledgement

               END

               ELSIF  ( bb = FALSE) THEN current_state := Idle

               END

          END

         ....

         END

END
```

Figure 11.38. *Implementation: TCS_LevelCrossingBehavior_n*

11.9. UML2B

We have been able to develop a UML to B translator (Figure 11.39) in the context of our work. This translator demonstrates the feasibility of the UML to B transformation. A formalized version of our work is given in [IDA 07, IDA 09] and [RAM 09, Chapter 19].

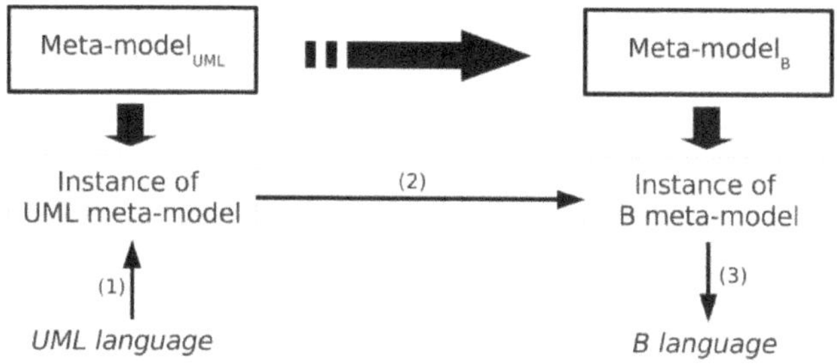

Figure 11.39. *UML2B transformation*

The UML2B environment was produced using developments made in the OpenArchitectureWare environment.

11.10. Conclusions

The aim of the B-RAIL project is to define a methodology for the development of rail transport systems. These systems are subject to strong operational safety constraints, as demonstrated in the CENELEC standards [CEN 01, CEN 11, CEN 00, CEN 03] governing the creation of rail transport systems (both from hardware and software perspectives).

The proposed methodology is based on the use of UML notation [OMG 07] and the B method [ABR 96]. UML notation is used in the acquisition of requirements and in describing the system. It takes an essentially graphical form, simplifying the understanding of models and assisting communications between project actors (clients, developers, verifiers, validators, etc.). The B method is a formal language which is used to express properties and allows us to detect incoherencies through the use of proof activities.

This example has demonstrated the feasibility and interest of transforming a UML model into B. Work is still needed to refine the process involved in generating B models from UML models. This refinement will involve in-depth analysis of the different UML to B generation processes which have already been proposed [MAR 04a, LED 01, LED 02, MAR 01, ABR 96].

This study has highlighted three considerations:

– risk analysis during the system design phase allows us to guarantee traceability throughout the whole process;

– UML notation is suitable for use in formalizing complex systems and for safety requirements. This second point is very important, and the graphical aspect of UML notation assists effective communication between different teams (development, validation and operational safety) on these subjects;

– the importance of highlighting requirements and traceability throughout the production cycle. UML notation offers a good means of representing and acquiring issues, but the coherency of this model in relation to the initial need still needs to be demonstrated.

In terms of perspectives for future development, note that we have integrated SysML [OMG 06] into our approach in order to model requirements and traceability connections using elements of the UML model. In the context of the RT3-TUCS project [OSS 07], we also designed a sub-set of UML2 notation [OMG 07] suitable for use in modeling critical and operationally safe systems.

In addition to this work, the generation of test scenarios based on sequence diagrams and use cases would allow us to respond to operational validation issues.

11.11. Glossary

FR	Functional requirement
FTA	Fault tree analysis
IDE	Integrated development environment
OCL	Object constraint language
OMG[13]	Object Management Group

13 http://www.omg.org/.

PRA Preliminary risk analysis

SIL Safety integrity level

UML Unified modeling language

11.12. Bibliography

[ABR 96] ABRIAL J.-R., *The B Book – Assigning Programs to Meanings*, Cambridge University Press, August 1996.

[BEH 93] BEHM P., "Application d'une méthode formelle aux logiciels sécuritaires ferroviaires", *Atelier Logiciel Temps Réel, 6ème Journées Internationales du Génie Logiciel,* 1993.

[BEH 96] BEHM P., "Développement formel des logiciels sécuritaires de METEOR", in HABRIAS H. (ed.), *Proceedings of the 1st Conference on the B method: Putting into Practice Methods and Tools for Information System Design*, IRIN Institut de recherche en informatique de Nantes, pp. 3–10, November 1996.

[BEH 97] BEHM P., DESFORGES P., MEIJA F., "Application de la méthode B dans l'industrie ferroviaire", *ARAGO*, vol. 20, pp. 59–88, 1997.

[BON 03] BON P., BOULANGER J.-L., MARIANO G., "Semi formal modelling and formal specification: UML & B in simple railway application", CNAM-Paris (ed.), *ICSSEA 2003*, 2–4 December 2003.

[BOO 99] BOOCH G., RUMBAUGH J., JACOBSON I., *The Unified Software Development Process*, Addison-Wesley, 1999.

[BOU 06] BOULANGER J.-L., BON P., "B-RAIL: Analyse et Modélisation des exigencies", *Revue Génie Logiciel,* vol. 79, pp. 18–24, December 2006.

[BOU 07] BOULANGER J.-L., "UML et les applications critiques", *Proceedings of Qualita '07*, Tangier, Morocco, pp. 739–745, 2007.

[CEN 99] CENELEC, EN 50126, "Railways application – specification and demonstration of reliability, availability, maintainability and safety (RAMS)", 1999.

[CEN 01] CENELEC, EN 50128, "Railways application – communication, signaling and processing systems – software for railway control and protection systems", 2001.

[CEN 11] CENELEC, EN 50128, "Railways application – communication, signaling and processing systems – software for railway control and protection systems", 2011.

[CEN 03] CENELEC, NF EN 50129, "Applications ferroviaires – systèmes de signalisation, de télécommunications et de traitement systèmes électroniques de sécurité pour la signalization", *Norme Européenne*, May 2003.

[CHO 01] CHOVEAU E., DE CHAZELLES P., "Application de l'ingénierie système à la définition d'une démarche d'ingénierie des exigences pour l'AIRBUS A380", *Génie Logiciel*, vol. 59, pp. 13–18, December 2001.

[EIA 98] EIA-632: Processes for Engineering a System, April 1998.

[FAA 04] FAA, *Handbook for Object Oriented Technology in Aviation (OOTiA)*, 26 October 2004. Available at http://www.faa.gov/aircraft/air_cert/design_approvals/air_software/oot/.

[GEO 90] GEORGES J.-P., "Principes et fonctionnement du Système d'Aide à la Conduite, à l'Exploitation et à la Maintenance (SACEM). Application à la ligne A du RER", *Revue Générale des Chemins de fer*, vol. 6, June 1990.

[GUI 90] GUIHOT G., HENNEBERT C., "SACEM software validation", *Proceedings of the 12th IEEE-ACM International Conference on Software Engineering*, March 1990.

[HAU 05] HAUSE M., THOM F., "Modelling high level requirements in UML/SysML", *INCOSE Symposium*, 2005.

[HUL 05] HULL E., JACKSON K., DICK J., *Requirement Engineering*, Springer, 2005.

[IDA 07] IDANI A., BOULANGER J.-L., PHILIPPE L., "A generic process and its tool support towards combining UML and B for safety critical systems", *CAINE is a congress 2007*, San Francisco, 7–9 November 2007.

[IDA 09] IDANI A., BOULANGER J.-L., PHILIPPE L., "Linking paradigms in safety critical systems", *Revue ICSA*, September 2009.

[IEC 90] IEC 61025, "Fault tree analysis – FTA", *International Electrotechnical Commission*, 1990.

[IEC 08] IEC 61508: Sécurité fonctionnelle des systèmes électriques électroniques programmables relatifs à la sécurité Norme internationale, 2008.

[ITU 03] ITU, "User requirements notation (URN) – language requirements and framework", February 2003.

[JAN 00] JANSEN L., SCHNEIDER E., "Traffic control systems case study: problem description and a note on domain-based software specification", *Institute of Control and Automation Engineering*, Technical University of Braunschweig, 2000.

[LEC 96] LECOMPTE P., BEAURENT P.-J., "Le système d'automatisation de l'exploitation des trains (SAET) de METEOR", *Revue Générale des Chemins de fer*, vol. 6, pp. 31–34, June 1996.

[LED 01] LEDANG H., "Des cas d'utilisation à une spécification B", *AFADL'2001: Approches Formelles dans l'Assistance au Développement de Logiciels*, 2001.

[LED 02] LEDANG H., SOUQUIÈRES J., "Contributions for modelling UML state-charts in B", *IFM 2002: The 3rd International Conference on Integrated Formal Methods*, LNCS 2335, Springer Verlag, 2002.

[MAM 01] MAMMAR A., LALEAU R., "An automatic generation of B specification from well-defined UML notations for database applications", *CNAM*, 2001.

[MAR 01] MARCANO R., LEVY N., "Transformation d'annotations OCL en expressions B", *Journées AFADL'2001: Approches formelles dans l'assistance au développement de logiciels*, June 2001.

[MAR 04a] MARCANO R., MARIANO G., BON P., "UML-based design and formal analysis of railway traffic control systems", *Formal Methods for Automation, Safety in Railway, and Automotive Systems*, FORMS '04, pp. 173–182, December 2004.

[MAR 04b] MARCANO R., COLIN S., MARIANO G., "A formal framework for UML modeling with timed constraints: application to railway control system", *Specification, Validation of UML Models for Real Time, and Embedded Systems (SVERTS'04)*, 2004.

[MEI 02] MEINADIER J.-P., *Le métier d'intégration de systèmes*, Hermes, 2002.

[MOT 05] MOTET G., "Vérification de cohérence des modèles UML 2.0", *1ère journée thématique "Modélisation de Systèmes avec UML – SysML et B-Système"*, French Association of Systems Engineering, Toulouse, France, June 2005.

[MUL 01] MULLER, P.-A., *Modélisation objet avec UML*, Eyrolles, 2001.

[OMG 06] OMG, OMG Systems Modeling Language (OMG SysML) Specification, Version 1.0, 2006.

[OMG 07] OMG, Unified Modeling Language (UML), Version 2.1.1, February 2007.

[OSS 07] OSSAMI D.O., MOTA J.M., BOULANGER J., "A model process towards modeling guidelines to build certifiable UML models in the railway sector", *The 7th International SPICE Conference (Software Process Improvement and Capability Determination)*, Seoul, Korea, 2007.

[RAM 09] RAMACHANDRAN M., DE CARVALHO R.M. (eds.), *Handbook of Software Engineering Research and Productivity Technologies: Implications of Globalisation*, August 2009.

[RAM 11] RAMACHANDRAN M. (ed.), *Knowledge Engineering for Software Development Life Cycles: Support Technologies and Applications*, April 2011.

[RET 07] RÉTIVEAU R., *La signalisation ferroviaire*, Presses de l'école Nationale des Ponts et Chaussées, 1987.

[STA 94] THE STANDISH GROUP, The CHAOS Report, 1994.

[STA 01] THE STANDISH GROUP, Extreme Report, 2001.

[SYS 05] SysML Partners, System Modeling Language (SysML) Specification, Version 1.0, 2005.

[ZOW 05] ZOWGHI D., COULIN C., *Requirements Elicitation: A Survey of Technique, Approaches and Tools*, Aurum A., Wohlin C. (eds.), Chapter 2, Springer, 2005.

12

Feasibility of the Use of Formal Methods for Manufacturing Systems

12.1. Introduction

In the manufacturing domain, if programmable logic controllers (PLC) are used to manage safety functions, these systems need to be more reliable when faced with software errors. One strategy often mentioned in software engineering, and also in the context of standards, is to use formal methods.

With a view to estimating the applicability of formal methods for the safety of the control systems of machines, the INRS[1] (*Institut National de Recherche et de Sécurité* – French Research and Safety Institute for the Prevention of Occupational Accidents and Diseases) has begun a research program which aims to develop the application software of a machine using these methods.

First, we describe the machine selected and its functions. After this, we present the different stages of the development, from specification to validation, of a software package installed on a safety PLC with two different methods: the B method [ABR 96] and a method which combines semi-formal models and model-checking verification techniques [BAI 08].

Chapter written by Pascal LAMY, Philippe CHARPENTIER, Jean-François PETIN and Dominique EVROT.

1 The INRS is a reference body in the prevention of occupational risks (accidents at work, work-related illnesses). To find out more about it, visit www.inrs.fr/.

For this second method, in view of the difficulty of defining *a posteriori* the safety properties which need to be formally verified at the level of the software components, we suggest a design process which makes it possible to identify and duplicate the safety properties from a high-level "system" view down to a low-level "component" view. The properties may then be formally verified *a posteriori*, using a proof tool. Finally, we conclude with some remarks concerning the applicability of these methods for the creation of software implemented on a safety PLC in a "machines" industrial context.

12.2. Presentation of the requirement

For more than a decade, in France, the use of safety PLC has been permitted by the authorities to handle the safety part of control systems for work equipment [CT5 98]. The embedded software in these control systems may contain bugs, caused by an incorrect interpretation of the specifications, for example.

Obviously, the same is true for the application software. If it is handling safety functions, an error in this software, more commonly known as a "PLC program", may lead to dangerous malfunctions: for example, to execute an incorrect instruction which has not been detected during the design phase is sufficient to activate an output which has an impact on the safety of the application. Therefore, it is essential to minimize the number of errors in this type of software, taking into account the stipulations of the machine's directive, which requires that no fault, due to a software error, for instance, should lead to a dangerous situation for the operator [DIR 06].

In response to this, the standards relevant to these new technologies, such as the standard IEC 61508 [CEI 10], recommend the use of development methods such as formal methods to guarantee a high level of software safety. The standard NF EN 62061 [NF 05], which is the application of the aforementioned standard in the domain of machines, mentions the use of formal methods as a way of reducing the number of tests.

Formal methods have been around for quite a while (since 1960), but have not been used in industry until relatively recently. These methods are currently used in critical systems (aeronautics, rail) for software development. In the manufacturing domain, to the best of our knowledge, no machine safety application software has yet been developed using formal methods. One possible explanation for this is that those involved in the sector are generally small companies with limited resources and short delivery times, e.g. a few weeks.

In order to confirm this state of affairs in the machine's sector, it is useful to be aware of the practices that automation technicians use to develop automated systems using PLC, and also to understand how the standard recommendations take the integration of prevention into the design into account. The contact that we have been able to have with industrial practice (through industrial conferences, relationships with suppliers to design workshops, discussions with experts) and some bibliographical references [NEU 02, LAM 03, VAL 10] has shown us that the methods currently being used in automation development do not facilitate the clear and unambiguous formalization of the specifications, nor, it follows, of the safety properties that the developed applications would need to verify, through a specification document. With current practices, the low-level programming is taken care of hurriedly, so the notion of safety properties disappears. In addition, even the safety properties are correctly formalized, their validation remains partial insofar as the current methods used, such as simulation or off-line tests, are generally by no means exhaustive. In fact, these test phases only facilitate the validation of a set of clearly defined situations and do not deliver any certainty that, whatever sequence of the situation is received by the controller, the operator will never be in danger.

INRS wished to evaluate the feasibility of using formal methods to develop application software for a machine control systems, with a view to determining whether this approach could work with existing practices in the sector.

In order to do this, the application software of a mechanical press with clutch-brake was developed using two types of formal methods:

– the formal B method [ABR 96], which makes it possible to progressively refine the requirements on the system under development up to the point where the code installed on the safety PLC which is driving the press is generated;

– an approach which combines the use of semi-formal methods at a system level for modeling control architectures and the safety properties that should be verified, with formal approaches, at a component level, for the proof of these properties and the generation of the code[2] [EVR 09].

The aim of this chapter is to present the results of the use of these different software development techniques, using formal verification.

12.3. The methods chosen and a brief description of them

12.3.1. *The B method*[3]

The B method [ABR 96], developed in 1996 by Jean-Raymond Abrial, uses the B language based on the mathematical concepts of set theory; this language includes proof mechanisms and can cover the whole of a development cycle without a break, up to an inclusion of the code of software elements.

It is an *a priori* design and specification method. The specifications are given using notations taken from set theory. Software tools or workshop software, supporting the B method, allow us to refine (the transition from formal specification to a detailed specification) and to prove, mostly automatically, that this transition is coherent. In this way, it is possible to generate programs that are certified correct in relation to the specifications.

The B method includes:

– a specification language (abstract machine notation (AMN)) with an added proof system;

– a refinement technique which makes possible the transition from a high-level design to a detailed design, while generating corresponding proof systems.

This method has a "development" flavor in the way that operations are specified: they are not specified in terms of pre- and post-conditions, but rather using generalized substitution of the type x:=x+1. This specification

2 This second possibility has been studied in a doctoral research project. The method which was developed in it has not yet been applied in industry.

3 This is not intended as a full presentation of B, but just to provide some context. Chapter 1 of this book contains more detailed information on B.

uses non-deterministic constructs and all of the power of set language. Algorithmic constructs of sequence or loop type, on the other hand, are not allowed. This is why those that feature this method are known as abstract machines.

As each stage of refinement passes, the structures of set data are replaced by the structures close to those of programming languages. These stages are subjected to proofs of maintaining the invariants (properties on control data which always hold and which are defined using logical conditions) and of conformity of refined machines in relation to more abstract machines. In this way, the final model is guaranteed to conform to the initial specifications.

There exist tools that facilitate the translation of an implementation expressed in AMN into C-code, and the generation of the object-oriented implementations or the creation of specification libraries.

There is a workshop software, sold as[4] "Atelier B", which lessens the workload for the designer, taking charge of:

– syntactic analysis and control of the type;

– generation of proof obligations;

– (partial) demonstration of proof obligations;

– translation into more widespread programming languages;

– management of the coherence of developments (in case of change).

Development in line with this method starts with the construction of a B model which takes on all the descriptions of the requirement. Following this, other models are developed in stages, using the B language each time, until the executable program is obtained. The coherence of the models at the different stages and the conformity of the program to the initial model are guaranteed by mathematical proofs, carried out automatically by the workshop software, or else by the intervention of the B expert.

At the final stage, the programs produced are corrected by construction, i.e. they conform to the specification of the requirement and there is no need to run tests on them to eliminate program errors. The only tests that remain

4 Chapter 3 contains a more detailed description of "Atelier B".

necessary are integration tests for the software in its hardware and software environment.

12.3.2. *Specification with SysML*[5] *and formal verification by model checking*

The second group of methods used for formal verification of properties is based on the techniques of model checking [CLA 00]. This technique involves constructing and exploring a state space so as to verify the respect of an expressed predicate in temporal logic for each of the achievable states.

These techniques were investigated by the INRS for the development of the control of the mechanical press by coupling a model-checking tool based on the use of the synchronous language signal with a PLC development tool which supported the languages of the standard NF EN 61131-3 [NF 03] (Ladder, SFC, Structured Text, Function Block) and by describing the control of the press in the form of a hierarchical set, structured from function blocks. This tool, which makes the simulation of all or a part of the developed models possible, thus withstands the validation:

– of elementary components and thus of unitary tests;

– of the integration of the different software components in the assemblies;

– of the application of the control itself.

In addition to this simulation stage, formal verification by model checking has made it possible to obtain a proof of the respect of certain safety properties by the control system. However, this proof has been limited by two main difficulties that we have demonstrated in the case of the press:

– the phenomenon of combinatorial explosion, which is well know because it is linked to the exhaustive exploration of state space;

– the difficulty of precisely identifying the local properties to be verified for each of the software components with regard to the safety requirements, often expressed at a system level.

---

5 SysML stands for systems modeling language. For more detailed information, see www.sysml.org/.

Therefore, the use of semi-formal methods, prior to formal methods, would seem to be necessary to cover a phase of "system" analysis which makes it possible to identify the smaller components together with their local properties [ACH 06, JOH 07].

To this end, INRS, in a thesis conducted in partnership with CRAN, studied an approach based on SysML [EVR 09, PÉT 10]. This language, which originated for system engineering, offers a set of formalisms such as static, dynamic, functional, structural or information diagrams. These diagrams make it possible to represent the different types of system objects: requirements, components and functions. Thus, they deliver a more complete view of the requirements widely used in the industry than might be obtained by using engineering tools.

The requirements can, in this way, be projected onto the constituents of the system (functions or components), which are modeled in the form of objects. SysML offers a definition diagram of blocks which allow us to model the physical structure of the system, and also to model diagrams of use cases and activities which define its functional architecture. By way of a principle similar to the B method, the suggested operation makes it possible to model the safety requirements and to verify starting from high-level or system requirements.

The operation makes it possible to draw and adapt these requirements throughout the modeling process in order to determine, for each unitary software component, the local safety requirement(s) which should be checked in the low-level software components: the PLC code. This SysML operation method results in a consensual vision of the functional and organic control architectures and the properties they should verify, in a formalism generic enough to be usable by all profession groups involved in the development of the press control. These models should then serve as an entry point to more specific models for each of the professions, and would be expressed in their specific languages, often called domain-specific languages (DSLs).

The automation technician would use the languages of the standard NF EN 61131-3. These models would be used for the modeling of the behavior of the press control, the verification of the properties by model checking, and, finally, for the generation of the code.

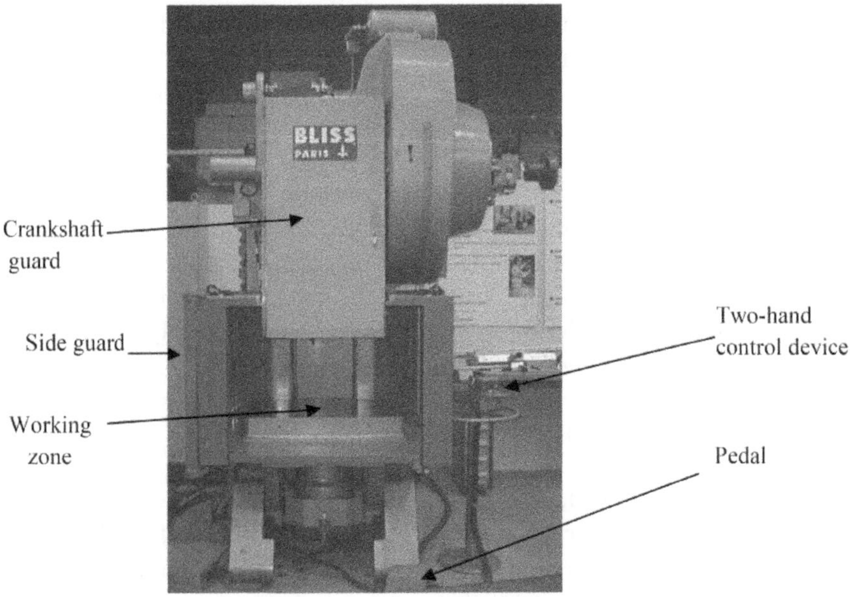

Figure 12.1. *An example of a mechanical press*

12.4. Description of the machine: mechanical press with clutch-brake

12.4.1. *Description of the press*

The function of this machine is to press the pieces positioned under the ram in the working zone. The movement of the ram is controlled by an operator through a control/command system. Two systems co-exist in this laboratory press, switched via a selector, based either on a technology incorporating relays or on a programmable safety PLC.

The photos in Figures 12.1–12.3 give an idea of this mechanical press.

The motor drives an inertia flywheel which provides the energy necessary for the ram to carry out a translational movement through a clutch-brake controlled by a solenoid valve. The position of the ram is determined by the operation of cams (one cam for the top dead center and a back-up cam for the bottom dead center).

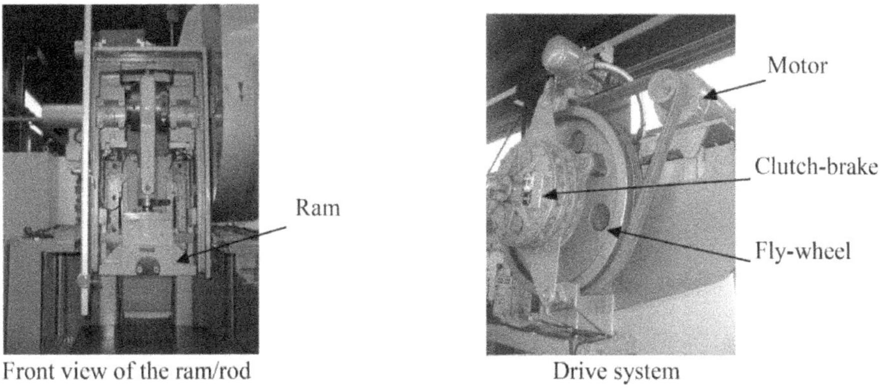

Figure 12.2. *Detailed views of the mechanical press*

Depending on the operating mode chosen, the movement of the ram may be controlled using different systems (e.g. pedal, two-hand control device), and guards (crankshaft guard, lateral guards and front guard) prevent the operator from accessing the working zone which presents a high level of risk.

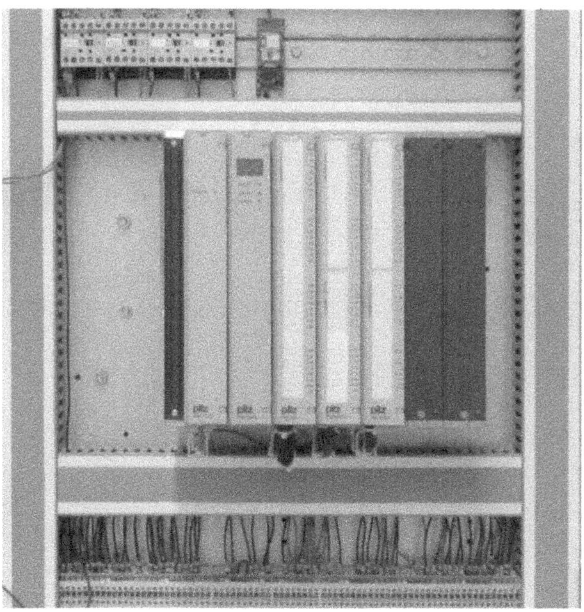

Figure 12.3. *Safety programmable logic controller installed in the switching cabinet*

12.4.2. *Brief description of the operating modes*

The press has five operating modes:

– Two setup modes:

- set-up with motor; the front and side guards and the crankshaft guard may be open; the pedal is operated to control the descent or ascent of the ram,

- set-up forward operation; the front and side guards and the crankshaft guard may be open; the two-hand control device is used to activate the movements of the ram.

– Two production modes:

- single-shot operation: the side guard and the crankshaft guard must be closed; the front guard may be open; the two-hand control device is used to control the ram, which makes a single movement, first descent and then ascent,

- continuous operation: all of the guards must be shut; the cycle is triggered using the two-hand control device.

– An off mode.

The selection of operating modes is done by a selector which may be locked with a key.

The arming of the machine, by pushing a button, is required:

– each time it is turned on;

– each time the operating mode is changed;

– after re-arming of an overrun braking angle[6];

6 Braking angle: angle traveled by the crankshaft during stopping at the upper dead point.

– after an emergency stop;

– for the “production” operating modes, each time the crankshaft guard is opened/shut.

12.4.3. *Brief description of the means of protection*

The dangerous zone considered is the working zone accessible by the sides and the front of the press. Access from behind is impossible.

There is an emergency stop button at the front of the press. If it is pushed, the clutch and the main motor are halted.

The braking performances of the machine are verified each time the ram stops at the upper dead point, for all “production” operating modes. If the normal braking angle is overrun by more than 15°, no new clutch request is possible. The control mechanism can be re-armed by pushing a key-operated button.

12.4.4. *Characteristics of the programmable logic controller*

The safety PLC uses the language of the standard NF EN 61131-3. In our case, a structured-text language is used. The PLC is certified SIL[7]3 in line with the standard IEC 61508.

12.5. Process followed for the design, validation and generation of the software using the B method

The different phases of this process applied in our case are shown in detail in Figure 12.4.

7 SIL stands for safety integrity level. The SIL may take the values 1, 2, 3 and 4.

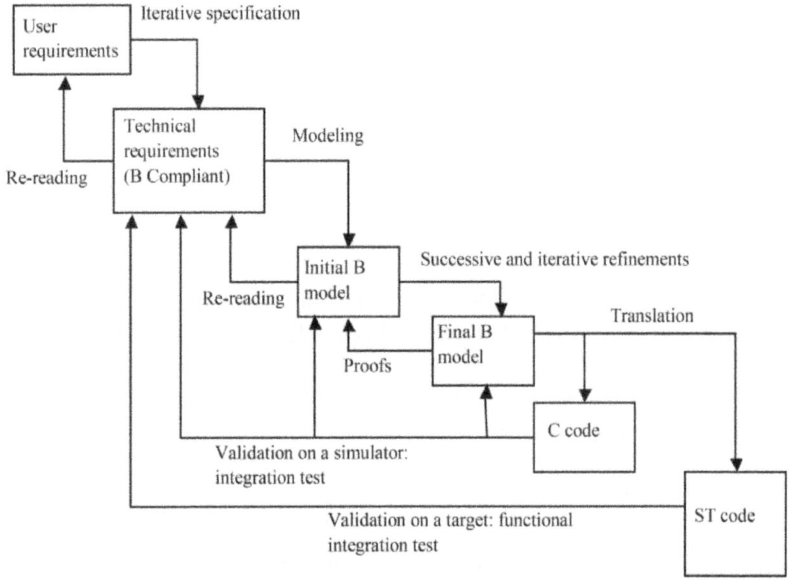

Figure 12.4. *Process followed with the B method*

12.5.1. *Creation of a B compatible specification*

This part consists of creating a B-compatible specification of the press which brings together all the information necessary for the development of the software, in natural language. This document must describe the system and present the requirements on the software clearly, unambiguously and as completely as possible.

This specification allows the B experts to make the operation of the machine their own, and to express the need so as to prepare the modeling work in B.

This B-compatible specification makes it possible to plot the functional requirements, the safety requirements and certain specific operating conditions. These will then be identified in the different refinements, in order to ensure that each of them has been properly taken into account.

At the outset of this study, we consulted a document written by the experts of the INRS, which serves as an initial specification. The writing of a B-compatible specification is based on this document and is supplemented by different interviews with experts who approve the new document as and when required.

The new specification contains both a descriptive part and a part which precisely defines the requirements of the software. The descriptive part serves to make it easier to learn the operating principles of the press for a person who does not know the machine. The part which defines the requirements serves as a reference during the development of the control software for the press, during the software specification and design phases, and during the integration test and validation phases.

12.5.1.1. *Factorization versus enumeration*

When several elements of the system have functions with common points, two approaches are possible: factorization and enumeration.

Factorization is a functional view which divides the elements of the system into two levels: an abstract level which describes the common behavior of the different elements, giving the general operating principles, and a sub-level which describes the characteristics of the elements. This approach reduces repetition.

In contrast, enumeration involves the description on a single level of each element of the system independently. This can lead to repetition.

12.5.1.2. *An example of factorization and enumeration*

In the case of the press, equipment such as the two-hand control device possesses the characteristics for each operating mode, but also its own characteristics. As far as possible, the B-compatible specification presents the information in factorized form, so as to avoid repetition and to make the system operating principles more visible. A compromise needed to be found to avoid the factorized description (abstract and particular) being less clear than an enumerated description.

12.5.1.3. *Part of the specification*

M1 Mode: Adjustment without motor

Nominal operating conditions in M1 mode

M1_F1: There is only one normal nominal operating condition in M1 mode: the motor must have been stopped for a certain time D4.

Actions to be carried out during selection of mode M1

M1_F2: When this mode is selected, if the motor is running, the controller must automatically halt the motor (section 12 of [CON 09]).

M1_F3: When this mode is selected, if the motor is running, a suitable period of time D4 must pass after its effective halt so that it is certain that the flywheel has stopped (see section 12 of [EVR 09] – the exact definition for the controller of the effective halt of the motor).

M1_F4: When this mode is selected, if the motor has already stopped, it is nonetheless necessary to wait until the same time period D4 has passed, so as to be sure that the flywheel itself has completely stopped.

The specification is a 34-page textual document, which contains 159 rules that are identified by a label: for example M1_F1.

12.5.2. *B Model: specification and design*

This part makes it possible to create a B model made up of several levels of completely proven refinement. This model gives an overall description of the press and its environment, formalizing the requirements of the B-compatible specification.

Specification and design using the formal method D involves describing the functional aspects of the system using a succession of points of view. This succession progresses from the most general to the most detailed.

This technique for describing how the system works, moving from the most abstract to the most concrete, is known as "refinement" in the B method. The initial B model consists of the creation of a high-level representation of the elements of the system that can be physically observed. In this initial model, there is no constraint, the elements are introduced to it as the refinement progresses during design.

The B model of the press is thus made up of a series of refinements:

– the first refinements formalize the system from a very abstract point of view, describing the parts which can be seen from the outside: the press, the hands of the operator, the direction of movement of the ram, the guards, the stop at the top dead center;

– the last few final levels of refinement describe how the system works in great detail. They formalize the detail of each individual operation of the software and each physical action which can be observed;

– at the final level of refinement, we find the scission between purely software events and B events modeling the mechanical parts of the press or the behavior of the operator.

What is particularly interesting about a B design is that it is necessary to bring proof of its coherence. This proof consists of showing that the processing described at a given level of refinement enforces all the properties of the preceding levels.

The refinement also serves to gradually introduce the different requirements given in the B-compatible specification document. It would not be possible to formalize all the requirements globally, one next to another. In this example, the usefulness of the B method is that it structures the modeling of the requirement in such a way that the consolidation brought by the proof corresponds to the demonstration of the salient properties of the system.

The proof is not only a tool for verification. It also allows us to refine the properties of the system, while revealing whether the properties formalized by the expert in charge of modeling are too restrictive or insufficiently so. Properties that are too restrictive mean that some conditions can never be met.

Insufficiently restrictive properties mean that some parts of the B model cannot be proved, due to a lack of information. In this case, the model needs to be supplemented with stronger properties so that the system as a whole can be described. This modeling process is iterative because the B model needs to be modified after a problem is discovered.

The proof mechanism operated during each of the series of refinements ensures the coherence of each new iteration with preceding models. It also ensures coherence within the refinement in progress. The usefulness of the B method is that we obtain a final model which is proved and coherent in relation to the initial model and its iterations.

12.5.2.1. *Characteristics of the B model generated for the press*

14 B models or B machines would be created:

– 1st model or initial model: Introduction of the abstract physical variables;

– 2nd model – 1st refinement: Operating and safety laws;

– 3rd model: Introduction of the motor and of the clutch;

– 4th model: The clutch commands, simplified;

– 5th model: Modeling of the movement, simplified;

– 6th model: The front guard;

– 7th model: The crankshaft;

– 8th model: Stopping and starting the motor;

– 9th model: Refinement of the movement (the cams);

– 10th model: Refinements of the clutch command;

– 11th model: Changing modes and emergencies;

– 12th model: Refinements of the preceding models (time frames and redundancy);

– 13th model: Refinement of the clocks for the PLC;

– 14th model or final model: Refinement of mode changes.

925 proofs were carried out, of which 60 could not be handled automatically by the prover in Atelier B and required with the intervention of the B expert. The number of lines in the 14th model is approximately 2,600.

The last few levels of refinement describe how the system works in a very detailed manner. They formalize the detail of each individual operation of the software and each physical action which can be seen.

12.5.2.2. *Example of refinement and adaptation to the target*

In the example in Figure 12.5, extracted from the initial model, an outside observer of the situation sees that the press is changing from working to stopping. The event which is the stopping of the press is thus described in a very general manner.

```
arreter_presse =
   SELECT PRESSE=en_marche
   THEN  PRESSE:=arrete END;
```

Figure 12.5. *Example of an event*

Figure 12.6 shows processing after refinement in the final B model.

```
arreter_presse =
  SELECT
   (mode:{M2,M3,M4} => MOTEUR=en_marche) &
    EMBRAYAGE=en_marche &
    sortie_embrayage=arrete &
   (CAME_PMH=OK or CAME_PMB=KO => ARRET=OK)
  THEN
    EMBRAYAGE:=arrete ||
    capteur_embrayage:=arrete ||
    capteur_embrayage_bis:=arrete
  END;
```

Refinement that corresponds to the conditions leading to stopping: function of the operating modes, position of the ram (cams), of the stop command

Refinement that corresponds to the stopping of the press: state of the sensors and real state of the clutch system

Figure 12.6. *Refinement*

A final level of refinement makes it possible to adapt the model depending on the target on which the code needs to be generated (15th model or B machine). This last refinement may be viewed as the preparation of the PLC for coding.

In this model, which is suited to the target, the example in Figure 12.6 becomes that of Figure 12.7.

```
arreter_presse =
        SELECT
                (MB_72_08__mode:{M2,M3,M4} => MOTEUR=en_marche) &
                EMBRAYAGE=en_marche &
                A_02_16__sortie_embrayage=FALSE &
                (CAME_PMH=OK or CAME_PMB=KO => ARRET=OK)
        THEN
                EMBRAYAGE:=arrete ;
                E_00_19__capteur_embrayage:=TRUE ;
                E_00_20__capteur_embrayage_bis:=TRUE
        END;
```

Figure 12.7. *From the point of view of the target*

12.5.3. *Generation of a C code and simulation*

Although it is not linked to the application of the B method, it was possible to create a mechanical press simulator, written by translation of the last level of refinement of the B model, and by adding a C code which carries out the sequencing of the B events and the input/output operations.

Some properties related to sequencing of the B model events were not integrated into the B model. The simulator makes it possible to carry out integration tests for the press software, to check if the behavior observed on the simulator complies with the written specification. The progress of the test scenarios for each of the five press operating modes allows us to verify that the software behaves in line with its specifications.

In practice, this simulation detects two types of problems:

– Deadlock problems: following application of the treatment of a B event, it may happen that the system is in a state such that no further event may occur, which means that the system is doomed to remain in the same state indefinitely. This type of problem could be covered by the B model, but the development of the model to prove this property would necessitate an intensive effort. As a result, the solution of using host simulation was preferred. An additional reason for this is that simulation also covers our second point.

– Problems in the specification and construction of the model: although much care may have been devoted to the writing of the new written specification, it may be that certain situations have been described with insufficient completeness or clarity. Simulation then serves to detect these problems. By conducting simulation tests, behaviors which seem troublesome can be found. We can then locate and re-examine the model B events and requirements from the written specification which are associated with these behaviors.

Unlike the proof of a B model, the test scenarios which can be conducted using a simulator do not cover all the possible cases. The number of different test scenarios necessary to run is much too large for it to be possible to run them all, in particular because of the treatment of breakdowns.

12.5.4. *Generation of the code for the PLC and validation*

12.5.4.1. *Presentation*

In order to generate the code for the PLC, it was first necessary to define the translation mechanisms for the pseudo B code, originating from the last B model, into the PLC language. These translation mechanisms were applied manually in order to generate the code in a format suited to the PLC (INSTRUCTION LIST type) and which clearly shows the possibility of automating this task.

12.5.4.2. *Example of a translation rule: the case of the B instruction "Select"*

The PLC software is based on the creation of an assembly of software blocks. Each of these blocks carries out a single function such as, for example, the treatment of the motor stoppage or the opening of the crankshaft guard.

The translation of a SELECT instruction corresponds to the creation of the body of a block. It begins with the positioning of the Begin label associated with segment 00. For the initialization event, the condition is not translated.

Otherwise, the pile of condition values is re-initialized, the condition is translated and inverted, making a pile following a de-piling of the inversion. In this way, if the condition, which represents the guard of the event, is false, then the RLO is worth 1 and the instruction of conditional jump will lead to a jump to reach the end of the block. If not, the instruction, which constitutes the body of the event, will be carried out.

The instruction is translated, and finally the segment with the label End is positioned by incrementing the number of the current segment.

```
TradSubst(SELECT ?P THEN ?S END, ?IsInit) ::=
Begin
    Write("Begin: NW ?NumSeg");
    ?NumSeg:=?NumSeg+1;
    if not ?IsInit then
        ResetPile;
        TradPred(?P);
        Push;
        Pop(LN);
        Write("SPB = End");
    end if;
    TradSubst(?S, ?IsInit);
    Write("End: NW ?NumSeg");
    ?NumSeg:=?NumSeg+1;
End;
```

Figure 12.8. *Example of a translation rule*

B0	PLC assembler
SELECT M_66_0 = TRUE THEN M_66_0 := FALSE END	Begin: NW 00 L M 66.0 = M (114.16) LN M (114.16) SPB = End L M 110.01 = M 66.0 End: NW 01

Table 12.1. *Example of translation*

The language in PLC format is then imported using the software programming workshop of the PLC.

A validation of the system in its environment is conducted. A validation using ControlBuild (see Chapter 8 of [BOU 12b]) to simulate the operative part (the press actioners) is conducted.

This platform acceptance test allows us, through ControlBuild, to communicate with the PLC and to go beyond the mechanical constraints of the machine. The software implanted in the PLC can be tested in this way. The advantage of this simulation by ControlBuild is that test scenarios can be rapidly reproduced.

This validation remains necessary, even if we use the B method, in order to validate:

– the interfaces: it should be verified that the software interfaces made up of 29 Boolean inputs and 4 Boolean outputs are coherent between the B model and the physical parts of the press. In particular, this should apply for the cabling of the inputs/outputs and the respect for the logics of each input/output;

– the initialization conditions: even if the B model is auto-coherent, it should be established that the initial state of the software is coherent with the initial state of the press;

– the real-time aspect: certain real-time constraints can be treated by the software package, others have not been specified or studied in this sense. For example, for the use of the two-hand control device, it was required that the command only be validated if pressure is applied to both buttons simultaneously (with a tolerance of 500 ms). As a result, it is possible that problems linked to the real-time aspect appear during this phase. The difficulties in perfecting set-up linked to real time should be studied by an expert in the press and the safety PLC, who should identify the requirements specifically linked to real time that need to be taken into account by the software.

Several problems were detected during the validation phase:

– errors in the generated code due to manual translation. Evidently, in the context of an industrial process, an automatic translator should be created;

– poor definition of the interface between the software variables and their material implementation (definition of the inputs/outputs);

– spreading out of the B events, which could have been avoided by segmenting the model into two B sub-models, one for the software and the other for the rest of the system;

– an error due to insufficient care taken during the definition of the B invariable.

That problems were discovered in validation should not make us question everything the B method contributes to the process.

For errors linked to translation mechanisms, prior tests should have been conducted on the PLC so as to validate these mechanisms and develop an automatic tool which, once validated, would have guaranteed the coherence of the automatic code generated. As these tasks had not been carried out, the validation of the software served to validate the translation mechanisms and the manual translation.

12.5.5. *Conclusion on the use of the B method for the creation of application software in an industrial and manufacturing context*

Several observations result from the use of the B method:

– The expert in B method plays a very significant role in the creation of the model. This is because many modeling choices need to be made. On the other hand, the use of the B method and the proof made it possible to ensure that these modeling options are coherent with the safety rules modeled as an invariant in B.

– Although INRS personnel were involved in the process (who had not been trained in the B method), it was necessary to also involve a B expert in order to understand the process that was followed;

– An extrapolation of these results for the development of software in the context of manufacturing industry could be attempted. This type of software is not generally created by significant research institutes as has been the case in applications of the B method created up till now. In addition, this study did not take into account the existence of functional blocks which had already been validated and certified (the management of the two-hand control device is, for example, carried out by a single block), which were already present in the PLC before the study.

– At present, it is difficult to evaluate the level of safety achieved by the software. This is the main concern of the INRS in its validation work on control systems [BLA 03]. The proof covers the unitary tests exhaustively, and makes it possible to improve the confidence level that we can have in the developed software.

– The use of the B method required around four weeks for the development of the complete software by people who were not experts in the press (without using the certified functional blocks) and one additional week to carry out the function tests.

– Manufacturers of this type of machine may not be ready to make the transition to a method such as B given the initial investment required (particularly in terms of training in the method). However, they could sub-contract certain critical functions such as the certified functional blocks.

– This method is a global design method which makes it possible to create a proven software.

12.6. Formalization of the requirements and properties helping SysML and verification of the unitary modules by model checker

In section 12.3.2, we have highlighted the importance of the specification phase of the system to be designed, in particular the definition of the requirements that it must satisfy and the properties that it must satisfy. The B method, discussed in the previous section, addresses this requirement by offering a modeling process by refinement, which makes it possible to begin modeling at a very abstract level, and to progressively add the levels of details necessary to the generation of the code.

However, our experience has shown that this requires a high level of expertise of the language, which is not always compatible with the practices of machine design professionals.

We thus have decided to develop a development process [EVR 09, PÉT 10] based on SysML [WIL 07] and on tools and languages dedicated to the modeling of the control, its formal verification by model checking and the generation of code. This process focuses on safety and aims to ensure the traceability of the safety requirements from the specification phase up to the stages of formal verification by model checking and generation of the code.

12.6.1. *Overall view of the design process for manufacturing systems*

The suggested process begins with the expression of the system needs and ends with a set of functional and safety requirements. Based on these requirements, a functional and organic architecture is suggested. Care is taken to associate each safety requirement with a functional and/or organic subset.

This first phase (see Figure 12.9) is concerned with the definition and the specification of the system, for the production functions as well as the protection measures linked to the safety of people who come into contact with the machine. What is important about this process is that it formalizes then plots the safety requirements based on a global risk analysis procedure, while, in the domain of machine safety, these aspects are not necessarily taken into account from the beginning of the design process.

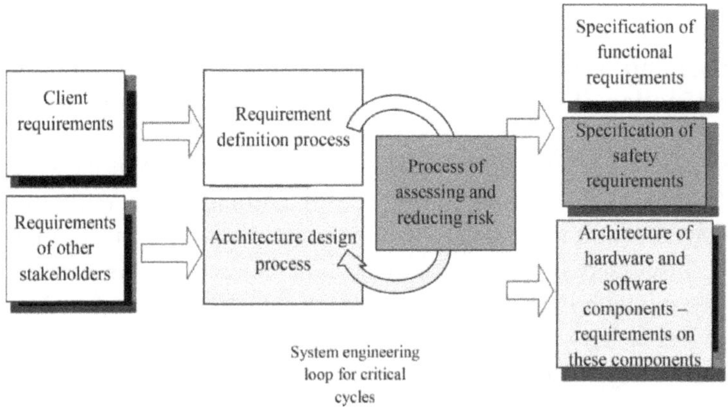

Figure 12.9. *System engineering loop: identification and allocation of the requirements, breakdown into components*

In the second phase (see Figure 12.10), these requirements are used as an entry point to a development phase of the command, which includes the verification and the generation of code on a programmable industrial safety PLC.

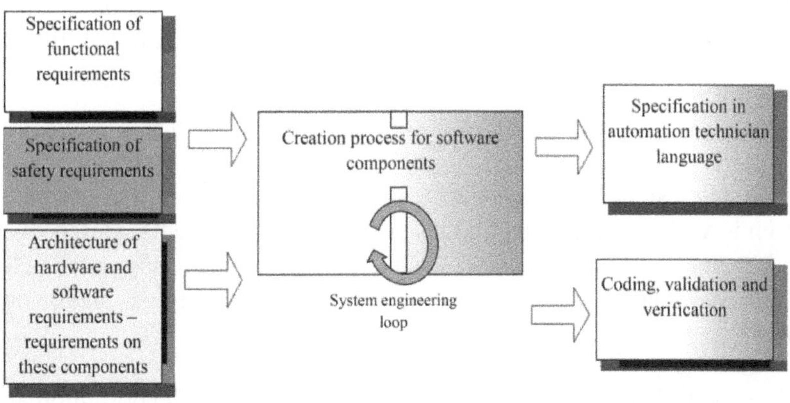

Figure 12.10. *Software engineering loop*

This phase is carried out using the automation technician's models and tools, which presupposes that it is possible to export the necessary knowledge expressed in the "system" specification stage to these workshops.

This includes:

– specification in automation technician language (Grafcet) of the behavior of the system, based on the outputs from the preceding level (functional and safety specifications and architecture of the components);

– coding of the associated functional and safety software components, in language compatible with the standard NF EN 61131-3;

– verification by emulation-simulation of the low-level functional components and of the software-PLC grouping;

– verification by model checking of the low-level safety components.

12.6.2. *Modeling the requirements*

The suggested process begins with the identification of the safety properties mentioned in the written specification of the machine. The aim of this stage is to separate the properties related to functional aspects and those which are concerned with the safety of the system. In this way, the proof will be limited to the subsets which are relevant to the safety requirements. This will reduce the size of the verified models and make it possible to avoid the phenomenon of combinatory explosion.

Modeling of the requirements is based on an incremental process founded on refinement and decomposition mechanisms which make it possible to perceive different levels of abstraction:

– the refinement consists of transforming a requirement into a new requirement which contains more precise information and levels of additional details; for example, a requirement such as "the two-hand control is activated by pushing the interfaces with both hands simultaneously" may be refined into the requirement "the two-hand control is activated by pushing the interface with both hands, the contact from each is separated by a maximum of 500 ms";

– the breakdown process consists of separating the requirements into several sub-requirements. This means that the composite requirement is satisfied if and only if all the sub-requirements are satisfied; for example, the requirement "operator protection" can be broken down into "protection by two-hand control device", and "lateral protection".

In SysML, the formalism used for the modeling and structuring of the requirements is the requirement diagram. It defines a requirement as an object which possesses attributes unique to it (ID, text, source of the requirement, type, level of priority, verification method, etc.). These objects may have a relationship with other requirements (links of composition and derivation to represent, respectively, the decomposition and refinement mechanisms) or other supporting objects (activities, components, etc.).

The functional requirements of the press are concerned with the job it is to carry out, its performance, its cost and its integration within a production chain. A first model, which of course requires further breaking down, is presented in Figure 12.11.

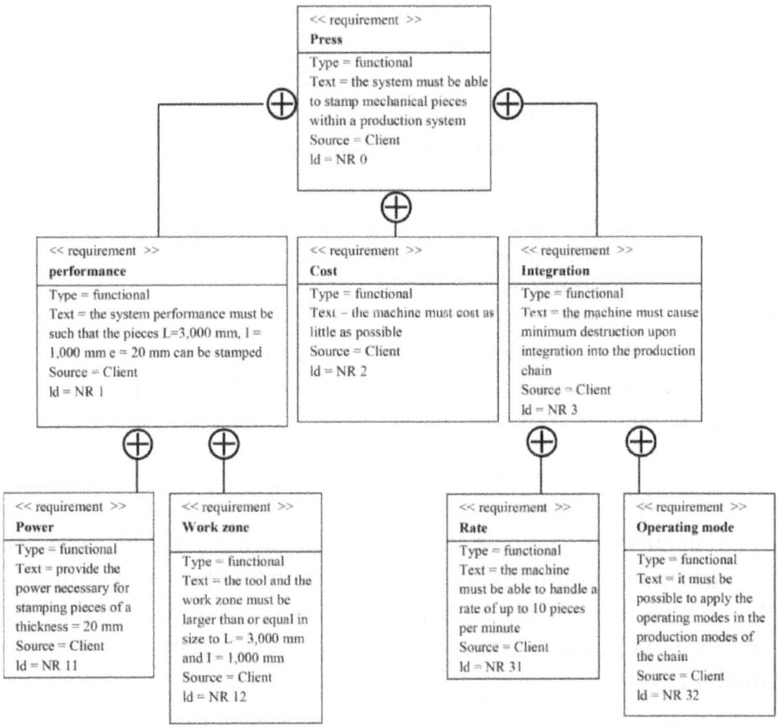

Figure 12.11. *Functional requirement*

The safety requirements are deduced from a risk analysis process as described in the ISO 12100 [NF 10], and which, in particular, includes:

– an identification of the dangers and a provisional evaluation of the risks based on methods such as failure tree analysis or failure modes, effects and criticality analysis (FMECA);

– a reduction in the risks based on the application of preventative measures, aimed at minimizing the occurrence of feared events, or on the application of protection which aims to minimize their consequences.

This study focuses on two principal risks (see Figure 12.12):

– crushing the operator's hands during the stamping movement;

– the ejection of a piece during stamping.

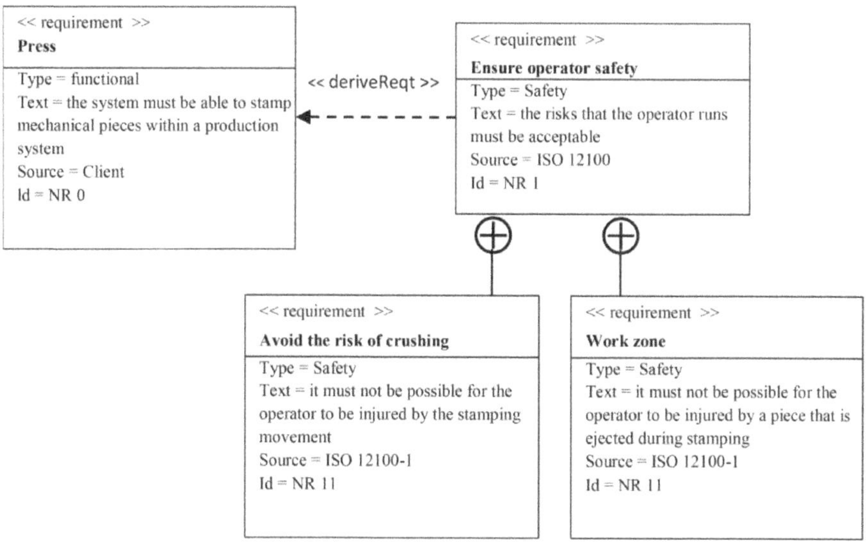

Figure 12.12. *Safety requirement (1)*

In the following, we will focus on the risk of crushing. Two access paths to the dangerous zone are identified: from the front and from the side of the machine. Due to the position of the crankshaft in the press architecture, access from the side may cause damage, not only during descent of the tool (stamping) but also during the re-ascent to the upper position of the press. Access by the side must be avoided whatever way the press is currently moving (requirement SR3) and access from the front must be avoided only in the descending phase (requirement SR1).

Following analysis of the risks, the measures chosen for prevention are, on the one hand, unmovable guards for access from the sides (SR3) and a two-hand control device (CB) for front access (SR1). The role of the two-hand control is to force the operator to apply both his/her hands to the apparatus during the entire descending movement. All of the protection measures are interlocked and conditioned by the movement of the press: if a protection measure is not activated during the stamping movement, the movement is halted (requirement SR2). These requirements are modeled in Figure 12.13.

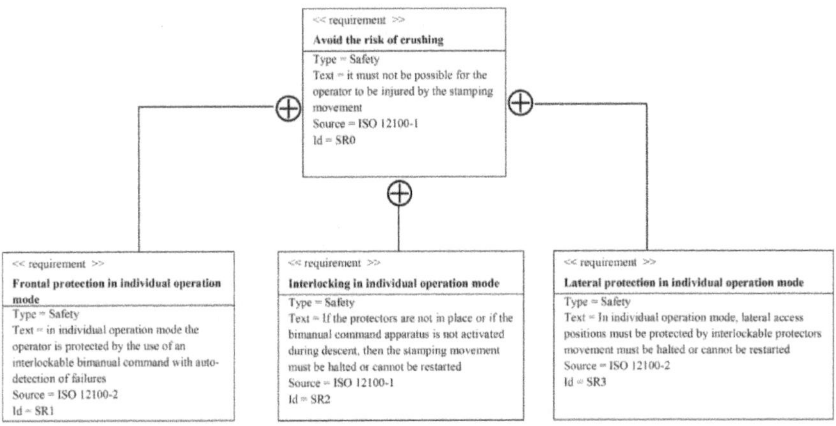

Figure 12.13. *Safety requirement (2)*

Let us consider the safety requirement related to the two-hand control device. This requirement SR1 can be broken down, according to the standards ISO 12100, ISO 13849-1 [NF 08a] and EN574 [NF 08b], into five sub-requirements related to:

– the physical design of the apparatus, particularly for preventing the two-hand control device from being activated with one hand, which is due to a separation hood (requirement SR1.2);

– auto-detection of failure (requirement SR1.4 dictates that the two-hand control device should be de-activated in the case of the detection of a fault);

– activation, de-activation and re-activation of the two-hand control device (requirement SR1.1 dictates that the two-hand control (BC) should not be re-activated unless both hands have been withdrawn, SR1.3 dictates that the BC is activated if both hands apply pressure to the apparatus within an interval of less than 0.5 s and SR1.5 means that the BC is de-activated if one of the hands is withdrawn).

These new requirements are modeled by the SysML diagram of Figure 12.14. The SysML constraints which make it possible to refine the requirements in the form of expressed properties in a predicate logic are also present in this diagram.

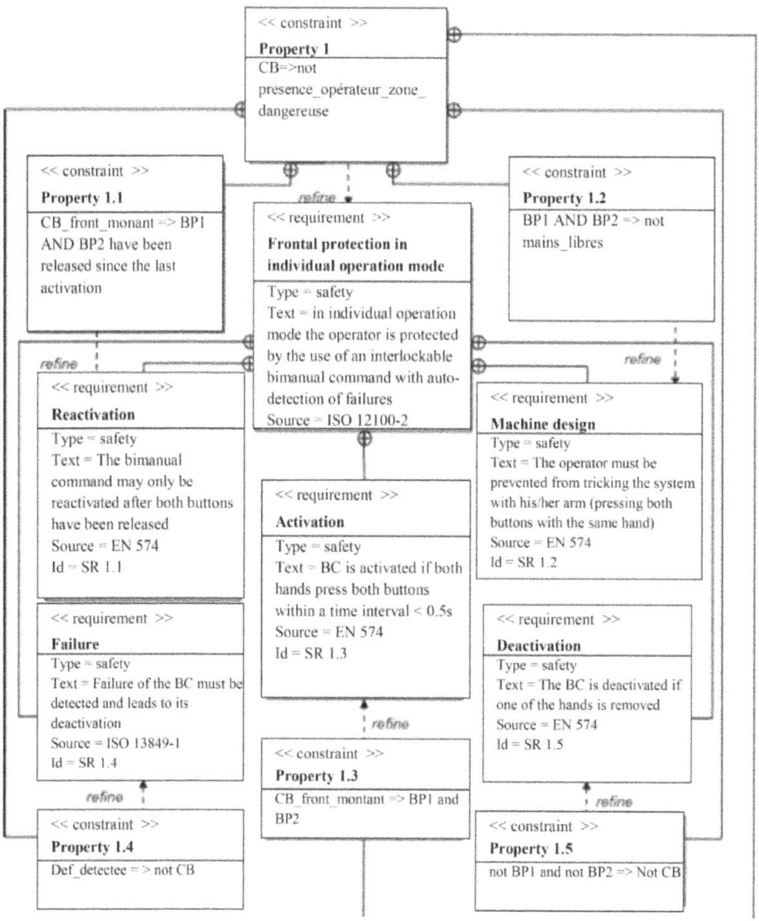

Figure 12.14. *Safety requirement (3)*

12.6.3. *Modeling functional and organic architectures*

The functional architecture describes and classifies all the functions that are supported by the system in development into a hierarchy. This functional analysis, equivalent to that which can be carried out with an SADT-type formalism[8] [LIS 90], is conducted during our process, using a SysML activity diagram with a restriction on the use of control streams.

Since the usual function of these diagrams is behavioral modeling, no control stream is used in the context of a functional analysis.

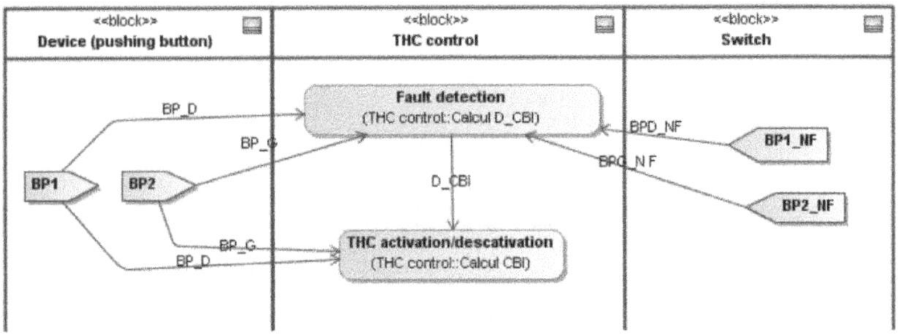

Figure 12.15. *Functional architecture of the two-hand control device (extract)*

As an example of this, Figure 12.15 shows two safety functions associated with the management of the two-hand control device: Two-hand control activation/deactivation and fault detection.

The structural architecture describes and arranges the components of the system in development into a hierarchy. In SysML, the component is described using the block concept, which is the class stereotype, and through two types of diagrams:

– The block definition diagram (BDD) makes it possible to represent the structure of the system through the composed/components relationships and those similar to what could be created using a class diagram.

– The internal block diagram (IBD) is a data stream type diagram which provides the detailed description of a composite element, in the spirit of data stream diagrams supported by command system design tools such as Simulink, SCADE or ControlBuild.

8 SADT stands for structured analysis and design technique.

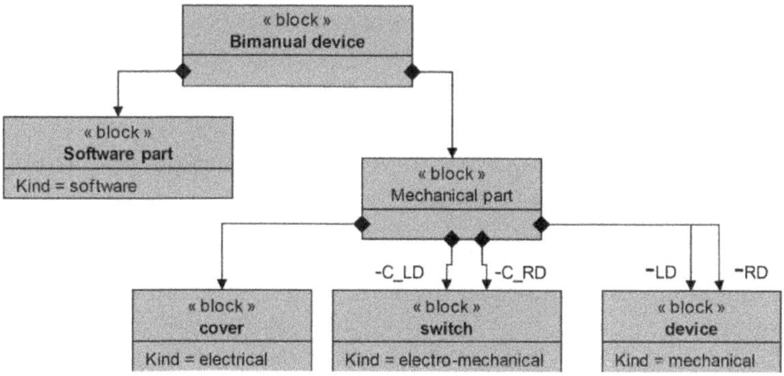

Figure 12.16. *Internal block diagram for the two-hand device (extract)*

For example, Figure 12.16 shows the architecture of the two-hand control device and all its components in the form of a BDD. Figure 12.17 provides details on the internal architecture of a software component related to the two-hand control device and its safety rules.

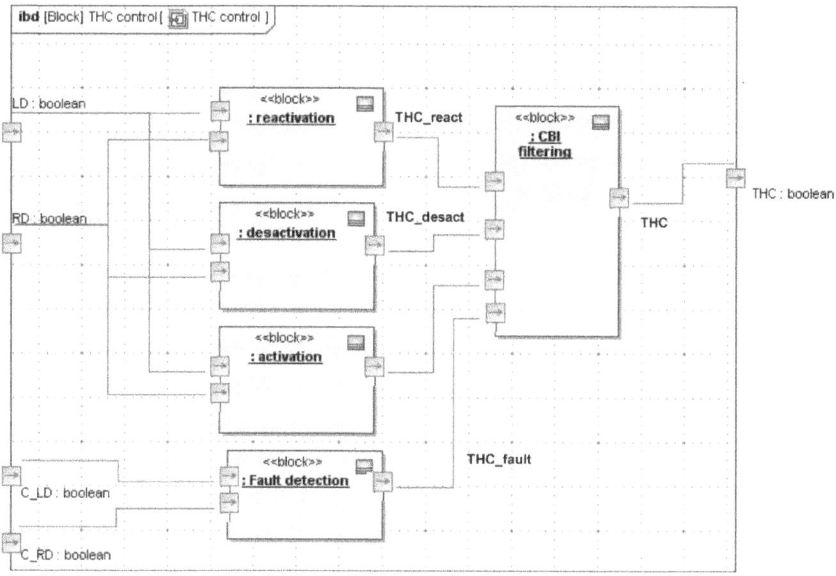

Figure 12.17. *Internal block diagram for the two-hand control device (extract)*

12.6.4. *Traceability of the requirements*

It must be possible to follow the requirements specified during this procedure throughout the development process. Three SysML relationships allow us to establish the common elements between functions, requirements and components (see Figure 12.18):

– the SysML "Allocate" relationship associates a function with one or several components (modeled in the form of a SysML block) which support its creation;

– the SysML "Refine" relationship associates a function (activity) with one or several requirements which it is supposed to fulfill;

– from the composition of these two previous relationships (function/component and function/requirement), we can deduce a component/requirement relationship which is represented by the SysML "Satisfy" relationship.

– at last, the SysML "Formalize" relationship associates a property described in the form of a SysML constraint with a requirement. This property corresponds to a formalization of the requirement in the form of a predicate.

Finally, it is necessary to establish the relationships between the variables manipulated by the constraint – i.e. the variables involved in the predicate which characterizes the property – and the variables manipulated by the components – i.e. the blocks' ports. The suggested solution is based on the use of a parametric diagram.

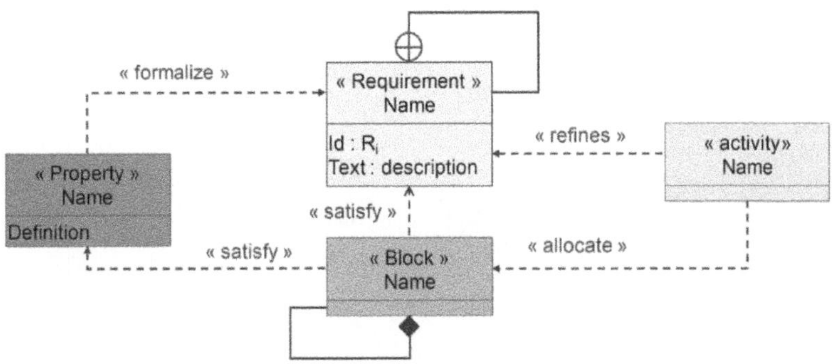

Figure 12.18. *Meta-model for traceability*

The meta-model of Figure 12.18 thus defines the interactions between all the objects present in the design process and structures the design process. This aids:

– Impact analyses: if, during validation, we notice that a requirement is not fulfilled, then we can go back down to the level of the constituent to identify the design faults. In the same way, if, during a unitary test, we notice that a constituent does not fulfill the function attributed to it, we can go back up to the level of the requirements in order to determine the impact of the constituent on the system.

– Re-use: if, during a new project, we identify a requirement that has already been fulfilled in a previous project, then we can seek the technical solutions used during this previous project and potentially re-use them. The database will serve as a library for future projects.

For example, Figure 12.19 shows an extract relating to the safety requirements for the two-hand control device.

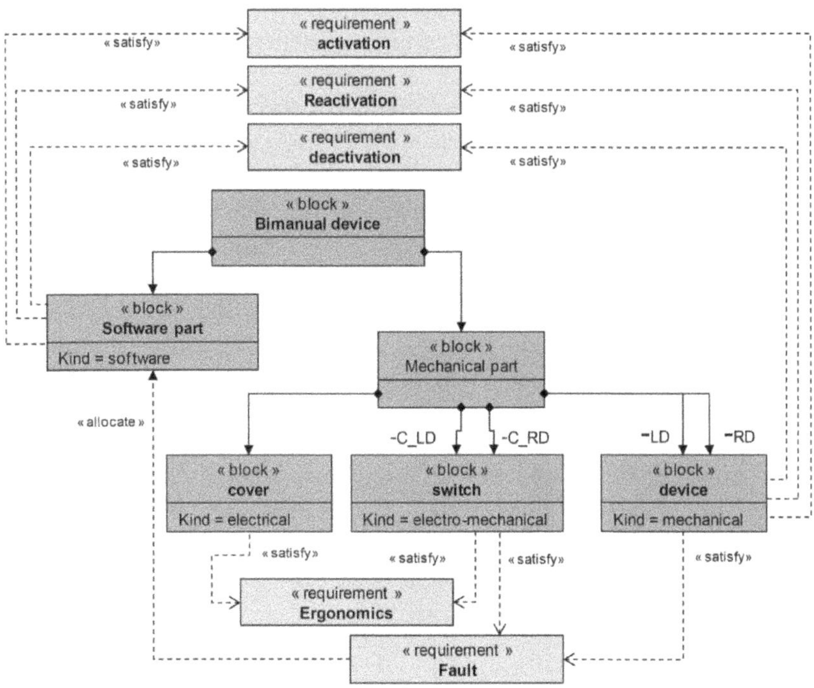

Figure 12.19. *Safety requirements of the two-hand control device (extract)*

12.6.5. *Development and verification of the software command components*

The detailed design of the control dynamics and the verification of its safety requirements necessitate the use of specific models and tools (using DSLs).

The main SysML objects re-used in input for these models are:

– IBD diagrams which provide the logical architecture of the control, and which can be interpreted in classical data stream tools such as Simulink, SCADE or ControlBuild as an interconnected network of components (or modules or nodes, depending on the tools used) with input ports and typed outputs;

– SysML constraints which make it possible to characterize the logical or temporal property(-ies) which should verify each of the components and composite elements;

– SysML functions which make it possible to characterize the functions which each of the components and composite elements should fulfill.

On the basis of this specification, engineers specialized in control system design can suggest dynamic models which satisfy the specifications. Then, the verification can be performed by using the SysML constraints as properties that need to be verified in the model checker or in the form of pre- and post-conditions that should be preserved during a test scenario.

In order to demonstrate the feasibility of the approach, model transformations have been simply implemented using import/export procedures based on SML and XSLT technology, and on a meta-model of shared concepts. Figure 12.20 shows an extract of these concepts.

The connected tools are Magic Draw and Artisan Studio for system modeling in SysML, ControlBuild for design and simulation of the command, and UPPAAL[9] for verification of properties.

9 UPPAAL: model checker developed during a shared project between the University of Uppsala in Sweden and the University of Aalborg in Denmark.

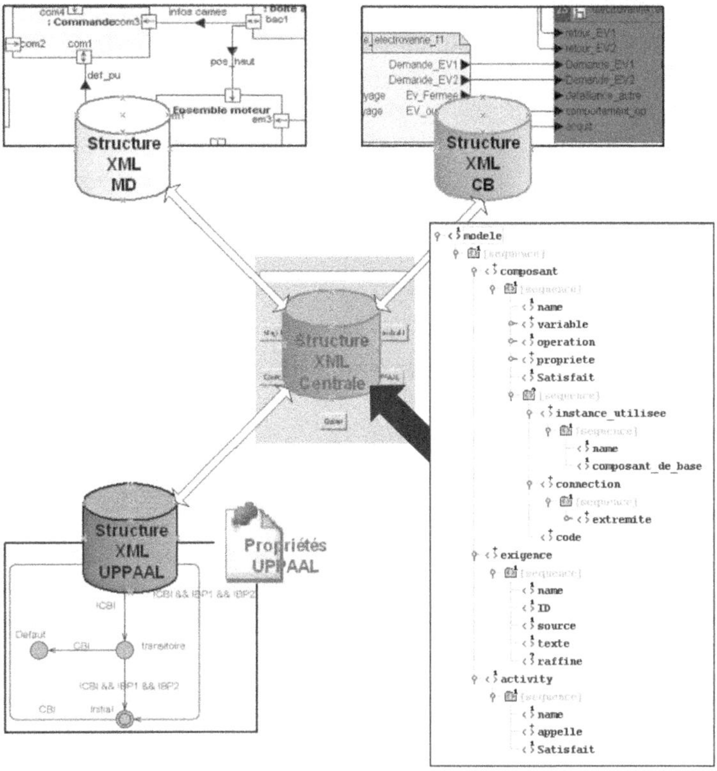

Figure 12.20. *Implantation of the suggested process*

For the case study related to the mechanical press, the set of SysML specifications provide:

– the press components, particularly the software components of the two-hand control device (BDD and IBD diagrams);

– the safety functions that each of these must ensure (allocate relationships);

– the properties that each of them must respect (satisfy and constraints relationships).

On the basis of this information, it is then possible to start creating each of the components. For the creation of software components which carry out safety functions for the two-hand control device, we chose ControlBuild data stream models. The structure of these is very close to that of the IBDs. The behavioral description is created on this tool, using the languages of the standard NF EN 61131-3. On the basis of the behavioral description created on this tool, an implementation stage allows us to generate a PLC code automatically.

Verification of the created components is carried out using the model-checker UPPAAL. Component properties are deduced from the SysML study through a transformation of the predicates contained in the constraints in the form:

– of a property expressed in a temporal logic, CTL* for UPPAAL, for properties that do not require state memorization;

– of an observer that memorizes state evolutions of the system and represents a forbidden sequence in the form of a blocking state.

For example, the property P1.5, expressed first in SysML in textual form (the two-hand control device is deactivated if one of the two hands is removed) and then in the form of a constraint (not BP1 or not BP2 ⇒ not CB), was expressed in the form "it is always true that ..." and translated into UPPAAL using the AG operator:

$$\text{AG (NOT(BP1) OR NOT(BP2)} \Rightarrow \text{NOT(CB))} \qquad \text{(P1.5)}$$

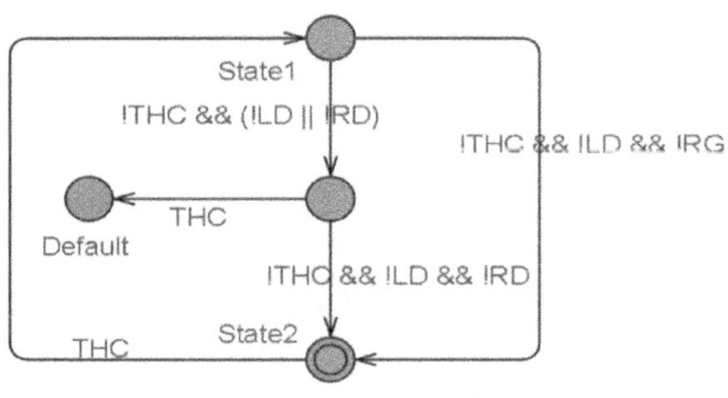

Figure 12.21. *Observer on UPPAAL for the property P1.1*

Let us now consider the property P1.1 which stipulates that the two-hand control device can only be reactivated if both buttons have previously been released. This property is represented by an observer which comprises four states: CB activated, CB deactivated with both buttons released, CB deactivated with one of the buttons released and finally an error state which corresponds to the forbidden sequence (see Figure 12.21). It is then necessary to verify, using the model checker, that the error state can never be reached through the AG property (not error).

A validation by simulation phase may be added to this formal verification stage. The validation by simulation phase would be conducted using the ControlBuild tool, and would increase the level of confidence that could be accorded to the development. It would proceed by running through a set of scenarios and by analyzing how the command responses matched with the needs that were initially expressed in the written specification.

12.6.6. *Discussion*

The approach that has been presented here is innovative in that it brings together two spheres of activity that do not always have the same concerns: on the one hand, industries that use industrial PLC for safety, and on the other hand, the software engineering and systems engineering community. This approach suggests a complete development process, which may be adapted to suit the skill level available in the industries, and which goes through from the expression of the need to the development of the PLC code. This process has been applied for the design and proof of the software or for certain parts of the command software of a mechanical press with a clutch-brake.

One of the advantages of this process is that with it we can formalize and plot the safety requirements that the system must fulfill. As SysML is only a toolkit, part of the process suggests usage rules for specifying high-level safety requirements, propagating them up to the lowest level software component, and plotting them throughout the process. This application guide, however, has some limitations with respect to operation safety, because the traceability of safety requirements is based on a data model informed by the machine's designer.

In order to increase our confidence level in the safety of the software, the principle of *a posteriori* formal verification was added to the development process. The principle allows us to be sure, at a low-level PLC code component, that the associated safety property has been respected. However, unfortunately, it is limited by the size of the components, because we cannot test/verify the entire software, but rather its use needs to be confined to sufficiently small software components (of a few variables). This principle could be completely automated in a tool.

The system requirements were wholly defined and the command software for the press was wholly created. In order to develop a complete application, it is currently necessary for the person carrying out the software development to know all of the system requirements so that they can understand the role of the software components that they will develop and validate by simulation. This is not necessarily a disadvantage because it means that the developer can play a more important role within the team and is not confined to a low-level role.

As for the proof, only a few software blocks, those involved in the properties regarding the safety of the machine, were proved by model checking. As it is necessary to formalize the safety properties that need to be verified in the language of the model checker, a certain level of expertise is required for this operation.

Various software tools might be developed to support this methodology. A demonstrator that ensures traceability between the different views (requirement, system, PLC code) has been created. It could have more functions added to it, and it could be incorporated into a development software suite. Also, in order for them to be effective, verification tools should be incorporated, in a manner which is transparent for the user, into a software development workshop for PLC.

This process, focused on safety, makes it possible to integrate prevention very early on in the design process for the command logic of machines that use programmable equipment. It thus provides a means of responding to some of the requirements of the European Directive 2006/42/CE. In addition, the use of formal verification guarantees that the safety property has been completely verified, and thus that the part of the software which carries out this property does not contain any errors which risk compromising the safety of the operator.

However, the process presented here is part of a design process: the descending part of a V software development cycle. A phase for validation and integration with the equipment, with integration tests on the machine, will also need to be conducted in addition to this process.

12.7. Conclusion on the use of formal techniques in the field of manufacturing

We have here applied two types of formal methods for the programming of a safety PLC which manages the safety functions of a machine.

The use of the B method is effective in the case of safety applications. In particular, it allows us to avoid validation of the various software modules individually (unitary tests). However, it does not treat the phase of equipment integration, which remains an essential step in any software development, even one which uses formal methods, in order to ensure that the software developed works sufficiently well with the equipment.

One of the potentially disadvantageous points regarding the use of this method in the manufacturing sector is that it is necessary to have people working on it who are trained and competent or even expert in the use of B, at the beginning of the project, but also for any change or modification in the software. This constraint means that this method will be used only by companies with design projects for new machines of sufficient scale that the initial investment might be repaid over several projects. A company choosing the B method for design would need to have consciously chosen this as part of a policy decision.

The use of formal verification methods *a posteriori* would seem to be a more approachable option for automation technicians. However, as far as we are aware, no integrated tool exists which could facilitate the use of this approach in the manufacturing sector. In addition, the formalization of the safety requirements which need to be verified requires a level of expertise, and the fact that its application is limited to small software modules is a strong constraint. The research work carried out at the INRS led to a design process which could be adapted to practices and could help designers to formalize the expressions which need to be proved. For example, as with the B method, an initial investment by the company for training and customization of the design method is required, for both the formalization of safety properties that need to be verified and for carrying out proofs with a model checker. In order for an integrated design tool for this sector to be available, some additional work is necessary from the providers of automation software design tools. Finally, the use of formal techniques is definitely a plus, but does not remove the necessity of conducting on-site tests to validate the integration of the developed software with the equipment. This might appear as "one more task" to be carried out.

Companies in the manufacturing domain have development cost constraints (the machines are often of limited commercial value) and a level of maturity in software development which makes it difficult, for example, for them to appropriate formal techniques of any kind. If there were a strong constraint from industry standards, as there is in the railway and aeronautic sectors, manufacturers might be obliged to use formal methods, but for the time being, and for the foreseeable future, this is not the case!

12.8. Glossary

AMN	Abstract machine notation
BDD	Block definition diagram
DSL	Domain-specific language
FMECA	Failure Modes, Effects and Criticality Analysis
IBD	Internal block diagram
IEC[10]	International Electrotechnical Commission
INRS	Institut National de Recherche et de Sécurité
ISO[11]	International Standards Organization
NF	French Standard
SADT	Structured analysis and design technique
SIL	Safety integrity level
SysML	Systems modeling language

12.9. Bibliography

[ABR 96] ABRIAL J.R., *The B-Book*, Cambridge University Press, 1996.

[ACH 06] ACHATZ R., "Requirements engineering: a key success factor", *Automation Technology in Practice*, no. 3, November 2006.

10 For information, see http://www.iec.ch/.

11 For information, see www.iso.org/.

[BAI 08] BAIER C., KATOEN J.-P., *Principles of Model Checking*, MIT Press, 2008.

[BLA 03] BLAISE J.C., BELLO J.P., BAUDOUIN J., "Validation du schéma de commande d'une presse utilisant un système électronique programmable", *Safety of Industrial Automated Systems (SIAS 2003)*, Nancy, 13–15 October 2003.

[BOU 12a] BOULANGER J.-L., (ed.), *Industrial Use of Formal Method: Formal Verification*, ISTE, London, and John Wiley & Sons, New York, 2012.

[BOU 12b] BOULANGER J.-L., (ed.), *Formal Methods: Industrial Use from Model to the Code*, ISTE, London, and John Wiley & Sons, New York, 2012.

[CEI 10] CEI 61508: Sécurité fonctionnelle des systèmes électriques/électroniques/électroniques programmables relatifs à la sécurité. Partie 1 à 7, April 2010.

[CLA 00] CLARKE E.M., GRUMBERG O., PELED D.A., *Model Checking*, MIT Press, Cambridge, MA, 2000.

[EVR 09] EVROT D., Contribution à la vérification d'exigences de sécurité: application au domaine de la machine industrielle, NS 277, INRS – PhD Thesis, UHP Nancy I, January 2009.

[CT5 98] CT5 – Ministère de l'Emploi et de la Solidarité. Note relative à l'acceptation de certains automates programmables pour gérer des fonctions de sécurité sur machines, e23/APIDS/26mai 1998, p. 5, May 1998.

[DIR 06] Directive 2006/42/EC of the European Parliament and of the Council of 17 May 2006 on machinery, p. 63, May 2006.

[JOH 07] JOHNSON T.L., "Improving automation software dependability: a role for formal methods"?, *Control Engineering Practice*, vol. 15, no. 11, pp. 1403–1415, November 2007.

[LAM 03] LAMY P., "Experience feedback concerning develoment methodology for programmable electronic system application software", *Actes du 3ème congrés international Safety of Industrial Automated Systems*, Nancy, October 2003.

[LIS 90] LISSANDRE M., *Maîtriser SADT*, Armand Colin, 1990.

[NEU 02] NEUGNOT C., KNEPPERT M., Logiciels applicatifs relatifs à la sécurité. Etude des problèmes liés à leur exploitation. Cahiers de notes documentaires – Hygiènes et sécurité du travail No. 187, 2002.

[NF 03] NF EN 61131 Partie 3 Automates programmables – Langages de programmation, August 2003.

[NF 05] NF EN 62061: Sécurité des machines – Sécurité fonctionnelle des systèmes de commande électriques/électroniques/électroniques programmables relatifs à la sécurité, July 2005.

[NF 08a] NF EN ISO 13849-1: Sécurité des machines – Parties des systèmes de commande relatives à la sécurité – Partie 1: principes généraux de conception, October 2008.

[NF 08b] NF EN 574: Sécurité des machines – Dispositifs de commande bimanuelle – Aspects fonctionnels – Principes de conception, August 2008.

[NF 10] NF EN ISO 12100: Sécurité des machines: Principes généraux de conception - Appréciation du risque et réduction du risque, December 2010.

[PÉT 10] PÉTIN J.F., EVROT D., MOREL G., *et al.*, "Traçabilité et vérification d'exigences de sécurité", *Génie logiciel*, vol. 95, pp. 27–37, 2010.

[VAL 10] VALKONEN J., BJÖRKMAN K., FRITS J., *et al.*, "Model checking methodology for verification of safety logics", *The 6th International Conference on Safety of Industrial Automated Systems*, Tempere, Finland, June 2010.

[WIL 07] WILLARD B., "UML for system engineering", *Computer Standard and Interfaces*, vol. 29, pp. 69–81, 2007.

13

B Extended to Floating-Point Numbers: Is it Sufficient for Proving Avionics Software?

13.1. Introduction

For a long time, formal methods did not pay much attention to calculations based on floating-point numbers. This started to change around 10 years ago, and today floating-point numbers can be used in most of the specification languages and proof tools used for research and industrial preparatory studies.

Better late than never: the B method [ABR 96] will soon be able to prove the correctness of floating-point calculations. Technically speaking, this is the only gap that needs to be filled before the method can be used in avionics. We will therefore give the rationale for the proposed extension of the B language.

However, first and foremost, we will reveal the new difficulties arising that make us believe that the application of the method to avionics will involve much more than a simple transposition of the railway success stories.

Chapter written by Jean-Louis DUFOUR.

13.2. Motivation

Industrial use of formal methods is highly context-dependent:

– in railways, from the middle of the 1990s onward, medium-sized applications (of around 20,000 code lines) have been proved to be functionally correct using the B method [DEH 94];

– in avionics, 10 years later, applications of a much greater size are proved free of execution error (division by 0, etc.) using the tool Astrée[1] [DEL 07, BOU 11a]; however, we are here far from the functional.

This would seem to be a "conceptual regression", and there are two reasons for it, which gradually become less important over time:

– culturally, avionics is not an easy client: the recommendation DO-178 in "B" edition [ARI 92] naturally does not facilitate the replacement of testing by proof. In fact, the only example of this is the use of CAVEAT[2] by Airbus [SOU 09]. Even if the general reasoning underpinning DO-178B [ARI 92] is the specification of the high-level objectives and not the techniques associated with these at a given time, the verification activity which checks for conformity between the product and the requirements is strongly "test" oriented. In the "formal methods" supplement to the "C" revision [ARI 12], published at the beginning of 2012, there is a significant framework for these methods as an alternative means of operation. When they rely on qualified tools, they can now naturally be used as a substitute for most tests. Economically speaking, this is necessary before they can gain widespread industrial use.

– Avionics is not, in technical terms, an easy client for two reasons:

- On complex equipment, at least, calculations on floating-point numbers are the norm, and not the exception (which is the opposite of the situation in railways). Floating-point numbers are numbers represented in the form: mantissa * base^{exponent}, where mantissa and exponent are signed

1 To find out more about Astrée, see http://www.astree.ens.fr/.

2 Here it was used with a special "unitary" proof which mimics unitary tests and cannot be transposed into B. The procedures which call for other procedures are "stubbed", i.e. their formal specification covers only the "linkage" between the calls for procedures and the procedures which result from these.

integers, and the base has a value, in practice, of 2 or 10; this is the computer science version of "scientific notation". Floating-point correction is one order of magnitude more complex than integer correction [MON 08]. Fortunately, proof technology for floating-point numbers is constantly improving[3]. This is due to, among other factors, the specification language ACSL[4] [BOL 07] and the multi-prover verification tool Frama-C[5] [AYA 10, BOU 11a].

- Second, the functional properties that need to be proved are more complex than with railways. We will discuss this in more depth later.

Therefore, it is now time to functionally prove avionics applications: a first "simple" step could be to transfer the existing technology for floating-point numbers into the B method [ABR 96]. Unfortunately, this transfer is not easy, because we need to ensure compatibility between the theoretical framework and the current practice (typing and base of rules), given the number of projects being maintained and developed.

However, before returning to this in more depth, it would be useful to gain an understanding of why the B method has always been limited to integers. To do this, we need to go back to the beginnings of the method [CHA 89, GUI 90].

13.3. Integers and the railway origins of the B method

13.3.1. *The SACEM project*[6]

The Parisian leg of RER (*Réseau Express Régional* – regional express network) Line A was opened in 1977, connecting the eastern and western suburbs of Paris. Line A very quickly became a victim of its own success, with passenger numbers increasing appreciably and constantly year by year.

In 1979, the operators (RATP in Paris and SNCF in the suburbs) launched preliminary studies on "intelligent" signaling which would bring

3 In [BOU 11a], abstract interpretation [COU 00] is presented, and several examples of uses are presented, which implement Frama-C, Astrée, POLYSPACE, etc.

4 ACSL stands for ANSI/ISO C specification language.

5 To find out more about Frama-C, see http://frama-c.com/.

6 SACEM stands for Système d'Aide à la Conduite, à l'Exploitation et à la Maintenance – assisted driving, operation and maintenance system.

about a significant increase in capacity through a reduction in headway between the trains on the central leg: SACEM see [GEO 90].

In 1982, the creation of this system was entrusted to a consortium made up of three industrial entities: Jeumont-Schneider[7]/Interelec[8]/CSEE[9]. In order to understand this, it is necessary to understand one key thing: "intelligent" of course refers to "software" here, but this was to be the first time that software would make a direct contribution to safety on a French railway system. Also, a certain level of complexity was involved (of 7,000 lines of code trackside and 14,000 lines onboard, 9,000 lines were critical).

13.3.2. *The need for an innovative software method*

There was no precedent (in France) even in the rest of the industry, and in fact other industries were faced with the same problem at the beginning of the 1980s:

– Merlin Gérin[10] needed to create software for part of the emergency stoppage for the new generation of French nuclear reactors: with the help of what was to become the laboratory Verimag[11], they created the SAGA environment[12] (the first forerunner of SCADE);

– Aérospatiale[13] needed to create software for a part of the electric flight commands of the A320: they created the SAO workshop (the other forerunner of SCADE[14], see Chapter 2 of [BOU 12]). It should thus be noted that when DO-178 appeared in 1982[15] and again in 1985 when its "A"

7 Jeumont-Schneider became Alsthom in 1987, and today is Alstom Transport.

8 Interelec became Matra Transport in 1985, and today is Siemens Mobility.

9 CSEE has now been replaced by Ansaldo STS France.

10 Today Schneider Electric.

11 Verimag is a laboratory that it is always at the forefront of the development of onboard systems. For more information, see http://www-verimag.imag.fr.

12 SAGA stands for "*Spécification d'Applications et Génération Automatisée*" – specification of applications and automatic generation.

13 Today Airbus.

14 The SCADE development environment is sold by the company ESTEREL-Technologies. To find out more about it, see http://www.esterel-technologies.com/.

15 Aeronautics "standard" on the development of critical software [ARI 92]; formally speaking, it is not actually a standard. This is the avionics equivalent of the railways standard CENELEC EN 50128 [CEN 01, CEN 11].

revision appeared, neither of these would have provided sufficient assurance to airline manufacturers.

These two manufacturing firms managed the complexity by introducing a solution that what was far removed from other solutions being offered at the time (at least in the software milieu), which today is called “model-based design”. Following this method, errors occur less frequently because the language is simple. Additionally, the errors that do occur are easier to detect because the language is graphic, and thus can be read by systems engineers.

However, these graphic languages are in fact a little too simple for them to be able to express SACEM algorithms, which require route track descriptions. Therefore, the SACEM consortium adopted a different response to this complexity. Under the leadership of Pierre Chapront (Alsthom), the consortium decided to replace unitary tests with proofs in Hoare logic [HOA 69].

This was a choice that brought with it a certain level of risk, because at the time this technique was only 15 years old, and there was no tool available to support it. However, just like SAGA and SAO (*Spécification Assistée par Ordinateur* – computer-assisted specification), this shows that already at that time the industry was fully aware of the weakness of the state-of-the-art faced with the power of expression of the software.

13.3.3. *The coded processor and integers*

For SACEM, this distrust of the current state of knowledge was to lead those involved in the project to question the classical safety method based on the calculator by redundancy: the “coded processor” invented in 1980 by Philippe Forin (Matra Transport) [FOR 89] during a preliminary study was chosen because it allows those involved in a project to:

– intrinsically make the problems associated with common modes and latent breakdowns disappear (including the problem of coverage of auto-tests);

– intrinsically ensure partitioning between the critical and non-critical software (without a “memory protection unit”);

– in practice, handle the issues associated with the evaluation of levels of failure and their variability from piece to piece (a level of failure is the

estimation of the average of a population. However, what is of real interest to a rail users who are aware of the issue is the probability of failure of the specific system on which they are travelling during the specific time they are travelling on it).

However, one of the disadvantages of this technique is that it cannot handle floating-point numbers. This means that it has to handle calculations of distances and speeds using integers (with fixed-point numbers).

13.3.4. *The limitations of Hoare logic and the beginnings of B*

The development of software began in 1983. Then, formal validation began later with a team completely separate to the development team. This is the classical "independent activity because different people are involved".

In 1987, the consortium signaled to its client that it was having significant problems in the application of Hoare logic. Their response to this situation came quite quickly: two independent experts, Jean-Raymond Abrial and Stéphane Natkin, were appointed to audit the development.

They both confirmed the weak point with Hoare logic: it cannot be scaled up. Formal specification and proof are well suited to leaf procedures; however, as soon as we go higher within the call graph, the formal specification becomes non-traceable with the informal specification, and the proof obligations become extremely large.

At that time, J.-R. Abrial, who was involved in the design of the Z specification method [SPI 89], had already gone on to the next stage and had begun defining what a formal development might be [ABR 84]. In addition, at the same time, but independently, the "missing link" was in the process of being developed: this was the refinement of control and data [BAC 81, MOR 90].

In his auditing report, Abrial summarized the situation and suggested bridging the gap between the informal specification and the preceding formal verification activities by a "formal re-expression" of the specification. This was to be the first application of the B method [ABR 96], which was performed manually in 1988 (the precursor of AtelierB, the "B tool", was at that point being developed at British Petroleum Research, and only became commercially available in 1992).

The launch of SACEM was (only) set back by a year, until autumn 1989 (and the significantly increased capacity was almost immediately exhausted, but that is another story).

13.3.5. *Successes of B, and integers once more!*

So thanks to B, something which could have been a fatal blow to program proving became the first in a long line of successes. However, these successes were almost always concerned with railway systems, where the typical applications are either signaling or speed control. The first of these only requires Boolean numbers, and for the second, fixed-point numbers are sufficient (in particular when the coded processor is used. In fact, until the present time, there has been bijection between the expressivity of B and the expressivity of the coded processor, which disappears when B is working with floating-point numbers).

13.3.6. *The positive influence of "fail-safe"*[16] *on complexity*

A train, like a car, a nuclear power station, a refinery, a press, etc., can stop in order to avoid a catastrophe. This is the safety paradigm known as "fail-safe", which allows a breakdown to result in degraded operation, as long as this is safe.

This principle is clearly unsuited to aircraft for which the "fail-operational" is required (see Chapter 6 of [BOU 11b]). For this to be attained, a breakdown must have no impact on operation (in general, this is limited to the first breakdown).

Fail-safe gives rise to redundant asymmetrical architectures [BOU 11b, BOU 11c], where the second track has only a supervisory function and cannot be substituted for the first in case of failure. As a result, in the language of the industrial safety standard CEI/IEC 61508[17] [IEC 98], the term that is used is command system/protection system, and the safety level

16 The terminology here is not fixed. For example, in aeronautics the circular FAA AC 25.1309 mentions a "fail-safe design concept" which is close to our "fail-operational". However, in railway, "fail-safe" is often translated, as into French, as "intrinsic safety", which means "absence of dangerous failure mode".

17 The European standards CENELEC EN 50126, 50129 and 50128 [CEN 01, CEN 11] for railways are derived from the generic standard [IEC 98].

of the overall system boils down to the level of coverage and availability of the protection sub-system. This level is quantified by 4 "safety integrity level" or "SIL" (the SIL scale goes from 1 to 4; 4 is the most sure (there is no need for SIL0[18] because if there is a protection, this means that there is a safety issue at play)).

Here, we use aeronautics terminology when referring to asymmetrical redundancy "COM/MON", COM for "COMmand" and MON for "MONitor", while remaining aware that the qualifier "asymmetrical" is very significant, because in the usual aeronautics COM/MON (for example, on a full authority digital engine control [FADEC]), MON actually means "passive": the redundancy is symmetrical and MON is involved whenever its state of health is better than that of COM.

Let us return to railways and take two examples:

– For a door command, COM will drive the opening/closing dependent on the driver's wishes, and the door lock dependent on speed. The MON will activate the emergency brake if the door is not locked beyond a certain speed or if the door opens at a time when this should not happen.

– For autopilot (AP), COM will calculate the speed set point and then the motor/brake torque set point. MON will only activate the emergency brake where the speed is not compatible with the next point at which the train needs to stop.

MON covers safety requirements. As a result, it is subject to an integrity requirement (SIL4 in AP). In this way, COM does not need to have an SIL, but it does need to be reliable (with regard to its hardware) and to be of a certain quality (with regard to its software); both of these need to be consistent with the service quality that the operator requested the manufacturer to provide. Obviously, it is MON that we will develop formally, and not COM.

13.4. The avionics context: floating-point numbers and complexity

In avionics, floating-point numbers are the norm, and integers the exception. The opposite is the case for railways. This is particularly true for

18 The CENELEC railway standards use SIL0 because they adopt a more general architectural viewpoint than the command/protection of the standard IEC 61508 [IEC 98].

navigation systems, where 64-bit floating-point numbers ("double precision" in the terms used by [IEE]) are what is in use.

Also, the algorithms are more complex. Let us examine two typical examples:

– A FADEC (motor control) drives the fuel flow through the set thrust through regulation loops which operate on temperatures, pressures, flows and rotation speeds. The relative precision of outputs must be around 10^{-3}, and to achieve this the relative precision of base operations must be around 10^{-6} (with a decent margin: 10 years ago, automobile motor controls carried out similar calculations with fixed-point numbers at 16 bits). A FADEC thus uses 32-bit floating-point numbers ("single precision" to use the terms of IEEE 754), which have a relative resolution of $2^{-23} \approx 1.2.10^{-7}$.

– An inertial navigation system (INS) calculates, among other things, its position on earth (sometimes in space) using 3D geometrical calculations (rotation matrices), trigonometry and statistical estimation (again matrices). An error of 1 m corresponds to a relative precision of 1 m/40,000 km = 2.5 10^{-8}, which is already better than simple precision. This could be compatible with a 32-bit fixed-point number (which was used in the first INSs based on Cardan). However, considering all the operations that are carried out by a modern "strap-down" INS (for example, integration of gyroscopic information at high frequency and Kalman filters), the precision required of basic operators is around 10^{-13}. (Fortunately, this is compatible with the resolution of double precision: $2^{-52} \approx 2.10^{-16}$). To the best of our knowledge, the only industrial case where double precision is insufficient is the representation of UTC time in a global positioning system (GPS), where the resolution is a fraction of a nanosecond and the interval that needs to be covered is several dozen years.

In addition, this algorithmic complexity cannot be mitigated by the safety paradigm, as is the case for railways with fail-safe and the associated architecture in asymmetrical COM/MON: avionics is synonymous with "fail-operational", and the architectures used are symmetrical COM/MON (FADEC) or triplication (INS). The notion of protection system no longer exists, and the SIL is replaced by the "development assurance level" or

"DAL" of the recommendation ARP 4754[19] : SIL4 becomes DAL A, SIL1 becomes DAL D and DAL E means that the system does not bring safety into play.

Let us return to our two earlier examples to see where this leads us to:

– A FADEC conceptually has two critical outputs: the fuel flow and the state of health (because if we falsely think we are in good health, we do not switch). Therefore, it is necessary to prove correctness. The complexity is similar to that of the COM part of a PA (therefore one order of magnitude greater than MON). The interesting approach of the automobile industry for motor controls should be noted (see [DUF 05]). The critical output (the equivalent of the outflow is the injection duration) is periodically recalculated according to a simplified formula which takes only the main parameters into account. Then, a comparison with tolerance is carried out in order to take the omitted parameters into account. This real-time approach could be transposed at verification, by proving a limited gap in relation to a simplified specification. In order to retain conformity with DO-178, which requires that everything that is implemented should be specified, and everything that is specified should be verified, the omitted parameters such as low-level derived requirements need to be taken into consideration:[20] under the current state of practice, this would probably not pass certification.

– An INS has, as its critical output position, speed and attitude (the state of health is less critical, because in everyday situations it is tripled, and therefore the choice can be made by majority vote). It calculates these by integration of the acceleration vector (produced by the three accelerometers) and of the rotation speed vector (produced by the three gyrometers). To improve performance, inertial data are fused with other information (air speed, Doppler or loch, GPS, etc.) through Kalman filters: the algorithmic complexity which results from this is even greater than that of a FADEC.

To summarize, the maturity that B has acquired in railways (its "TRL") cannot be transposed to avionics for the three following reasons:

19 Aeronautics "standard" on systems development; formally speaking, it is not actually a standard. This is the avionics equivalent of the railway standard CENELEC EN 50126 [CEN 00].

20 False friend: according to ARP 4754, derived requirements are "additional requirements resulting from design or implementation decisions during the development process which are not directly traceable to higher-level requirements".

– proofs on floating-point numbers are more complex than proofs on integers;

– the codes are more complex;

– the specifications are more complex.

13.5. Barking up the wrong tree: separation between integer and floating-point calculations

Let us now return to our initial issue: proving an avionics application with the B language [ABR 96]. In order to do this, we can ask if it is really indispensable to extend B to floating-point numbers. In fact, particularly within an INS, the predominance of floating-point numbers compared to other types of data is such that it may suggest us a path to follow which will not deliver useful results.

To illustrate this predominance, here are three observations on a typical INS application (the lower layers are excluded):

– more than half of the atomic variables (the variables of base type and the terminal elements of structures and of tables) are floating-point numbers (exclusively "double" in recent systems);

– practically no integer variable contains "navigation" information (e.g. position or altitude). The only exception is for tabulated functions, within which integer indexes are conversions of floating-point numbers;

– practically all of the integers represent states. The only two exceptions are

- counters (which may often be considered to be a state);
- table indices for matrix calculations.

This means that, at least conceptually, such an application may be viewed as two weakly coupled tasks: an "algorithmic" or "continuous" or "physical" task which carries out all the floating-point calculations and these alone, and a "piloting" or "discrete" or "logical" task which calculates the INS mode.

These two tasks exchange only enumerated values, for example the algorithmic task sends the piloting task the Boolean "Speed ≤

THRESHOLD_LOW" and the piloting task sends the algorithmic task the Boolean "Status_altitude_baro = VALID".

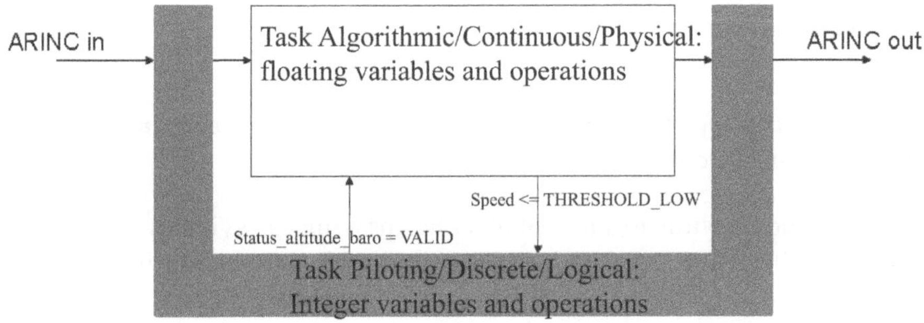

Figure 13.1. *Integer/floating-point number segregation*

This conceptual segregation may give the impression that it is also possible to segregate design and correctness (see Figure 13.1):

– a B model will specify/design only the pilot portion, and the algorithmic part will be viewed through "basic" machines, that is, machines which are not refined. In this way, as the interfaces are discreet, the floating-point numbers would not need to be introduced in B;

– the algorithmic part is specified and proved with a tool that is more suited to it, such as Frama-C, and informal traceability is achieved between the basic machines and the ACSL specification.

The problem is that:

– this segregation is purely conceptual, and the application is never designed in this way: the gap between the model and the (existing) software would be substantial;

– traceability between B and ACSL is informal, because the specification languages are different;

– this traceability may not be so simple to establish, because the levels of abstraction are different between the two methods: ACSL currently does not have much refinement capacity.

For these reasons, the introduction of floating-point numbers, and we will also see of real numbers, would seem to be indispensable.

13.6. IEEE 754 Floating-point numbers

13.6.1. *Scope of the standard*

The standard IEEE 754 ("IEEE" in what follows) was published in 1985 and revised in 2008. Its main aim is the portability of floating-point algorithms, but because it does not go beyond the provision of a "mathematical library", it is not the only contributor to this aim: languages and compilers are also involved.

The portability is not attained essentially due to them: on embedded software the effect that it produces is target/host non-representivity, which more generally is the reason why DO-178 requires that tests cover the code on target. As for its technical scope, the IEEE is only missing a portable specification of non-arithmetic functions (sin, log, etc.), which is a subject reaching maturity in academic research, and which is not a problem in critical avionics, because DO-178 obliges us to re-write the mathematical library (in DAL A, the arguments "proved in use" and "COTS"[21] are difficult to use).

The IEEE "library" firstly specifies types of floating-point data, then rounding functions of "real to floating-point numbers", and finally the associated operations.

Two types of data are fundamental: "single precision" with base 2 in 32-bit format and "double precision" in 64 bits.

We should note two things:

– the mantissa is in the form "signe * integer_not_sign", which means that the floating-point numbers are symmetrical in relation to the negation (as sets of numbers, "single = –single" and "double = –double");

– IEEE numbers are not only floating-point numbers: the smallest numbers (in double,]-2-1022 , 2-1022[) are coded in fixed-point format and are called "sub-normals" or "denormalized". Their practical plus-value is not

21 COTS stands for commercial off-the-shelf.

obvious. In fact, no system implemented them before the IEEE (and still today the architectures Intel x86 and Motorola/IBM PowerPC allow us to exclude them with a CPU gain at the key). However, their theoretical plus-value is clear:

- Fundamentally, without them, the gap between a real number and its rounded number would demonstrate a strong discontinuity around 0, because the exponent is limited (to -1022 in double). There is a sort of "no float's land" around 0, where in order to create a topology that pleases the punters, 0 is "isolated":]-2-1022, 2-1022[only contains 0, whereas just below 2-1022 there is a high density of population;

– formally, the inhabitation of this "no float's land" by 2×2^{52} denormalized (positive and negative) brings about:

– a simple bound of the rounding error: 2^{-52} * max(|x|, 2^{-1022}) in double;

– the property x <> y => x-y <> 0.

Denormalized numbers are the great technical contribution of the IEEE, which is due to the pugnacity of William Kahan (Turing Award 1989, for "his fundamental contributions to numerical analysis").

As regards the 4 or 5 rounding modes (depending on whether we refer to the 1985 or 2008 version), these associate each real number with a "close" floating number. This gives a second semantics to floating-point numbers: each floating-point number can be viewed as the set of real numbers that it represents. The standard rounding is "round to nearest, ties to even", which means, we choose the closest floating-point number, and if two floating-point numbers are equally close, we take the one which has the bit of weak weight of the mantissa equal to 0. This rounded value is said to be "unbiased" because a sum of rounded values of random real numbers does not present a bias in relation to the real sum (which is in general a sought-after property; other rounded values are said to be "directed" and have specific non-embedded applications).

As regards the associated operations, the only thing that needs to be noted is the way in which the four arithmetic operations and the square root are specified:

– the operation is firstly "carried out" in real numbers;

– the real number result is rounded in floating-point numbers (according to the rounding which has been selected).

What is necessary to understand is that the background presence of real numbers (through the rounding functions) makes it possible to obtain an "intensional" definition of operations, which is much simpler than an algorithmic definition, and upon the basis of which further reflection may be conducted.

Between the initial 1985 version and the 2008 revision, there were many clarifications and additions, but no fundamental change was made except on a point which involves portability: the decimal → binary conversion which, in particular, allows compilers to read floating-point constants. This is one of the most complex subjects dealt with by the standard, and it only reached maturity in 1990 (see [PAX 91, MUL 10], section 2.7). The 1985 version thus did not require that a floating-point decimal constant be translated into binary exactly as its rounded value, which means that two compilers could generate different numerical values. The 2008 revision corrected this. However, it remains a delicate point in practice, as implementations also have bugs which are difficult to identify (but are without significant consequences: in C, the function responsible is called "strtod", proving it formally far from simple). In addition, the standard now requires that it should be possible to write floating-point numbers in hexadecimal notation: in C, 0x1.8p10 means $1.5*2^{10} = 1{,}536$.

13.6.2. *The behavior of floating-point numbers is complex*

Compared to real numbers, the behavior of floating-point numbers is more complex. There are many examples in the literature [MUL 10]; here are a few selected cases:

– In algebraic terms, sum and product are commutative; they have as their neutral element, respectively, 0 and 1, and 0 is absorbent for the product, but this is all. They are not associative, multiplication is not distributive on addition, subtraction (and respectively division) is not the inverse of addition[22] (and respectively multiplication), etc.

---

22 a + (-a) = 0, but a+(b-a) = b and (b+a)-a = b are false, and we do not even have a * (1/a) = 1!

– A real vector of norm 1, once rounded into a floating-point vector, has a pretty high probability of having a floating-point norm which is different from 1. The following figure shows the random walk which the norm of the product of a million "standardized" random complex floating-point numbers follows[23] (it is the discrepancy with 1 that is shown). Of course, the norm of the product is not equal to the product of the norms.

– The same is true for the norm of the column vectors or the determinant of a rotation matrix. What is worse, if we multiply them among themselves many times, we see elements outside [–1,1] appearing, which is a problem when we want to extract a Euler angle with an arc-sine.

The examination of this random walk may give us the impression that the discrepancy between a floating-point calculation and the same calculation with real numbers could be simply modeled by a random noise, which has a standard deviation which regularly increases with the number of elementary operations carried out.

This is false due to

– the changes in execution path due to branching (x > 0, etc.);

– calls for partial functions outside their domain of definition (1/x in 0, square root on negative numbers, etc.).

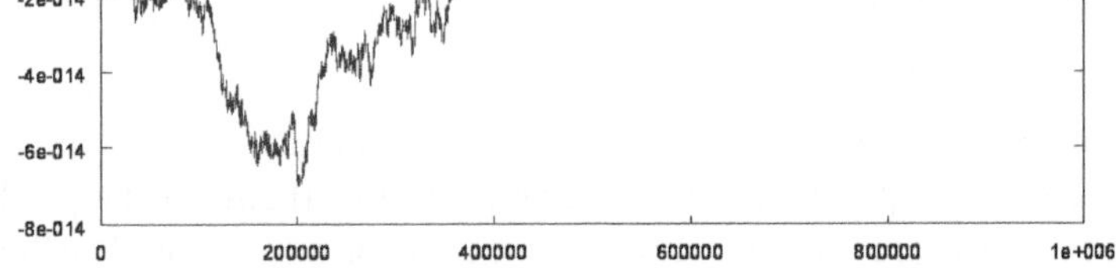

Figure 13.2. *The random walk of the norm of a product of unitary complex numbers*

23 "normed" in an algorithmic sense: here we generate a non-normed complex, and then we divide it by its norm (using the tools Matlab or Octave: « c = complex(rand(),rand()) ; c = c/norm(c) »). The distribution of the norm around 1 strongly depends on the method of generation (other possibilities: (cos θ, sin θ), $(x,\sqrt{1-x^2})$, …).

13.6.3. *Infinities and NaNs*

A fundamental aspect of the standard IEEE is that the floating-point operations are "total" functions: they are defined for all the input values, due to the addition of two "infinite" numbers ±INFINITY and the "NaN" (not a number).

For example, addition behaves in the following way (in double precision):

– 1E308 + 1E308 = INFINITY, because the largest finite number which can be represented is less than 2E308;

– INFINITY + x = INFINITY, for any number x greater than – INFINITY;

– INFINITY + (– INFINITY) = NaN;

– NaN + x = NaN, for any object x (number or not).

This requirement to continue to calculate whatever happens is impossible to understand for embedded critical software; however, it is obviously required in scientific calculation. When we ask the tools Matlab or Octave to find the minimum of the fun function around x0 "x = fminsearch(fun,x0)", we do not wish the search to be interrupted for the reason that fun has an asymptote or behaves chaotically around x0.

For proof, as early as 1938 and 1941, Konrad Zuse's programmable calculators Z1 and Z3 managed overflows without interruption by using the special values ±INFINITY (however, the calculators did not yet have the NaN: INFINITY – INFINITY stopped the machine: see [ROJ 97]).

We must, however, remain prudent. That a "normal" result has been obtained does not necessarily mean that everything has gone well. In fact, INFINITYs and NaNs are destroyed by comparisons. Here are a few examples in the C language:

– The evaluation of the predicate "+INFINITY ≥ 0.0" must in absolute terms either halt execution (this is the safe method) or give a Boolean: by default, we obtain a Boolean (TRUE, as it happens); therefore, we forget that we have passed through the stage INFINITY.

– More difficult to handle, but in fact identical, "fmin(+INFINITY, 0.0)" equals 0.0.

– Also due to going through Booleans, because "+INFINITY ≥ +INFINITY" is evaluated as TRUE, the expression C "2*1E308 ≥ 3*1E308 ? 1.0: 2.0" yields 1.0, whereas the result in real numbers is 2.0[24].

To work against this covering up of an anomaly, when an operation generates an infinity or a NaN, a "sticky" bit is placed at 1 in a state register ("sticky" means that it is not returned to 0 by the operations that follow). The consultation of sticky bits is the only way to be sure that there has not been a problem.

Finally, obtaining a +INFINITY does not mean that the "real" result is a large positive number: "(2*1E308 – 1.5E308) –1.5E308" yields +INFINITY, even though the result in real numbers is –1E308. Therefore, no certain information can be drawn from an INFINITY. This "safety of the calculation" aspect is further developed in the appendix.

13.7. Reasons underlying extension to floating-point numbers

13.7.1. *Overview*

Considering the discussion above, we clearly cannot speak of floating-point numbers without the support of real numbers.

More precisely, we maintain that real numbers have a role to play for two different purposes:

– they allow us to handle floating-point numbers: they thus have a role to play within the properties of a B model (invariants, pre-conditions, etc.) and within abstract objects;

– given the complexity of floating-point properties (a determinant of a rotation matrix is "nearly" equal to 1, etc.), given the complexity of the proof of these properties (modeling of the rounded value), modeling in real numbers will be easier to write, check and prove: as far as we see it, they may well belong to the concrete objects of a B model.

However, this second role naturally begs the question: "what does this prove?" In fact, a proven "implementation in real numbers" can give rise, in

---

24 If the careful reader wishes to check this with gcc on a PC, it is important to establish IEEE mode with the options "-mfpmath=sse –msse2".

real life, to the evaluation of 1/0 or √- ε. We will return to this topic in the conclusion, section 13.9.

13.7.2. *Real numbers*

We thus add a new set called REAL to the B language, with literal numbers in decimal and hexadecimal notation and with arithmetic and comparison operations that make it into an ordered field. The only issue which needs to be addressed is the relationship between REAL and INTEGER: in ACSL, for example, integers are included in real numbers.

For B, we make the opposite choice, for the following reasons:

– it is necessary to ensure ascending compatibility with existing projects. However, a certain number of current rules are false when they are applied in real numbers;

– in practice, as we have seen previously, the two worlds are quite well segregated: conversions are rare.

REAL is thus a new basic type, and is far removed from INTEGER. This implies that it is necessary to provide the formal bridge which ensures that INTEGER is (isomorphous to) an ordered sub-ring of REAL, and which allows us to make the following explicit conversions:

– INTEGRAL_REAL is the subset of REAL which contains the integer values;

– INTEGRAL_PART(r) is the "integer part" function of REAL toward INTEGRAL_REAL;

– REAL(i) and INTEGER(r) are the conversion functions between INTEGRAL_REAL and INTEGER.

On the other hand, in order to ensure good legibility of models, it is better to maintain the traditional syntax of comparisons and arithmetic: a < b, a + b, ... We thus overload the comparison predicates (">", "≥", "<", "≤"; equality is already polymorphous) and the operators "+", "–", "*", "**", "mod", "max", "min", "SIGMA", "PI".

The logic to authorize the overload is to have one of the following two properties:

– REAL(i1) o REAL(i2) = i1 o i2, where “o” is a predicate;

– REAL(i1) o REAL(i2) = i1 o i2, where “o” is an operator.

As a result, “/” is not overloaded, because the integer and real number divisions give different results on the integers: it is replaced by the new infix operator “rdiv”.

In the same way, “..” is not overloaded, because a real interval is denser than an integer interval. European notation “[a,b]” and American notation “(a,b)” are already taken, and it is also necessary to express semi-open intervals such as [a,b[= [a,b). Therefore, we suggest four new infix operators “++”, “+-”, “-+”, “—”, with the convention “+”=included and “–”=excluded ([a,b[is written “a +- b”).

In order to facilitate resolution of the overloading, we require that the real literal numbers are differentiated from integer literal numbers by a point (“.”) or an exponent: real zero is written “0.0”, “0e36” or “0p-49”.

Of course, a library defines all the useful functions: √, log, sin, etc.

13.7.3. *Concrete floating-point numbers*

“Concrete” floating-point numbers are those that are found in silicon (and by extension in the C source) and that are in line with the IEEE; this being opposed to “abstract” floating-point numbers, which are those that are found in the B model and the basis for rules. An embedded application only uses a small portion of the variants and services provided by the IEEE library.

In order to better meet the needs of critical avionics software, we suggest the following framework:

– With regard to numbers:

- The application contains only simple floating-point numbers (32 bits, for example, a motor control) or double floating-point numbers (64 bits, for example an inertial unit); there is no mixing between these two precision levels. This simplification is possible due to the generalization of external 64-bit buses and 64-bit floating-point units, which bring the CPU cost of 32-bit and 64-bit floating-point numbers closer together.

- The numbers ±INFINITY and the NaNs are forbidden as functional values: we cannot mention them. However, because if they appear, it indicates that there is a problem (software or equipment), we should always be able to detect this. In a critical system, if they appear, it leads to the deletion of the task, and if this task is indispensable, it therefore also leads to the loss of the equipment. To do this, we could use the predicate IEEE "isFinite" or simulate it with "–MAXFLOAT ≤ x && x ≤ MAXFLOAT".

– With regard to rounded values:

- The only rounding mode is "to nearest, ties to even"[25], which is the mode at compilation and by default at execution in the C language (the C library allows this to be changed during execution, for very specific non-embedded applications).

– With regard to operations:

- From the standard IEEE, we retain only the four arithmetic operations, the comparisons, the "floor" function (which returns the floating-point number which has the integer value immediately below or equal: the official name is "roundToIntegralTowardNegative") and conversions out of and into the integers ("convert" and "convertToIntegerTowardNegative").

- The IEEE "remainder" function is not used (a "modulo" function is used instead, typically to maintain the angles in the interval [0 2*pi[; it is a library function and does not need to be "built-in").

- The IEEE "square root" function is not used, because it is much more precise than the need, and alignment with the need allows us to make a CPU gain.

13.7.4. *Abstract floating-point numbers*

These concrete numbers are modeled in B by a subset of REAL which we will call FLOAT, with the three following further details:

Of course, – +/-INFINITY and NaNs are not included, because they are not real, and also because they are not useful: instead of proving "x <

25 We should note that in domains other than onboard software (accounting), other modes of rounding may be obligatory: see [MUL 10] p. 95. In this particular case, we will use the base 10 and not the base 2.

INFINITY" or "x <> NaN", we prove "x ≤ MAXFLOAT", or, more generally, we prove that the functions are called in their domain of definition. This means that the floating-point operators, which are total functions in reality, become partial functions (with pre-conditions) in the model.

– The +0 and –0 IEEE (this peculiarity is due to the signed representation of the mantissa) are both modeled by "0.0".

– We can consider that "floating-point" literal numbers do not exist: there are real literal values (which are written in decimal or binary finite form); only some of these correspond exactly to a floating-point number (for example, in double, all the integer values on 32 bits are exactly represented). These are authorized in a context where we expect a floating-point number (notion needs to be formally defined), the others give rise to a typing error. This does have an impact on the typing algorithm, which currently only verifies belonging to the basic types (REAL, INTEGER, BOOL and user types) and which delegates sub-typing to the proof obligations.

The important point is that FLOAT is a subset of real numbers, which is not the case for IEEE floating numbers (to find out more about this, see the appendix). Nevertheless, the evaluation identity demonstration between a B expression and its translation into C should not be very demanding (if we evaluate strictly following the standard ANSI C).

As for the rounded value, the partial function ROUND models the rounded value of REAL toward FLOAT, and the following property should hold: ROUND([–MAXFLOAT, MAXFLOAT]) = FLOAT.

For predicates and operations, predicates on FLOAT are simply the restriction to FLOAT of predicates on REAL; therefore, we do not need to redefine them. On the other hand, for operations, only "max" and "min" are suitable and are unchanged, because they satisfy the property

f1 o f2 : FLOAT [13.1]

The others behave differently depending on whether they operate on real or floating-point numbers, and as a result, they need to be renamed:

– "+", "–", "*", "**", "++", "+-", "-+", "—" are prefixed with a ".": ".+", ".–", etc.

– “rdiv”, “mod”, “SIGMA”, “PI” must begin with “f”: “fdiv”, “fmod”, “FSIGMA”, “FPI”.

For example, the specification IEEE of the addition is written:

$$f1 \;.\!+ f2 = \mathrm{ROUND}(f1 + f2) \qquad [13.2]$$

13.8. Returning to the useful properties that need to be proved

If we were to finish with floating-point numbers, we would run the risk of imparting a false impression that the situation has been mastered: the real problem is with the properties that need to be verified. For this reason, we will discuss them further.

13.8.1. *In avionics, specifications are complex*

We have seen, above, how an asymmetrical COM/MON architecture makes it possible to naturally express the security properties on MON in the form of invariants:

– on the ground, an occupied section of the track must be followed by a free section, protected by a red light, etc.

– onboard, the distance before the next stopping point must be compatible with the deceleration guaranteed by emergency braking, the doors must be locked above a certain speed except during emergency braking, etc.

The invariant is an ideal means of specification in terms of abstraction, because it allows us to say almost nothing about the evolution of the state of the system.

On a fail-operational system, the invariants are much less natural, because safety is synonymous with availability. It is true that we have seen how, on a motor control, it is technically possible to formalize a simplified specification. However, for an INS, the simplification is not at all obvious. Let us take the function “integration of the attitude” (attitude is the inclination with respect to the horizontal plane, or more generally, orientation in space), the only simplification which comes to mind is to place oneself on a flat Earth which does not turn, this gives:

– "the attitude in relation to the initial position is the integral of the elementary rotations detected by the gyroscopes since initialization".

Of course, this cannot be directly expressed in B; therefore, a stage of informal refinement brings us back to a unique execution of the function:

– "at initialization, the attitude is the identity rotation";

– "at each cycle, the attitude is multiplied by the elementary rotation detected by the gyroscopes".

This is an evolution property, and the only invariant that we can extract from it is

– "the attitude is a rotation"

which is already a complex property, especially when it is expressed in floating-point numbers. These invariants are generally sufficient to prove the pre-conditions of low-level procedures, and therefore to prove that the execution will take place without incident. However, they are insufficient for expressing the desired functionality.

If this example taken from an INS seems too complicated or insufficiently representative of the "average" avionics algorithm, it is enough to take a low-pass filter: the two obvious specifications are:

– at the one end, an exact transfer function is specified (no abstraction);

– at the other end, it is sufficient to type the output.

Finding an intermediary and useful specification is less straightforward (these do exist: for example the behavior on a constant input).

13.8.2. *Can vector data be abstracted?*

Let us return to the INS and the invariant: "the attitude is a rotation". This makes another problem appear: it is not easy to abstract this type of data. We could also refer to this as linear application of R^3 in R^3, which preserves the norm and the orientation, but this would not necessarily help simplify the specification. However, it is the case that, at least for a part of railway applications, the refinement of data is a fundamental aspect for having specification at a useful level of abstraction.

13.8.3. *The gap between algorithmic specifications and pre-conditions of leaf procedures*

Also in an INS, at the bottom of the call graph, we find the operations "scalar_product", "matrix_vector_product", "matri_matrix_product", etc. These operations are sums of products, which are partial functions in FLOAT; therefore, there are pre-conditions. Depending on the context, this may raise different issues.

First context: kinematic calculations. In order to simplify the operation, we imagine that we are working not in 3D but in 2D, and therefore we are able to represent the rotations using complex numbers.

The operation "c ← complex_product (a,b)" should have a pre-condition which ensures that a'r*b'r-a'i*b'i and a'r*b'i+a'i*b'r are correctly evaluated. The simplest way of achieving this is to require that for a and b:

$$\max(\,|x'r|, |x'i|\,) < \text{sqrt}(\text{ MAXFLOAT} / 2\,) \qquad [13.3]$$

The term on the left is called the norm l_∞ or "Chebyshev's", written as $||x||_\infty$ (see [HIG 02]). To demonstrate the pre-condition within the calling procedure, we use the fact that

– the rotations are (Euclidean) norm 1 complexes: $||x||_2 = 1$ (in R, not in FLOAT);

– the Euclidean norm is greater than or equal to the infinite norm: $||x||_2 \geq ||x||_\infty$ (in R, but also in FLOAT).

This last theorem cannot be demonstrated immediately (and thus will enrich the basis of rules).

Also, in order to prove the invariant that "the attitude has 1 as its norm", we need the theorem "the norm of the product is equal to the product of the norms", which is similar in complexity to the preceding theorem (and is only valid in R).

13.8.4. *Integrators and the formalization of the system boundaries*

Second context: Kalman filter. The state covariance matrix, "P", evolves at each propagation cycle in accordance with the formula:

$$P := \Phi * P * \Phi^T + Q \qquad [13.4]$$

where Φ represents the evolution of the system and Q the uncertainty of the modeling. Here, this raises not only the issue of mathematic formalization (in particular, which matrix norm should be chosen for the product?) but also the physical formalization: what is the dynamics of Φ and of P?

The problem is that Φ and P are *a priori* unbounded integrators (as opposed to attitude, which is also an integrator, but is limited to the space of the rotations):

– Φ is the integral in the wider sense of movement, and it is limited because the system moves in a limited space (around earth, at a limited altitude) at limited speeds;

– P is the integral in the wider sense of measurement and modeling errors, and it is limited in function of the mission time, which it is therefore necessary to limit.

These limits are currently determined by an informal system analysis, and then used by the software team to test robustness. In the future, this informal system analysis should be integrated into the formal specification. This is probably the greatest challenge which awaits us.

To summarize, in addition to the three reasons identified in section 13.4, avionics has three further reasons to distrust the strong railway TRL of B:

– the abstraction of data may not apply to "signal treatment"-type algorithms;

– the formalization of these algorithms will lead us to complex mathematics;

– it will probably be necessary to formalize the part of the system analysis which determines the dynamics of computerized objects.

13.9. Conclusion

Currently, in the railway sector, the economic balance between test and proof is neutral: it has not been proven that B reduces costs, but it clearly reduces technical risk and increases confidence levels. In the future, in avionics, in order to maintain this balance, the introduction of formal methods must be sufficiently prepared, beginning with projects of limited complexity, and gradually increasing this complexity. We have identified six potential stumbling blocks, and the complexity of floating-point numbers in relation to real numbers or integers is far from the most serious of these: the complexity of specifications and algorithms is the difficulty that we really need to bear in mind.

This is not to say that the complexity introduced by floating-point numbers can be neglected, even temporarily. We believe that a proof in real numbers, even if it is not *a priori* usable in a DO-178 certification, lends significant technical credit, and that then the transition to floating-point numbers can be carried out "in delta" with tools specialized in numeric precision, such as Fluctuat (developed by the CEA).

In order to make an on-the-ground assessment of this additional complexity brought about by floating-point numbers and the possibility of an approach in delta, Sagem has asked Clearsy[26] to create an AtelierB prototype which would implement a part of the written specification expressed in section 13.7 (see [BUR 12]).

A final point which has not been addressed is that AtelierB currently generates code. It is thus considered by the DO-178 to be a "development tool" which can introduce bugs, and is thus subject to a very demanding qualification process. Therefore, before any industrial use, it is essential to ensure that the code is an input into the Atelier (and not an output from it; for example, by translating it into B0). If this is the case, then the Atelier may be categorized as a "verification tool".

I would like to thank Philippe Baufreton, an expert from Sagem's Division Safran Electronics, for his detailed and constructive feedback on this chapter, and for sharing his DO-178 expertise [ARI 92, ARI 12].

26 To find out more about Clearsy and AtelierB, see http://www.clearsy.com/.

13.10. Appendix: the confusion between overflow, infinity and illegal parameters

13.10.1. *Presentation of the issue*

We have seen above that the value "infinity" appeared right at the beginnings of information technology. However, it did not immediately become widespread. In the 1950s, calculators treated overflows and illegal parameters using exceptions and sticky bits, and the results were insignificant (for example, an overflow gives rise to a "truncated" exponent, and a 1/0 leaves the registers as they were at the input of the division).

Completion by the concept of NaN, making it possible to have total functions, only appeared for the first time (as far as we are aware) in 1963, in the floating-point arithmetic of CDC 6600, under the name "INDEFINITE". Table 13.1 describes the associated addition table, and for the four basic operations, the behavior of INFINITY and INDEFINITE is identical to the IEEE (0*INF = 0/0 = NaN, see [THO 70]).

		Xk			
		W	+∞	–∞	±IND
Xj	W	W	+∞	–∞	IND
	+∞	+∞	+∞	IND	IND
	–∞	–∞	IND	–∞	IND
	±IND	IND	IND	IND	IND

Table 13.1. *Addition table*

The aim of this appendix is to show why these calculation rules are not as "safe" as they might be, and that if they may seem natural from the perspective of numerical analysis (which was the major preoccupation of the years 1950–1980), they are not natural from the perspective of formal semantics. This is also why the B floating-point numbers suggested do not contain these objects, and we think that it is necessary to be very careful if it is intended to extend the model.

13.10.2. *Confusion between overflow and infinity*

An addition, subtraction or multiplication generates an "infinity" from two normal arguments if the result overflows: INFINITY thus represents a (too) large number in the interval]MAXFLOAT, ∞[.

However, according to the IEEE: "INFINITY – x = INFINITY", for any finite x. If

– the first INFINITY comes from MAXFLOAT+1;

– and if x is 2;

– then INFINITY – x represents MAXFLOAT–1. This number is normal and should not be represented by INFINITY.

This first peculiarity is due to the fact that as regards this rule "INFINITY – x = INFINITY", the IEEE interprets INFINITY as the "true infinity" ∞: we could say that IEEE floating-point numbers are not an abstraction of the real numbers R but of the "extended" real numbers R ∪ {+∞,–∞}.

This explains the behavior remarked upon in section 13.6.3: "(2*1E308 – 1.5E308) –1.5E308".

If we could change the definition of floating-point numbers, we could easily ensure "safe" behavior, by performing what is known as "interval arithmetic" and "abstraction":

– We forget NaN, and replace INFINITY with BIG, which represents any number in]MAXFLOAT, ∞[(and especially not ∞).

– What is BIG+BIG? In terms of interval, it is]2*MAXFLOAT, ∞[, but we are not going to add to this all of the intervals of this type: they are contained in BIG, thus we decide that BIG + BIG = BIG.

– What is BIG + x, x finite? In terms of interval, it is]0, ∞[. Let us call this POS. We could add it, but we decide to proceed simply by rather adding ALL =]-∞, ∞[: POS is contained in ALL, thus we decide that for finite x, BIG + x = ALL.

The new system of numbers is now complete: we naturally have BIG + (–BIG) = ALL and for any x, ALL + x = ALL. We can even refine a little, with the following (symmetrical) addition in Table 13.2.

The subtraction table is similar (but more "anti-symmetrical"), and with this system, which is not more complicated than the IEEE, "(BIG – 1.5E308) –1.5E308" is evaluated in ALL (which is obviously a safe result, whereas the IEEE goes a bit too far forward with +INFINITY).

+	N	BIG	–BIG	ALL
M	If there is no overflow. n + m Otherwise BIG or –BIG	If m ≥ 0, BIG If not, ALL	If m ≤ 0, -BIG If not, ALL	ALL
BIG	.	BIG	ALL	ALL
– BIG	.	.	–BIG	ALL
ALL	.	.	.	ALL

Table 13.2. *New addition table*

This system extends without problem to total functions, such as absolute value, exponential, cosinus, etc. Here, for example, is a possible multiplication table (also symmetrical):

*	N	BIG	–BIG	ALL
M	If there is no overflow, n * m Otherwise BIG or –BIG	If m ≥ 1, BIG If m ≤ –1, – BIG If m == 0, 0 If not, ALL	If m ≥ 1, –BIG If m ≤ –1, BIG If m == 0, 0 If not, ALL	If m == 0, 0 If not, ALL
BIG	.	BIG	–BIG	ALL
–BIG	.	.	BIG	ALL
ALL	.	.	.	ALL

Table 13.3. *Multiplication table*

The fundamental difference between this and the IEEE is: 0*BIG = 0*ALL = 0.

We can simplify the system by bringing together BIG and –BIG in a BIG_IN_ABSOLUTE_VALUE, and we can further simplify by only retaining ALL: this is the minimal system of "safe" arithmetic (on total functions).

Conversely, we can make the system more complex, for various different reasons: for example, we can define a system which tells us that "(2*1E308 – 1.5E308) –1.5E308" is in the interval [–MAXFLOAT, MAXFLOAT], or even in the interval [–MAXFLOAT, –MAXFLOAT/2[, etc. This search for a set of intervals that are not too complex, but are informative, is the crux of "abstract interpretation" [BOU 11a], technology which is at the heart of the tools Astrée and POLYSPACE.

The fundamental point is that these systems are abstractions of R: the "infinity" does not exist.

13.10.3. *Confusion between infinity and illegal parameters*

The systems above cannot handle partial functions: the manipulated objects are either numbers or intervals of numbers. Therefore, when the program requires the evaluation of √–1, we do not know how to answer this, because no real number squared gives –1. The solution to this is to introduce the empty set ∅ as a value, which we will call NONE (in contrast to ALL), and which means that because we have asked a stupid question (√–1), there will be no answer.

NONE may be classed as "not-a-number" and it satisfies the same rule as NaN: as soon as it appears as one of the parameters of an operation, it is also the result. However, it only signifies the call of a function outside of its domain of definition, and not a result which may exist but would be "indefinite":

– INFINITY – INFINITY = NaN becomes BIG – BIG = ALL, and NONE is not involved;

– 0 * INFINITY = NaN becomes 0 * BIG = 0, and NONE is not involved;

– 1/0 = INFINITY becomes 1/0 = NONE, because there is no solution to the equation "1 = 0 * x";

– 0/0 = NaN becomes 0/0 = NONE, because there is more than one solution to the equation "0 = 0 * x" .

This last point is important: "/" is a partial function of R^2 in R. Therefore, it must associate a unique value with any couple from its domain of definition, and (0,0) cannot be within its domain of definition.

Another point: infinity still has no place in this system.

Even if, for a mathematician, the equation "1/0 = INFINITY" might seem reasonable, it is important to bear in mind that the IEEE has "+0" and "–0", and that we also have "1/–0 = –INFINITY". Because "+0 = –0", therefore "+INFINITY = –INFINITY", etc. Or therefore the axiom "x = y => f(x) = f(y)" must be abandoned, and in this case it is not inconsistency that matters, but incompleteness.

To summarize, we have removed the infinity of INFINITY to obtain BIG, and we have distributed NaN between NONE and ALL. The system { +/- BIG, ALL, NONE } is only a little more complicated than the IEEE, completely codable in the IEEE binary representation, and if we could rewrite history and add a logician to the IEEE standardization group begun in 1977, it is likely that INFINITYs and other NaNs would not have the same definition (in fact, do they actually really have one?), nor the same behavior.

13.11. Glossary

ACSL	ANSI/ISO C specification language
CENELEC[27]	*Comité Européen de Normalisation ELECtrotechnique* – European Committee for Electrotechnical Standardization
COM	Command
COTS	Commercial Off-The-Shelf
CPU	Central Processing Unit
DAL	Development Assurance Level
FADEC	Full Authority Digital Engine Control
GPS	Global Positioning System

27 For information, see http://www.cenelec.eu/.

IEC[28]	International Electrotechnical Commission
INS	Inertial Navigation System
MON	Monitor
NaN	Not a Number
PA	*Pilote Automatique* – autopilot
RER	*Réseau Express Régional* – regional express network
SACEM	*Système d'Aide à la Conduite, à l'Exploitation et à la Maintenance* – assisted driving, operation and maintenance system
SAGA	*Spécification d'Applications et Génération Automatisée* – specification of applications and automatic generation
SAO	*Spécification Assistée par Ordinateur* – computer-assisted specification
SIL	Safety Integrity Level

13.12. Bibliography

[ABR 84] ABRIAL J.-R., "The mathematical construction of a program", *Science of Computer Programming,* vol. 4, pp. 45–86, 1984.

[ABR 96] ABRIAL J.-R., *The B Book – Assigning Programs to Meanings*, Cambridge University Press, Cambridge, August 1996.

[ARI 92] ARINC, Software considerations in airborne systems and equipment certification, DO 178B and l'EUROCAE, no. ED12, ed. B, 1992.

[ARI 12] ARINC, Software considerations in airborne systems and equipment certification, DO 178C, RTCA, ed. C, 2012.

[ARP 96] ARP 4754 Certification considerations for highly-integrated or complex systems, publié par le SAE, et par l'EUROCAE, no. ED79, 1996.

[AYA 10] AYAD A., MARCHÉ C., "Multi-prover verification of floating-point programs", *5th International Joint Conference on Automated Reasoning,* 2010; see also the latest specification ACSL at http://frama-c.com/download.html.

28 See http://www.iec.ch/.

[BAC 81] BACK R.-J., "On correct refinement of programs", *Journal of Computer and System Sciences*, vol. 23, pp. 49–68, 1981.

[BOL 07] BOLDO S., FILLIÂTRE J.-C., "Formal verification of floating-point programs", *18th IEEE International Symposium on Computer Arithmetic*, Montpellier, France, pp. 187–194, June 2007.

[BOU 11a] BOULANGER J.-L. (ed.), *Utilisations industrielles des techniques formelles – interprétation abstraite*, Hermes-Lavoisier, 2011.

[BOU 11b] BOULANGER J.-L., *Sécurisation des architectures informatiques industrielles*, Hermes-Lavoisier, 2011.

[BOU 11c] BOULANGER J.-L., *Utilisation industrielles des techniques formelles – interprétation abstraite*, Hermes-Lavoisier, 2011.

[BOU 12] BOULANGER J.-L., *Outils de mise en œuvre industrielle des techniques formelles*, Hermes-Lavoisier, 2012.

[BUR 12] BURDY L., DUFOUR J.-L., LECOMTE T., *The B Method Takes up Floating-Point Numbers*, ERTS, Toulouse, 2012.

[CEN 00] CENELEC, EN 50126, Applications Ferroviaires. Spécification et démonstration de la fiabilité, de la disponibilité, de la maintenabilité et de la sécurité (FMDS), January 2000.

[CEN 01] CENELEC, EN 50128, Railway applications – communications, signalling and processing systems – software for railway control and protection systems, May 2001.

[CEN 11] CENELEC, EN 50128, Railway applications – communications, signalling and processing systems – software for railway control and protection systems, January 2011.

[CHA 89] CHAPRONT P., "Christian Galivel, results of a safety software validation: SACEM", *Proceedings of the IFAC CCCT'89 Symposium (Control, Computers, Communication in Transportation)*, 1989.

[COU 00] COUSOT P.. "Interprétation abstraite", *Technique et Science Informatique*, Hermès, Paris, vol. 19, no. 1–3, pp. 155–164, January 2000.

[DEH 94] DEHBONEI B., MEJIA F., "Formal methods in the railways signalling industry", *FME '94: Industrial Benefit of Formal Methods, LNCS*, vol. 873, pp. 26–34, 1994.

[DEL 07] DELMAS D., SOUYRIS J., "Astrée: from research to industry", *14th International Static Analysis Symposium,* LNCS, vol. 4634, pp. 437–451, 2007.

[DUF 05] DUFOUR J.-L., "Automotive safety concepts: 10-9/h for less than 100€ a piece", *6th AAET Conference*, 2005.

[FOR 89] FORIN P., "Vital coded microprocessor principles and application for various transit systems", *Proceedings of the IFAC CCCT'89 Symposium (Control, Computers, Communication in Transportation)*, 1989.

[GEO 90] GEORGES J.-P., "Principes et fonctionnement du Système d'Aide à la Conduite, à l'Exploitation et à la Maintenance (SACEM), application à la ligne a du RER", *Revue Générale des Chemins de fer*, vol. 6, June 1990.

[GUI 90] GUIHO G., HENNEBERT C., "SACEM software validation", *Proceedings of the International Conference on Software Engineering (ICSE'90)*, 1990.

[HIG 02] HIGHAM N.J., *Accuracy and Stability of Numerical Algorithms*, 2nd ed., Society for Industrial & Applied Mathematics, 2002.

[HOA 69] HOARE C.A.R., "An axiomatic basis for computer programming", *Communications of the ACM*, vol. 12, no. 10, pp. 576–580, 583, 1969.

[IEC 98] IEC 61508: Sécurité fonctionnelle des systèmes électriques électroniques programmables relatifs à la sécurité, International Standard, 1998.

[IEE 85] IEEE 754-1985 and IEEE 754-2008, IEEE standard for (binary) floating-point arithmetic.

[MON 08] MONNIAUX D., "The pitfalls of verifying floating-point computations", *ACM Transactions on Programming Languages and Systems (TOPLAS)*, vol. 30, no. 3, May 2008.

[MOR 90] MORGAN C., *Programming from Specifications*, Prentice Hall, 1990.

[MUL 10] MULLER J.-M., and coll., *Handbook of Floating-Point Arithmetic*, Birkhaüser, 2010.

[PAX 91] PAXSON V., A program for testing IEEE decimal-binary conversion, May 1991.

[ROJ 97] ROJAS R., "Konrad Zuse's legacy: the architecture of the Z1 and Z3", *IEEE Annals of the History of Computing*, vol. 19, no. 2, 1997.

[SOU 09] SOURYIS J., WIELS V., DELMAS D., *et al.*, "Formal verification of avionics software products", *Formal Methods*, LNCS 5850, 2009.

[SPI 89] SPIVEY J.M., *The Z Notation- A Reference Manual*, Prentice Hall, 1989.

[THO 70] THORNTON J.E., *Design of a Computer: The Control Data 6600*, Scott Foresman and Company, 1970.

14

From Animation to Data Validation: The ProB Constraint Solver 10 Years On

We present our 10 years of experience in developing and applying the PROB validation tool. Initially, the tool provided animation and model checking capabilities for the B-method. Over the years, it has been extended to other formal specification languages and provides various constraint-based validation techniques. The tool itself was developed in SICStus Prolog, and makes use of the finite domain library together with newly developed constraint solvers for Booleans, sets, relations and sequences. The various solvers are linked via reification and Prolog co-routines. The overall challenge of PROB is to solve constraints in full predicate logic with arithmetic, set theory and higher-order relations and functions for safety critical applications. In addition to the tool development, we also provide details about various industrial applications of the tool as well as about our efforts in qualifying the tool for usage in safety critical contexts. Finally, we also describe our experiences in applying alternate approaches, such as SAT or SMT.

14.1. The problem

The B-method [ABR 96] is a formal method for specifying safety critical systems, reasoning about those systems and generating code that is correct by construction. The first industrial usage of B was the development of the software for the fully automatic driverless Line 14 of the Paris Métro, also called Météor (*Metro est-ouest rapide*) [BEH 99]. This was a great success; quoting [SIE 09]: "*Since the commissioning of Line 14 in Paris in 1998, not a single malfunction has been noted in the software developed using this principle*". Since then, many other train control systems have been developed and installed worldwide [DOL 03, BAD 05, ESS 07].

Chapter written by Michael LEUSCHEL, Jens BENDISPOSTO, Ivo DOBRIKOV, Sebastian KRINGS and Daniel PLAGGE.

Initially, the B-method was supported by two tools, BToolkit [BCO 99] and Atelier B [CLE 09], which provided mainly both automatic and interactive proving environments, as well as code generators. To be able to apply the code generators, one has to *refine* the initial high-level specifications into lower-level B (called B0). This process is illustrated in Figure 14.1. Every refinement step engenders proof obligations; if all proof obligations are discharged one has the guarantee that the final B0 specification correctly implements the initial high-level specification.[1]

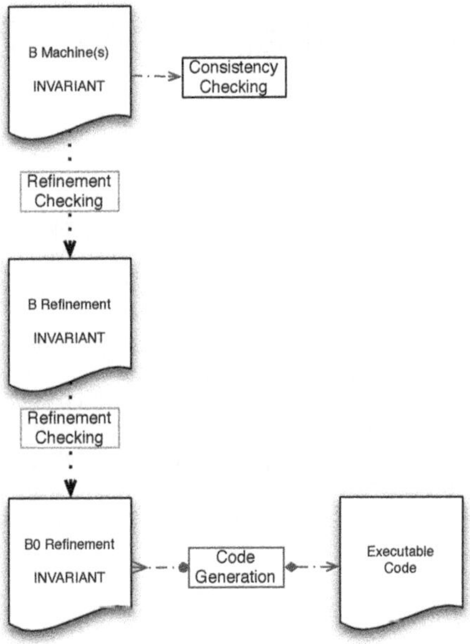

Figure 14.1. *B Development process*

14.1.1. *Animation for B*

In this "correct-by-construction" approach, it is of course vital that the initial high-level specification (at the top of Figure. 14.1) correctly covers the intended application. To some extent, this can be ensured by providing

1 The correctness of the code generation phase is of course also critical; here the industrial users typically use two different, independently developed code generators, targeting different hardware platforms which are both in operation in the final system.

invariants and assertions, but it quickly became obvious that additional validation of the high-level specification is important. In 2003, only very limited additional validation was available. The BToolkit provided an interactive animator with some strong limitations. Basically, the user had to provide values for parameters and existentially quantified variables, the validity of which was checked by the BToolkit prover. This approach was justified by the undecidability of the B language, but was tedious for the user and prevented automated validation.

The PROB validation tool was developed to fill this gap in the tooling landscape. The first problem that PROB set out to solve was to provide automatic animation, freeing up the user from providing values for parameters and quantified variables. This was to be achieved by developing the animator in logic and constraint logic programming.

14.1.1.1. *Challenge*

Indeed, the major challenge of animating or validating B is the expressiveness of its underlying language. B is based on predicate logic, augmented with arithmetic (over integers), (typed) set theory, as well as operators for relations, functions and sequences. As such, B provides a very expressive foundation which is familiar to many mathematicians and computer scientists. For example, Fermat's Last Theorem can be written in B as follows:

$$\forall n.(n > 2 \Rightarrow \neg\exists a, b, c\,.\, a^n + b^n = c^n).$$

In B's ASCII syntax (AMN), this is written as follows:

```
!n.(n>2 => not(\#(a,b,c).(a{*}{*}n
+ b{*}{*}n = c{*}{*}n)))
```

A more typical example in formal specifications would be the integer square root function, which can be expressed in B as follows:

$$isqrt = \lambda n.(n \geq 0 \mid max(\{i \mid i^2 \leq n\})).$$

As another example, let us express the fact that two graphs g_1, g_2 are isomorphic in B:

$$\exists p . p \in 1..n \rightarrowtail\!\!\!\!\twoheadrightarrow 1..n \wedge \forall i.(i \in 1..n \Rightarrow p[g_1[\{i\}]] = g_2[\{p(i)\}])$$

where, $1..n \rightarrowtail\!\!\!\!\twoheadrightarrow 1..n$ is the set of all permutations between the set of integers $1..n$ and itself, and $g_k[\{x\}]$ stands for the relational image of g_k for $\{x\}$, i.e. the set of all successor nodes of x in the graph g_k. This predicate is also more typical of the kind of predicates that appear in high-level B specifications. In B, these predicates can appear as invariants over variables, assertions, guards of operations, conditions of conditional statements and many more.

Due to arithmetic and the inclusion of higher-order functions, the satisfiability of B formulas is obviously undecidable. As such, animation is also undecidable, as operation pre-conditions or guards in high-level models can be arbitrarily complex. We cannot expect to be able to determine the truth value of Fermat's Last Theorem automatically, but PROB *is* capable of "solving" the graph isomorphism predicate for reasonably sized graphs,[2] without the user providing a value for the permutation p. It is also capable of computing the integer square root function above, e.g. determining that $isqrt(101) = 10$ or $isqrt(1234567890) = 35136$.[3] The tool has now also been extended to animate Z and TLA$^+$, whose logical foundations share a large common basis.

14.1.2. *Model checking B*

Once implemented, the automatic animation capabilities also enabled a second kind of validation, namely systematically exploring the state space of a B specification, i.e. *model checking*. Initially [LEU 03], PROB allowed us to examine the state space of a B model for invariant violations, deadlocks and assertion violations. Later [PLA 10], this was extended to check temporal (LTL and CTL) properties of the high-level models. Model checking provides additional guarantees of correct behavior of a high-level specification. In addition, the combination of model checking and constraint solving can provide a more elegant approach in specifying and solving certain problems than either technique alone.

2 E.g. 0.2 s for solving a "hard" isomorphism between two graphs with 30 nodes and 90 edges or 40 s for determining that two random graphs with 1,000 nodes and 1,500 edges are not isomorphic.

3 This is one of the specifications which is given as an example of a non-executable specification in [HAY 89].

14.1.2.1. *Challenge*

From a constraint solving perspective, the challenges are very similar to those for animation. One additional complication is, however, that we now need to find *all* solutions to the constraints. This is important for ensuring that *all* possible executions of a B model are analyzed, and that solutions are normalized (to avoid duplicate states in the state space). Also, if we want to deal with large state spaces we need state space reduction techniques (e.g. detecting symmetries), fast animation steps and optimized memory usage.

14.1.3. *Data validation*

In order to avoid multiple developments, a safety critical program is often made from a generic B-model and data parameters that are specific to a particular deployment. In other words, the initial B machine in Figure 14.1 is very generic and requires various parameters to be provided at runtime. For example, in railway systems, these parameters would describe the tracks, switches, traffic lights, electrical connections and possible routes. Adapting the data parameters is also used to "tune" the system. The proofs of the generic B-model rely on assumptions about the data parameters, e.g. assumptions about the topology of the track. It is vital that these assumptions are checked when the system is put in place, as well as whenever the system is adapted (e.g. due to line extension or addition or removal of certain track sections in a railway system).

Before 2009, this validation of the parameters was basically conducted by using automated provers. Siemens, for example, was using Atelier B along with custom proof rules and tactics, dedicated to dealing with larger data values [BOI 00, BOI 02].[4] This approach had two major shortcomings. First, if the proof of a property fails, the feedback of the prover is not very useful (and it may be unclear whether there actually is a problem with the data or just with the power of the prover). Second, the data parameters became so large that the provers ran out of memory, even with maximum memory allocated. This led us [LEU 11] to apply PROB's constraint solving engine to validate those data properties automatically. This turned out to be very successful: full validation

4 Standard provers have not been developed with large, concrete values in mind. For example, many proof rules will duplicate parts of the goal to be proven. This frequently leads to out-of-memory problems when the duplicated parts contain large constants.

was now achieved in minutes rather than weeks or months. The tool is now used by various companies for similar data validation tasks, sometimes even in contexts where B itself is not used for the system development process. In those cases, the underlying language of B turns out to be very expressive and efficient to cleanly encode a large class of data properties.

14.1.3.1. *Challenge*

From a constraint solving perspective, the challenge here is clearly to deal with big data: one has relations containing tens of thousands or hundreds of thousands of elements and these should not *per se* grind the constraint solving engine to a halt. Also, numbers tend to be very large (e.g. positions of beacons expressed in millimeters).

Another challenge is validation of the output of the tool itself. In safety critical environments, we need to provide a case of why a validation tool itself can be trusted. Many standards, such as the EN 50128 in the railway domain, provide criteria that have to be met for a tool to be usable for certain applications. For PROB this meant the development of a rigorous testing and validation process, along with the generation of a validation report which is actively maintained alongside the tool itself.

14.1.4. *Constraint-based checking and disproving for B*

Over the years, PROB's constraint solving capabilities have increased and as such new possibilities for validation have opened up. Some of these applications use the constraint solver as a complement to the prover:

– check if an invariant of a B machine is inductive, i.e. check if it is possible to prove the B machine correct by induction. If a counter example is found, we know that any proof attempt will be futile.

– check if an invariant of a B machine ensures that no deadlock can appear [HAL 11].

– check whether the refinement proof obligations are provable or not.

These applications are complementary to proof; the main difference is that counter examples can be provided which can be inspected within the animation interface. In addition, many other applications arise: test-case generation, understanding certain aspects of a B model, such as control flow.

14.1.4.1. *Challenge*

The main challenge for this application is to deal with complicated constraints and possibly very big constraints (as is the case for deadlock checking [HAL 11]). In addition, we want to try and provide counter-examples even if some of the variables are not bounded to a finite domain. Finally, we want to detect when the result of the constraint solver (i.e. the fact that no counter example was found) can be used as a formal proof.

14.1.5. *Summary*

In essence, the challenge and ultimate goal of PROB is to solve constraints:

– for an undecidable formal method with existential and universal quantification, higher-order functions and relations, unbounded variables;

– very large data;

– infinite functions to be dealt with symbolically;

– in a reliable way, e.g. so as to satisfy standard EN50128;

– fast solving, with minimal overhead and memory consumption;

– being able to find all solutions for predicates;

– dealing with big constraints and complicated constraints.

14.2. Choice of implementation technology

14.2.1. *What was used before?*

14.2.1.1. *Proof*

Before the development of PROB, the validation of B models relied solely on the B provers. For animation, the user had to provide values for quantified variables; the correctness of the values were checked by the prover in automatic mode. When the prover failed, it was not necessarily clear whether this was due to the weakness of the prover or because the user had chosen wrong values. Similarly, data validation relied on automatic proof, along with custom proof rules.

All this meant that animation was very tedious for the user and no automated validation, such as model checking, (section 14.1.2) was possible. Concerning data validation (section 14.1.3) meant that about a month of work was necessary to validate new configuration data.

14.2.1.2. *Naive enumeration*

Tools for other languages, such as the TLC model checker for TLA, [YU 99] use naive enumeration for solving constraints. These tools can be very fast when no constraint solving is necessary, but are obviously very bad at solving constraints and thus bad for animating or model checking high-level specifications or for constraint-based checking.

The power of using logic programming was realized by several works: Bowen [BOW 98] developed an animator for Verilog in Prolog, [KIN 01] pursued a Horn logic approach to encode denotational semantics, [WIN 98] presents an animator for Z implemented in Mercury. None of these works, though, used the potential of coroutines or constraint logic programming.

14.2.2. *Why was constraint logic programming used?*

When moving into the formal methods field and coming from a logic programming background it quickly become obvious that the existing tools had severe limitations and that those could be overcome by constraint logic programming. From within the field of formal methods, there was also the feeling that certain specifications were inherently not executable [HAY 89]. But when moving from a logic programming group to a formal methods group (as was the case for the first author) it was obvious that one could do much better than the state-of-the-art at the time using Prolog and constraint solving.

Unknown to us at the time (around 2000), another team pursued similar ideas leading to the CLP-S solver [BOU 02] and the BZTT tool [AMB 02] based on it. This work also gave rise to a company (Lerios), which concentrated on model-based testcase generation and later ported the technology to an imperative programming language. Unfortunately, the development of BZTT and CLP-S has been halted; the tool is no longer available.

In this context, we could mention many other works (such as, e.g. [DEL 01]) which used constraint solving for validation of formal models.

Another interesting related work is the Setlog [DOV 00] constraint solver. Compared to PROB, Setlog has powerful unification procedure, but only deals with sets and has problems dealing with larger sets.[5]

14.3. Implementation of the PROB constraint solver

14.3.1. *Architecture*

14.3.1.1. *Overview*

The PROB kernel can be viewed as a constraint solver for the basic datatypes of B (and Z) and the various operators on it. It supports Booleans, integers, user-defined base types, pairs, records and inductively: sets, relations, functions and sequences. These datatypes and operations are embedded inside B predicates, which are made up of the usual logical connectives ($\wedge, \vee, \Rightarrow, \Leftrightarrow, \neg$) and typed universal ($\forall x.P \Rightarrow Q$) and existential ($\exists x.P \wedge Q$) quantification. An overview of the various solvers residing within the PROB kernel can be seen in Figure 14.2. We explain these parts and their history in the following sections.

14.3.1.2. *Coroutines and determinism*

All versions of PROB have been developed using SICStus Prolog. The initial versions of PROB tried to delay enumeration and give priority to deterministic computations. This was first implemented using coroutines via the `when` metapredicate. More precisely, choice points (such as a predicate $x \in \{1, 2\}$) were guarded by a `when` predicate to ensure that:

– either enough information was available to resolve the choice point deterministically;

– or the solver has switched to enumeration mode.

Later, most of the uses of `when` were replaced by the more restricted but much faster `block` declarations.

14.3.1.3. *Controlling choice points via waitflags*

It was identified very quickly that a more fine-grained enumeration was required, in order to prioritize the choice points once the solver had switched

5 E.g. computing the union of two intervals `un(int(1,10),int(2,15),R)` takes minutes in setlog (4.6.17), while computing the B equivalent $1..10 \cup 2..15$ in PROB is instantaneous.

to enumeration mode. This led to the development of a *waitflags* library which stores choice points and their expected number of solutions. The idea was that whenever the PROB kernel was to create a choice point it would have to:

1) estimate the number of solutions for the choice points;

2) obtain a "waitflag" variable from the library;

3) block on this variable and only execute the choice point once this variable had been grounded.

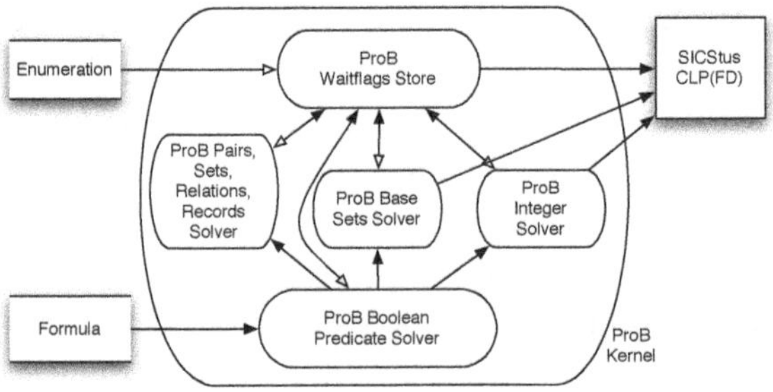

Figure 14.2. *A view of the* PROB *kernel*

The grounding of the waitflags was conducted and explicitly controlled by the kernel in the enumeration phase.

14.3.1.4. *Coping with large datavalues*

This scheme was later refined further driven by the requirements of the data validation application (see section 14.1.3), in particular the requirement to deal with large integers and large relations. Indeed, initially PROB represented sets using Prolog lists. This scheme clearly breaks down for larger sets, and a second representation for fully known sets was introduced. This representation used the AVL library of SICStus and guaranteed for instance membership checks with logarithmic complexity (in the size of the set). It is vital that the PROB kernel uses the AVL representation rather than the list representation whenever possible. For this, a special priority of 0 was introduced in the waitflags library: it is used for those operations that are deterministic *and* are guaranteed to produce data values in an efficient representation.

14.3.1.5. *Integrating CLP(FD)*

Initially, ProB provided its own support for arithmetic. This was obviously less efficient than the built-in CLP(FD) library of SICStus Prolog. However, at the time SICStus discouraged the joint use of coroutines and CLP(FD). This issue was solved in version 4.1 of SICStus Prolog and we then started to integrate CLP(FD) into the ProB kernel. After the introduction, a few more issues were uncovered which led to erroneous results or segmentation faults when CLP(FD) was used in conjunction with coroutines. These issues have now been sorted out, and CLP(FD) can now be reliably used for improved solving of arithmetic constraints. ProB still has the option of being able to run without CLP(FD), falling back on the more limited Prolog implementation of arithmetic in the ProB kernel. This can have two uses: in case a B specification manipulates large numbers the CLP(FD) library will generate overflow exceptions. (The ProB kernel catches those exceptions when they occur directly upon posting an arithmetic constraint. In this case ProB falls back to the Prolog implementation, which uses Prolog's arbitrary precision integers. However, this scheme cannot be applied if the exception occurs later, e.g. due to some instantiation of an unbound variable.) Also, for low-level B machines, which do not require constraint solving, the posting of CLP(FD) constraints induces a certain overhead, which can be avoided by turning CLP(FD) off.

We also investigated using the CLP(B) solver from SICStus Prolog 4. This, however, was less successful. The solver often had problems with larger formulas. For example, CLP(B) runs out of memory after about 5 min on the most complicated SATLIB example in [HOW 10] (flat200-90 with 600 Boolean variables and 2237 Clauses), whereas ProB solves it under 2 s.

14.3.1.6. *Linking solvers via reification*

Much later, inspired by an industrial case study [HAL 11] requiring solving very big constraints, we realized the importance of reification as a way of linking various parts of the ProB kernel. Indeed, propagation of information from one solver of ProB to another was often suboptimal, which became apparent in this case study.

CLP(FD) provides reification for certain constraints. For example, one can post the constraint `R #<=> (Y #> 0)`. This can serve as a way to link CLP(FD) with another solver:

– We can block a coroutine on the variable R; this coroutine will be triggered when the truth value of the test Y #> 0 is known. This way information propagates from CLP(FD) to the other solver.

– In turn, if this coroutine can decide that Y #> 0 must either be true or false it can simply set the variable R to either 0 or 1. This way information propagates the other solver to CLP(FD).

We have provided reification for the arithmetic operators via CLP(FD) and for the basic set operators of B $x \in S$, $x \notin S$, $S \subseteq S'$, $S \subset S'$, $S \not\subseteq S'$, $S \not\subset S'$ as well as $x = y$ and $x \neq y$ in the PROB kernel itself. The kernel tries to avoid setting up choice points whenever possible, using reified versions instead. For example, to compute $f(x)$ with $f = \{1 \mapsto 0, 2 \mapsto 2\}$ we could reify $x = 1$ and wait until the result of this test is known. Once it is known, we can compute the result of $f(x)$.[6] This mechanism is used in many places of the kernel, providing support for operators such as ∪, ∩, ...

14.3.1.7. *Challenges*

One challenge is that PROB tries to catch well-definedness errors, such as division by zero, the application of a function outside of its domain or applying the maximum operator to an empty set. To some extent, this hinders constraint propagation (e.g. from $10/y = 5$ we cannot infer that $y = 2$ unless we also know that $y \neq 0$) and makes the implementation of the solver more complicated.

Another issue is that upon encountering something like $x/y = 10 \wedge y = 0$, the PROB kernel cannot directly raise an error; it could be that some other constraint restricts y to be non-zero. The solution here is to post-pone raising an error until enumeration is complete. Other technical challenges are related to graceful treatment of timeouts.

14.3.2. *Validation*

PROB is being used as a tool of class T2 according to the norm [CEN 11] for data validation within Alstom and Siemens. A tool of class T2 "supports the test or verification of the design or executable code, where errors in the

6 Obviously, we would also wait on the output value being known and propagate information backwards. i.e. once we know that $f(x) = 0$ we can infer that $x = 1$.

tool can fail to reveal defects but cannot directly create errors in the executable software" [CEN 11, section 3.1.43]. However, we strive for PROB to be also used as a tool of class T3, i.e. a tool that "generates outputs which can directly or indirectly contribute to the executable code (including data) of the safety related system" [CEN 11, section 3.1.44]. To achieve this, a validation report is being maintained along with extensive testing and validation infrastructure.

14.3.2.1. *Testing and continuous integration*

PROB contains unit tests, integration and regression tests as well as model check tests for mathematical laws. All of these tests are run automatically on our continuous integration platform "Jenkins".[7] When a test fails, an email is sent automatically to the PROB development team.

14.3.2.2. *Self- model check with mathematical laws*

With this approach, we use PROB's model checker to check itself, in particular the PROB kernel and the B interpreter. The idea is to formulate a wide variety of mathematical laws and then use the model checker to ensure that no counterexample to these laws can be found. Definitively, PROB now checks itself for over 500 mathematical laws. These even uncovered several bugs in the underlying SICStus Prolog compiler using self model check, e.g.:

– The Prolog `findall` sometimes dropped a list constructor, which means that instead of `[[]]` it sometimes returned `[]`. In terms of B, this meant that instead of $\{\varnothing\}$ we received the empty set $\varnothing$. This violated some of our mathematical laws about sets. This bug was reported to SICS, and it was fixed in SICStus Prolog 4.0.2.

– A bug in the AVL library (notably in the predicate `avl_max` computing the maximum element of an AVL-tree) was found and reported to SICS. The bug was fixed in SICStus Prolog 4.0.5.

14.3.2.3. *Test coverage*

The above validation techniques are complemented by code coverage analysis techniques. In particular, we try to ensure that the unit tests and the self-model checks (section 14.3.2.2) above cover all predicates and clauses of the PROB kernel.

7 See http://en.wikipedia.org/wiki/Jenkins_(software).

14.3.2.4. *Positive and negative evaluation*

For data validation, all properties and assertions are checked twice, both positively and negatively. Indeed, PROB has two Prolog predicates to evaluate B predicates: one positive version which will succeed and enumerate solutions if the predicate is true and the another is a negative version, which will succeed if the predicate is false and then enumerate solutions to the negation of the predicate. The reason for the existence of these two Prolog predicates is that Prolog's built-in negation is generally unsound and cannot be used to enumerate solutions in case of failure.

For a formula to be classified as true the positive Prolog predicate must succeed *and* the negative Prolog predicate must fail, introducing a certain amount of redundancy (admittedly with common error modes). In fact, if both the positive and negative Prolog predicates would succeed for a particular B predicate then a bug in PROB would have been uncovered. If both fail, then either the B predicate is undefined or we have again a bug in PROB.

This validation aspect can detect errors in the predicate evaluation parts of PROB i.e. the treatment of the Boolean connectives $\vee$, $\wedge$, $\Rightarrow$, $\neg$, $\Leftrightarrow$, quantification $\forall$, $\exists$, and the various predicate operators such as $\in$, $\notin$, $=$, $\neq$, $<$, ... This redundancy can not detect bugs inside expressions (e.g. $+$, $-$, ...) or substitutions (but the other validation aspects mentioned above can).

14.4. Added value of constraint programming

14.4.1. *Cost of development*

The first version of PROB was made available about 10 years ago. Before that, various experimental prototypes had been under development since about 1999. A reasonably large team of researchers has since then helped in developing, maintaining and improving the tool. Initial usage concentrated on animation and model checking. The first industrial usage for data validation started at the end of 2008, and PROB has been used in industry to that effect since 2009.

14.4.2. *User feedback*

The animation and model checking capabilities have helped many users understand and debug their specifications. On many occasions, errors were found in proven models. Various other tools and techniques have been built on top of PROB, leading to over 400 citations of the two main articles about PROB[LEU 03, LEU 08].

For data validation, the tool has achieved a reduction from one man-month to several minutes for validating a new railway configuration [LEU 11]. The tool has also discovered errors that were not previously seen. The PROB tool is now in relatively widespread use in the railway domain (Siemens, Alstom, ClearSy, Systerel, ...), and the university spin-off company Formal Mind has been created for commercial exploitation.

14.4.3. *Was it difficult/necessary for the end user to understand constraint technology?*

The goal of PROB was always (and still is) to provide automated validation of high-level specifications without the user having to understand constraint solving. For many industrial specifications, this goal has now been achieved, but obviously sometimes debugging is still necessary. Maybe surprisingly, many B specifications can be animated by PROB out of the box. The tool now provides external B predicates which can be inserted into a specification to help debug a B specification when run by PROB and help identify (performance) problems. Also, sometimes user annotations are required to mark certain infinite B functions as symbolic, so as to prevent PROB from trying to expand them.[8] But the long-term goal is to further increase the automation, and even to be able for ordinary users to describe their own constraint solving problems in B and have them solved using PROB.

14.4.4. *Comparison with non-constraint solving tools*

We have already discussed the proof-based BToolkit animator earlier in the paper. In the meantime, a variety of other tools have been developed for animating or model checking high-level specifications. These tools, such as Brama [SER 07] and AnimB [MÉT 10] for Event-B or TLC [YU 99] for TLA$^+$, rely on naive enumeration. They can be used if the models are

8 In particular in Event-B [ABR 10] users currently have to axiomatize their own transitive closure, which poses problems if not dealt with symbolically.

relatively concrete, possibly by providing additional animation values in the setup of the tools. However, there is little chance in using such tools for constraint-based checking (section 14.1.4). For example, TLC takes hours to find an isomorphism for two graphs with 9 nodes (using a specification similar to the one seen in section 14.1.1.1; see [LEU 11] for more details). TLC however, can be very efficient for concrete models, where the overhead of constraint solving provides no practical advantage.

14.4.5. *Comparison with other technologies*

In the past few years, we have also investigated a variety of alternate technologies to replace or complement the constraint solver of ProB: BDD-Datalog- based approaches, SAT- and SMT-solving techniques. We have given up the BDD-approach very quickly (see, e.g. [PLA 09]): due to the lack of data types that are more abstract than bit vectors, the complexity of a direct translation from B was too high, even for small models.

For SAT, we have implemented an alternate backend for first-order B in [PLA 12] using the Kodkod interface [TOR 07]. For certain complicated constraints, in particular those involving relational operators, this approach fared very well. The power of clause learning and intelligent backtracking are a distinct advantage here over classical constraint solvers. However, for arithmetic the SAT approach usually has problems scaling to larger integers.

As an example, take the following set comprehension with 49,646 solutions. The ProB solver takes 1.36 s to find the solutions, while the Kodkod-SAT approach takes 145 s on the same hardware:

```
{x,y,z|x:1..10000 \& z = x/y \& z:200..500 \& y : 10..20}
```

Quite often, the SAT approach is better for inconsistent predicates, while the ProB constraint solver often fared better when the predicates were satisfiable. Also, the SAT approach often has problems dealing with large data and cannot deal with unbounded values or with infinite or higher-order functions. Here, an SMT-based approach could be more promising. We have also experimented with SMT-solvers, in particular a SMT-plugin for Event-B [DEH]. So far, the results were rather disappointing, but this may be due to the translation rather than the SMT solvers used. For a cruise control case study of [HAL 11], the SAT and SMT alternatives were not successful in solving the constraints.

14.4.6. *Future plans*

We are working on reducing the overhead of using B compared to directly encoding problems in a lower-level language such as Prolog. To that end, a partial evaluator has already been developed, which can specialize the PROB interpreter for a particular B specification. A long-term research challenge is to be able to use B and PROB as a programming language and as a constraint solving language.

Other avenues that are being pursued are parallel versions of PROB improved symmetry breaking during constraint solving, better constraint solving over unbounded integers (i.e. without a finite domain) using CHR or CHR-like techniques.

14.4.7. *Lessons*

Constraint logic programming in particular and constraint solving in general has a lot to offer for formal methods, and new applications are popping up all the time. Constraint solving can be made to deal with large data, something which is very difficult with SAT-based approaches. The combination of model checking and constraint solving can be very useful, allowing to express certain problems very concisely. Constraint solving is often good at finding solutions; but not so good at detecting unsatisfiable predicates.

The use of Prolog to implement PROB was both a blessing and a curse. SICStus Prolog is a very efficient Prolog engine, and the efficiency and memory consumption of PROB was often very satisfactory. Indeed, in the context of Event-B PROB often had fewer efficiency problems with large specifications than Java-based tools. However, in some aspects the use of Prolog prevents certain optimizations: we cannot easily re-order lists on the fly (e.g. to keep them sorted and remove duplicates); it is difficult to cache results (e.g. when expanding set comprehensions) because backtracking undoes bindings and assert/retract is expensive.

In conclusion, constraint solving has provided the foundation for many novel tools and techniques to validate formal models. While SAT- and SMT-based techniques have also played an increasingly important role in this area, constraint solving approaches have advantages when dealing with large data.

PROB is available for download at `http://www.stups.uni-duesseldorf.de/ProB`. An online logic calculator with examples is available at: `http://www.stups.uni-duesseldorf.de/ProB/index.php5/ProB_Logic_Calculator`.

14.5. Acknowledgments

We would thank all those people who have contributed toward the development of PROB and without whom the tool would not be where it is now: Michael Butler, Fabian Fritz, Marc Fontaine, Corinna Spermann and many more.

14.6. Bibliography

[ABR 96] ABRIAL J.-R., *The B-Book*. Cambridge University Press, 1996.

[ABR 10] ABRIAL J.-R., *Modeling in Event-B: System and Software Engineering*. Cambridge University Press, 2010.

[AMB 02] AMBERT F., BOUQUET F., CHEMIN S., *et al.*, "BZ-testing-tools: a tool-set for test generation from Z and B using constraint logic programming", *Proceedings FATES'02*, Technical Report, INRIA, pp. 105–120, August 2002.

[BCO 99] B-Core (UK) Ltd, Oxon, UK, *B-Toolkit, On-line manual*, 1999. Available at http://www.b-core.com/ONLINEDOC/Contents.html.

[BAD 05] BADEAU F., AMELOT A., "Using B as a high level programming language in an industrial project: Roissy VAL", in TREHARNE H., KING S., HENSON M., *et al.*, (eds.), *Proceedings ZB'2005*, LNCS 3455, pp. 334–354. 2005.

[BEH 99] BEHM P., BENOIT P., FAIVRE A., *et al.*, "Météor: a successful application of B in a large project", in WING J. M., WOODCOCK J., DAVIES J. (eds.), *World Congress on Formal Methods*, LNCS 1708, pp. 369–387. 1999.

[BOI 00] BOITE O., Méthode B et validation des invariants ferroviaires, Master's Thesis, Denis Diderot University, 2000.

[BOI 02] BOITE O., "Automatiser les preuves d'un sous-langage de la méthode B", *Technique et Science Informatiques*, vol. 21, no. 8, pp. 1099–1120, 2002.

[BOU 02] BOUQUET F., LEGEARD B., PEUREUX F., "CLPS-B – a constraint solver for B", in KATOEN J.-P., STEVENS P., (eds.), *Proceedings TACAS'02*, LNCS 2280, pp. 188–204, 2002.

[BOW 98] BOWEN J., "Animating the semantics of VERILOG using Prolog", UNU/IIST Technical Report no. 176, United Nations University, Macau, 1999.

[CEN 11] CENELEC, Railway applications – communication, signalling and processing systems – software for railway control and protection systems, Technical Report EN50128, European Standard, 2011.

[CLE 09] CLEARSY, Atelier B, user and reference manuals, Aix-en-Provence, France, 2009. Available at http://www.atelierb.eu/.

[DEH] DEHARBE D., FONTAINE P., GUYOT Y., *et al.,* "Smt solvers for rodin", *Proceedings ABZ'2012*, LNCS. Springer.

[DEL 01] DELZANNO G., PODELSKI A., "Constraint-based deductive model checking", *STTT*, vol. 3, no. 3, pp. 250–270, 2001.

[DOL 03] DOLLÉ D., Essamé D., Falampin J., "B dans le tranport ferroviaire, L'expérience de Siemens transportation systems", *Technique et Science Informatiques*, vol. 22, no. 1, pp. 11–32, 2003.

[DOV 00] DOVIER A., PIAZZA C., PONTELLI E., *et al.,* "Sets and constraint logic programming", *ACM Transactions on Programming Languages and Systems*, vol. 22, no. 5, pp. 861–931, 2000.

[ESS 07] ESSAMÉ D., DOLLÉ D., "B in large-scale projects: the Canarsie line CBTC experience", in JULLIAND J., KOUCHNARENKO O., (eds.), *Proceedings B'2007*, LNCS 4355, pp. 252–254, Springer-Verlag, 2007.

[HAL 11] HALLERSTEDE S., LEUSCHEL M., "Constraint-based deadlock checking of high-level specifications", *TPLP*, vol. 11, nos. 4–5, pp. 767–782, 2011.

[HAY 89] HAYES I., JONES C.B., "Specifications are not (necessarily) executable", *Softw. Eng. J.*, vol. 4, no. 6, pp. 330–338, November 1989.

[HOW 10] HOWE J.M., KING A., "A pearl on SAT solving in Prolog", in BLUME M., KOBAYASHI N., VIDAL G., (eds.), *Proceedings FLOPS'10*, LNCS 6009, pp. 165–174, Springer, 2010.

[KIN 01] KING L., GUPTA G., PONTELLI E., "Verification of a controller for BART", in WINTER V.L., BHATTACHARYA S., (eds.), *High Integrity Software*, Kluwer Academic Publishers, pp. 265–299, 2001.

[LEU 03] LEUSCHEL M., BUTLER M., "ProB: a model checker for B", in ARAKI K., GNESI S., MANDRIOLI D., (eds.), *FME 2003: Formal Methods*, LNCS 2805, pp. 855–874, Springer-Verlag, 2003.

[LEU 08] LEUSCHEL M., BUTLER M.J., "ProB: an automated analysis toolset for the B method", *STTT*, vol. 10, no. 2, pp. 185–203, 2008.

[LEU 11] LEUSCHEL M., FALAMPIN J., FRITZ F., *et al.*, "Automated property verification for large scale b models with ProB", *Formal Asp. Comput.*, vol. 23, no. 6, pp. 683–709, 2011.

[MÉT 10] MÉTAYER C., AnimB 0.1.1, 2010. Available at http://wiki.event-b.org/index.php/AnimB.

[PLA 10] PLAGGE D., LEUSCHEL M., "Seven at a stroke: LTL model checking for high-level specifications in B, Z, CSP, and more", *STTT*, vol. 11, pp. 9–21, 2010.

[PLA 12] PLAGGE D., LEUSCHEL M., "Validating B, Z and TLA+ using ProB and Kodkod", in GIANNAKOPOULOU D., MÉRYD. (eds.), *Proceedings FM'2012*, LNCS 7436, pp. 372–386. Springer, 2012.

[PLA 09] PLAGGE D., LEUSCHEL M., LOPATKIN I., *et al.*, "SAL, Kodkod, and BDDs for validation of B models, lessons and outlook", *Proceedings AFM 2009*, pp. 16–22, 2009.

[SER 07] SERVAT T., "Brama: a new graphic animation tool for B models", in JULLIAND J., KOUCHNARENKO O., (eds.), *Proceedings B'2007*, LNCS 4355, pp. 274–276. Springer-Verlag, 2007.

[SIE 09] SIEMENS, "B method - optimum safety guaranteed", *Imagine*, vol. 10, pp. 12–13, June 2009.

[TOR 07] TORLAK E., JACKSON D., "Kodkod: a relational model finder", in GRUMBERG O., HUTH M., (eds.), *Proceedings TACAS'07*, LNCS 4424, pp. 632–647, Springer-Verlag, 2007.

[WIN 98] WINIKOFF M., DART P., KAZMIERCZAK E., "Rapid prototyping using formal specifications", in *Proceedings of the 21st Australasian Computer Science Conference*, pp. 279–294, Perth, Australia, February 1998.

[YU 99] YU Y., MANOLIOS P., LAMPORT L., "Model checking TLA$^+$ specifications", in PIERRE L., KROPF T., (eds.), *Proceedings of CHARME'99*, LNCS 1703, pp. 54–66, Springer-Verlag, 1999.

15

Unified Train Driving Policy

A patchwork of railway modernization poses the challenge of developing a uniform description and modeling method capable of capturing, on the same semantic ground and in faithful terms, the logic of outdated, modern and emerging signaling and train operation principles and, at the same time, offering a foundation to experiment with some yet unexplored directions. This paper presents a domain-specific formal modeling language uniformly addressing fixed and moving block principles in both discrete and continuous (inertial) contexts.

15.1. Introduction

Low rolling resistance makes railways highly efficient for hauling heavy loads over large distances. It also means that a train cannot be stopped at short notice. To avoid accidents, trains must be separated in temporal or spatial dimensions. Both approaches are applied albeit at differing levels [PAC 09, VLA 09]. The spatial model is dominant at the microscopic level, also known as railway signaling and interlocking. Temporal analysis is primarily aimed at the network-level optimization and the construction of train schedules. The two are closely interlinked: over-zealous safety margins may result in uneconomical capacity while a high-performance yet potentially unsafe railway is never acceptable. The situation is further complicated by the fact that there is no single approach to signaling and even within national boundaries it is not uncommon to see a mixture of diverse signaling solutions.

Chapter written by Alexei ILIASOV, Ilya LOPATKIN and Alexander ROMANOVSKY.

An objective of this work is to help signaling engineers to reason about safety and performance within the scope of a single railway model and thus help them to design safe railway networks that achieve higher capacity. To achieve this goal, we propose a modeling notation called Unified Train Driving Policy (UTDP). It captures in a uniform manner and exposes interrelations of concepts that are often treated separately: track topology and gradients, signaling, fixed speed regime, platform assignment, dynamic rerouting, train schedules and dwelling times, dynamic train headway control, acceleration and deceleration curves, automated train operation, real-time rescheduling, etc.

The power of the approach arises from a few simple yet expressive modeling concepts. We apply the hybrid systems modeling approach that interleaves discrete state changes with continuous evolution [AKH 07, RIV 08, PLA 10]. This makes it possible to capture the interaction of a physical phenomenon such as a moving train with a discrete control system such as the interlocking control and the route reservation systems.

A train considered in isolation is not challenging to understand: one sensible abstraction is an interval (a train) on a ray (train path). Interval length remains constant while the position monotonically increases. In other words, a train is completely characterized by its speed function $v(t)$, length l and some initial speed and position values. A great deal of complexity arises when there is a multiplicity of trains traveling over intersecting paths. Unconstrained train progress may lead to collisions or derailments. In addition, the equipment needed to realize diverging and converging paths must also be protected. Thus, there needs to be some form of coordination between trains.

Train speed may be under the direct control of a driver or controlled automatically by an onboard train computer communicating with infrastructure area control computers.

There is a number of such coordination approaches. The contemporary ones focus on spatial separation between trains and point protection. Depending on the way train proximity control is realized, one can distinguish two major approach classes: fixed block signaling and moving block signaling. Each class is composed of a considerable number of unique approaches owing primarily to independent development within national boundaries. UTDP attempts to give a common foundation over which all such approaches may be formulated and fruitfully reasoned about.

Railway computerization and advances in train proximity control make railway operation less dependent on unreliable human driving. An onboard train computer is capable of assessing the dangers and speed restrictions on the horizon of a train and generating acceleration and deceleration curves. Such systems are already realized in protected environments such as underground and in airport rapid transit systems. It is envisaged in [TSL 12] that by 2030 the whole UK rail network will be based on virtual signals – a form of fully digital interface between infrastructure and trains.

15.2. Overview

The primary subject of UTDP is the definition of laws of train movement that result in a safe railway operation, achieving optimum capacity. The reasoning about capacity on the same level as safety means that one is able to formulate a range of Quality of Service (QoS) criteria such as average train speed, minimum speed at a given location and maximum separation between trains.

UTDP is used to model, verify and analyze fixed block and moving block signaling, or some combination of the two, in the context of partial or completely automated train operation [PAC 09, VLA 09, WIN 09]. It is an evolution of a previous approach based on Event-B [ILI 12, ILI 13].

At the core of UTDP is a formal notation used to express both static and dynamic properties of railway. The static part is based on a formal domain-specific language [ROM 12] and captures railway topology, route boundaries and track side equipment. The dynamic part describes train properties and the way trains move over the track. UTDP has an *executional semantics* which is the simulation of railway operation; it also offers a *proof semantics* to verify safety and QoS conditions. The aspects of the latter are the focus of this paper. We will now briefly overview the essential concepts of UTDP.

In UTDP, all stateful parts of railway are known as actors. A train and a point (a track switching device) are two possible examples of an actor. New actor types may be defined in a model (i.e. a station controller) and all actors are permitted to interact with each other through some shared state.

An actor lifecycle is split into three stages: continuous *evolution* (e.g. a train moving in accordance with the laws of physics), *mutation* (a step change due to a logical trigger) and *hibernation* (inability to evolve or mutate).

The evolution of a train is described by a continuous or piece-wise continuous function of the effective longitudinal force. It defines a smooth progression from one position to another and accounts for effects such as air drag, gradient, rolling resistance and variable tractive effort. A mutation is a change of law governing an actor evolution; it may be dictated, for instance, by signaling logic or speed regime. An actor goes into hibernation when it is unable to evolve. One example is a stationary train waiting for a permissive (i.e. green or yellow) signal aspect.

UTDP tries to balance the terseness and expressiveness of notation by offering several modeling layers: a high-level, *constraint-based* definition indirectly characterizing actor evolution and mutation laws; construction of custom actor types from scratch or on the basis of existing ones; and a fine-grained specification level for a direct definition of evolution and mutation rules.

For all but the tiniest of networks, it is impractical to attempt to characterize a train actor by directly defining its evolution function as this amounts to an infinitely accurate prediction of future train behavior. Mutation allows the composition of an actor from simpler actors where each constituent actor is constructed dynamically in reaction to the evolution of other actors. This activity is central to the UTDP *modeling notation* – a high-level specification layer operating in terms of *mutation constraints*: rules from which concrete actor mutations are computed on the fly.

The following is an example of a UTDP *constraint* applying to a train actor.

$$\boxed{\textbf{stop on}\ \text{entering}(\mathsf{L.R1})\ \textbf{when}\ \text{occ}(\mathsf{AA}, \mathsf{AB}) \vee \text{reverse}(\mathsf{P102})}$$

The constraint influences train speed to ensure that the train stops at a certain position. Term $\text{entering}(\mathsf{L.R1})$ is a predicate binding a set of trains, specifically those trains on line L that have the beginning of route $\mathsf{R1}$ on their *horizon*, i.e. can potentially travel over the route. Predicate $\text{occ}(\mathsf{AA}, \mathsf{AB}) \vee \text{reverse}(\mathsf{P102})$ is a *guarding* condition defining states where the constraint applies. In this case, it speaks about the states of train detection circuits (equipment for detecting sectional track occupation) AA, AB and the state of point P102. On the whole, the rule requires a train traveling over line L to be stationary when its head reaches the start of route R1 provided circuits AA, AB report occupation (presence of another train or a fault) or point P102 is set to reverse. This is a trivial example of a control table rule expressed in UTDP.

It is possible to reason about signaling based on the moving block principle where train separation is controlled by real-time proximity sensing and speed control. For instance, constraint

$$\boxed{\textbf{stop on } \mathrm{entering}(\textbf{any } \mathrm{train})}$$

states that a train must stop when its head is about to enter a region occupied by another or the same train.

To verify safety, a signaling engineer must define applicable *hazards*. By a hazard, we understand a negative form of constraint – one that should never be satisfiable for any valid configuration. One example of a hazard is train collision. With the "brick-wall" principle[1], it may be stated as follows:

$$\boxed{\textbf{hazard proceed on } \mathrm{entering}(\textbf{any } \mathrm{train})}$$

i.e. two trains may be adjacent only when the following train is stationary. One may also want to complement this rule with the prohibition of a train driving backwards:

$$\boxed{\textbf{hazard} \ \ldots \ \textbf{any } t \textbf{ where } t \in \mathrm{train} \textbf{ in } t.\mathrm{speed} < 0}$$

Notation $a.\mathrm{prop}$ denotes a labeled state component of actor a.

It is important to determine the appropriate level of model fidelity. The following are the three major classes that we have learned to distinguish:

---

1 The brick-wall safety principle states that a train in front may stop instantaneously irrespective of its current speed.

– a model of movement permissions; such a model describes safe positions of a train without stating how fast a train may go and how quickly it must get to the destination; there is no train inertia in this model – train acceleration and deceleration are unbounded;

– a refinement of the above overlays a movement permission with a discrete speed profile; train inertia is modeled by constant acceleration and deceleration values while resistance and gravity forces are disregarded;

– train behavior is modeled to utmost precision including weight distribution, specific engine performance, gradients and carriage couplers.

The first layer captures the *fixed block* principle realized over train detection circuits determining the train's position in large, discrete steps. It also addresses the *moving block* principle based on continuous detection of the train's position. Safety properties of the first layer may be translated into set-theoretic propositions in the first-order logic, amenable to automated verification.

The second layer crudely captures the effect of train inertia and thus makes reasoning about upper and lower speed bounds meaningful. Acceleration and deceleration forces must be defined to overapproximate train acceleration and braking distances so that the safety proofs hold in respect to a more accurate model.

The final layer may be used for safety analysis when the margins must be tight but its primary application is likely to be the assessment, via a computer-based simulation, of capacity, energy efficiency, operational costs and other dynamic parameters. Crucially, such an assessment is based on the same model as the proof of operational safety, thus removing a potential mismatch between dynamic and static models.

15.3. Semantics

A UTDP specification defines a *world* of *actors* where a world is a set of actors $\mathrm{W} \in \mathbb{P}(\mathrm{A})$ and an actor A is a five-tuple (D, S, h, e, m) made of the following components:

– actor *state* (D, S) composed of discrete, D, and continuous, S, components; D may have an arbitrary type while S must be a tuple of real values: $S \subseteq \mathbb{R} \times \cdots \times \mathbb{R}$. D and S may be read by any actor but updated only by their owning actor. An indexed set of all D's, $\{D_i\}_{i \in \mathrm{A}}$ is denoted by $\mathbf{D}$.

– a *horizon* h defined as a function $h \in \mathrm{W} \to \mathbb{R}_+ \cup \{*\}$. A current horizon value $h(w)$ defines for how long, if at all, an actor may evolve:

- value $h(w) \in \mathbb{R}_+, h(w) > 0$ defines the longest extent of time the actor may evolve before experiencing a mutation (however, evolutions and mutations of other actors may force an earlier mutation point);

- $h(w) = 0$ demands an immediate mutation;

- $h(w) = *$ indicates that the actor is *hibernating*, that is, not able, in the current state w, to evolve or mutate.

– a continuous in $\mathbb{R}$ *evolution* function $e \in \mathbf{D} \times \mathbb{R}_+ \to S$. Value $e(w, t)$ gives the result of an evolution starting from world state w and lasting for t units of time;

– a *mutation* function $m \in \mathrm{W} \to \mathrm{A}$ which replaces the current actor with a different one. In addition to complete actor change, it is also used to express an update of discrete state component D and change the laws of horizon, evolution and mutation.

World behavior is fully determined by the behavior of individual actors. An actor behavior is given by its horizon, evolution and mutation functions and thus both world and actors are *determinate*.

A behavior $B(w_0)$, $B \in \mathrm{W} \to \mathrm{seq}^{\omega}(\mathrm{W})$, of a world w_0 is an infinite chain of worlds $B(w_0) = \langle w_0 \rangle \frown B(w_1) = \langle w_0, w_1 \rangle \frown B(w_2) = \langle w_0, w_1, \ldots, w_n, \ldots \rangle$

In such a chain, some w_i may be obtained from a predecessor w_{i-1} following these steps:

1) compute actor horizons, $H = \{a \mapsto h(w_i) \mid a \in w_i \wedge a = (D, S, h, e, m)\}$;

2) filter out hibernating actors, $H' = H \setminus (\mathrm{A} \times \{*\})$;

3) if set H' is empty, then there is no change and $w_i = w_{i-1}$;

4) otherwise, determine the smallest horizon value, $l = \min\{h \mid a \mapsto h \in H'\}$, and a set of actors defining horizon l, $H'' = H'^{-1}[l]$;

5) if l is non-zero, compute a new world w_i by applying the evolution functions of all non-hibernating actors H' to the current world w_{i-1}. Since

evolution functions update disjoint parts of a world state, actor evolutions may be computed in any order or even concurrently;

6) if l is zero then w_i is defined by applying the mutation functions of actors H'' to world w_{i-1}. As in the case of evolution, mutations may be applied in any order.

The above steps (1–6) define a *world change function* F, $w_i = F(w_{i-1})$. We are interested in such definitions of F that world changes eventually stabilize and the chain defined by $B(w_0)$ is *stationary*. A stationary chain may be expressed as a concatenation of some finite prefix and an infinite sequence $\{u\}^\omega$, $u \in$ W:

$$B(w_0) = \langle w_0, w_1, \ldots, w_k, u \rangle \frown \langle u, \ldots, u, \ldots \rangle \qquad [15.1]$$

Equivalently, we require that there exists a world u such that it is a fixed point of F, $u = F(u)$.

DEFINITION 15.1 (Well-formedness).– *A UTDP specification is* well-formed *if there exists a fixed point of world change function F.*

The actor model provides a semantic underpinning for the *modeling language* of UTDP.

15.4. Modeling notation

The actor model is not adequate for constructing models of any complexity. In this section, we introduce the UTDP *modeling notation* based on the *constraint* concept and show how to use it to indirectly define horizon, evolution and mutation of actors, in particular actors modeling train progress through a railway network. A UTDP constraint defines a mutation law specific to a given actor. In other words, a combination of an actor and a constraint are used to compute how an actor mutates. Since constraints are shared by a class of actors, it turns out that an actor mutation function is dependent, in some non-trivial manner, on mutation functions of other actors.

As a simple illustration consider the diagram in Figure 15.1. The diagram depicts a *speed regime* (dashed line) overlaid by a train speed profile. Logically, a speed regime is fully defined by a speed constraint interval. However, a train must start braking some distance before the restriction applies and the exact point where this happens is dependent on the braking capability and the current train speed. In the diagram, the distance between advance warning (dashed triangle) and the actual start of restriction is exactly the braking distance $BD(t, u, x)$ of some train t approaching restriction x at speed u. The point where braking initiates may be different for some other train. UTDP constraints hide such details by offering a mechanism to dynamically determine appropriate actor mutation and evolution laws.

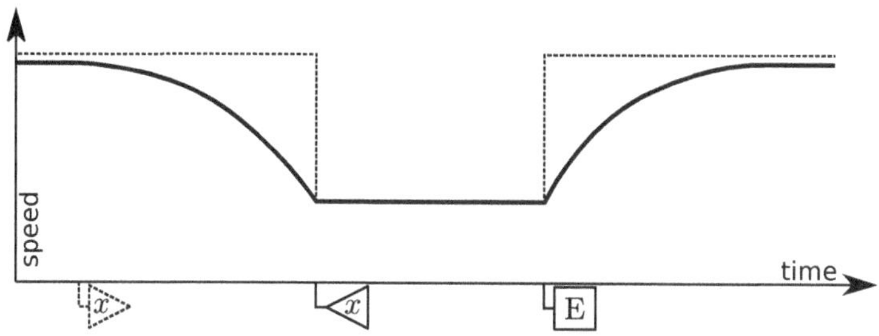

Figure 15.1. *Train progress in presence of speed restrictions. A dashed triangle is a forward restriction warning, a solid triangle is the start of a speed restriction and 'E' in square marks the restriction cancellation point*

The overall structure of a UTDP model is given in Figure 15.2.

frame *frm*	import of UTDP frame model
track *sch*	import of track topology
vehicles *tt*	import of a vehicle dynamic library
service *sp*	import of a service pattern
identifiers v	model constants and variables
attractors a	attractor definitions
actors Q	custom actor types
axioms $A(a, v, Q)$	axiomatic statements over identifiers and attractors
invariant $I(a, v, Q)$	an invariant predicate defining valid states
hazard H	actor constraints defining hazards
behavior B	actor constraints defining behaviour

Figure 15.2. *A summary of core UTDP notation*

Clauses **frame**, **track**, **vehicles** and **service** import definitions of UTDP actor types, railway topology (physical track graph overlaid with logical structuring pertinent to considered signaling laws), rolling stock properties (weight, length, acceleration and deceleration curves) and train schedules. All of these may also be defined programmatically in UTDP.

identifiers v are the model constants and variables. They have fixed types and may be used to construct expressions and predicates. In addition, variables may be dynamically updated to model the on-line update of signaling laws. Logically, model variables represent the discrete part of the state of an implicit *infrastructure* actor. Such an actor does not experience evolution (it has no continuous state) but can mutate to simulate the substitution of model variables. Constant and variable identifiers are initialized deterministically.

attractors define a set of labeled spatial or temporal locations. An attractor location may be fixed or dependent on an actor state. When it is fixed or changes in discrete steps aligned with actor mutation it is called a *peg* attractor. If an attractor position changes continuously (in time or space) and is aligned with an actor evolution then it is known as a *pin* attractor. The attractor concept plays the central role in binding constraints to actors. An example of a pin attractor is some fixed position on a track (where, for instance, a speed restriction sign – a form of constraint – is permanently placed). One example of a pin attractor is a location linked to a train position.

actors Q is a list of explicit class-like definitions describing UTDP actors. For actor types not defined via constraints, hibernation and evolution functions must be provided explicitly. Parts of an actor state are accessed using notation $actor.property$, e.g. t.speed.

axioms $A(a, v, Q)$ are labeled predicates over identifiers v, attractors a and states of actors Q. They postulate properties of v and a that help to reason about model well-formedness (Definition 15.1) and safety (section 15.5.3).

invariants $I(a, v, Q)$ state the invariant properties of actor states, including the infrastructure actor. They may refer to both discrete and continuous state parts. Both axioms and invariants are formulated in the first-order logic and are only given interpretation in the proof semantics.

hazard H is a set of constraints defining undesirable actor evolutions and mutations. It is the main objective of the proof semantics to demonstrate that that no actor evolution or mutation leads to the manifestation of a defined hazard.

Finally, the **behavior** section provides definitions of behavior constraints governing actor mutation.

The standard UTDP model of a train defines one or more actors per logical train. In the case of moving block, they are an actor modeling the physical train itself and *reservation* actor. Fixed block also requires an *unlocking* actor.

Each actor type is attracted by a certain class of *attractions*. An attraction limits the horizon of an actor and, generally, forces an actor mutation.

The role of a reservation actor is to maintain some movement authority (an extent of *safe* track onto which the train may move); it is positioned some distance in front of its train and its position changes in discrete steps during mutations. A reservation actor is attracted by station control boundaries, points and, in the case of the route-based signaling, route boundaries. An unlocking actor stays behind a train tail and unlocks train detection circuits one by one. Its position jumps from one detection circuit boundary to another. Note that there is no point actor: the point movement is modeled as an evolution of a reservation actor.

The rest of the section is organized as follows. In the first part we show how to reason about fixed block signaling using peg attractors. The second part shows some examples of pin attractors in the context of the moving block principle.

Consider the following UTDP specification.

track T
attractors peg a **to** entering(L.5)
behavior stop on a

It states that any train whose head is about to arrive at location L.5 must have speed zero. Location L.5 is 5 m from the start of line L – a line which must be defined in track topology T.

peg a **to** entering(L.5) is a *peg* attractor – an attractor whose position changes only during an actor mutation. There are other predefined train binders such as leaving(..) and over(..) and new ones may be defined by a user. We may also use the proposition logic to construct complex binders. For instance, **peg** a **to** entering(L.5) $\wedge$ over(L) states that a train must be entering L.5 and be on line L. An attractor may be associated with several physical locations at once, e.g. **peg** a **to** entering(L.5) $\vee$ leaving(L.920) matches a train head position at L.5 or a tail position at L.920.

One possible translation of constraint **stop on** entering(L.x) into the actor model is shown in Figure 15.3. A train experiences three mutations while approaching and driving past the location of the constraint. The second diagram in the figure has another constraint at L.y that forces a different acceleration curve.

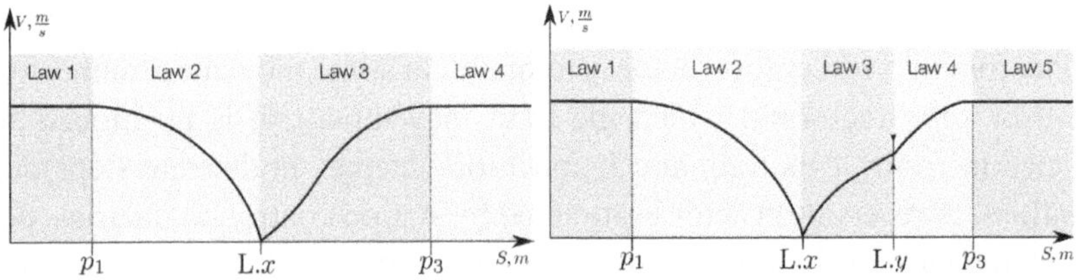

Figure 15.3. *A train speed profile determined by an attractor* **stop** *at location* L.x. *Locations* p_1, L.x, p_3 *are the train mutation points where the driving law changes*

Often two constraints positioned at a distance less than the maximum train braking distance logically overlap and may not be considered in isolation. An actor model must be generated in such a manner that it satisfies both constraints. For instance, in model

```
behavior
    stop on entering(L.x)
    speed 15..20 on entering(L.y)
```

location L.x is a short distance after L.y so that the second attractor makes a train go a bit slower for some time. If the speed constraint of the second attractor (in this case a speed region of 15 to 20 mph) was wider it might have had no effect on the choice of evolution law and speed profile would stay exactly the same as in the first figure. There is a simple iterative algorithm to determine the most constraining attractor on a horizon.

An attractor position may change dynamically. In the following example, a passing train "captures" a speed limit and, each time the train tail reaches the limit attractor position, moves it to the position of the train head.

```
identifiers s : Real
attractors peg a to entering(L.s)
behavior
    speed 10 on entering(a)
    set s ← self.head on leaving(a)
```

One possible application of dynamic reconfiguration is the modeling of a transport corridor where trains gradually level their speeds to reduce time spent braking and accelerating.

Peg attractors may be used to model various forms of the fixed block train signaling. A layout example and an excerpt of its signaling in UTDP are given in Figure 15.4 (the model uses a short-cut notation for in-place attractor definition). In fixed block signaling, a simple program (called a control table) helps a driver to maintain safe speed. The program observes the infrastructure state (points and train detection circuits) and interacts with a driver via track-side signals that communicate commands to a driver via color-coded messages. If a driver obeys the commands then, assuming the control table is correct, it may be shown that a train is never within a dangerous proximity to another train.

We can also change the position of an attractor by first attaching an attractor to a location associated with a model variable and then changing the variable value with the **set**:

```
identifiers
    p : Real
invariants
    p ∈ L.interval
behavior
    speed 10 on entering(L.p)
    set p ← min(self.head + 200, L.interval.to) on entering(L.p)
```

The model defines a constraint **speed** 10 at a variable position p: the position jumps forward when a train head arrives at p. This has the effect of a train constantly driving to a speed limit 10, located short (less than 200 m) distance ahead.

UTDP is not specific to fixed block; using pin attractors one may express various forms of the moving block principle. For instance,

```
behavior
    stop on entering(any train)
```

states that a train must stop when its head is about to enter a region occupied by another or same train. This avoids train collision and also satisfies the “brick-wall” safety principle.

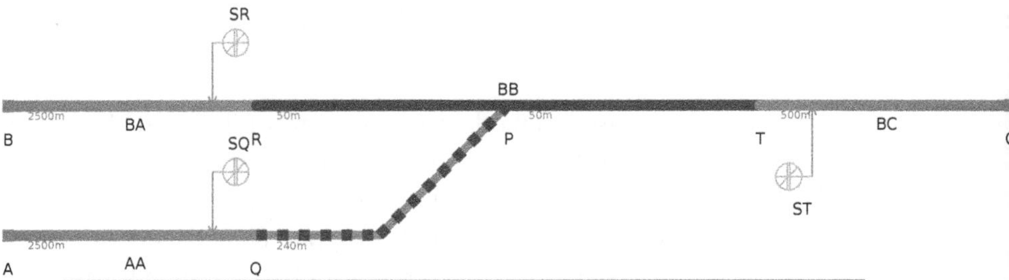


```
track flyout
behavior
    stop on entering(B_C.B_SR) when occc(BA) ∨ reverse(P)
    stop on entering(B_C.SR_C) when occ(BB, BC)
    stop on entering(A_C.A_SQ) when occ(AA)
    stop on entering(A_C.SQ_C) when occ(BB, BC) ∨ normal(P)
    stop on entering(C_A.C_ST) when occ(BC)
    stop on entering(C_A.ST_A) when occ(BB, AA) ∨ normal(P)
    stop on entering(C_B.C_ST) when occ(BC)
    stop on entering(C_B.ST_B) when occ(BB, BA) ∨ reverse(P)
    ...
```

Figure 15.4. *The layout of a simple junction and its fixed block signaling in UTDP. In the layout, the valid paths through the junction are* A_C, B_C, C_A *and* C_B*; signals* SR, SQ *and* ST *define routes* B_SR, SR_C, ...*;* AA, BB, ... *are the train detection circuits that report the presence of absence of a train; point* P *is located on train detection circuit* BB*; finally,* R, Q, T *are the labels of train detection circuits boundaries*

A variation of the above allows a following train to track the speed of a train in front while maintaining a gap of g meters:

```
behavior
    any t where t ∈ train in speed t.speed on entering(t.rear − g)
    any t where t ∈ train in speed t.speed/2 on over[t.rear − g, t.rear]
```

The two constraints define a safety gap and force a following train to fall behind if it appears, from an adjoining route, too close to another train. One of the reasons for UTDP development is its ability to quickly assess the viability (safety and capacity) of non-conventional laws like the above.

15.5. Verification

Verifying railway operation safety – properties such as the avoidance of collision and absence of derailment – is an essential part of railway control and signaling. UTDP, being a formal notation, is well suited to serve as a foundation for the formulation and verification of formal correctness conditions. Our approach is based on the derivation, from a given UTDP specification, of a set of verification conditions, expressed in the first-order logic, that demonstrate the required safety properties.

To enable a meaningful verification process, UTDP defines notational constructs that introduce redundancy into a model. By comparing such redundant elements it becomes possible to detect problems such as omissions or underspecified constraints. Redundancy comes in the form of *invariants* and *hazards*. An invariant is a predicate over model constants, variables and attractors. Such a predicate must hold in an initial actor world and in all subsequent worlds. An additional role of an invariant is the propagation of assumptions about important actor states.

A hazard is a mirror symmetry of a behavioral constraint – the definition of a hazard uses the same notation but defines actor behavior that must not be present in a model. UTDP does not provide any implicit hazards and it is imperative that a user lists all the hazards deemed applicable in a given context.

In addition to demonstrating invariants and hazards, we must also prove that a given UTDP specification satisfies the well-formedness condition [15.1] and behavioral constraints are satisfiable.

In this chapter, due to space constraints, we focus on the latter and the related subject of hazards while omitting the discussion invariant-based reasoning and concrete verification conditions for proving well-formedness.

The *well-formedness* condition aims to establish the property of definition 15.1. The strategy is to insist on the existence of a global "bottom" world $\bot_W$ initializing a UTDP model and also requires that for each actor a there is an upper bound of evolution/mutation cycle $\top_a$. Thus an actor world eventually reduces to the *terminal* world $\top_{\mathrm{W}} = \{\top_i\}_{i \in \mathrm{A}}$ which is the maximum element in poset (W, F) and hence a fixed point of F:

$$B(w_0) = \left\langle \bot_{\mathrm{W}}, F^1(w_0), \ldots, F^k(w_0), \top_{\mathrm{W}} \right\rangle \frown \langle \top_{\mathrm{W}}, \ldots, \top_{\mathrm{W}}, \ldots \rangle \qquad [15.2]$$

We only briefly sketch the proof strategy. The existence of $\bot_{\mathrm{W}}$ is established by a syntactic constraint requiring that all actor states are initialized. The reachability of $\top_{\mathrm{W}}$ is shown by requiring that each actor $a \in \mathrm{A}$ eventually turns into $\top_A$. For this, we ask to exhibit, for every such actor a, a well-founded relation $R(a)$. For a train actor, as an example, such a relation is taken to be $R \in (\mathbb{R} \times \mathbb{R}) \leftrightarrow (\mathbb{R} \times \mathbb{R})$ where for some $(d, t) \in R$, d is the distance traveled and t is the time spent waiting while stationary. The existence of such R is predicated by the existence of upper bounds on time and distance components[2]. The latter is trivial as we consider only non-cyclic train paths. The former requires a proof that a is obstructed by other actors for a finite duration of time.

15.5.1. *Constraint satisfiability*

A constraint C is a tuple of $(\mathcal{A}, R, G)$ where:

– $\mathcal{A}$ is an attractor, $\mathcal{A} \in \mathrm{A} \leftrightarrow (\mathrm{A} \times \mathcal{L})$; here A is the set of actors and $\mathcal{L} = \mathbb{R} \times \{\mathtt{t}, \mathtt{s}\}$ is a temporal or spatial location;

– R is a mutation rule, $R \in \mathrm{A} \times \mathrm{W} \rightarrow \mathrm{A}$;

– G is a guard, $G \in \mathrm{W} \rightarrow \mathrm{BOOL}$.

For some actor $p \in \mathrm{A}$ expression $\mathcal{A}\langle p \rangle$ where $\mathcal{A}\langle p \rangle \subseteq \mathrm{A} \times \mathcal{L} = \mathcal{A}[\{p\}]$ defines the *attraction set* of actor p with respect to attractor $\mathcal{A}$. An attractor $\mathcal{A}$ and its declaring constraint are said to be *on the horizon* of p if the attraction set $\mathcal{A}\langle p \rangle$ is not empty. It is sometimes necessary to refer to the components of an attraction set: we write $\mathcal{A}^a\langle p \rangle$ to denote $\mathrm{prj}_1[\mathcal{A}\langle p \rangle]$ and $\mathcal{A}^l\langle p \rangle$ to denote $\mathrm{prj}_2[\mathcal{A}\langle p \rangle]$.

The set of attractor locations $\mathcal{A}^l\langle p \rangle$ has type $\mathcal{A}^l\langle p \rangle \in \mathbb{R} \times \{\mathtt{t}, \mathtt{s}\}$ where tags $\mathtt{t}$ and $\mathtt{s}$ define whether the location is temporal or spatial.

---

2 In addition, we must also take care to avoid certain cases of Zeno behavior that would otherwise pass the test of a well-founded R.

A set of constraints define a mutation program. For such a program to exist, constraints must satisfy certain feasibility properties. Intuitively, from some current non-terminal world $w \in \mathrm{W}$ it should be possible to compute the next world w' by mutating some or all of the world actors. Assume some non-terminal world w and consider a set of constraints,

$$\boxed{\textbf{behavior } C1, \ldots, Cn}$$

Each C_i defines a partial mutation rule R_i that may mutate some or none of the actors. To compute a next world w', it must hold that such a constraint set defines at least one actor mutation and whenever several constraints apply to a single actor it must be possible to *reconcile* such constraints by choosing one constraint out of the set. Assuming some world w, we can write this down as follows:

$$\begin{array}{l} \exists a, D \cdot a \in \mathrm{A} \wedge \varnothing \subset D \subseteq \{C_1, \ldots, C_n\} \wedge \\ \quad (\forall c \cdot c \in D \wedge c = (\mathcal{A}_c, R_c, G_c) \Rightarrow G_c(w) \wedge \mathcal{A}_c\langle a \rangle \neq \varnothing) \wedge \\ \quad \mathbf{rec}(w, D, a) = \{R\} \wedge \\ \quad a \mapsto w \in \mathrm{dom}(R) \end{array} \qquad [15.3]$$

The above guarantees the existence of at least one new actor $R(a, w)$ in w'. The well-formedness property requires that $a \neq R(a, w)$ and thus w differs from w', i.e. w evolves to w'. It is impractical to apply condition [15.3] directly. Instead, we use a stronger criterion requiring that (1) at all times there exists at least one pair of an actor and an applicable constraint,

$$\begin{array}{l} \forall w \cdot w \in \mathrm{W} \Rightarrow \\ \quad \exists a, c \cdot a \in \mathrm{A} \wedge c \in \{C_1, \ldots, C_n\} \wedge \\ \qquad c = (\mathcal{A}, R, G) \wedge G(w) \wedge \mathcal{A}\langle a \rangle \wedge a \mapsto w \in \mathrm{dom}(R) \end{array} \qquad [15.4]$$

and (2) it is possible to reconcile an arbitrary non-empty subset of constraints:

$$\begin{array}{l} \forall w, a, D \cdot w \in \mathrm{W} \wedge a \in \mathrm{A} \wedge \varnothing \subset D \subseteq \{C_1, \ldots, C_n\} \wedge \\ \quad (\forall c \cdot c \in D \wedge c = (\mathcal{A}_c, R_c, G_c) \Rightarrow G_c(w) \wedge \mathcal{A}_c\langle a \rangle \neq \varnothing) \Rightarrow \\ \quad \mathrm{card}(\mathbf{rec}(w, D, a)) = 1 \end{array} \qquad [15.5]$$

Together [15.4] and [15.5] establish a sufficient criterion for [15.3].

Condition [15.4] may be discharged by supplying a witness actor shown to experience some further mutation with a given constraint set. This is straightforward with train actors when there are no opposing routes (opposing routes are train paths going over the same track in opposite directions). In general, opposing routes may lead to a deadlock so we need to build a proof by case analysis over applicable worlds.

For condition [15.5], the strategy depends on the concrete definition of $\mathbf{rec}(..)$ which is unique to each class of constraints. Currently, UTDP defines two constraint classes: *plain* and *speed*. The plain class is used solely to model updates of the infrastructure actor state (that is the model variables) and the speed class are the constraints defining speed limits for train classes. Reconciliation may only be done over constraints from the same class. In practice, this is not a limitation as such a test is already encoded as $a \mapsto w \in \mathrm{dom}(R)$ in [15.3] and [15.4].

Recall that attractors define locations, temporal or spatial. Within each class there is a linear order but a temporal location may not be compared with a spatial one. Thus, for any $x, y \in \mathcal{A}^l\langle a\rangle, x = (p, i), y = (q, j)$, we have $x \leq y \Leftrightarrow (p \leq q \wedge i = j)$. The infinum of a partial order on the set of all attractor locations gives a set of certain "nearest" locations. Then the reconciliation set is the set of compatible mutation rules corresponding to these locations:

$$
\begin{aligned}
&l(w) = \inf\{\mathcal{A}^l_c\langle a\rangle \mid c \in D \wedge c = (\mathcal{A}_c, R_c, G_c) \wedge G_c(w) \wedge \mathcal{A}^l_c\langle a\rangle\} \\
&\mathbf{rec}(w, D, a) = \{R_c \mid c \in D \wedge c = (\mathcal{A}_c, R_c, G_c) \wedge \mathcal{A}^l_c\langle a\rangle \in l(w) \wedge \mathbf{comp}(D)\}
\end{aligned}
\qquad [15.6]
$$

where $\mathbf{comp}(D)$ defines the compatibility of constraints D. With this definition, there are two possibilities for contradicting $\mathrm{card}(\mathbf{rec}(w, D, a)) = 1$: having to choose between incomparable spatial and temporal locations, and failing the $\mathbf{comp}(C)$ criterion. In the former case, conflicting locations are necessarily defined by distinct constraints and must be made mutually disjoint through constraint guards.

Note that we may conclude $\mathbf{rec}(w, D, a)$ for an arbitrary non-empty D by considering all possible pair-wise reconciliations $\mathbf{rec}(w, \{g, h\}, a)$ where $\{g, h\} \subseteq D, g \neq h$. This means that condition [15.5] needs to be instantiated, to consider all cases of $\mathbf{rec}(..)$, at most $\mathrm{card}(C)(\mathrm{card}(C) - 1)/2$ times.

The compatibility criterion requires that each constraint pair defines a feasible evolution program for an actor class these that constraints may bind.

This may be stated as follows

$$\begin{aligned}\mathbf{comp}(C) \Leftrightarrow (\forall w, a, g, h \cdot w \in \mathrm{W} \wedge a \in \mathrm{A} \wedge g, h \in \{C_1, \ldots, C_n\} \wedge g \neq h \wedge \\ g = (\mathcal{A}, r_1, G) \wedge h = (\mathcal{B}, r_2, H) \wedge \\ (\mathcal{A} \cap \mathcal{B})^l \langle a \rangle \neq \varnothing \wedge G(w) \wedge H(w) \Rightarrow \\ \vartheta(a, \mathcal{A}, \mathcal{B}, r_1, r_2))\end{aligned} \qquad [15.7]$$

where $\vartheta(a, \mathcal{A}, \mathcal{B}, r_1, r_2)$ is a compatibility criterion of mutation rules r_1 and r_2 with respect to actor a and attractors $\mathcal{A}$, $\mathcal{B}$. Since rule classes may be user defined, the concrete definition of $\vartheta(..)$ is given in a UTDP specification together with the definition of an attractor rule class. UTDP has a built-in *speed rule* class (e.g. **stop**) which provides a definition of $\vartheta(..)$, denoted as $\vartheta_S(..)$, for this class.

Intuitively, $\vartheta_S(..)$ requires that a train actor be able to satisfy, in all situations, a pair of constraints g and h (see equation [15.7]), i.e. a train can be driven to meet the constraint requirements. One reason this might not be the case is when a train is required to accelerate or decelerate harder than it is capable of, thus leading to an overrun (and, potentially, a collision) or violation of a QoS requirement. Formally expressing the condition, we state that a pair of locations of some two distinct constraints g, h define an interval such that assuming a given train actor a satisfies one constraint at one edge of the interval it is also able to satisfy the other constraint at the opposing edge:

$$\vartheta_S(a, \mathcal{A}, \mathcal{B}, r_1, r_2) \Leftrightarrow \Big(\forall i, j \cdot (i, j) \in \mathcal{A}^l\langle a \rangle \times \mathcal{B}^l\langle a \rangle \Rightarrow \theta_S(a, i, j, r_1, r_2)\Big) \qquad [15.8]$$

and predicate $\theta_S(a, i, j, S_1, S_2)$ states whether train a is able to meet the speed goals set by mutation rules r_1, r_2 on interval defined locations i, j:

$$\theta_S(a, i, j, r_1, r_2) = \begin{cases} \begin{pmatrix} \exists s_1, s_2 \cdot (s_1, s_2) \in \mathrm{spd}(r_1) \times \mathrm{spd}(r_2) \wedge \\ \mathsf{DD}(a, s_1, s_2) \leq j - i \end{pmatrix}, & i \leq j \\ \begin{pmatrix} \exists s_1, s_2 \cdot (s_1, s_2) \in \mathrm{spd}(S_1) \times \mathrm{spd}(S_2) \wedge \\ \mathsf{DD}(a, s_2, s_1) \leq i - j \end{pmatrix}, & i > j \end{cases}$$
$$\mathsf{spd}(\mathbf{speed}\ x) = \{x\},\ \mathsf{spd}(\mathbf{stop}) = \{0\},\ \mathsf{spd}(\mathbf{proceed}) = \{x \mid x \geq V_{\min}\},\ \ldots \qquad [15.9]$$

where $\mathsf{spd}(..)$ converts a speed mutation rule into a set of speeds permitted by the rule:

$$\mathsf{spd}(\mathbf{speed}\ x) = \{x\},\ \mathsf{spd}(\mathbf{stop}) = \{0\},$$
$$\mathsf{spd}(\mathbf{proceed}) = \{x \mid x \geq V_{\min}\},\ \ldots \qquad [15.10]$$

Value $V_{\min} \in \mathbb{R}_+$ is a small arbitrary positive real number denoting the minimum train speed we can register.

Expression $\mathsf{DD}(a, u, v)$ defines either an acceleration or a braking distance of a train a currently traveling at speed u and trying to achieve target speed v:

$$\mathsf{DD}(t, u, v) = \begin{cases} \mathrm{BD}(t, u, v) & \text{when } v < u \\ \mathrm{AD}(t, u, v) & \text{when } v > u \\ 0 & \text{when } v = u \end{cases} \qquad [15.11]$$

To define BD(..) and AD(..) we need some notion of train dynamics. Let t be a train actor; then its acceleration $a_t(v) = F_t(v)/m_t$ depends on current speed v (due to, as an example, the air drag force) and train characteristics such as mass m_t. Assume that i and j in [15.9] are spatial locations; the differential of speed over distance and the consequent braking or acceleration distance may be given as

$$v\frac{dv}{dx} = a(v) \qquad S = \int_{u_1}^{u_2} va^{-1}(v)dv$$

These provide the following definitions for train acceleration and braking distances:

$$\mathsf{BD}(t, u, u') = \int_{u'}^{u} va_{-,t}^{-1}(v)dv \qquad \mathsf{AD}(t, u, u') = \int_{u}^{u'} va_{+,t}^{-1}(v)dv \qquad [15.12]$$

where $a_{-,t}(v)$ and $a_{+,t}(v)$ are the maximum deceleration and acceleration of train t, respectively. Temporal i and j are treated symmetrically.

15.5.2. *Hazard avoidance*

A hazard is a negative form of a constraint; it is a mutation program describing a mutation that should never happen to an actor of a given system.

More precisely, a hazard is a constraint that cannot be reconciled with any existing behavioral constraint. The proof technique is based on the reconciliation criteria [15.6] and [15.7]. Consider the following model template.

hazard H
behavior $C1, \ldots, Cn$

It must be the case that H is irreconcilable with any subset of C,

$$\forall w, D, a \cdot w \in \mathrm{W} \wedge D \subseteq C \wedge a \in \mathrm{A} \Rightarrow \mathrm{card}(\mathbf{rec}(w, D \cup \{H\}, a)) \neq 1$$

The above may be replaced by the following sufficient criterion:

$$\forall i \cdot i \in 1..n \Rightarrow (\forall a \cdot a \in \mathrm{A} \Rightarrow (\mathcal{A}_H \cap \mathcal{A}_i)^l \langle a \rangle = \varnothing) \vee \neg \mathbf{comp}(\{H, C_i\}) \qquad [15.13]$$

where $\mathcal{A}_H$ and $\mathcal{A}_i$ are the attractors of constraints H and C_i, respectively. Term $(\mathcal{A}_H \cap \mathcal{A}_i)^l \langle a \rangle = \varnothing$ excludes vacuous compatibility of H and C_i as a hazard indication.

15.5.3. *Example*

Consider the moving block principle where train paths do not intersect (there are no points). We showcase a safety proof demonstrating the absence of train collisions and, thus, the viability of the moving block principle.

hazard @h **proceed on** entering(**any** train)
behavior @a **stop on** entering(**any** train)

Hazard @h (@? is UTDP syntax for attaching labels to model elements) defines a constraint expressing the "brick-wall" safety law and @a is the familiar moving block constraint. Expanding the syntactic sugar, we obtain @$h = (\mathcal{A}, r_2, \top)$, @$a = (\mathcal{A}, r_1, \top)$ and

$$\mathcal{A} = \{t \mapsto (t', t'.\mathrm{head} \mapsto \mathbf{s}) \mid t' \in \mathrm{train} \wedge t.\mathrm{head} \leq t'.\mathrm{tail} \wedge t.\mathrm{line} = t'.\mathrm{line}\}$$

where $r_1 = \textbf{proceed}$ and $r_2 = \textbf{stop}$. From [15.13], we derive a safety proposition stating absence of train collisions

$$\neg\mathbf{comp}(\{@h, @a\}) \Leftrightarrow \\ (\forall t \cdot t \in \mathrm{A} \Rightarrow \mathcal{A}^l\langle t\rangle = \varnothing) \vee \neg(\forall t \cdot t \in \mathrm{A} \wedge \mathcal{A}^l\langle t\rangle \neq \varnothing \Rightarrow \vartheta_S(t, \mathcal{A}, \mathcal{B}, r_1, r_2))$$

We go through the proof in small steps to give a feeling of how it could be done in an automated procedure. The predicate above is equivalently stated as

$$t \in \mathrm{A}, \mathcal{A}^l\langle t\rangle \neq \varnothing \vdash \neg\,\vartheta_S(t, \mathcal{A}, \mathcal{B}, r_1, r_2) \qquad [15.14]$$

First, expand the definition of $\vartheta_S(..)$ using [15.8]:

$$t \in \mathrm{A}, \mathcal{A}^l\langle t\rangle \neq \varnothing \vdash \exists i, j \cdot (i, j) \in \mathcal{A}^l\langle t\rangle \times \mathcal{A}^l\langle t\rangle \wedge \neg\,\theta_S(t, i, j, r_1, r_2) [15.15]$$

Notice that $\mathcal{A}^l\langle t\rangle \neq \varnothing$ is same as $\exists z \cdot z \in \mathcal{A}^l\langle t\rangle$, we obtain $z \in \mathcal{A}^l\langle t\rangle$ in hypothesis and use z to instantiate both i and j:

$$t \in \mathrm{A}, z \in \mathcal{A}^l\langle t\rangle \vdash \neg\,\theta_S(t, z, z, r_1, r_2) \qquad [15.16]$$

From definition [15.9] of $\theta_S(..)$ we have

$$t \in \mathrm{A} \vdash \neg(\exists s_1, s_2 \cdot (s_1, s_2) \in \mathrm{spd}(r_1) \times \mathrm{spd}(r_2) \wedge \mathsf{DD}(t, s_1, s_2) \leq 0) [15.17]$$

Expressions $\mathrm{spd}(r_1)$ and $\mathrm{spd}(r_2)$ are replaced with sets of speed values according to definition [15.9]:

$$t \in \mathrm{A} \vdash \neg(\exists s_1, s_2 \cdot (s_1, s_2) \in \{0\} \times \{x \mid x \geq V_{\min}\} \wedge \mathsf{DD}(t, s_1, s_2) \leq 0) \qquad [15.18]$$

The next step instantiates s_1 and s_2 with 0 and $V_{\min}$ (see [15.9]) and, since $s_2 > s_1$, $\mathsf{DD}(t, s_1, s_2)$ turns into acceleration distance $\mathsf{AD}(t, s_1, s_2)$ (see [15.11]):

$$t \in \mathrm{A} \vdash \neg\mathsf{AD}(t, 0, V_{\min}) \leq 0 \qquad [15.19]$$

It is a statement about the acceleration distance required to reach $V_{\min}$ from 0:

$$t \in \mathrm{A} \vdash \int_0^{V_{\min}} v a_{+,t}^{-1} dv > 0 \qquad [15.20]$$

This is trivially correct for any meaningful definition of $a_{+,t}$. A proof like this must be delegated to an automated proof environment. The proof is elementary except, to some degree, steps [15.17] and [15.19], which require heuristics to instantiate variables.

The fixed block safety proof follows a similar pattern but requires the consideration of a wider context to capture route reservation. Modeling points necessitates the consideration of an additional actor type simulating point locking and setting activities, however the principal technique stays the same.

15.6. Discussion

Ensuring and demonstrating railway safety is crucial for the way our society operates. Formal methods have been successfully used in developing various railway control systems. The best-known examples include the use of the B method [ABR 96] for designing various metro and suburban lines, and airport shuttles all over the world [BEH 99, ESS 07]. The formal methods in these works are used to trace the requirements to system models and to ensure and demonstrate system safety. Our work builds on this experience and introduces a generalized approach for the verification of various types of signaling.

UTDP is developed as part of a railway modeling environment – the SafeCap Platform [SAF 13]. In the Platform it has replaced Event-B and Classical B formalisms previously used for specification and validation of operational safety [ILI 13].

Figure 15.5 gives a general picture of the role UTDP plays in the Platform. Railway schema (track topology, optional signaling rules for route-based signaling, static speed limits and track gradient) is combined with the definition of rolling stock dynamics and a UTDP specification. The UTDP engine is responsible for syntax and type checking UTDP models (a part of the type checking requires matching against schema and rolling stock definitions), generation of verification conditions and filling the template code of C-based railway simulator. Proof obligations use the syntax of Why3 [BOB 11] and Classical B [ABR 96]. Why3 manages a range of provers and solvers such as Z3, CVC4 and SPASS. ProB [LEU 03] handles the B part and, although nominally a model checker, is used in the capacity of a Satisfiability Modulo Theories (SMT) solver. All the conditions are generated in both styles.

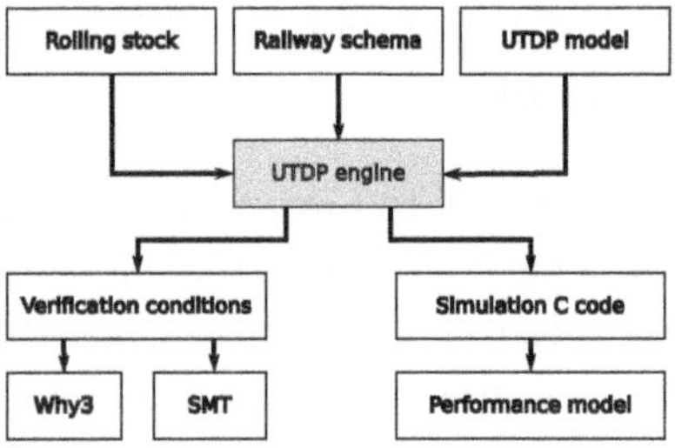

Figure 15.5. *UTDP tooling*

An experiment with two-aspect route-based signaling of an average-size station (8 platform, 63 points and several miles of track) with constant acceleration and deceleration functions resulted in 603 conditions of which 41% were discharged automatically by a combination of Why3 and ProB. Manual experiments that a direct translation into Z3 may help to discharge the majority of the remaining conditions (also the number of conditions they are based on few distinct schemas).

A symbolic solution of [15.12] even for a crude approximation of train physics yields complex non-linear terms. Some initial experiments with constraint solvers produced no encouraging results and, as we see at the moment, the most viable strategy would be to use a provably safe approximation of $a_{\_,\_}$ in conjunction with the Computer Algebra System (CAS) (e.g. Mathematica) or logic + CAS (e.g. KeYmaera [PLA 10]) system. However, dropping all the retardation force components and using constant acceleration/deceleration values produces conditions that are easy to handle with automated constraint solvers and provers. There is a class of safety proofs, as demonstrated in the example below, that does not require expansion of the integral term. We may also expect that a *resa* can apply theorem proving and constraint solving to filter out vacuously correct instances of [15.3].

There are several reasons we thought it necessary to develop a new modeling language. Event-B and Classical B, as well as comparable model-based languages such as Z and Vienna Development Method (VDM), are not friendly for industrial users. It is difficult for a railway expert to read such a model (and thus confirm its adequacy) and almost impossible to independently modify it. Failed verification conditions are often difficult to interpret for non-expert users.

UTDP offers a compact specialized vocabulary and friendly but terse syntax. It hides most of the aspects of formal modeling and lets an engineer operate with familiar operational concepts. Its executable side (railway simulation) offers immediate feedback to confirm model viability. This makes a development pattern possible where a railway engineer develops signaling model and then lets a formalist add the missing parts necessary to ensure safety (or demonstrate absence of safety). Verification conditions are formulated at a higher conceptual level leading to fewer identifiers and simpler expressions. For trains, these conditions also capture continuous train dynamics, something that is not expressible directly in the modeling languages we have previously applied.

Signaling rules expressed in UTDP are central to the analysis of dynamic performance: assessment of various capacity utilization metrics for given train schedules and train characteristics. There is an automatic translation routine from a UTDP model into a high-performance event-based railway simulator. The simulator executes train runs and collects a wide range of data for later analysis, mainly from the viewpoint of optimal track utilization and energy efficiency.

During UTDP development we have studied a number of railway modeling languages [BIØ 95, BLØ 00]. Many of the UTDP ideas were carried over from our previous work on a railway Domain Specific Language (DSL) [ILI 12].

15.7. Conclusions

We have presented a domain-specific method for modeling railway signaling laws. The method may be used to demonstrate the operational safety of a combination of signaling rules and track topology. It is equally applicable to the formulation and analysis of non-functional properties such as railway network capacity, stability (the ability to recover from unforeseen disruptions), operational costs and energy efficiency. Some of these properties may be proven using symbolic theorem proving while others are confirmed via simulation. Our experience in working with Invensys Rail and the analysis of the strategic plans for developing the UK railway show the pressing need for a rigorous approach to modeling of unconventional and highly specialized signaling solutions with strong guarantees of operational safety.

Automation of train operation (essentially a driver-less train) is the most promising way to improve capacity with tighter safety margins and it is the principal guiding aspect in the design of UTDP. Definition 15.2 gives one concrete strategy for executing UTDP models. An efficient simulation of UTDP models critically depends on the ability to discover fix-point u in definition 15.1 without going through each individual actor evolution. Such an algorithm exists and is already realized in the SafeCap Modeling Platform [SAF 13].

The railway domain has always been one of the areas in which formal methods are successfully deployed and used in a substantial way. For example, in France, RATP (a major rail operator) with a considerable experience in formal methods, looks favorably on using formal methods to conform to the development standards that they require. From the mid-90s, in France, RATP, the main rail operator with considerable experience of formal methods, has been approving various developments that use the B method as meeting the development standards RATP requires [ESS 07]. There are now several tool development companies supporting the use of the B [ABR 96] and Event-B [ABR 98] methods in the railway domain: ClearSy, Systerel and Formal Mind. Model checking has been successfully used by railway companies to assess safety and data integrity (see, for example, [FER 10, LEU 11]).

15.8. Bibliography

[ABR 96] ABRIAL J.-R., *The B-Book*, Cambridge University Press, 1996.

[ABR 98] ABRIAL J.-R., MUSSAT L., "Introducing dynamic constraints in B", *2nd International B Conference*, Lecture Notes in Computer Science, Springer-Verlag, vol. 1393, April 1998.

[AKH 07] AKHMET M., *Nonlinear Hybrid Continuous/Discrete-Time Models*, Atlantis Press, 2007.

[BEH 99] BEHM P., BENOIT P., FAIVRE A., *et al.*, "Météor: a successful application of B in a large project", *Proceedings of the Wold Congress on Formal Methods in the Development of Computing Systems (FM '99)*, Springer-Verlag, London, UK, vol. 1, pp. 369–387, 1999.

[BLØ 00] BJØRNER D., Formal Software Techniques in Railway Systems, pp. 1–12, 2000.

[BIØ 95] BJØRNER D., GEORGE C., PREHN S., "Scheduling and rescheduling of trains", 1995.

[BOB 11] BOBOT F., FILLIÂTRE J.-C., MARCHÉ C., *et al.*, "Why3: shepherd your herd of provers", *Boogie 2011: 1st International Workshop on Intermediate Verification Languages*, pp. 53–64, August 2011.

[ESS 07] ESSAMÉ D., DOLLÉ D., "B in large-scale projects: the Canarsie Line CBTC experience", in JULLIAND J., KOUCHNARENKO O. (eds.), *B 2007: Formal Specification and Development in B*, Lecture Notes in Computer Science, Springer, vol. 4355, pp. 252–254, 2007.

[FER 10] FERRARI A., MAGNANI G., GRASSO D., *et al.*, "Model checking interlocking control tables", in SCHNIEDER E., TARNAI G. (eds.), *FORMS/FORMAT*, Springer, pp. 107–115, 2010.

[ILI 12] ILIASOV A., ROMANOVSKY A., SafeCap domain language for reasoning about safety and capacity, Technical Report CS-TR-1352, Newcastle University, September 2012.

[ILI 13] ILIASOV A., LOPATKIN I., ROMANOVSKY A., "The safecap platform for modeling railway safety and capacity", in BITSCH F., GUIOCHET J., KAÂNICHE M., (eds.), *SAFECOMP*, Lecture Notes in Computer Science, vol. 8153, Springer, 2013.

[LEU 03] LEUSCHEL M., BUTLER M., "ProB: a model checker for B", in KEIJIRO A., GNESI S., DINO M. (eds.), *Formal Methods Europe 2003*, Lecture Notes in Computer Science, Springer-Verlag, vol. 2805, pp. 855–874, 2003.

[LEU 11] LEUSCHEL M., FALAMPIN J., FRITZ F., *et al.*, "Automated property verification for large scale B models with ProB", *Formal Aspects of Computing*, vol. 23, no. 6, pp. 683–709, 2011.

[PAC 09] PACHL J., *Railway Operation and Control*, VTD Rail Publishing, 2009.

[PLA 10] PLATZER A., *Logical Analysis of Hybrid Systems: Proving Theorems for Complex Dynamics*, Springer, 2010.

[RIV 08] RIVERA G. ANGEL J., Reasoning about co-evolving discrete, continuous and hybrid states, PhD Thesis, Electrical Engineering and Computer Science, Syracuse University, 2008.

[ROM 12] ROMANOVSKY A., ILIASOV A., "Safecap domain language for reasoning about safety and capacity", *IEEE CS*, pp. 1–10, 2012.

[SAF 13] SafeCap Project, SafeCap Platfrom website, Available at http://safecap.sf.net, 2013.

[TSL 12] TSLG, "The rail technical strategy (RTS)", Available at http://www.futurerailway. org/RTS/Pages/Intro.aspx, 2012.

[VLA 09] VLASENKO S., THEEG G. (eds.), *Railway Signalling and Interlocking – International Compendium*, Eurailpress, 2009.

[WIN 09] WINTER P. (ed.), *Compendium on ERTMS – European Railway Traffic Management System*, Eurailpress, 2009.

Conclusion

C.1. Introduction

This series of five books (three books already published [BOU 11, BOU 12a, BOU 12b] and this book, plus another published in 2014 [BOU 14]) have presented a large number of methods known as "formal" (SCADE, B Method, etc.) and techniques (e.g. abstract interpretation, proof and model-checking). The series has also shown their application in large-scale industrial projects in various different domains (railway, nuclear, automation, spatial, aeronautics, etc.).

Table C.1 provides an outline of projects using formal methods in railways.

C.2. B Method

The present book has shown various uses of the B Method [ABR 96], from both an industrial and an academic approach, in different sectors (railway, automation, etc.). It should be noted that there have been various other experiments conducted using this method in the automobile, spatial and aeronautics domains. Table C.2 gives an idea of the size of different B models, which makes it possible to check whether the models involved are real-sized models.

Conclusion written by Jean-Louis BOULANGER.

It should be noted that this book is more focused on the so-called "classical" B, which corresponds to the B-Book [ABR 96]. Classical B makes it possible to build a formal model and to refine it until a translatable implementation is obtained in a classic language such as JAVA, ADA and C.

Project	Onboard equipment	Ground equipment	Commissioning
CdG VAL	Atelier B (Siemens)	Atelier B (Siemens)	04/2007
CBTC in China	Atelier B (Alstom)	Atelier B (Alstom)	2008
OCTYS L3	Atelier B (Siemens)	SCADE–Proof Toolkit (Ansaldo STS)	12/2009
SAET L1	Atelier B (Siemens)	Atelier B (Siemens)	12/2011
OURAGAN L13	SCADE (Thales RSS)	SCADE (Thales RSS)	2012
OCTYS L5	SCADE (Areva-TA)	Atelier B (Siemens)	2012
PMI L1, L2	N.A.	SCADE–Proof Toolkit (Thales)	2009, 2010
CdG VAL extension	Atelier B (Siemens)	Atelier B (Siemens)	06/2012
PMI L4	N.A.	SCADE–Proof Toolkit (Thales)	2012
LYON	SCADE 5 (Areva-TA)	– SCADE 6 + Atelier B – (Areva-TA)	2013

Table C.1. *List of railway projects using formal methods*

Classical B makes it possible to create software applications (complete or integrating manual code). Classical B also makes it possible to create models that enable the modeling of a problem and the verification that properties are respected under certain assumptions. There are even some examples of classical B models which are focused on the demonstration of a mathematical theorem.

In the context of the management of the modeling of system aspects, several approaches allow the definition of models based on the notion of an action system. In the context of this type of modeling, we are more concerned with the link between the people involved and the system, and there are events on these links.

After delivering a solution for the creation of a safely functioning software application, J.-R. Abrial addressed the system aspects, suggesting a new version of the B language called EVENT-B, which is focused on the notion of an event and on refining these events. A new book was published [ABR 10], and the language is supported by the tool called RODIN[2].

Instead of a changeover to EVENT-B, several projects have suggested coupling Classical-B with a form of graphics such as UML and/or SysML. This is so that the form of Classical B can be maintained in the modeling of the algorithms. The graphic aspects are useful for creating a better description and for taking the systems aspects into account.

Name of the system	Lines of B code	Lines of generated code	Language	Number of proof obligations
CDTC	5,000	3,000	ADA	700
KVB	60,000	22,000	ADA	10,000
KVB-SN	9,000	6,000	ADA	2,750
KVS	22,000	16,000	ADA	6,000
SACEM- simplified	3,500	2,500	Modula 2	550
SAET-METEOR	115,000	90,000	ADA	27,800
Eurocoder	10,000	4,500	ADA	4,200
CdG-VAL	PADS: 186,440	30,632	ADA	62,056
	UCA: 50,085	11,662	ADA	12,811

Table C.2. *Example of the complexity of B models ([BOU 06])*

In this book, various tools that make it possible to apply the B method have been presented, both industrial (Atelier B) and academic (ABTools, BRILLIANT, etc.).

Chapter 13 is particularly interesting in that it allowed us to identify the conditions under which the B method can be used in the aeronautical domain. The first of these conditions involves the introduction of real numbers and the second condition is linked to the qualification of the component on the shield COTS. These two points show that there are still

2 More information is available at http://www.event-b.org/.

elements requiring development and that making an open and free tool available is an important direction for future work.

C.3. Conclusion

This book is part of a series of five books that cover different aspects of formal techniques: static analysis of code, formal methods and tools.

The formal techniques and methods are now successfully being used for projects of various sizes in industry. The associated tools have reached a maturity so that we can account for the complexity of such applications. Note that the complexity of industrial applications very often has an impact on the processing time: within the context of the SAET-METEOR, it took longer than a week in 1998 to analyze 100,000 lines of ADA code with the Polyspace tool (see [BOU 11, Chapter 4] for more information), whereas maintaining that would take 1 or 2 h.

Taking account of the techniques and formal methods has an impact on the implemented process, and it is therefore necessary to build a new referential that conforms to the quality standards being enforced. The construction of this referential must take into account the fact that the model can replace documents that were initially to be produced; however, it is necessary to account for the system's lifespan and the objectives of associated maintenance. Indeed, if the tool is no longer maintained and formalism is proprietary, it is difficult or even impossible to update the application without the model.

Another difficulty of the *model-centered* approach is bringing the software application's level of safety to that of the implemented tools.

Although it is difficult to show that a compiler C is SSIL4, it is even more difficult to show than a prover is SSIL4. Within the context of compilers, it was possible to set up strategies based on redundancy and diversity. As for specific tools such as provers, *model-checking* tools, and/or tools for abstract interpretation, it is difficult to have two tools of similar effectiveness within the same field[3]. Therefore, it is necessary to set up tool qualification files.

The different standards (DO 178, ISO 26262, CEI/IEC 61508, CENELEC EN 50128) show the concept of a *qualification report*. The qualification of a tool depends on its impact on the final product.

Concerning formal techniques and methods, the question of tool qualification is of primary importance because the complexity of the implemented technologies (prover, *model-checking*, etc.), the confidentiality aspect (licensed algorithm, etc.), the innovation aspect (new technology, few users, etc.) and the maturity aspect (product resulting from research carried out under a "free" license, etc.) do not allow confidence to be built easily.

C.4. Bibliography

[ABR 96] ABRIAL J.-R., *The B Book: Assigning Programs to Meanings*, Cambridge University Press, Cambridge, August 1996.

[ABR 10] ABRIAL J.-R., *Modeling in Event-B System and Software Engineering*, Cambridge University Press, Cambridge, 2010.

[BOU 11] BOULANGER J.-L. (ed.), *Static Analysis of Software*, ISTE, London and John Wiley & Sons, New York, 2011.

[BOU 12a] BOULANGER J.-L. (ed.), *Industrial Use of Formal Method: Formal Verification*, ISTE, London and John Wiley & Sons, New York, 2012.

[BOU 12b] BOULANGER J.-L. (ed.), *Formal Methods: Industrial Use from Model to the Code*, ISTE, London and John Wiley & Sons, New York, 2012.

[BOU 14] BOULANGER J.-L. (ed.), *Formal Methods Applied to Industrial Complex Systems,* ISTE, London and John Wiley & Sons, New York, 2014.

[CEN 00] CENELEC – EN 50126, Applications Ferroviaires, Spécification et démonstration de la fiabilité, de la disponibilité, de la maintenabilité et de la sécurité (FMDS), January 2000.

[CEN 01] CENELEC – EN 50128, Railway applications, Communications, signalling and processing systems, Software for railway control and protection systems, May 2001.

3 Recall that for several of the tools currently in use, the algorithms are not public and are even under copyright.

[CEN 11] CENELEC – EN 50128, Railway applications, Communications, signalling and processing systems, Software for railway control and protection systems, January 2011.

[IEC 08] IEC 61508, Sécurité fonctionnelle des systèmes électriques électroniques programmables relatifs à la sécurité, Norme internationale, 2008.

[ISO 08] ISO 9001, Systèmes de management de la qualité – Exigences, 2008.

[ISO 09] ISO, ISO/CD-26262, Road vehicles – functional safety, 2009. [Unpublished]

Glossary

AADL	Architecture Analysis and Design Language
ACATS	Ada Conformity Assessment Test Suite
ACU	Alarm Control Unit
AFIS	*Association Française d'Ingénierie Système* (French Association of Systems Engineering)
AMN	Abstract Machine Notation
ANSI	American National Standards Institute
APU	Auxiliary Power Unit
ASA	Automata and Structured Analysis
ASIL	Automotive SIL
ATO	Automatic Train Operation
ATP	Automatic Train Protection
ATS	Automatic Train Supervision
BDD	Binary Decision Diagram
CAN	Controller Area Network
CAS	Computer-Assisted Specification
CBTC	Communication Based Train Control
CbyC	Correct by Construction

CCP	Centralized Control Point
CdCF	*Cahier des Charges Fonctionnel* (Functional Requirements Specification)
CENELEC[1]	European Committee for Electrotechnical Standardization
CMMI	Capability Maturity Model Integration
CPU	Central Processor Unit
DAL	Design Assurance Level
DoD	Department of Defense
DV	Design Verifier
E/E/PE	Electric/Electronic/Programmable Electronic
EAL	Evaluation Assurance Level
ECU	Electronic Control Units
ERTMS	European Rail Traffic Management System
FADEC	Full Authority Digital Engine Control
FBD	Function Block Diagram
FC	Failure Condition
FDA	Food and Drug Administration
FMECA	Failure Mode and Effects Criticality Analysis
FT	Functional Testing
GPS	GNAT Programming Studio
GSL	Generalized Substitution Language
GUI	Graphical User Interface
HIL	Hardware In the Loop
HR	Highly Recommended
IDE	Integrated Development Environment

1 See www.cenelec.eu.

IEC[2]	International Electrotechnical Commission
iFACTS	interim Future Area Controls Tools Support
IL	Instruction List
IMAG	*Institut de Mathématiques Appliquées de Grenoble* (Institute of Applied Mathematics of Grenoble)
IPSN	*Institut de Protection et de Sûreté Nucléaire* (Institute of Nuclear Protection and Safety)
IRSN	*Institut de Radioprotection et de Sûreté Nucléaire* (Radioprotection and Nuclear Safety Institute)
ISO[3]	International Organization for Standardization
ISSRE	International Symposium on Software Reliability Engineering
IT	Integration Testing
KCG	Qualifiable Code Generator
KLoC	1000 LoC
LaBRI	*Laboratoire Bordelais de Recherche en Informatique* (Bordeaux Laboratory for Computer Research)
LD	Ladder Diagram
LoC	Lines of Code
MaTeLo	Markov Test Logic
MBD	Model-Based Design
MBT	Model-Based Testing
METEOR	*METro Est Ouest Rapide* (Train operation system used by the Paris metro)
MISRA[4]	Motor Industry Software Reliability Association
MMI	Man-Machine Interface
MPU	Main Processor Unit

2 See www.iec.ch.

3 See www.iso.org/iso/home.htm.

4 See www.misra.org.uk.

MTC	Model Test Coverage
MTTF	Mean Time To Failure
MU	Multiple Unit
NHMO	NATO HAWK Management Office
NR	Not Recommended
NSA	US National Security Agency
NSE	No Safety Effect
OCR	Optical Character Recognition
OFP	Operational Flight Plan
OMG[5]	Object Management Group
OOTIA[6]	Object Oriented Technology in Aviation
OPRI	*Office de Protection contre les Rayonnements Ioisants* (Office of Ionizing Radiation Protection)
OS	Operating System
PADS	*Pilot automatique double sense* (two-way autopilot)
PAI-NG	*Poste d'aiguillage informatisé de nouvelle génération* (Next Generation Computerized Signaling Control)
PO	Proof Obligation
PTS	Problem of the Traveling Salesman
PWM	Pulse With Modulation
QTP	Quick Test Professional
R	Recommended
R&D	Research and Development
RAMS	Reliability, Availability, Maintainability and Safety

5 See www.omg.org.
6 See www.faa.gov/aircraft/air_cert/design_approvals/air_software/oot.

RAT	Ram Air Turbine
RATP[7]	*Régie Autonome des Transports Parisiens* (Autonomous Operator of Parisian Transports)
RER	*Réseau Express Régional* (Regional Express Network)
RFT	Rational Functional Tester
RM	Requirement Management
ROM	Read Only Memory
SACEM	*Système d'Aide à la Conduite, à l'Exploitation et à la Maintenance* (Assisted driving, Control, and Maintenance System)
SADT	Structured Analysis and Design Technique
SAET	*Système d'Automatisation de l'Exploitation des Trains* (Automation system of train operations)
SAO	*Spécification Assistée par Ordinateur* (Computer-aided Design)
SAS	Software Architecture & Design
SCADE	Safety Critical Application Development Environment
SFC	Sequential Function Chart
SHOLIS	Ship/Helicopter Operational Limits Instrumentation System
SIL	Safety Integrity Level
SIS	Safety Instrumented System
SMDS	Software Module Design Specification
SMTP	Software Module Test Plan
SOC	System On a Chip
SPIN	*Système de Protection Intégré Numérique* (Digital Integrated Protection System)
SRS	Software Requirement Specification
SSIL	Software SIL

7 See www.ratf.fr.

ST	Structured Text
SU	Single Unit
SUT	Software Unit Test
TCMS	Train Control Management System
TCO	*Tableau de Contrôle Optique* (Visual Control Panel)
TFTA	Terrain Following Terrain
TIS	Tokeneer ID station
TOR	*Tout ou Rien* (hit-or-miss)
UML	Unified Modeling Language
UT	Unit Testing
V&V	Verification and Validation
WCET	Worst-Case Execution Time
WP	Weakest Precondition

List of Authors

Jens BENDISPOSTO
Formal Mind GmbH
Dusseldorf
Germany

Jean-Louis BOULANGER
Certifer
Anzin
France

François BUSTANY
Systerel
Aix en provence
France

Néstor CATAÑO
School of Engineering and Informatics
University EAFIT
Medellín
Colombia

Philippe CHARPENTIER
National Institute of Research and Safety (INRS)
Vandoeuvre-lès-Nancy
France

Mathieu CLABAUT
Systerel
Aix-en-Provence
France

Samuel COLIN
Saferiver
Paris
France

Ivo DOBRIKOV
Formal Mind GmbH
Dusseldorf
Germany

Daniel DOLLE
Siemens SAS I MO
Chatillon
France

Jean-Louis DUFOUR
Sagem, Safran group
Division Avionique
Eragny
France

Dominique EVROT
LPO
Louis Marchal de Molsheim
Molsheim
France

Alexei ILIASOV
Newcastle University
UK

Sebastian KRINGS
Formal Mind GmbH
Dusseldorf
Germany

Pascal LAMY
National Institute of Research and Safety (INRS)
Vandoeuvre-lès-Nancy
France

Thierry LECOMTE
Clearsy
Aix-en-Provence
France

Michael LEUSCHEL
Formal Mind GmbH
Dusseldorf
Germany

Ilya LOPATKIN
Newcastle University
UK

Dominique MÉRY
Henri Poincare University
Nancy
France

Christophe METAYER
Systerel
Aix-en-Provence
France

Jean-François PETIN
Research Centre in Automatic Nancy (CRAN)
Nancy University US
Vandoeuvre-lès-Nancy
France

Dorian PETIT
University of Valenciennes
France

Daniel PLAGGE
Formal Mind GmbH
Dusseldorf
Germany

Alexander ROMANOVSKY
Newcastle University
UK

Víctor RIVERA
Madeira Interactive Technologies Institute (M-ITI)
University of Madeira
Funchal
Portugal

Camilo RUEDA
Department of Computer Science
Pontificia Universidad Javeriana
Cali
Colombia

Neeraj Kumar SINGH
Henri Poincare University
Nancy
France

Tim WAHLS
Department of Mathematics and Computer Science
Dickinson College
Carlisle, PA
USA

Index

I

M, N

O, P

R

S

T

V, W